MODERATE AND SEVERE DISABILITIES

A Foundational Approach

BELVA C. COLLINS

University of Kentucky

PEARSON

Merrill
Prentice Hall

Upper Saddle River, New Jersey
Columbus, Ohio

Library of Congress Cataloging-in-Publication Data

Collins, Belva C.
  Moderate and severe disabilities : a foundational approach / Belva C. Collins.—1st ed.
    p. cm.
  Includes index.
  ISBN 0-13-140810-0
  1. Children with disabilities—Education. 2. Special education teachers—Training of. I. Title.
  LC4015.C595 2007
  371.91—dc22

               2006003613

Vice President and Executive Publisher: Jeffery W. Johnston
Senior Editor: Allyson P. Sharp
Editorial Assistant: Kathleen S. Burk
Production Editor: Sheryl Glicker Langner
Production Coordination: TechBooks/GTS York, PA
Photo Coordinator: Sandy Schaefer
Design Coordinator: Diane C. Lorenzo
Cover Design: Linda Sorrells-Smith
Cover Image: Corbis
Production Manager: Laura Messerly
Director of Marketing: David Gesell
Marketing Manager: Autumn Purdy
Marketing Coordinator: Brian Mounts

This book was set in Garamond by TechBooks/GTS Companies, York, PA, Campus. It was printed and bound by Hamilton Printing Company. The cover was printed by The Lehigh Press, Inc.

Photo Credits: Tom Watson/Merrill, p. 2; David M. Grossman/PH College, p. 26; Laura Dwight/PhotoEdit, p. 46; Scott Cunningham/Merrill, pp. 72, 146; © Bob Daemmrich/PhotoEdit, p. 94; Laura Bolesta/Merrill, pp. 118, 224, 250; Paul Conklin/PhotoEdit, p. 178; Barbara Schwartz/Merrill, p. 200; Anthony Magnacca/Merrill, p. 276; Mark Richards/PhotoEdit, p. 302; Stone/Getty Images, Inc., p. 336.

Pearson Education Ltd.
Pearson Education Singapore Pte. Ltd.
Pearson Education Canada, Ltd.
Pearson Education–Japan

Pearson Education Australia Pty. Limited
Pearson Education North Asia Ltd.
Pearson Educación de Mexico, S.A. de C.V.
Pearson Education Malaysia Pte. Ltd.

10 9 8 7 6 5 4 3 2 1
ISBN: 0-13-140810-0

*To my cousin, Jeffrey Scott Boggs, and
his wonderful family, who have supported
him with love for so many years*

PREFACE

Recent legislation, including No Child Left Behind and the recent reauthorization of the Individuals with Education Disabilities Act, has raised questions as to the content that a special education teacher needs to be highly qualified. This text provides a foundation in best practices for working with persons with moderate and severe disabilities across the life span based on both logic and the research literature. Providing a strong foundation is the first step to building a personal philosophy that will result in successful collaboration with general educators in inclusive settings who have expertise in core content.

Over time my own philosophy has evolved as best practices have evolved. As a budding professional in special education in the early 1970s, I was inspired by the enthusiasm of the late Dr. Albert S. Levy as I was introduced to the field of moderate and severe disabilities. In the mid-1980s I was privileged to have my mentor and friend, Dr. David L. Gast, guide me through the writings of the leaders in the field and teach me to review the research literature before drawing conclusions. Since that time I have taught an introductory course twice each year for both undergraduate and graduate students first entering the field of moderate and severe disabilities or related areas, such as early childhood special education, communication disorders, or rehabilitation counseling. Each semester I have updated the class readings to reflect current practices while retaining those readings that have provided the basis for best practices in the field. This text is based on my course as it has evolved for over 15 years and includes the content, examples, activities, and assessments I have used to provide my students with a foundation to develop their own philosophies through critical thinking and research.

It is my opinion and experience that it is insufficient to tell students what to think. Rather, guiding them through the research literature and helping them analyze their and others' experiences enables them to build a firm foundation that gives them the strength to work in the field with less danger of "burnout." Although many of the activities in this text are drawn from my own experiences, they are intended to be similar to those that students will encounter in the real world. Sometimes professionals in the field of moderate and severe disabilities are quick to assume that those outside of our field are familiar with best practices and should accept them without question. Even in today's world, however, I am surprised again and again to discover that many people outside of the field of special education do not understand why we do what we do. To illustrate this, I offer the following example.

In a conversation during the past year, a childhood friend confided that she was shocked when she learned that her sister had a new job as a classroom assistant in which she worked with an adolescent male with significant cognitive and multiple severe disabilities who lacked basic self-care skills. "I can't understand why kids like this are in school," she told me. "How can they benefit?" When I explained to her that this was my area of expertise and that all children are entitled to an appropriate public school education, she replied, "I knew you worked in special education, but I thought that was for kids who had trouble reading and writing; I never dreamed that these were the kinds of students you taught." Her surprise was understandable, given that the only students who were served in school settings when we were children were those with mild disabilities.

This is but one example of how those outside of special education think about persons with moderate and severe disabilities. In recent years I repeatedly have found myself justifying expenditures for special education services for students with moderate and severe disabilities and explaining the reasoning behind inclusive services to both family and friends. "Shouldn't they be in institutions?" or "What can they learn?" come up in conversations with people of all ages from all geographic regions. In addition to knowing methodology, today's teachers in the field of moderate and severe disabilities need to be able to articulate the logic and research that has led to current best practices in inclusive school and community settings.

To provide this foundation, this text is divided into three sections. Part one focuses on building a foundation for best practices in moderate and severe disabilities by explaining the evolution and proper use of terminology, discussing the issues involved in educating students with the most severe disabilities, addressing the needs of families of children with moderate and severe disabilities, and reviewing the reasoning for appropriate educational practices. Part two delves into appropriate practices by introducing functional skills, systematic instruction, inclusion, and community-based instruction; examining the issues involved in working with students with healthcare needs and with challenging behaviors; and discussing longitudinal transition from birth to adulthood. Finally, Part three addresses difficult issues that are related to the basic human rights of persons with moderate and severe disabilities, including sexual fulfillment, personal safety, and life, before ending with an optimistic note focusing on the practice of self-determination.

It is my hope that after reading this text students will have been given a thorough introduction to a variety of topics in the field of moderate and severe disabilities that will prepare readers for more advanced study in specific areas, such as assessment, instructional methodology, behavior management, and transition. In addition, readers should be able to articulate a strong philosophy for working with persons with moderate and severe disabilities, be able to use terminology associated with the field, and be able to defend best practices based on data-based research. If the reader can accomplish these outcomes, then the text will have been successful.

ACKNOWLEDGMENTS

In the preparation of this text, I am indebted to several individuals. First, I dedicate this text to my cousin, Jeffrey Scott Boggs, who was born with multiple severe and significant cognitive disabilities, including complex health care needs, and who grew up prior to the laws that mandated an education for all children regardless of ability. I have been inspired by the love and dedication of his family, especially his mother, Grace, who told me to feel free to write about Jeffrey and his family throughout this text if it would help others learn from their experiences. Second, I am grateful for the research assistance of the following students in my courses on moderate and severe disabilities as I prepared this text: Jennifer Cornish, Carey Creech-Galloway, Erin Eilerman, Autumn Gadlage, Renee Hollinger, Melanie Howard, Lisa Marlak, Jennifer Potts, and Bethany Smith. Their enthusiasm for their topics came across in their own position papers and literature reviews. They are assets to the field, and I know their work will have a positive influence on the lives of their students. Finally, I thank my husband, Ted Collins, for his patience during the hours I spent writing this text and for his unwavering belief that I was up to the challenge.

For their helpful suggestions and constructive feedback, I would like to thank the following reviewers of this text: Judy Castles-Bentley, Southwest Texas State University; Denise M. Clark, University of Wisconsin Oshkosh; Harry L. Fullwood, Texas A&M University–Commerce; Nora Griffin-Shirley, Texas Tech University; Chris Hagie, San Jose State University; Helen Hammond, University of Texas at El Paso; Kelly Heckaman, Northwestern State University of Louisiana; Linda Medearis, Texas A&M International; Robert W. Ortiz, California State University, Fullerton; Sara Pankaskie, Florida Atlantic University; Crystal Pauli, Dakota State University; Barbara Phillips, University of South Alabama; Judith Presley, Tennessee State University; Michael Shaughnessy, Eastern New Mexico University; Qaisar Sultana, Eastern Kentucky University; Carolyn Talbert-Johnson, University of Dayton; Diane T. Woodrum, Waynesburg College; Donna Wandry, West Chester University; and Gwen Williams, West Texas A&M University

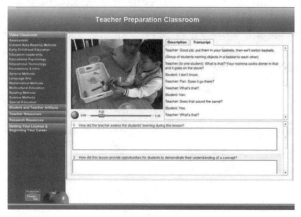

DISCOVER THE MERRILL RESOURCES FOR SPECIAL EDUCATION WEBSITE

Technology is a constantly growing and changing aspect of our field that is creating a need for new content and resources. To address this emerging need, Merrill Education has developed an online learning environment for students, teachers, and professors alike to complement our products—the *Merrill Resources for Special Education* Website. This content-rich website provides additional resources specific to this book's topic and will help you—professors, classroom teachers, and students—augment your teaching, learning, and professional development.

Our goal with this initiative is to build on and enhance what our products already offer. For this reason, the content for our user-friendly website is organized by topic and provides teachers, professors, and students with a variety of meaningful resources all in one location. With this website, we bring together the best of what Merrill has to offer: text resources, video clips, web links, tutorials, and a wide variety of information on topics of interest to general and special educators alike. Rich content, applications, and competencies further enhance the learning process.

The *Merrill Resources for Special Education* Website includes:

- Video clips specific to each topic, with questions to help you evaluate the content and make crucial theory-to-practice connections.

- Thought-provoking critical analysis questions that students can answer and turn in for evaluation or that can serve as basis for class discussions and lectures.

- Access to a wide variety of resources related to classroom strategies and methods, including lesson planning and classroom management.

- Information on all the most current relevant topics related to special and general education, including CEC and Praxis™ standards, IEPs, portfolios, and professional development.

- Extensive web resources and overviews on each topic addressed on the website.

- A search feature to help access specific information quickly.

To take advantage of these and other resources, please visit the *Merrill Resources for Special Education* Website at

http://www.prenhall.com/collins

BRIEF CONTENTS

CONTENTS

PART TWO

CREATING APPROPRIATE PROGRAMMING FOR PERSONS WITH MODERATE AND SEVERE DISABILITIES   93

PART THREE

IDENTIFYING ISSUES THAT AFFECT THE LIVES OF PERSONS WITH MODERATE AND SEVERE DISABILITIES   301

NOTE: Every effort has been made to provide accurate and current Internet information in this book. However, the Internet and information posted on it are constantly changing, and it is inevitable that some of the Internet addresses listed in this textbook will change.

PART ONE

BUILDING A FOUNDATION IN MODERATE AND SEVERE DISABILITIES

CHAPTER ONE

DEFINING THE TERM:
Moderate and Severe Disabilities

On completion of this chapter, the reader will meet the following objectives:

- State the differences between terms and definitions used to define mental retardation and developmental disabilities.
- Describe the differences between the 1983 American Association on Mental Deficiency classification system and the 1992 American Association on Mental Retardation supports system in regard to mental retardation.
- Use person-first language and explain the rationale for doing so in most cases.
- Provide a working definition for moderate and severe disabilities.
- Describe the diversity that exists within a group of individuals labeled as having moderate and severe disabilities.

This text surveys the underlying principles for establishing a philosophical foundation for working with persons with moderate and severe disabilities. The intent is to explain where we have been, where we are, and where we are going as a field in working with persons who fall into this diverse category. Before the issues can be addressed, however, it is necessary to clearly define the terminology and explain the classifications that are used in working with persons with mental retardation and developmental disabilities. The purpose of this chapter is to describe the evolution of terminology, define relevant terms, explain classification systems, illustrate appropriate language in reference to persons with disabilities, and enable the reader to formulate a working definition for moderate and severe disabilities.

Although there are a number of persons who argue that we should drop all labels and classification systems and lump everyone together as "people," the ability to define and describe types and levels of disabilities is a powerful tool for communication and advocacy. You would not have opened this book and read this far if you were not interested in learning more about a group of people who manifest certain characteristics and have needs that require specialized services.

Unfortunately, labels that are used to describe and categorize disabilities often must be replaced because they become stigmatizing over time. Thus, the creation of terminology is an evolutionary process, as is evident in the changing names of professional organizations and their publications. For example, the members of the Division on Mental Retardation of the Council for Exceptional Children changed their name to the Division on Developmental Disabilities in 2002 and also changed the title of the division's journal from *Education and Training in Mental Retardation and Developmental Disabilities* to *Education and Training in Developmental Disabilities*. Likewise, TASH, in 2002, changed the name of its journal from *Journal of the Association for Persons with Severe Handicaps* to *Research and Practice for Persons with*

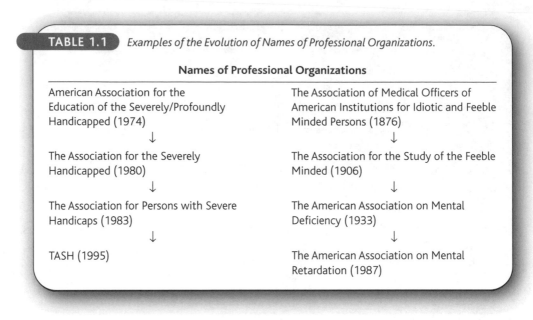

| TABLE 1.1 | *Examples of the Evolution of Names of Professional Organizations.* |

Names of Professional Organizations

American Association for the Education of the Severely/Profoundly Handicapped (1974)	The Association of Medical Officers of American Institutions for Idiotic and Feeble Minded Persons (1876)
↓	↓
The Association for the Severely Handicapped (1980)	The Association for the Study of the Feeble Minded (1906)
↓	↓
The Association for Persons with Severe Handicaps (1983)	The American Association on Mental Deficiency (1933)
↓	↓
TASH (1995)	The American Association on Mental Retardation (1987)

Severe Disabilities after several changes to the name of the organization (Weiss, 2000). As shown in Table 1.1, the changes in the names of organizations reflect a movement away from using terms that became stigmatizing over time as well as a movement toward using terms that more accurately and positively describe a diverse group of persons.

The following sections describe the evolution of terminology, definitions, and classification systems in the field of moderate and severe disabilities. Before reading further, however, stop and complete Activity 1.1.

ACTIVITY 1.1 Listing Terms

As noted in this chapter, many terms have been used to describe persons with disabilities over the past 200 years. Generate a list of terms that immediately come to mind. Afterward, look at your list with a critical eye. Which terms sound degrading or have an attached stigma? Which may be heard in daily conversation to describe something in a derogatory way? Which are the most acceptable? Which convey information that may be beneficial? How would you feel if these terms were used to describe a member of your family or a close friend? Would any of the terms be a positive or fair way to describe a person who is close to you? Now compare your lists to the terms found in Table 1.1. Is there an overlap? Do you have terms listed from both the past and the present?

LABELING PERSONS WITH DISABILITIES

Past Terminology

Over the past 200 years, many terms have been used to describe those who currently are labeled as having moderate and severe disabilities. Table 1.2 contains past terms that professionals in the field of disabilities (Gelb, 2002; Luckasson & Reeve, 2001; Turnbull, Turnbull, Warren, Eidelman, & Marchand, 2002; Vergason & Anderegg, 1997) have identified.

TABLE 1.2	*Past and Present Terminology Used in the Area of Moderate and Severe Disabilities.*

Past Terminology

Autistic; Constitutional Inferiority; Cretin; Feeblemindedness; Idiocy, Imbecility, Moronity; Low Level; Mental Defective, Mental Deficiency; Mongolism; Retard, Retarded, Retardate; Subnormality; Trainable Mentally Handicapped, Severely/Profoundly Handicapped

Present Terminology

Autism, Autism Spectrum Disorder; Cognitive Disability, Cognitive-Adaptive Disability, Cognitive Impairment; Significant Cognitive Disability; Developmental Delay, Developmental Disability; Down syndrome; Intellectual Disability; Mental Retardation; Moderate Disability, Severe Disability, Profound Disability

When first adopted, many of these terms were not meant to be stigmatizing, but acquired a stigma over time by being attached to people that society did not deem "desirable." Once this happened, society adopted many of the terms for use in a derogatory way. For example, Gelb (2001) noted that today's teenagers may use the word *retarded* to describe something inanimate that they do not like (e.g., "Those shoes are retarded.")

Some past terms were coined out of a lack of respect for diversity and have been replaced over time with less demeaning terms. Vergason and Anderegg (1997) illustrated this phenomenon in the labeling of persons with Down syndrome. In the past it was common for this diagnosis to be labeled as *mongolism* and for persons with Down syndrome to be called *mongoloids* by the general public, based on the characteristic of almond-shaped eyes. Occasionally, these terms still can be heard today even though *Asian* has become the acceptable term in referring to ethnicity. An example of a term that became acceptable although it was used in a demeaning way to describe physical characteristics can be found in Example 1.1.

EXAMPLE 1.1 THE EVOLUTION OF TERMINOLOGY

Some terms, unfortunately, evolve from slang and gain acceptance through repeated use, as demonstrated through the following story.

During an activity in an introductory college class on disabilities, the instructor asked students to list all of the terms—good or bad—that they had heard used to describe persons with disabilities. The class was being offered through the use of distance education technology. As the discussion progressed and the class began to list a number of terms, the distance education technologist could not contain himself and chimed from the back of the room, "No one has listed 'FLK.'"

All heads turned toward the technician. "I'm not familiar with that term," the instructor responded, adding it to the list on the overhead.

"Funny-looking kid," he responded. "We called them FLKs when I was in high school."

When the instructor later shared this story with a colleague, he voiced surprise that the instructor had never heard the term. "More than 20 years ago, I had a physician lecture my introductory class on the various types of disabilities," he said. "He told us that it was common practice to write 'FLK' down on a child's chart when a diagnosis could not be made."

Amazed, the instructor asked a physician if this was still standard practice. "I saw it all the time in medical school," was his reply.

Present Terminology

As society evolves, the search continues to identify terms that show respect for individual differences in a positive light while communicating important information. This can be seen in the labels that are used to describe differences in ethnicity and sexual preference. For example, the term *Negro* was replaced by *Black* then replaced by *African American.* The field of special education is no different. Advocacy groups need terms to effect change, as do service providers to identify appropriate means of working with persons with disabilities. The problem comes when the intent to show respect and not stigmatize causes confusion in communication. Wolfensberger (2002) stated the position that such terms as *differently abled, profoundly gifted*, and *people with different learning and communication styles* are ineffective as tools in honest communication. These terms fail to name the different abilities, gifts, or styles of learning of individuals or to even provide information if the difference is or is not advantageous or beneficial to the person.

The question arises as to whether it is possible to find the perfect terminology in the field of disabilities. Many professionals in the field, however, continue to make the effort to build on and improve the language we use to communicate differences and similarities. One only has to thumb through recent issues of *Mental Retardation* to realize that the debate over appropriate terminology is alive and well.

As shown in Table 1.2, present terms that have been cited by professionals in the field (Schalock, 2002; Vergason & Anderegg, 1997; Walsh, 2002) are the result of honest efforts to avoid the stigma attached to older terminology. Vergason and Anderegg (1997) noted that teachers who do not keep up with and use current terminology reveal that they have not remained current in their field. In spite of efforts in the field to replace past terminology with current terminology, old habits are hard to break, and it is often difficult to persuade people to adopt a new uniform set of terminology.

To illustrate the evolution of terminology in the professional literature, Sandieson (1998) analyzed three computer bases containing professional articles in the field of special education (i.e., PsycINFO, ERIC, MEDLINE) and found 67 terms used to label persons with mental retardation or developmental disabilities. Of the 67 identified terms, 5 were used with the highest frequency. These included (a) mental retardation/mentally retarded, (b) cognitive impairment/cognitively disabled, (c) learning disability/learning disabled, (d) developmental disability/developmentally disabled, and (e) developmental delay/developmentally delayed. During the 15-year period from 1981 to 1995, the term *mentally retarded* was most prevalent. When this range of time was further analyzed, the terms most prevalent in the 5-year period from 1991 to 1995 were *cognitive impairment* and *developmental disability.* Although this shows a change to the use of terms that may be more universally acceptable, cognitive impairment and developmental disability apply to a larger range of persons than those who can be described by the term *mental retardation*; thus, they communicate less about the specific group of persons being described in journal articles for purposes of generalizing information from one group to the next.

Consumers of research should note the evolution of terminology used by researchers to communicate when sharing the results of investigations. The term *vegetative human organism* used by Fuller in 1949 would be replaced in today's world by a less offensive term, such as *person with a significant cognitive disability*. Because journals are not revised as time passes, the substitution of current terminology for the old is a responsibility that is placed on consumers as they interpret the professional literature.

Issues in Assigning Labels to Persons with Disabilities   There are both advantages and disadvantages to using labels to identify persons with disabilities. Labels can be important tools when they communicate information, allowing knowledge gained through scientific investigation to facilitate advances in the field of special education (Luckasson & Reeve, 2001). Labels also are needed to advocate for persons with disabilities (Turnbull et al., 2002). Research, diagnosis, and treatment require labels to improve the lives of persons with disabilities while entitlements require labels to secure services (e.g., social security, special education) (Goode, 2002). The loss of labels can result in the loss of rights, entitlements, and services (Luckasson & Reeve, 2001; Turnbull et al., 2002).

Although labels can be beneficial, they are not without problems. First, assigning a term or a label to a person with a disability can have the unwanted outcome of devaluing that person (Luckasson & Reeve, 2001). Simply replacing labels that have become stigmatizing over time does not prevent this (Turnbull et al., 2002). In assigning new names or terms to persons with disabilities, Luckasson and Reeve (2001) suggested asking if the name or term (a) applies to a certain disability and nothing else, (b) provides consistent nomenclature, (c) facilitates communication, (d) incorporates current and future knowledge, (e) meets the purpose for which it was proposed, and (f) contributes positively to the portrayal of people with disabilities.

Person-First Language

Regardless of which term is used to describe persons with disabilities in a respectful manner, the purpose is defeated if the disability is allowed to dominate or overshadow the person (e.g., disabled person). One way to avoid identifying a person by his or her disability alone is to name the person before the disability. In addition, we should refer to persons as individuals rather than as a collective group (e.g., the disabled) because individual differences exist within groups. This is referred to as *person-first language*. Examples of acceptable language include *persons with disabilities*, *students with mental retardation*, and *children who have epilepsy*. These terms are preferable to their counterparts that include *the disabled, mentally retarded child*, or *epileptic*. Snow (1998) stated that it is common for society to misuse the terms *disabled* and *handicapped* in describing accommodations, making the point that it is more accurate to focus on accessibility. For example, it would be more appropriate to state that a restroom or parking lot is accessible, taking into consideration that not all people with disabilities will need all accommodations (e.g., a deaf person does not need the restroom accommodations needed by a person in a wheelchair).

The effort to use language that is not offensive can be a difficult undertaking. Some find it cumbersome, whereas others think it may send the wrong message. In his position paper on the language wars, Wolfensberger (2002) argued that the rules of political correctness are applied inconsistently to persons with and without disabilities. This practice can defeat the purpose of person-first language by drawing attention to a disability as if it devalued a person. For example, the rules of political correctness allow one to say "a person with a mental disability" or "a child with a developmental delay" and, at the same time, say "a smart woman" or a "gifted child." The message is that some terms come after the person because they are considered undesirable whereas other terms come before the person because they are considered desirable. Another practice questioned by Wolfensberger is putting the disability in quotation marks, such as describing a child in writing as *a child "labeled as having autism"* or in speech as "a child, quote, labeled as having autism, unquote." In this case, the use of quotation marks draws attention to the label as being something that is undesirable.

Some groups have combated stigmatizing labels by campaigning to make them a source of pride. For example, the Deaf community put the label before the person and refer to themselves in the collective with pride. This practice sends the message that the Deaf community recognize their difference in the ability to communicate and find it acceptable.

It is the responsibility of advocates for persons with disabilities to model the use of nonoffensive language in their speech and writing. In compiling a history of the terminology used in special education, Vergason and Anderegg (1997) stated that using person-first language (i.e., putting the child before the disability) avoids derogatory language and shows respect for the individual. However, Wolfensberger (2002) cautioned that, when people become too concerned with using the wrong term, they quit talking, and that can be dangerous. Therefore, even though persons in the field of disabilities should make an effort to model acceptable language, they should not be condescending to those (e.g., parents, members of the community) who, through lack of exposure and in absence of malice, express themselves in a way that may not seem preferable. Example 1.2 provides an illustration of a difference of opinion on person-first language from a person with a disability in the community.

EXAMPLE 1.2 A DIFFERENCE OF OPINION IN THE APPLICATION OF PERSON-FIRST LANGUAGE

Several years ago, a committee met to plan the program for a local conference that would focus on the inclusion of persons with disabilities in the community (Collins, Epstein, Reiss, & Lowe, 2001). The ground rules were that the planning committee should consist of an array of interested persons from the community, with the majority being persons with disabilities or their family members.

During the initial planning meeting, the committee members introduced themselves and told how they came to be involved in the project. Each person was being careful in the wording they used to describe their connection to the conference (e.g., "I am a special education teacher who works with students with moderate to severe disabilities.").

One gentleman, who was eager to voice his opinion, began by stating his occupation. Although his disability was apparent, he concluded his introduction by saying, "Furthermore, I am a blind person, and I don't want to be known as a person who is blind or has a visual impairment. I'm blind and I'm proud of it!"

Before continuing with this chapter, give some thought to your position on the language that is used in our society in referring to persons with disabilities. An example for your consideration can be found in Activity 1.2.

ACTIVITY 1.2   Identifying Appropriate Language

The media do much to influence the language used by society to describe persons with disabilities. The following excerpts are from articles that appeared in a newspaper in the months following the publication of an editorial stressing the importance of positive terminology in relation to disabilities. As you read through each excerpt, note the terminology and the way it is used. In most cases the writers are trying to be advocates for persons with disabilities. Is this purpose accomplished? What suggestions, if any, do you have for changing the language in each piece?

"The 11-year-old Shelby County middle-schooler was kicked out of his Scout troop last month because he is autistic and has 'special needs'" ("Intolerance Badge," 2002).

"The prom, with the theme 'An Enchanted Evening,' is for all mentally or physically disabled adults, ages 16 or older" ("Prom for Disabled," 2002).

"Down syndrome dolls help children identify" (Knight-Ridder News Service, 2002).

"[The television program] tells how two developmentally disabled individuals overcame extraordinary circumstances to forge a life together as husband and wife" (Your Sunday, 2003).

"A 37-year-old mother and her mentally handicapped 22-year-old daughter were found in a back bedroom of their house . . ." (Lannen, 2003).

"[The school] district must reimburse a couple's expenses for private tutoring because it failed to meet the needs of their disabled son . . . (Schreiner, 2003).

DEFINING THE TERMINOLOGY USED IN THE FIELD OF DISABILITIES

Chapter 1, to this point, has noted that there are a number of terms used in the field of moderate and severe disabilities and that care should be exercised in selecting and using those terms that are most appropriate. It should be clear that a number of past terms have been replaced over time with new terms that are less stigmatizing, while having the advantage of more accurately describing a condition and providing more information that is useful in communication. This section will explain why all terms are not interchangeable and will provide definitions of acceptable terms.

It may be most useful to begin by describing the differences among three common terms: (a) impairment, (b) disability, and (c) handicap. An **impairment** indicates a lessening or weakening in ability or state of health (Graziano, 2002). For example, a person with a visual impairment may have an eye that is misshapen or may have loss of vision due to a physical condition, such as glaucoma, that affects the ability to see. A person with a motor impairment may have a physical diagnosis of cerebral palsy, with the motor impairment resulting from damage to the brain tissue that controls motoric ability resulting in difficulty in walking.

A **disability** refers to a reduction of function or absence of a body part or organ. The disability may be physical or cognitive, but it produces the possibility of limitations (Vergason & Anderegg, 1997). A person with a communication disability may have a reduction in the capacity of the oral musculature to produce speech or a reduction in the capacity of the brain to process language. A person with a cognitive disability may have a reduction in the function of the brain to process information in his or her environment. The cause may be genetic, as in Down syndrome; acquired, as in a birth trauma; or social, as in poor nutrition due to low socioeconomic status.

A **handicap** refers to the problems that persons with impairments or disabilities have in interacting with their environment. In other words, a handicap is a limitation imposed in part by a lack of accommodations within the environment (Vergason & Anderegg, 1997). For example, a person with a motor impairment or physical disability may have difficulty manipulating a staircase in a wheelchair but experience no problems in performing academic tasks. It is interesting to note that everyone (with or without a disability or impairment) can be viewed as having a handicap in certain environments. Just imagine a golfer who is blind and a golfer who is sighted who are playing golf at midnight without artificial lighting. Who has the handicap?

With these terms defined, it follows that mental retardation is a disability that may or may not be accompanied by an impairment (e.g., sensory impairment) and, while it is cognitive in nature, may or may not be a handicapping condition across all adaptive areas (e.g., communication, mobility). Luckasson and Reeve (2001) asserted that, once a term is named or assigned, it must be explained; once defined, it can result in further classifications or divisions into subgroups. The American Association on Mental Retardation (AAMR) has struggled with accepting mental retardation as an appropriate term, defining the term in an accurate manner, and further classifying the term into subgroups. However, mental retardation has been the term most commonly used in the United States for more than 50 years (Luckasson & Reeve, 2001).

Once a term is deemed appropriate, Luckasson and Reeve (2001) also stated that there are questions that should be asked before deciding on a corresponding definition. These questions include determining if the definition (a) indicates the boundaries of the term, (b) indicates the class of things to which it belongs, (c) differentiates from other members of the class, (d) uses words that are no more complicated than the term, (e) defines what the term is and is not, (f) allows for generalization of characteristics of the individual or group named by the term, (g) remains consistent with the desired framework, and (h) contributes positively to portrayal of people within the term.

To illustrate the difficulty of defining the term used for a category of disability, AAMR has had 10 editions of definitions for mental retardation since 1908 (AAMR, 2002). The most recent definition was written in 2002 when AAMR defined mental retardation in the following manner:

> **Mental retardation** is a disability characterized by significant limitations both in intellectual functioning and in adaptive behavior as expressed in conceptual, social, and practical adaptive skills. This disability originates before age 18 (AAMR, 2002).

After defining mental retardation, AAMR listed the five assumptions that follow as being essential in applying the definition:

1. Limitations in present functioning must be considered within the context of community environments typical of the individual's age, peers, and culture.
2. Valid assessment considers cultural and linguistic diversity as well as differences in communication, sensory, motor, and behavioral factors.
3. Within an individual, limitations often coexist with strengths.
4. An important purpose of describing limitations is to develop a profile of needed supports.
5. With appropriate personalized supports over a sustained period, the life functioning of the person with mental retardation generally will improve (AAMR, 2002).

The definition of mental retardation raises a number of questions. These include the ability of teacher training programs to prepare teachers for the whole continuum of mental retardation and effects on teacher certification, funding, and class size (Smith, 1997).

Mental retardation defines a more specific group than the broader term *developmental disabilities*. As written in the Developmental Disabilities Act (P.L. 95:602), **developmental disability** is defined as a

> severe, chronic disability which is attributable to a mental and/or physical impairment or combination of mental and physical impairments; is manifested before the person attains age 22; is likely to continue indefinitely; results in substantial functional limitations in three or more of the following areas of major life activity: self-care, receptive and expressive language, learning, mobility, self-direction, capacity for independent living and economic self-sufficiency; and reflects the person's need for special services that are of lifelong or extended duration and are individually planned and coordinated (Handleman, 1986, p. 153).

Handleman (1986) proposed **severe developmental disabilities** as "an umbrella term for those with autism, severe mental retardation, and multiple disabilities" (p. 89).

To determine a preference in the field for the terms *mental retardation* and *developmental disabilities*, Conyers, Martin, Martin, and Yu (2002) analyzed the subjects sections of data-based articles focusing on persons with disabilities in four journals published in the years 1993 to 2001 *(American Journal on Mental Retardation, Education and Training in Developmental Disabilities, Journal of the Association for Applied Behavior Analysis,* and *Research in Developmental Disabilities).* They found that the authors of these studies used the older 1983 AAMR terms, definitions, and classifications for mental retardation in two thirds of the articles. The authors rarely used the term *developmental disabilities,* even where that term appeared in the title of the journal. Conyers et al. hypothesized that, because *developmental disabilities* is a broad term and the 1983 classification system is more specific, the authors chose to use the 1983 terms to facilitate generalization of research to practice. (It should be noted that reviewers from journals often ask authors to change the terms they use to describe the participants with disabilities in their studies before they are published; again, this is probably to facilitate generalization from research to practice.)

CLASSIFYING PERSONS WITH DISABILITIES

Once a term has been defined, there is sometimes a need to provide further classifications under the term. Classifying allows coding, facilitation of record keeping, consistent nomenclature, better communication, generalization of research to practice, positive portrayal of persons within categories, an organization system for incorporating knowledge, better planning, and predictability about outcomes of treatments (Luckasson & Reeve, 2001). As they did with labeling and defining, Luckasson and Reeve (2001) also listed questions that should be asked in developing classification systems. These include asking if the classification system (a) allows grouping on consistent, meaningful criteria; (b) facilitates record keeping; (c) provides consistent nomenclature; (d) facilitates communication; (e) allows generalization about the group; (f) facilitates organization of new knowledge; (g) promotes planning and allocation of resources; (h) contributes to meaningful prediction for groups; (i) is consistent within the theoretical framework; and (j) contributes positively to the portrayal of groups.

Past systems of classification for mental retardation that, in most cases, have been dropped because they became stigmatizing include (a) moron, imbecile, and idiot; (b) high grade, middle grade, and low grade; and (c) educable mentally handicapped or retarded, trainable mentally handicapped or retarded, and severely/profoundly handicapped or retarded. Ignacy Golberg's story of a classification system within an institution for persons with disabilities illustrates how a classification system can be both degrading and sarcastic (Smith, 2002; Smith & Mitchell, 2001). The institutional system he described had three classifications for the persons with cognitive disabilities who resided there: (a) the retarded who were in need of constant care and attention, (b) the normal retarded who cared for themselves and functioned in a relatively independent fashion within the group, and (c) the minimally gifted who were rewarded by staff for doing things they were paid to do.

In illustrating how absurd classification systems can be, Smull (1998) questioned what would happen if college students were placed in college dorms and assigned roommates according to SAT scores that ran a continuum of borderline clever (SAT score of 850–1000) to profoundly clever (1451–1600). Because classification systems can be problematic in labeling persons, they must be used with care, making certain that they are used only to provide information that improves lives instead of stigmatizing people. The following sections discuss the issues in classifying by IQ scores, support levels, and state certification.

Classification by IQ Scores

Although AAMR acknowledges mental retardation as having an upper IQ limit of 70–75, the 1992 and 2002 definitions omitted the further classifications by IQ found in the 1983 version of the definition. The 1983 version of the American Association on Mental Deficiency (AAMD) definition of mental retardation had four classifications based on IQ. The bell curve shown in Figure 1.1 demonstrates these classifications and the percentage of the population in each. As depicted, the majority of the population can be expected to score an average of 100 on standardized IQ tests. The further the IQ score falls from the mean in either direction, the smaller the percentage of the population falling within a particular range of classification. **Mild mental retardation** fell within an IQ range of 55 to 75 (i.e., 2 to 3 standard deviations below the mean), **moderate mental retardation** fell within an IQ range of 35 to 55 (3 to 4 standard deviations below the mean), **severe mental retardation** fell within an IQ range of 20 to 35 (4 to 5 standard deviations below the mean), and **profound mental retardation** fell below an IQ of 20 (more than 5 standard deviations below the mean).

Some have viewed the classification by IQ range as being problematic. For example, at the upper end of the IQ range, Smith (1997) questioned if a cutoff of 75 instead of 70 would increase the population of students needing special education services beyond the capacity of school districts and whether those with mild disabilities would be jeopardized in advocacy and protection services.

In the past, professionals in the field of special education have proposed further categories when describing persons with severe to profound disabilities. For example, Switzky, Haywood, and Rotatori (1982) broke the profound range into two classifications: (a) relative and (b) absolute. They viewed those classified in the **relative profound range** as being more competent than those falling in the absolute range and as having some degree of ambulation, language, communication, and self-help skills. They viewed those in the **absolute profound range** as lacking all adaptive

FIGURE 1.1

The bell curve showing the distribution of mental retardation by IQ score across the population.

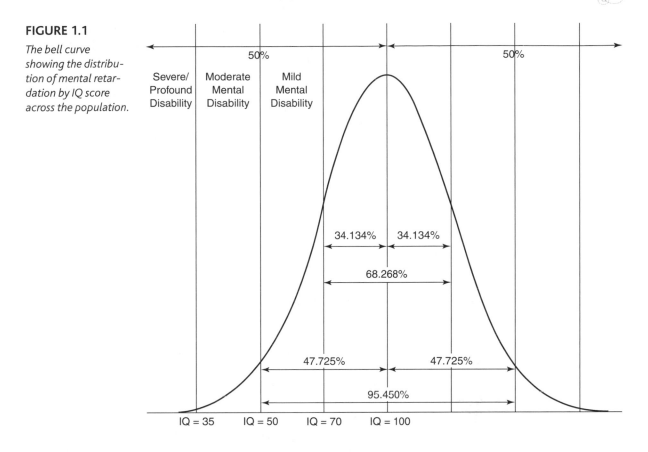

behavior skills and as being in a medically fragile state. In another example, Sailor, Gee, Goetz, and Graham (1988) described characteristics of persons with the most severe disabilities or those who would fit in the absolute range of profound mental retardation by stating that these individuals

> (a) have a wide range of multiple impairments; (b) have profound loss of functioning; (c) may have various orthopedic and sensory disabilities; (d) may have little or no voluntary control over movements; (e) may be medically at risk, chronically ill, or medically dependent; (f) may have severe behavior disorders; (g) may not demonstrate any obvious choices or preferences; (h) may show no signs of anticipation or have little affect; (i) and may have restricted participation in other environments due to self-injurious behavior or assaultive behavior (p. 89).

Issues in Assigning IQ Scores to Persons with Mental Retardation According to Evans (1991), the problems encountered in using IQ tests are numerous. Assigning an IQ score to a person influences the expectations one makes of that person. Most IQ tests were normed on persons without disabilities, making the validity of IQ scores for persons with disabilities suspect. In addition, there is a tendency to misuse IQ tests normed on certain age groups. For example, the *Bayley Scales of Infant Development*, although designed for young children, may be administered to older children with severe mental retardation.

Evans (1991) further noted a numbers of issues, as follow, that make dependency on IQ scores to classify degrees of mental retardation a dangerous practice, particularly in working with persons with severe cognitive disabilities or mental retardation. First, IQ tests are inappropriate to use with persons with severe intellectual disabilities. Persons falling into this category may have sensory, motoric, or communicative disabilities that preclude their ability to respond to test items and cognitive disabilities that preclude their ability to process directions. Second, tests that were standardized on infants often are used to assess older persons with severe disabilities and scores are extrapolated. This practice is hazardous because the tests were designed for a younger population and the scores would be inaccurate. Third, inaccurate IQ scores render them useless. More meaningful information is obtained by assessments that determine educational and service needs. Fourth, adaptive behavior assessments are questionable because they often consist of scales of poorly defined competencies. This makes reliability of scoring an issue. Fifth, tests and other measures are only as useful as the ways in which they are used. Many items on scales do not yield useful information for programming. For example, teaching a child to stack one block on another or to balance on one foot may increase the score on an IQ test or adaptive behavior scale but serve no useful purpose in the child's life. Finally, persons with severe mental retardation have an array of related and unrelated challenges, as would be found in the general population. These challenges (e.g., behavior disorders) may influence the outcome of assessments and result in labels (e.g., dual diagnosis of mental retardation and mental illness) that create issues in determining appropriate services.

Finally, Evans (1991) stated that there have been inconsistencies in assignments of IQ scores to categories. For example, AAMR set the range of severe mental retardation at IQ scores of 20–35, whereas the American Psychological Association (APA) set the range at IQ scores of 20–25.

It is clear that classifying persons by IQ scores alone can be problematic. To err on the side of caution, Vergason and Anderegg (1997) suggested that children near the limiting borders of diagnosis or classification should be given the benefit of the doubt and placed in the higher category. Because IQ scores can be inaccurate, assignments to labels must be flexible and curricula must be adapted appropriately regardless of the label. Luckasson and Reeve (2001) pointed out that using IQ scores alone for classification is problematic in that IQ scores do not predict the sophistication of learning that persons will achieve during life or the supports they will need.

Classification by Supports

The 1992 AAMR definition of *mental retardation* omitted classification by range of IQ scores in lieu of a classification system based on supports (Luckasson et al., 1992, p. 26). This was meant to be a flexible system of classification in which levels of needed support were assigned to adaptive areas on an individual basis, recognizing that the level of needed support can change over time. **Intermittent support** was that which could be provided on an "as needed" basis and was episodic in nature. For example, a person may need intermittent support in securing employment or during a medical crisis. **Limited support** was that which could be delivered consistently over time. For example, a person would need limited support during the secondary school years to complete a seamless transition to adulthood. **Extensive support** was that which could be provided on a regular basis for long periods of time. For example, a student may need daily special education services to participate in academic classes throughout the school years or daily support from an assistant to perform domestic tasks during adulthood. **Pervasive support** was that which could be provided consistently with high intensity over time. For example, life-sustaining procedures, such as suctioning or gastrointestinal tube feeding, would be pervasive in nature and needed on a continuous schedule to sustain life.

The benefits of using levels of support for classification are numerous. The support system allows persons to change from one level of support to another over time. In addition, persons may need various levels of support across adaptive areas. For example, a person with mental retardation who is transitioning to adulthood might need intermittent support in adapting to a new residential placement (e.g., learning a new neighborhood), limited support in training for a job, sustained support in budgeting and money management, and pervasive support in managing a medical condition (e.g., epilepsy or diabetes).

Smith (1997) questioned the system of classification by levels of support, wondering if the four categories would be considered equivalent to IQ subgroups, whether using them in placement meetings would be cumbersome, and how they would be measured. Vergason and Anderegg (1997) asserted that the 1992 system of classification by supports has been ignored in the field of special education because the previous 1983 classification terms using IQ scores facilitate communication and help prospective special education teachers find jobs in their areas of expertise and licensure.

In 2002 AAMR simplified the support system by stating in simple terms that persons with mental retardation need a profile of "appropriate personalized supports over a sustained period" (AAMR, 2002). The association further clarified that supports can be implemented across domains (e.g., education, domestic, recreation, vocational) and provided by a variety of sources (e.g., family, friends, agencies) in the following nine areas: (a) human development activities, (b) teaching and education activities, (c) home living activities, (d) community living activities, (e) employment activities, (f) health and safety activities, (g) behavioral activities, (h) social activities, and (i) protection and advocacy activities (AAMR, 2002).

Recognizing the benefits of a system that revolves around the need for supports, TASH (an advocacy group for persons with disabilities) avoids applying a label to its target group by instead describing a diverse group of individuals with needs for supports who may or may not fall under the definitions of developmental disabilities or mental retardation. Instead of defining a term, the mission statement of TASH describes the target group in terms of advocacy and support needs. The following was stated on the TASH Web site in 2005:

> TASH's focus is on those people with disabilities who. (a) are most at risk for being excluded from the mainstream of society; (b) are perceived by traditional service systems as being most challenging; (c) are most likely to have their rights abridged; (d) are most likely to be at risk for living, working, playing, and/or learning in segregated environments; (e) are least likely to have the tools and opportunities necessary to advocate on their own behalf; (f) historically have been labeled as having severe disabilities; and (g) are most likely to need ongoing, individualized supports in order to participate in inclusive communities and enjoy a quality of life similar to that available to all citizens.*

Like the 2002 definition from AAMR, the TASH mission implies that levels of support will be individualized in order to meet the needs of the diverse group of individuals they represent.

Classification by State Certification

States appear to have as difficult a time as professional organizations in determining appropriate terminology and classification systems. With 50 states, there are a minimum of 50 possibilities, causing confusion when teachers apply for certification across

---

*Printed with permission from TASH. For more information about TASH, visit www.tash.org.

states or when students with disabilities move from one state to another. For example, Kentucky certifies teachers in two areas: high-incidence or mild disabilities fall under the umbrella label of *Learning and Behavior Disorders* whereas low-incidence disabilities fall under the umbrella label of *Moderate and Severe Disabilities*. To compound the problem, there is inconsistency in the language used in certification and in placement; Kentucky teachers with certification in moderate to severe disabilities serve students who are classified as having *Functional Mental Disabilities*. In contrast, Utah groups students and certifies teachers in the collapsed areas *of Mild/Moderate Disabilities* and *Severe/Profound Disabilities*.

DEMOGRAPHICS OF PERSONS WITH DISABILITIES

Discrepancies in terminology, labels, and classification systems create problems in determining the demographics of persons with disabilities. Larson et al. (2001) described the results of the National Health Interview Survey of 1994 to 1995, which was based on face-to-face or telephone interviews. The recipients were from the United States and identified themselves as having mental retardation or developmental disabilities. The definitions for categorization included having limitations in adaptive skills or having a condition related to a deficit in learning requiring special education services, such as autism, Down syndrome, spina bifida, or hydrocephalus. The results showed that 14.9 per 1,000 noninstitutionalized persons fell into the categories of developmental disabilities or mental retardation. This was equivalent to 1.9 percent of the noninstitutionalized U.S. population. Noting the differences between mental retardation and developmental disabilities, Larsen et al. found the prevalence of those with mental retardation to be 7.8 per 1,000 and the prevalence of those with developmental disabilities to be 11.28 per 1,000. When combined with those who were institutionalized, the prevalence of those with mental retardation increased to 9.7 per 1,000.

In breaking the data into specific groups, Larson et al. found the prevalence of specific disabilities in the noninstitutionalized population as follows: (a) cerebral palsy, 4.02 per 1,000; (b) spina bifida, .62 per 1,000; and (c) autism, .40 per 1,000. Each of these specific disabilities may or may not be accompanied by mental retardation. Those with autism (87 percent) were the most likely to have mental retardation or developmental disabilities. In contrast, 26% of those with cerebral palsy and 23% of those with spina bifida reported having mental retardation or developmental disabilities. The percentage of those meeting the criterion for developmental disabilities without mental retardation was 16% of those with autism, 9% of those with cerebral palsy, and 3% of those with spina bifida. The overlap of mental retardation and developmental disabilities was more pronounced in those who resided in institutions.

Larson et al. also analyzed the data for differences in children and adults and found that children are more likely to be identified with mental retardation or developmental disabilities than are adults. Specifically, 3.84% of children age 5 years and younger and 3.17% of children ranging in age from 6 to 7 years met the criterion for mental retardation, developmental disabilities, or both. In contrast, only .79 percent of adults met this criterion. This supports the assertion that, once the demands of learning in school end, many persons no longer meet the definition of having a cognitive disability, particularly those who had limitations in only learning or economic sufficiency. In addition, Larson et al. noted that many adults attempt to rid themselves of labels they consider stigmatizing. Finally, the increase of mortality with age also can account for the difference in prevalence between children and adults. This appears to be supported by the fact that 9% of those in the 25- to 34-year age range had mental retardation or developmental disabilities as opposed to .4% of those over the age of 65 years.

Graziano (2002) listed more recent estimates for the prevalence of developmental disabilities in the United States in 2000 as being 14 million. He also estimated an incidence of mental retardation as being 250 to 300 of every 10,000 births. In addition, McClean (2002) cited the prevalence of autism as affecting 15 out of every 10,000 people and noted that most are children under the age of 10.

MODERATE AND SEVERE DISABILITIES

The purpose of this book is to provide the reader with a foundation in the study of moderate and severe disabilities. Thus far this chapter has presented the term *disability*, provided a definition for that term, and presented the classifications of *moderate* and *severe* as they relate to the term *mental retardation*. This section will elaborate on *moderate and severe disabilities* as a term and classification and will lead the reader through a working definition.

The category of high-incidence disabilities contains a large number of persons with mild disabilities. This category can contain persons who are eligible for services because they have mild mental retardation, specific learning disabilities, health impairments (e.g., attention deficit hyperactivity disorder), certain physical or sensory impairments (e.g., cerebral palsy, astigmatism), and behavior disorders (e.g., aggressive or disruptive behaviors) that require adaptations and accommodations in an academic setting. Most of the children in this group can participate in an academic curriculum with minimal support. In other words, they focus on academic tasks, such as reading and math, during the school years with the assumption that they will master the content to the extent that they will be able to apply it in their daily lives. With appropriate adaptations and accommodations, students with high-incidence disabilities may reach or even surpass the academic achievement level of students without disabilities. The next assumption is that the students will transition to an adulthood in which they may hold jobs; develop personal, committed relationships; have families; and participate in the community without further support or with minimal support. It is not uncommon for persons with mild mental retardation to lose their label once they are no longer in need of educational services.

The category of low-incidence disabilities contains a smaller percentage of the population (see the bell curve described earlier). Persons with moderate, severe, and profound cognitive disabilities or mental retardation fall into this category. The category also contains persons with severe developmental disabilities that include autism and multiple disabilities (e.g., sensory impairments, physical disabilities, severe behavior disorders) that cause them to function within the moderate to profound disability range. The category is diverse, with students who exhibit a great number of abilities on one end of the continuum and students with a minimal number of abilities on the other. What binds them together is their need for a functional curriculum focusing on the life skills they will need when they transition to adulthood. Thus, a person with moderate or severe disabilities might be considered to have a **functional mental disability.** Persons with moderate and severe disabilities will need lifelong support and services in more than one area of adaptive skills once they leave the school environment. As in the 1992 and 2002 definitions of mental retardation, the level of support across adaptive skill areas can vary in intensity and length of delivery.

It is important to note that some high-incidence disabilities, such as behavior disorders, health impairments, sensory impairments, physical disabilities, and specific learning disabilities also can be present in persons with moderate and severe disabilities. On the other hand, significant sensory impairments, such as deafness and blindness, are considered low-incidence disabilities due to the low frequency with which they are found in the population, although they are not tied to cognitive functioning.

The diversity of persons falling within the moderate and severe disability classification creates a challenge for those who work with them. Whereas persons in the moderate range may become proficient in a number of domains such as functional academics (e.g., reading sight words, computing with a calculator), domestic skills (e.g., cooking with picture recipes), and community skills (e.g., using a next dollar strategy to make purchases), persons in the severe and profound range may struggle to perform basic skills in areas such as communication (e.g., using picture symbols or adaptive devices) and self-help (e.g., eating, toileting, dressing). Switzky et al. (1985) described the diversity of persons with the most severe disabilities (i.e., significant cognitive or profound disabilities) when they stated that they are more likely to have delayed puberty, active seizures, enuresis, poor communication, pica, self-biting, fecal smearing, public masturbation, mutism, echopraxia, lack of self-recognition, rumination, encopresis, lack of social skills, and a higher pain threshhold. Jacobson and Janicki (1985) stated that persons with profound disabilities are more likely to be institutionalized. Example 1.3 describes two young men who are similar in age and family background who represent the diversity of persons to fall in the category of moderate and severe disabilities.

EXAMPLE 1.3   TWO PERSONS WITH MODERATE AND SEVERE DISABILITIES WHO DEMONSTRATE THE DIVERSITY IN THE CATEGORY

Blake is a 25-year-old man with moderate disabilities. He also has Down syndrome. He has a large functional sight word vocabulary and the functional math skills to make purchases in the community. In spite of speech that can be difficult to understand, he has excellent social skills and is well liked by people in the community. Blake attended a high school in a school district with an inclusive philosophy. In addition to receiving functional skill instruction in the special education classroom, Blake attended general education classes, such as chorus and language arts. Before transitioning from school services at the age of 21, he held several jobs in his community (e.g., fast food restaurant, farm equipment store) and attended college classes (e.g., weight lifting, radio broadcasting) with same-age peers. Blake currently holds a full-time job in the community and is waiting for an opening for supported living within his home community.

Jeremy is a 40-year-old man with severe disabilities. His disabilities include blindness, profound mental retardation, severe epilepsy, a cleft palate, and a congenital heart condition. He communicates by smiling, and he explores his environment by rolling back and forth on the floor. His caregiver performs self-help activities for him. Although he cannot stand, he can sit upright with the support of adaptive equipment. Because his birth was prior to the laws that mandated school services for all children, Jeremy remained at home instead of going to school. His family used respite services that were offered through social services when they needed to be away from Jeremy. Jeremy resided at home until the intensity of caregiving caused his aging parents to place him in a nearby rest home, where they can visit him on a daily basis.

Based on the earlier definitions of mental retardation and developmental disabilities covered in this chapter, the label of *moderate and severe disabilities,* as used in this text, includes persons who have cognitive disabilities consistent with an IQ below 50–55 or a severe developmental disability that limits their functional ability to this range. It is common for persons with moderate and severe disabilities to have two or more disabilities that contribute to their ability to function (e.g., mental retardation with a communication or motor impairment, deafblindness, autism with a severe behavior disorder). The onset of the disability occurs before adulthood, ruling out those who acquire a severe disability as a result of a medical condition, such as a stroke, or an injury, such as a head trauma, in adulthood. Varying levels of lifelong support are needed in two or more areas of adaptive behavior (i.e., communication, functional academic, self-help, motor, self-determination, or social skills) across domains (i.e., community, domestic, educational, leisure/recreation, vocational). Persons with moderate and severe disabilities benefit from individualized adaptations and accommodations, a functional curriculum, and support services that facilitate the ability to access less restrictive environments. (It should be noted that, throughout this text, the term *moderate and severe disabilities* will be used as a broad term to include persons with significant cognitive disabilities because the principles and strategies that will be described apply to persons within the moderate to profound range of mental retardation.)

DESCRIBING PERSONS WITH MODERATE AND SEVERE DISABILITIES

O'Brien and Mount (1991) told two stories about the same individual with severe disabilities. In the first version, Mr. Davis was described in clinical terms (age, IQ, gender) in three short, curt paragraphs. In the second, Ed (the same individual) was described through examples in terms that highlighted both his abilities and disabilities. The two stories drove home the point that clinical terms, such as IQ, do little to help practitioners identify appropriate services in terms of needed support. Describing capacities instead gives practitioners information that can be used as a starting point for developing appropriate services and identifying appropriate interventions, adaptations, and accommodations. Activity 1.3 illustrates this point with two new stories. Stop and complete this activity before finishing this chapter.

ACTIVITY 1.3   Telling the Stories of Persons with Moderate and Severe Disabilities

The following example provides the opportunity to examine the way persons with disabilities are described. During a school consultation for Ned (Collins, Schuster, & Grisham-Brown, 2002), the director of special education provided the consultants with the following information.

Ned was a male student with Down syndrome, a chronological age of ten years, a mental age of 2 years, and a minimal expressive signing vocabulary. He no longer was allowed to attend school while other students were present due to the severity of his aggressive behavior (e.g., hitting, throwing tantrums) and the classroom disruption caused by his noncompliant behavior. Before reading further, stop and find a discussion partner. Based on the information above, what do you know about Ned, and what do you still need to learn?

After interviewing Ned's teacher and staff and observing Ned in the school environment, the consultants discovered new pieces to Ned's story that enabled them to develop an appropriate program in the months that followed. This included the following information. Although the speech therapist stated that Ned did not have a functional communication system, his mother reported that he could use more than 40 meaningful manual signs in the home environment. The consultants also found that Ned could match pictures to objects and activities and that he was imitative. Some of Ned's aggressive behavior (e.g., hitting, spitting) appeared to be an attempt to get the attention of peers. Some of his disruptive behavior (e.g., throwing tantrums, lying down in the floor and refusing to move) appeared to be a way to communicate his preferences and nonpreferences for tasks he was asked to perform.

Over time the consultants discovered that Ned liked spending time in the cafeteria with both staff and peers. He liked playing games on the computer, listening to music, and looking at books. He liked physical activity with peers on the playground and in the gym. He adored his older brother and liked to roughhouse with him at home. He had definite preferences in the foods he ate. Ned liked to go into the community and to take part in classes with peers, and he had better behavior in those settings. His behavior was better also when he had little downtime, had a choice in activities, and knew in advance what activity came next in his schedule. How does this information portray Ned in a different light? How would this information help a teacher who might have Ned as a student prepare an appropriate curriculum and schedule?

TRENDS AND CURRENT ISSUES

As this chapter concludes, it may be helpful to note other changes that have accompanied the way in which we view persons with mental retardation and developmental disabilities as a prelude to the remainder of this text. Polloway, Smith, Patton, and Smith (1996) have identified three paradigm shifts. In the early 1900s, a facility-based paradigm existed in which persons with disabilities were institutionalized or lived in residential programs. By the 1950s this shifted to a services-based paradigm in which persons with disabilities entered special schools or school programs and group homes in their communities where they could be clustered together to receive specialized services (e.g., speech therapy). With the advent of the 1992 AAMR definition of mental retardation, the shift was to a supports-based paradigm where the thrust was for persons with disabilities to be included, not just physically integrated, in the same settings where they would attend classes, reside, or work if they did not have disabilities. The most recent shift is to an empowerment paradigm where persons with disabilities have the right to practice self-determination, making their own choices in school, work, community living, and recreation instead of having choices made for them.

On a final note, it should be mentioned that there are current issues that have raised the stakes in labeling, classifying, and categorizing children with disabilities. With the implementation of the No Child Left Behind Act in 2002, all children are expected to make progress across general education core content (Browder & Cooper-Duffy, 2003). Those children who fall in the range of moderate and severe disabilities are permitted to participate in alternate assessment procedures. Because of the high stakes associated with performance and progress, schools may be tempted to place borderline students in the alternate assessment category, where their scores will be weighted in a different manner even though standard assessment procedures are more appropriate. Thus, it is important that families continue to work with school systems to ensure that the labels put on children are correct and appropriate.

Best Practices
Labeling Persons with Disabilities

1. Stay current on terminology and use it in a respectful manner that does not demean others.
2. When speaking about persons with disabilities, model person-first language by putting the person before the disability.
3. Recognize that, while IQ scores, mental ages, and labels serve a purpose in identifying individuals who require special services and in securing those services, more useful information for programming comes from describing persons in terms of strengths and weaknesses and needs for support.
4. Never assume that a person with a specific label will fit a preconceived mold because persons with moderate and severe disabilities are a heterogeneous group with a broad array of characteristics.

Conclusion

This chapter has defined and described the classification of moderate and severe disabilities through reviewing the evolution of terminology from past to present and through comparing the definitions of mental retardation and developmental disabilities. Issues, such as the advantages and disadvantages of labeling and classifying and the dangers of relying on IQ scores, have been discussed. With an understanding of moderate and severe disabilities as it is used in this text, the reader is ready to begin to explore the issues and the thinking that provide a foundation for working with persons with moderate and severe disabilities (including those with significant cognitive disabilities). Before proceeding, however, readers should stop and check their understanding through the performance-based assessment question at the end of this chapter.

Questions for Review

1. In what ways has terminology evolved over the past decades? Why?
2. How do the broad categories of mental retardation and developmental disabilities differ?
3. Contrast the classification systems for mental retardation used by AAMD in 1983, AAMR in 1992, and AAMR in 2002. What remained the same and what changed?
4. Why is the practice of classifying by IQ scores problematic? Is it useful in any way?
5. Give an example of person-first language and explain the rationale for using it. Is there a time when person-first language may not be used? If so, when?
6. In your own words, provide a working definition for moderate and severe disabilities that highlights the diversity within the group.

Performance-Based Assessment
Defining and Describing Moderate and Severe Disabilities

Professionals in the field of moderate and severe disabilities often find themselves in situations where they must define or describe the persons with whom they work in terms that create a clear picture for the general public without using offensive language or terminology that is unfamiliar. Pick one of the scenarios below and write a brief overview of how you would provide an explanation to your audience.

1. You are working with a family who are transitioning their child from preschool to elementary school services. Until this point the family has heard the term *developmental delay* used to describe their child. Your job is to explain the classification system used by the school district and the label of moderate and severe disabilities that the district has placed on their child in order to receive services.

2. You have been invited to address a community civic group that wants to donate time and funds to a project in the school system that focuses on children with special needs. Your job is to explain the type of children you serve under the label of moderate and severe disabilities and how they should be addressed during the project.

3. You have read an article in the paper that describes persons with moderate and severe disabilities in outdated, stigmatizing language and terminology. As an advocate for persons with disabilities, your job is to write a response that explains appropriate language and terminology.

4. Services for persons with disabilities in your community and state are under consideration for serious financial cutbacks. As a representative from your district or agency, you have been asked to describe the students with whom you work and make a case for continued funding. Your job is to come up with a working definition for moderate and severe disabilities that will be used in a position paper to be submitted to provide a rationale for continued funding.

References

AAMR Definition of Mental Retardation (2002). Retrieved June 6, 2005, from www.aamr.org/Policies/faq_mental_retardation.shtml.

Browder, D. M., & Cooper-Duffy, K. (2003). Evidence-based practices for students with severe disabilities and the requirement for accountability in "No Child Left Behind." *Journal of Special Education, 37,* 157–163.

Collins, B. C., Epstein, A., Reiss, T., & Lowe, V. (2001). Including children with mental disabilities in the religious community. *Teaching Exceptional Children, 33*(5), 52–58.

Collins, B. C., Schuster, J. W., & Grisham-Brown, J. (2002). *Success story: Ned.* Unpublished manuscript.

Conyers, C., Martin, T. L., Martin, G. L., & Yu, D. (2002). The 1983 AAMR Manual, the 1992 AAMR Manual or the Developmental Disabilities Act: Which do researchers use? *Education and Training in Mental Retardation and Developmental Disabilities, 37,* 310–316.

Evans, I. M. (1991). Testing and diagnosis: A review and evaluation. In L. H. Meyer, C. A. Peck, & L. Brown (Eds.), *Critical issues in the lives of people with severe disabilities* (pp. 25–44). Baltimore: Brookes.

Fuller, P. R. (1949). Operant conditioning of a vegetative human organism. *Journal of Psychology, 62,* 587–590.

Gelb, S. A. (2002). The dignity of humanity is not a scientific construct. *Mental Retardation, 40,* 55–56.

Goode, D. (2002). Mental retardation is dead: Long live mental retardation! *Mental Retardation, 40,* 57–59.

Graziano, A. M. (2002). *Developmental disabilities: Introduction to a diverse field.* Boston: Allyn & Bacon.

Handleman, J. S. (1986). Severe developmental disabilities: Defining the term. *Education and Treatment of Children, 9,* 153–167.

Intolerance badge: Disabled boy's explosion discredits Scouts [Editorials] (2002, September 6). *Lexington Herald-Leader,* p. A10.

Jacobson, J. W., & Janicki, M. P. (1985). Functional and health status of characteristics of persons with severe handicaps in New York state. *Journal of the Association for Persons with Severe Handicaps, 10,* 51–60.

Knight-Ridder News (2003, February 4). Down syndrome dolls help children identify. *Lexington-Herald Leader,* p. E8.

Lannen, 3. (2003, March 7). Mother, daughter found dead in home: Property manager discovers apparent murder-suicide. *Lexington Herald-Leader,* p. B4.

Larson, S. A., Lakin, K. C., Anderson, L., Kwak Lee, N., Lee, J. H., & Anderson, D. (2001). Prevalence of mental retardation and developmental disabilities: Estimates from the 1994/1995 National Health Interview Survey disability supplements. *American Journal on Mental Retardation, 106,* 231–252.

Luckasson, R., Coulter, D. L., Polloway, E. A., Reiss, S., Schalock, R. L., Snell, M. E., et al. (Eds.). (1992). *Mental retardation: Definition, classification, and systems of supports* (9th ed.). Washington, DC: American Association on Mental Retardation.

Luckasson, R., & Reeve, A. (2001). Naming, defining, and classifying in mental retardation. *Mental Retardation, 39,* 47–52.

McClean, T. (2002, October 2). *All alone no longer: Parents of autistic child form support group in Versailles. Lexington Herald-Leader,* p. E1.

O'Brien, J., & Mount, B. (1991). Telling new stories: The search for capacity among people with severe handicaps. In L. H. Meyer, C. A. Peck, & L. Brown (Eds.), *Critical issues in the lives of people with severe disabilities* (pp. 89–92). Baltimore: Brookes.

Polloway, E. A., Smith, J. D., Patton, J. R., & Smith, T. E. C. (1996). Historic changes in mental retardation and developmental disabilities. *Education and Training in Mental Retardation and Developmental Disabilities, 31,* 3–12.

Prom for disabled. (2002, October 26). *Lexington Herald-Leader,* E8.

Sailor, W., Gee, K., Goetz, L., & Graham, N. (1988). *Progress in educating students with the most severe disabilities: Is there any?* Journal of the Association for Severe Handicaps, 13(2), 87–99.

Sandieson, R. (1998). A survey on terminology that refers to people with mental retardation/developmental disabilities. *Education and Training in Mental Retardation and Developmental Disabilities, 33,* 290–295.

Schalock, R. L. (2002). What's in a name? *Mental Retardation, 40,* 59–61.

Schreiner, B. (2003, March 8). Fayette must reimburse parents for special education, court rules. *Lexington Herald-Leader,* p. B1.

Smith, J. D. (1997). Mental retardation as an educational construct: Time for a new shared view? *Education and Training in Mental Retardation and Developmental Disabilities, 32,* 167–173.

Smith, J. D. (2002). The myth of mental retardation: Paradigm shifts, disaggregation, and developmental disabilities. *Mental Retardation, 40,* 62–64.

Smith, J. D., & Mitchell, A. L. (2001). "Me? I'm not a drooler. I'm the assistant": Is it time to abandon mental retardation as a classification? *Mental Retardation, 39* (2), 144–146.

Smull, M. W. (1998, October). Escaping from the label trap. *TASH Newsletter, 24*(10), 22–23.

Snow, K. (1998, October). To achieve inclusion, community, and freedom for people with disabilities, we must use people first language. *TASH Newsletter, 24*(10), 14–16.

Switzky, H. N., Haywood, H. C., & Rotatori, A. F. (1982). Who are the severely and profoundly mentally retarded? *Education and Training of the Mentally Retarded, 20,* 268–272.

TASH Mission (2005). Retrieved June 7, 2005, from www.tash.org/misc/index.htm

Turnbull, R., Turnbull, A., Warren, S., Eidelman, S., & Marchand, P. (2002). Shakespeare redux, or *Romeo and Juliet* revisited: Embedding a terminology and name change in a new agenda for the field of mental retardation. *Mental Retardation, 40,* 65–70.

Vergason, G. A., & Anderegg, M. L. (1997). The ins and outs of special education terminology. *Teaching Exceptional Children, 29* (5), 35–39.

Walsh, K. K. (2002). Thoughts on changing the term mental retardation. *Mental Retardation, 40,* 70–75.

Weiss, N. (1998, March). What does TASH stand for? *TASH Newsletter.* Retrieved September 9, 2002, from www.tash.org/misc/index.htm

Wolfensberger, W. (2002). Needed or at least wanted: Sanity in the language wars. *Mental Retardation, 40,* 75–80.

Your Sunday (2003, February 9). *Lexington Herald-Leader,* p. A2.

CHAPTER TWO

WORKING WITH PERSONS WITH SIGNIFICANT COGNITIVE DISABILITIES:

Educational Issues and Challenges

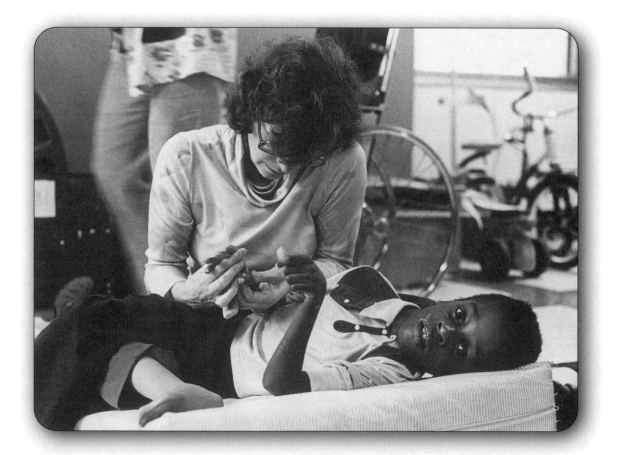

On completion of this chapter, the reader will meet the following objectives:

- Describe historical educational issues in regard to persons with significant cognitive disabilities.
- List skills that have been acquired by persons with significant cognitive disabilities as documented in the professional literature.
- Provide an overview of the skills needed to work with persons with significant cognitive disabilities.
- State the least dangerous assumption in regard to education.

The efficacy of special education has been debated for more than 20 years, in spite of laws that declare that all children have the right to a free and appropriate public school education. When members of the community question whether special education is effective or whether it is worth the cost, it is easy to respond, "It doesn't matter; it's the law." This response, however, passes up an opportunity to educate the public as to what constitutes an appropriate education and what the benefits might be.

In recent years, the debate has centered on special education in its entirety. This is evidenced by two nationally syndicated editorials from the daily news. Nolan (2002), a congressional liaison for the arts for children with disabilities in Washington, D.C., wrote in support of special education. He supplemented his argument with figures showing that, after three decades of special education, 6.5 million children received special education services in inclusive settings. Specifically, inclusive services increased to 96% in 1997 from 20% in 1970. In addition, early childhood intervention more than tripled since its inception. Also, 60% of the states reported an increase in the participation of students with disabilities in state tests. In addition to having higher achievement rates, students with disabilities were staying in school longer. These figures carried over to postsecondary education, with a 30% increase in the enrollment of students with disabilities. Based on these figures, Nolan made the assumption that students receiving special education services will be better prepared for independent community living.

Soifer (2002), executive vice president of the Lexington Institute in Arlington, VA, countered Nolan's arguments by questioning the benefits, placements, funding, and regulations of special education. He noted that 12% of students in the United States were enrolled in special education, causing a high rise in its cost, and cited figures showing that special education funding accounted for 22% of all school spending. Soifer also cited an estimate that one-half of all special education students were inappropriately placed. He argued that many students in special education did not have disabilities but received services because they had been failed by general education. Thus, he reasoned that these students diverted special education funds from those with real disabilities who needed them more. He also cited a nationwide statistic that only one in four students receiving special education services received diplomas and that 75% of black students with disabilities and 47% of white students with disabilities were unemployed two years after they left school. He noted other problems in special education such as laws that required teachers to complete paperwork, decreasing the time they had to teach, and laws that prevented the expulsion or suspension of students who were school safety risks.

Clearly, there is a continuing debate over the benefit of special education. While some people debate the value of special education across a continuum of disabilities, this chapter will narrow the focus to the benefits of special education to those with the most severe disabilities, including significant cognitive and severe multiple disabilities. As noted in Chapter 1, the term *moderate and severe disabilities* is used in this text to include persons with profound mental retardation because the principles and strategies to be discussed are applicable to this group. In 1991 Orelove concluded a chapter focusing on the education of those with the most severe or signficant (i.e., profound) cognitive disabilities by stating that it would be magnificent to write a follow-up chapter in 2000 that stated the advances in this area. This chapter will review some of those advances.

This chapter is included in this text because the majority of students with moderate and severe disabilities function in the upper range of ability. Indeed, much of the research reported in texts focusing on low incidence disabilities was conducted with students with moderate disabilities. Thus, if their prior field experiences did not provide adequate exposure, teachers who obtain certification to work with students with moderate and severe disabilities may not be prepared to work with students with the most severe disabilities (i.e., significant cognitive and severe multiple disabilities) who inevitably appear on their caseload. Members of the community, even in the 21st century, may continue to question the benefits of public school services for these students. Because students with significant cognitive disabilities are entitled to appropriate individualized educational services, the purpose of this chapter is to acquaint the reader with the issues that are involved in delivery of those services before continuing with the remainder of the text.

HISTORICAL ISSUES IN THE EDUCATION OF PERSONS WITH SIGNIFICANT COGNITIVE DISABILTIES

In 1988 Sailor, Gee, Goetz, and Graham focused on deficits in describing persons with the most severe, or significant cognitive, disabilities as those who (a) are likely to be unresponsive, (b) have no understanding of daily routines or communication, (c) have no recognition of significant persons, (d) have no purposeful movement, (e) have little observable response to stimuli, (f) have a wide range of multiple impairments, (g) are medically at risk or medically dependent, (h) have severe behavior disorders, (i) show no preferences or choices, (j) show no anticipation, (k) show little affect, and (l) are restricted to a small range of environments. Likewise, Reid, Phillips, and Green (1991) described persons with significant multiple disabilities as being untestable on intelligence tests, exhibiting signs of serious neuromuscular dysfunction, having frequent medical complications, and being totally dependent on caregivers. In Chapter 1 this group of persons was described by

Switzky, Haywood, and Rotatori (1982) as functioning in the absolute range of profound mental retardation.

The passage in 1974 of Public Law 94-142 giving the right to all children to receive a free and appropriate public school education sparked a debate on the educability of persons with significant cognitive disabilities. This historic debate was the catalyst for establishing principles that continue to provide a foundation for working with persons with the most severe, or significant, disabilities. The following sections summarize the conflicting points presented by Bailey (1981) and Baer (1981) in position papers on this topic. Before continuing, however, stop and complete Activity 2.1.

ACTIVITY 2.1   Identifying Issues in Educability

Have you ever questioned the ability of all children with disabilities to benefit from an education? Have you ever heard anyone else question this? Make a list of arguments that question the ability of all children, regardless of the severity of a disability, to benefit from an education.

When you finish, read over your list. Can you think of counterarguments? If so, list them. As you continue reading, check off those points that your lists have in common with Bailey's or Baer's position.

Issues in the Educability Debate

Bailey (1981) based his arguments on his intense experience working for a summer as a consultant to an institution housing more than 700 persons with significant cognitive disabilities that fit the description by Sailor et al. (1988) of those with the most severe, or profound, disabilities. His job was to provide suggestions to improve the quality and quantity of services for these persons. When he turned to the professional literature for help, he found that it was lacking in data-based studies to document effective procedures for persons with the ability to make only minimal responses. Most of the literature focused on the teaching of skills to those with a higher level of cognitive functioning, while a smaller body of literature focused on reducing detrimental behaviors (e.g., self-abuse, physical aggression) under controlled laboratory conditions. Bailey reasoned that the most appropriate intervention for persons with significant disabilities might be stimulation programming (e.g., physical or occupational therapy) that possibly could result in the prerequisite skills needed for future instruction. For example, therapy to improve fine motor skills or visually focusing on an object might lead to instruction on augmentative communication skills. Even if the therapy never leads to future instruction, it may prevent deterioration of motor skills as in permanent contractions or atrophied muscles and lead to an increase of sensory ability, such as vision and hearing, to experience the environment. Based on these arguments, Bailey asserted that persons with significant disabilities should have the "right to be left alone" (p. 49) just as persons with medical conditions have the right to deny life support when there is no hope of recovery.

With these points made, Bailey proceeded to question the use of limited resources to educate persons with significant cognitive disabilities. He reported the custodial care of persons with significant cognitive disabilities to be $15,000 to $20,000 per client per year in 1980 and wondered if it was justifiable to spend this amount of money to teach someone to have eye contact for ten seconds or to raise an arm. (Current figures on residential services are reported in Chapter 12.) Bailey concluded by stating that our enthusiasm to teach all persons outweighs our expertise and that **stimulation programming,** such as occupational or physical therapy, is more appropriate for persons with significant cognitive disabilities than **teaching programming** that focuses on the instruction of basic skills.

On the other hand, Baer (1981) argued that it is incorrect to assume that education means attaining a skill; rather, education means making progress toward attaining a skill. He also stated that teaching skills is not aversive or demeaning because a student receives reinforcement for working toward the attainment of the skill. For example, successive approximations are reinforced in the shaping of communication or mobility skills. In regard to the lack of studies that show acquisition of skills by persons with profound disabilities in the professional literature, Baer argued that it is impossible to apply all procedures shown to be effective to all behaviors. Thus, the literature has not shown that persons with significant cognitive disabilities cannot be taught. Baer's experience had led him to believe that continual applications of variations of procedures eventually lead to a procedure that will result in at least some progress. Thus, he concluded that the **least dangerous assumption** is to proceed in providing an education in the event that a child might learn, noting that the acquisition of only one response can improve the quality of life. For example, a consistent eye blink can be used for communication. In terms of cost, Baer argued that it costs no more to educate a child than to provide custodial care, and it may actually be cost effective if the education results in a skill that promotes independence, reducing caregiving or making caregiving easier. In Baer's opinion, dollars were better spent on education than on other pursuits (e.g., buying designer clothing, photographing planets, increasing a supply of weapons). Baer concluded by reaffirming the Scottish verdict of "not proven" used in the title of his paper because it has not been proven that all children cannot learn.

To summarize, Bailey (1981) and Baer (1981) addressed the following points.

1. *Stimulation versus teaching programming:* Do persons with significant cognitive disabilities benefit more from therapies that maintain the status quo and possibly lead to prerequisite skills for instruction or from instruction on skills needed for independence even if they never acquire a skill or only acquire a portion of a skill?

2. *Cost versus benefits:* Is the cost of educating persons with significant cognitive disabilities worth the outcome if it is small or nil, given that resources are limited and needed in other areas?

3. *Enthusiasm versus expertise:* Does our enthusiasm to educate all children outweigh our expertise in effective procedures, given the limited base of data-based studies documenting skill acquisition in the professional literature?

4. *Progress versus result:* If our efforts to educate persons with significant cognitive disabilities never result in the desired outcomes, is it a sufficient outcome that progress was made toward the acquisition of a skill?

5. *Aversiveness of instruction versus the right to be left alone:* If the behavior of a person with a significant cognitive disability indicates that instruction is aversive (e.g., resists physical prompting, cries when touched) and it is unlikely that the person will make even minimal progress in acquiring a skill, does that person have the right to be left alone and, instead, receive services that focus on making his or her existence more pleasant (e.g., music, soft lighting)?

6. ***Ability of the person versus ability of the program:*** Is it less dangerous to assume that persons with significant cognitive disabilities cannot learn or that we have not yet learned how to teach all persons?

In looking back, these questions do not address whether all children are entitled to special education services. This already has been determined and made law, whether or not all of society has been in agreement. The root of the educability issue, rather, is in what constitutes appropriate services. In 2002 the President's Commission on Excellence in Special Education noted that the needs of students with moderate and severe disabilities and those with mild disabilities may be different and raised the concern that this difference might result in segregation of students with severe disabilities. Thus, the President's Commission stated a commitment to inclusion in general education to the maximum extent appropriate for all students.

Do students with significant cognitive disabilities benefit more from stimulation programming or from teaching programming? Should their days focus on therapies that improve the quality of their ability to experience their environment or on instruction that improves the quality of their ability to participate in their environment to whatever extent possible? Example 2.1 provides a parent's perspective on this issue. In addition, Activity 2.2 offers the reader the opportunity to consider educational issues as they relate to a child with severe multiple and significant cognitive disabilities. The following sections describe what has been learned about providing an education to persons with signficant cognitive disabilities since Bailey's and Baer's debate. Before reading the following sections, contemplate the issues raised by Bailey and Baer by reading through Example 2.1 and completing Activity 2.2.

EXAMPLE 2.1 A PARENT'S PERSPECTIVE ON EDUCABILITY

Example 1.3 in Chapter 1 described Jeremy as a young man with significant cognitive and severe multiple disabilities. During the 1960s Jeremy's family received training in the Doman-Delacoto program, a popular program at the time, in an effort to increase Jeremy's capacity to learn during his early childhood years. When they began the program, Jeremy's family provided for all of his caregiving needs (e.g., feeding, bathing, dressing, positioning). At that point in time, Jeremy showed no affect (e.g., laughing or crying), displayed no efforts to communicate (e.g., making eye contact, babbling), and performed limited motor skills (e.g., swallowing, moving head back and forth). In accordance with the program, the family enlisted volunteers from the community to come into their home on a set schedule several times each day to put Jeremy through a patterning sequence that simulated moving the limbs in order to crawl. The hypothesis was that the motor activity would stimulate the brain cells needed to learn. Their involvement in the program continued for several months, with family life completely revolving around being home and having enough volunteers for Jeremy's daily sessions.

When Jeremy showed minimal progress over the course of several months, his family discontinued the program and began to rebuild a semblance of normalcy in their life with Jeremy. Years later Jeremy's mother affirmed that the family's involvement in the program had been a worthwhile experience because "Jeremy learned to smile." Whether this could be attributed to the program or to the fact that Jeremy received consistent and prolonged attention from those who loved him is irrelevant. What is important is that the acquisition of a skill as small as a smile was significant to the family and made all of their effort worth the price they paid.

ACTIVITY 2.2   Seeing Two Points of View

Several years ago a teacher reported being faced with a dilemma that centered on the educational program of a student in her elementary classroom who had significant cognitive disabilities and was medically fragile. Because the student had a poor prognosis for surviving the school year, the teacher found that she and the parent had philosophical differences as they designed the child's Individual Education Plan (IEP). The teacher's perspective was that the child should be treated as other students and put through an educational program with the assumption that the prognosis might be wrong and the child would live longer than expected. At the very least, she wanted the child to receive therapy that might improve his quality of life. Although the parent agreed that the child should be in the school environment each day, the parent's perspective was that the child should be made as comfortable as possible (e.g., frequently repositioned, fed, and changed) but not disturbed for any type of instructional or therapeutic programming. When observed, the child showed no alertness or awareness of his surroundings and cried when touched.

In another case, a parent requested a change from a segregated to an inclusive placement for a middle school child with Down syndrome and a significant cognitive disability. The teacher and school administrators argued that the child had severe challenging behaviors (e.g., hitting, kicking, pinching, biting, spitting) that put others in his environment at risk and that the child needed to be segregated from other students until behavior improved. The parent argued that with better role models, a more appropriate curriculum, functional communication training, and an appropriate positive behavioral support plan the child's behavior would improve. When the placement team reached a stalemate, the parent requested an advocate and a due-process hearing.

Pretend that you are in the position of each of these teachers. What do you see as appropriate services for each child? What goals and objectives would you write in their IEPs? How would you work with the child and with the parent? Is a compromise possible? Now look at the situation from the point of view of each of the parents. Has your position changed?

PROGRESS IN EDUCATING PERSONS WITH SIGNIFICANT COGNITIVE DISABILITIES

Orelove (1991) described **education** as being meaningful progress in a positive direction and **meaningful skills** as those that produce an effect on the environment, noting that progress may be small. In 1974 federal law (PL 94-142) mandated a position of **zero reject** in education. This asserts that, even though a child will never become self-sufficient, the child still can benefit from services that maintain the status quo and provide a stable quality of life.

The paragraphs that follow document the paucity of research in the area of significant cognitive disabilities (i.e. profound mental disabilities). For those who have attempted research in this area, the process can be daunting. Example 2.2 highlights one of the reasons that more research has not been conducted in the area of profound and/or severe multiple disabilities that may help the reader put the following reviews of the professional literature in perspective.

EXAMPLE 2.2   CONDUCTING RESEARCH WITH CHILDREN WITH PROFOUND DISABILITIES

With federal funding secured through a student-initiated research grant to teach self-feeding skills to children with significant disabilities, Collins, Gast, Wolery, Holcombe, and Leatherby (1991) focused their efforts on Victor and Sabrina, two preschoolers with deaf/blindness and severe developmental delays. The goal of the project was to use a new instructional strategy (i.e., constant time delay procedure with a physical prompt and multiple exemplars) in a natural setting to teach the children to use a spoon, cup, and napkin with independence within the timeframe of a single school year. After nine months, both children had acquired the single skill of independently using a spoon, and one of the children was using a cup following multiple procedural modifications (i.e., adapted materials and task sequence, differential reinforcement, graduated guidance).

The limited outcomes of this research investigation illustrate why researchers with limited time and support might choose to focus their efforts on conducting research with persons where the expectation for meeting criteria might be within a shorter timeframe and have more generalizable results. Research in the area of significant cognitive and severe multiple disabilities requires a large commitment in time and resources for what might be perceived as a very small amount of progress.

Was the result of the investigation worth its cost of $8,000? While some people may question this, it is possible that the limited result of that year-long investigation added one more piece of information to the body of research in teaching persons with significant disabilities that may impact the lives of a large number of persons with disabilities and their caregivers.

Research on Significant Cognitive Disabilities Prior to 1991

In 1983 Stainback and Stainback reviewed the educational research conducted with persons with significant cognitive disabilities. They noted that teaching someone to perform a behavior that may seem insignificant to others is still meaningful to the person who cannot perform it. Through their review of the literature, they found that persons with significant cognitive disabilities have acquired motor, self-help, social, and communication skills and maladaptive behaviors have been effectively reduced when systematic behavioral procedures were used. Based on their analysis, Stainback and Stainback concluded that enough progress had been made in teaching those with significant cognitive disabilities to face the future with optimism and to proceed with continued research under the assumption that all children can learn and that all lives have worth.

In 1988 Sailor et al. continued to review the literature on teaching those with significant cognitive disabilities. Their research showed progress when using several independent variables that included (a) peer instruction, (b) instruction in fully integrated settings, (c) systematic instruction, (d) naturally distributed trial delivery, and (e) positive behavioral interventions. In addition, they found progress across several dependent variables that included (a) vocational skills, (b) communicative behaviors, (c) community mobility, and (d) community living. Based on their review of the literature, Sailor et al. offered several recommendations:

1. A zero reject or zero exclusion policy should continue.
2. The movement toward integrated settings should be accelerated.
3. Humane and ethical behavioral interventions should be facilitated in community settings.
4. Quality education outcomes should be created that include family input.
5. An inclusive, interdisciplinary model should be adopted that includes peers, multiple settings, distributed trial instruction, integrated therapy, and adaptations.
6. Transition from school should be to the workplace.

In 1991 Reid et al. added to the previous reviews of the professional literature by analyzing behavioral research in teaching persons with significant cognitive disabilities. Consistent with the review by Stainback and Stainback (1983), they found the early research (1949–1979) to focus on demonstrating that behaviors could be changed (e.g., raising arm, touching/pulling ring, blinking eyes, moving head/limbs, pressing lever, decreasing self-injury, patting foot, smiling, vocalizing) through the manipulation of reinforcers. They found the advent of research on postural control (1975–1982) to demonstrate that more relevant behaviors could be changed (e.g., holding head erect, making purposeful arm/hand movements). This paved the way for research investigations that focused on teaching adaptive skills.

In discussing their review of the published literature through 1988, Reid et al. concluded that the investigations to that point demonstrated the teaching of meaningful skills on a small and inconsistent basis without causing substantial changes in the lives of participants over time. They further noted that, even when studies had successful outcomes, the assistance of a caregiver still was needed for the participant to exhibit the acquired skill; thus, independent skills were not obtained. Furthermore, they questioned the degree to which a person must partially participate in an activity in order for it to be considered meaningful. Reid et al. concluded that the field did not possess an adequate research base for teaching those with significant cognitive disabilities, noting that the 39 investigations they reviewed were conducted over a 40-year period, yielding an average of less than one investigation per year. Even though persons with significant cognitive or profound disabilities constitute a small percentage of the population, this is a low number. Reid et al. concluded by stating that future research in the area of significant cognitive disabilities is needed in behavioral assessment protocol, behavioral teaching procedures, neuromotor behavioral interventions, alertness and responsiveness, and the development of alternate treatment programs (e.g., focus on enhanced quality of living environments over skill instruction).

Reid et al.'s final point returns the reader to one of the original arguments of the 1981 debate between Bailey and Baer, that of teaching programming versus stimulation programming. In spite of Bailey's position that instruction may be aversive and ill-spent, Reid et al. supported Baer's position to proceed as if all children can learn by urging researchers to continue to investigate instructional strategies. It is clear that future research is warranted, whether the focus is on stimulation programming or on teaching programming, if the quality of the lives of persons with significant cognitive disabilities is to improve. This case, in fact, can be made for all persons with moderate and severe disabilities. It is through systematic research that we advance our ability to improve the quality of lives of persons with disabilities, regardless of their severity. Our creed should be that, until we have evidence to the contrary, we should never assume that a person cannot learn because of his or her disability; rather, we should assume that we have not yet discovered the means by which to teach him or her. This is the least dangerous assumption (Donnellan, 1984).

Tables 2.1 through 2.6 provide an overview of the early research in significant cognitive disabilities reviewed by Stainback and Stainback (1983), Sailor et al. (1988), and Reid et al. (1991) and summarized in the previous paragraphs. The tables contain a sample of the investigations reviewed by these authors and are grouped for comparison into (a) challenging behaviors, (b) communication, (c) leisure skills, (d) motor skills, (e) self-help skills, and (f) social skills. It is recognized that some of these domains may overlap (e.g., communication and social skills, leisure and motor skills), some of the skills may appear better suited in an unlisted domain (e.g., community), or some of the skills may not be placed in the domain originally assigned to them

TABLE 2.1 *Sample of Investigations on Challenging Behaviors Reviewed by Stainback and Stainback (1983), Sailor et al. (1988), and Reid et al. (1991).*

Reviewer	Behaviors	Strategies	Years
Stainback & Stainback (1983)	Self-stimulation (e.g., stereotypy), self-injury (e.g., hitting), aggression (e.g., throwing objects, turning over furniture, biting grabbing, pinching, pulling hair)	Contingent reinforcement, overcorrection, time-out, differential reinforcement	1972–1978
Sailor et al. (1988)	Reduction of severe problem behaviors (not specified), increasing compliance	Communication skills, variation in tasks, natural cues & contexts, pretask requesting	1985–1987
Reid et al. (1991)	Not reviewed	Not reviewed	Not reviewed

by their reviewers. The tables, however, provide a brief overview of a sampling of the target skills and instructional strategies that have received attention in the research literature from 1949 to 1991. Although the research design is not specified in the tables, the majority of the research with persons with significant cognitive disabilities has been conducted using single-subject research designs (e.g., multiple

TABLE 2.2 *Sample of Investigations in Communication Skills Reviewed by Stainback and Stainback (1983), Sailor et al. (1988), and Reid et al. (1991).*

Reviewer	Communication Skills	Strategies	Years
Stainback & Stainback (1983)	Manual signing	Modified incidental teaching	1982
Sailor et al. (1988)	Smiling, activating recorded message, prompting caregiver attention	Increasing communication awareness through body contact and movement, graduated prompting, switch activation, systematic instruction on functional tasks	1983–1988
Reid et al. (1991)	Smiling, activating recorded message, prompting caregiver attention	Increasing communication awareness through body contact and movement, graduated prompting, switch activation, systematic instruction on functional tasks	1983–1988

TABLE 2.3 *Sample of Investigations in Leisure Skills Reviewed by Stainback and Stainback (1983), Sailor et al. (1988), and Reid et al. (1991).*

Reviewer	Leisure Skills	Strategies	Years
Stainback & Stainback (1983)	Performing fitness routines, playing game		1981–1983
Sailor et al. (1988)	Play skills	Peer interactions	1984–1985
Reid et al. (1991)	Interaction with toys and leisure materials, activating switch	Specified positions, switch manipulation graduated prompting, systematic instruction on functional tasks	1984–1988

TABLE 2.4 *Sample of Investigations in Motor Skills Reviewed by Stainback and Stainback (1983), Sailor et al. (1988), and Reid et al. (1991).*

Reviewer	Motor Skills	Strategies	Years
Stainback & Stainback (1983)	Raising arm, controlling head & arm, walking upright	Continuous, contingent reinforcement & fading; restraint; prompting & fading	1949–1981
Sailor et al. (1988)	Basic motor movements, mobility	Distributed trials in ongoing routines & natural contexts	1987
Reid et al. (1991)	Reach/grasp	Graduated prompting	1984

TABLE 2.5 *Sample of Investigations in Self-Help Skills Reviewed by Stainback and Stainback (1983), Sailor et al. (1988), and Reid et al. (1991).*

Reviewer	Self-Help Skills	Strategies	Years
Stainback & Stainback (1983)	Eating (e.g., controlling tongue thrust, chewing, using utensils, cooking), toileting (e.g., day and night)	Contingent reinforcement & mild punishment, physical guidance, modeling, fading	1973–1980
Sailor et al. (1988)	Partial participation in toothbrushing & eating in restaurant	Systematic instruction	1987
Reid et al. (1991)	Self-feeding	Behavioral instruction, systematic instruction on functional tasks	1985–1986

TABLE 2.6   *Sample of Investigations in Social Skills Reviewed by Stainback and Stainback (1983), Sailor et al. (1988), and Reid et al. (1991).*

Reviewer	Social Skills	Strategies	Years
Stainback & Stainback (1983)	Smiling, sharing, cooperating	Modeling, prompting, contingent reinforcement	1975–1981
Sailor et al. (1988)	Social skill development (not specified)	Peer social initiations	1986
Reid et al. (1991)	Head orientation, vocalizations, gestures during communication	Increase in physical proximity	1984

baseline) with single participants or a small number of participants. Single-subject research designs have the advantage of allowing the researcher to analyze formative data as an intervention is applied and to make modifications as needed (Horner et al., 2005). Generalizability is built through systematic replications of the effect of the intervention.

Research on Significant Cognitive Disabilities Since 1991

An analysis of the literature since 1991 shows that research investigations continue to be conducted in the area of significant cognitive disabilities. Although, as found by Reid et al., the average number of studies conducted per year remains low. The following paragraphs describe a sampling of current (1991–2002) research investigations. As with previous investigations, single-subject research designs have been used to establish experimental control. The specific systematic instructional procedures listed in these overviews will be presented in detail in Chapter 6.

Challenging Behaviors   Borrero, Vollmer, Wright, Lerman, and Kelley (2002) conducted a functional analysis on the self-injurious behavior (e.g., head hitting and banging) of an eight-year-old male with profound mental disabilities and found that the helmet he wore made it difficult to determine the function of the behavior (e.g., to get attention, to escape from tasks). The authors recommended that a fading procedure be developed when protective equipment is used. This investigation shows how the emphasis in behavior reduction has shifted from treating the behavior to identifying the cause of the behavior. More about functional behavioral assessment and positive behavioral support is discussed in Chapter 10.

Communication Skills   Investigators have taught communication skills to persons with profound disabilities in two areas: (a) augmentative communication and (b) functional communication. In augmentative communication, Mechling and Langone (2000) taught two persons with severe to profound disabilities to recognize photographs to be used with an augmentative communication system. The materials consisted of a computer-based presentation program with embedded video anchors; when a participant touched a picture on the screen, the action activated a video of the picture (e.g., walking with mother). The investigators used a least to most prompting system (e.g., verbal, gesture, or physical prompt, as needed) to teach the participants to perform the skill. The participants learned the skill and generalized it to an augmentative communication system.

In functional communication Duker and Jutten (1997) established a yes/no response using gestures in three adults with profound disabilities through a most-to-least prompting procedure. The procedure began with physical guidance and faded over time to verbal instruction. The participants maintained the yes/no responses, although they did not generalize the responses across settings.

Domestic Skills   Some domestic skills have the advantage of generalizing to the community or vocational domains. For example, Neef, Lensbower, Hockersmith, DePalma, and Gray (1990) focused on domestic skills in teaching four adults with severe to profound disabilities to use a washing machine and dryer. The investigators used a least-to-most prompting procedure (e.g., model, gesture, physical guidance) to teach the skills using artificial machines in classroom simulations and real machines in community settings. They found that using several examples of machines (i.e., general case instruction) resulted in generalization to untrained machines. Generalization of laundry skills could enable participants to use home machines or laundromats and could result in employment doing laundry.

Leisure Skills   The acquisition of leisure skills facilitates the ability of persons with profound disabilities to participate in community activities with peers and to avoid large periods of inactive, passive downtime (e.g., watching television) that increase the opportunity for self-stimulatory or self-injurious behaviors to occur. Bolton, Belfiore, Lalli, and Skinner (1994) taught putting on a golf green to three adults with severe to profound disabilities. The investigators started with 152-centimeter guides leading from the ball to the cup and systematically faded the length of the guides as putting accuracy increased. The skill maintained over time, giving the participants a skill that they could perform with peers at a putting green or putting course.

Motor Skills   As noted earlier, motor skills can overlap with other domains. Saunders et al. (2001) focused on the use of electronic switches (e.g., button, grip, leaf, pillow, or treadle switch) by eight women with profound, multiple disabilities to activate leisure items (e.g., audiotape player, mechanical bird, radio, or vibrator) while in a sitting or side-lying position. They found that prompting was not necessary to teach the women to activate the switches; the women learned to depress the switch through trial and error when the leisure items were contingent on the switch activation.

Motor skills overlapped with social skills when Anderson and Brady (1993) used peers without disabilities to encourage two elementary students with profound, multiple disabilities to perform motor skills (e.g., using adapted walker, holding head upright when prone over a wedge). The investigators found that peer-initiated social interactions were as effective as adult instruction in getting the students with disabilities to perform the target motor skills. Social and instructional interactions centered around leisure materials (e.g., cassette player, computer, electric piano, guitar, magazines, radio, video game), some of which were adapted with electronic switches.

Self-Help Skills   Self-help skills typically focus on those skills (e.g., dressing and feeding) that make caregiving easier. Hughes, Schuster, and Nelson (1993) taught two children with severe to profound disabilities to dress themselves. The procedure consisted of a constant time delay procedure with oversized clothing in which a physical guidance prompt was used when a student failed to initiate a step of the dressing chain within five seconds. The students maintained the ability to dress themselves in four articles of clothing (jacket, pants, shirt, and socks).

As described in Example 2.2, Collins et al. (1991) taught two preschool students with severe to profound multiple disabilities to feed themselves. Like Hughes et al., the investigators used a constant time delay procedure in which the child received a prompt of physical guidance if he or she could not initiate a step of the self-feeding chain within three seconds. After several modifications to the procedure (e.g., differential reinforcement, graduated guidance), both children learned to use a spoon, and one child also learned to use a cup. The skills maintained over time.

Munk and Repp (1994) focused on children with severe to profound multiple disabilities who could not feed themselves when they assessed feeding problems. Through systematic presentation, they were able to identify the textures and types of foods that the target children would accept or reject. This process allowed the investigators to later implement a program to increase food intake in one of the children through interspersing preferred and nonpreferred foods.

Social Skills Smalley, Certo, and Goetz (1997) were successful in increasing the social integration of five adults with severe to profound disabilities by teaching the staff of a day treatment center to identify and facilitate appropriate activities in a vocational site. The investigators noted a correlational decrease in challenging behaviors as valued activities increased.

Quality of Life Both Sailor et al. (1988) and Reid et al. (1991) suggested that future research should focus on improving the quality of life for persons with significant cognitive disabilities and suggested that quality of life can be quantified. Recent investigations in this area are described in the following paragraphs.

Green and Reid (1996) addressed the factor of happiness in the lives of six students with profound multiple disabilities (e.g., nonambulatory, absence of functional communication skills, dependency on caregivers for basic needs, varying medical diagnoses, sensory impairments) in an adult education class. The authors used facial expressions to measure happiness (e.g., smiling, laughing) and unhappiness (e.g., frowning, grimacing, crying). After conducting preference assessments, the investigators observed the participants during systematic presentations to determine happiness in the presence of individualized preferred stimuli (e.g., juice, toy, verbal interaction, vibrator) and unhappiness in the presence of individualized nonpreferred stimuli (e.g., vibrator, pudding, juice, colored lights). Two of the participants displayed more unhappiness than happiness, and two of the participants displayed more happiness than unhappiness. To follow up, the investigators showed videotapes of the participants to naive observers and had them rate degrees of happiness and unhappiness on a Likert scale. Their responses validated the state of the participants during the investigation.

In a second experiment conducted in the same investigation, Green and Reid increased happiness in the same participants by instituting one to three minutes of "fun time" at frequent intervals during classtime. Fun time consisted of the preferred stimuli from the first experiment as well as blowing air on, tickling, and rubbing arms and bouncing the wheelchair. The results of these two experiments indicated that the happiness of persons with profound multiple disabilities can be defined, observed, and increased, which should, in turn, increase quality of life.

Logan et al. (1998) also investigated the happiness of students with profound multiple disabilities (e.g., cerebral palsy, sensory impairments, seizures). Instead of the effect of materials or activities on happiness, Logan et al. were interested in the effect of interactions with peers without disabilities. In their investigation, they defined happiness as smiling (i.e., lips open and curving upward to show teeth for three seconds) or keeping the eyes open (i.e., eyelid open with pupil and two thirds of iris visible). The authors had two peers with moderate disabilities and eight peers without disabilities interact with five elementary students with profound multiple disabilities during activities (e.g., music, art, game) within the special education classroom. All of the target students exhibited more happiness when interacting with the peers without disabilities during these activities. The authors correlated happiness with alertness and a better quality of life and suggested that placement in a general education classroom would result in more opportunities for happiness.

Finally, Yu et al. (2002) compared happiness indexes during the work (e.g., sorting, shredding) and leisure (e.g., listening to music, watching television) activities of 19 adults with severe to profound disabilities. They measured happiness through facial expressions and vocalizations (e.g., smiling, laughing) and found that more happiness occurred during leisure activities. The group with profound disabilities, however, demonstrated lower rates of happiness than the group with severe disabilities.

Summary of Recent Research in the Most Severe Disabilities

The investigations reviewed since 1990 show that research is continuing in the field of significant cognitive disabilities and that several patterns are emerging. First, investigations are occurring in more natural settings (in lieu of clinical settings) that give the participants access to natural stimuli and interactions with peers. This, in turn, facilitates the usefulness and meaningfulness of the skills taught and increases the likelihood that the results of the investigations will be generalizable to the real world. Second, social integration with peers without disabilities occurs in some investigations, making it evident that persons with significant cognitive disabilities can benefit from both interacting with and being taught by their peers. This may facilitate instruction by providing a natural reinforcer (e.g., interaction with a peer) and by providing a natural model (e.g., the peer's behavior). Third, behavioral assessment is being used to identify appropriate individual interventions. The systematic presentation of variables can identify reinforcers, preferences, and communicative functions of behaviors that can be used in designing interventions. Fourth, systematic instructional procedures continue to build on the research base established in earlier studies. For example, the least-to-most and constant time delay procedures grew out of more intrusive prompting procedures, such as graduated guidance and most-to-least prompting. The addition of such procedures expands the instructional technology base for practitioners. Finally, continual developments in assistive technology (e.g., electronic switches, augmentative communication devices, computer-based instruction) provide more options for increasing communication and motor skills in persons with significant cognitive and severe multiple disabilities. This, in turn, provides persons with significant disabilities greater access to the community. All of these variables result in one important outcome: an improvement in the quality of life for persons with significant cognitive disabilities.

TEACHING STUDENTS WITH SIGNIFICANT COGNITIVE DISABILITIES

As noted in Chapter 1, working with students with moderate and severe disabilities requires teachers to be able to work with a diverse population. As evident in the review of the research literature, target skills for students with moderate and severe disabilities may include communication, functional academic, motor, self-help, and social skills that can be embedded across community, domestic, educational, recreation/leisure, and vocational domains. Working with students with significant cognitive and severe multiple disabilities may require a broader range of skills than teaching students with less severe disabilities. To address the issues involved in providing an education for students with moderate and severe disabilities, including those with significant or profound cognitive disabilities, teachers need to be skilled in applied behavioral analysis and systematic instructional strategies. They also need skills in the strategies used for assessment (e.g., ecological inventory, functional analysis), inclusion, community-based instruction, embedded therapy (e.g., occupational, physical, speech/language), and the sustenance of health and vitality (e.g., nursing, nutrition). Finally, they need the skills to analyze the research base for information as well as the skills to conduct research in their own classrooms in an effort to determine effective practices for each student. These topics will be described in subsequent chapters.

According to Orelove (1991), an appropriate education for students with significant cognitive disabilities consists of an increase in any meaningful skill and the replacement of unwanted behaviors with others that serve the same function (e.g., physical aggression or self-injury replaced by communication skill that indicates hunger or discomfort). Significant progress occurs when a student participates at least partially in activities and has access to peers without disabilities. Orelove listed several factors that can contribute to an appropriate education that continue to be relevant today.

1. Research investigations focusing on the feelings and beliefs of persons with significant disabilities and their families
2. Teacher awareness of history, law, and policy
3. Parent participation in the IEP process
4. State-of-the-art models for delivery of instruction
5. Focus on functional skills (e.g, domestic, vocational) needed in future environments
6. Attention to those in the environment who influence and are influenced by students with significant disabilities (e.g., peers)
7. Understanding of the function or communicative intent of behavior
8. Research in quality-of-life issues

Best Practices
Educational Issues for Students with Significant Disabilities

1. Following a policy of zero reject, be an advocate for all students, recognizing that even those with significant cognitive disabilities can benefit from an education.
2. Use the criterion of least dangerous assumption in working with students with significant cognitive disabilities by assuming that, in the absence of conclusive data, it is the fault of the program, and not the child, if a child fails to make progress.

3. Be aware that a beneficial program for students with significant cognitive disabilities may contain goals for stimulation programming as well as for instructional or teaching programming.

4. Continue to advocate for research to find better ways to teach all students with disabilities, including teacher-based research in classroom settings.

Conclusion

This chapter has presented issues in the education of students with significant cognitive or severe multiple disabilities. In addition, an overview of the research literature in teaching those with significant disabilities has been presented. Closing comments focused on the need for a wide range of skills in providing an appropriate education for students with the most severe disabilities, in particular. The foundation has been laid for the content of the following chapters that will focus on the underlying principles of providing an appropriate education for students with moderate and severe disabilities, including those with significant cognitive disabilities, and describing the methods and strategies that have been effective. With the passage of No Child Left Behind, educators continue to be faced with new challenges in working with students with moderate and severe disabilities. As will be discussed in later chapters, this includes determining appropriate access to the core content of the general education curriculum as well as appropriate assessment. Before continuing, the reader should determine his or her own perspective on educational issues regarding persons with significant cognitive disabilities by reflecting on the performance-based assessment question at the end of this chapter.

Questions for Review

1. What are some of the historical issues that have been debated regarding the education of persons with significant or profound cognitive disabilities?

2. What are some of the skills that persons with significant cognitive disabilities have been taught? Has the emphasis on the type of skills taught changed over time?

3. What factors contribute to an appropriate education for persons with significant disabilities? Which of these are mandated by law?

4. What is the least dangerous assumption and how does it apply to educational programming?

Performance-Based Assessment:
Responding to Issues in Educability

Although public law mandates that all children, regardless of their disabilities, are entitled to a free and appropriate public education, teachers often encounter people who do not understand how all children can benefit from an education, especially those with significant cognitive disabilities. Several questions teachers may be asked are listed below. Pick one of the questions, and formulate a response that is informative without being defensive, rude, or condescending. Remember that your job as an advocate is to gain support from, rather than alienate, the public. (Feel free to use the terms *most severe disability, severe multiple disabilities, profound disability,* or *significant cognitive disability* interchangeably.)

1. "I just don't understand what children with significant disabilities can learn in school. How do they benefit?"
2. "I can't believe it can take years to teach a single skill to a child with a significant cognitive disability. How do you justify the cost when there are so many underfunded programs for typical children?"
3. "Is there any proof that children with significant cognitive disabilities can actually acquire meaningful skills?"
4. "Even when children with significant cognitive disabilities learn simple skills, they still cannot function independently. How then do they benefit from instruction?"
5. "Why would you continue to work with a child whose behavior—crying, screaming, withdrawing—indicates that he or she wants to be left alone?"
6. "Isn't it true that there are certain disabilities that indicate a child cannot learn?"

References

Anderson, N. B., & Brady, M. P. (1993). Improving motor responses in students with severe disabilities using adult instruction and peer social interactions. *Education and Training in Mental Retardation and Developmental Disabilities, 28,* 47–56.

Baer, D. M. (1981). A hung jury and a Scottish verdict: "Not proven." *Analysis and Intervention in Developmental Disabilities, 1,* 91–97.

Bailey, J. S. (1981). Wanted: A rational search for the limiting conditions of habilitation in the retarded. *Analysis and Intervention in Developmental Disabilities, 1,* 45–52.

Bolton, J. L., Belfiore, P. J., Lalli, J. S., & Skinner, C. H. (1994). The effects of stimulus modification on putting accuracy for adults with severe or profound mental retardation. *Education and Training in Mental Retardation and Developmental Disabilities, 29,* 236–242.

Borrero, J. C., Vollmer, T. R., Wright, C. S., Lerman, D. C., & Kelley, M. E. (2002). Further evaluation of the role of protective equipment in the functional analysis of self-injurious behavior. *Journal of Applied Behavior Analysis, 35,* 69–72.

Collins, B. C., Gast, D. L., Wolery, M., Holcombe, A., & Leatherby, J. (1991). Using constant time delay to teach self-feeding to young students with severe/profound handicaps: Evidence of limited effectiveness. *Journal of Developmental and Physical Disabilities, 3,* 157–179.

Donnellan, A. (1984). The criterion of the least dangerous assumption. *Behavior Disorders, 9,* 141–150.

Duker, P. C., & Jutten, W. (1997). Establishing gestural yes-no responding with individuals with profound mental retardation. *Education and Training in Mental Retardation and Developmental Disabilities, 32,* 59–67.

Green, C. W., & Reid, D. H. (1996). Defining, validating, and increasing indices of happiness among people with profound multiple disabilities. *Journal of Applied Behavior Analysis, 29,* 67–78.

Horner, R. H., Carr, E. G., Halle, J., McGee, G., Odom, S., & Wolery, M. (2005). The use of single-subject research to identify evidence-based practice in special education. *Exceptional Children, 71,* 165–179.

Hughes, M. W., Schuster, J. W., & Nelson, C. M. (1993). The acquisition of independent dressing skills by students with multiple disabilities. *Journal of Developmental and Physical Disabilities, 5,* 233–252.

Logan, K. R., Jacobs, H. A., Gast, D. L., Murray, A. S., Daino, K., & Skala, C. (1998). The impact of typical peers on the perceived happiness of students with profound multiple disabilities. *Journal of the Association for Persons with Severe Handicaps, 23,* 309–318.

Mechling, L., & Langone, J. (2000). The effects of a computer-based instructional program with video anchors on the use of photographs for prompting augmentative communication. *Education and training in Mental Retardation and Developmental Disabilities, 35,* 90–105.

Munk, D. D., & Repp, A. C. (1994). Behavioral assessment of feeding problems of individuals with severe disabilities. *Journal of Applied Behavior Analysis, 27,* 241–250.

Neef, N. A., Lensbower, J., Hockersmith, I., DePalma, V., & Gray, K. (1990). In vivo versus simulation training: An interactional analysis of range and type of training exemplars. *Journal of Applied Behavior Analysis, 23,* 447–458.

Nolan, E. (2002, June 23). Special Education: Programs are succeeding, but more effort, money is needed to continue. *Lexington Herald-Leader,* p. F2.

Orelove, F. P. (1991). Educating all students: The future is now. In L. H. Meyer, C. A. Peck, & L. Brown (Eds.), *Critical Issues in the Lives of People with Severe Disabilities* (pp. 67–87). Baltimore: Brookes.

President's Commission on Excellence in Special Education (2002). *A new era: Revitalizing special education for children and their families, July 2002.* Jessup, MD: ED Pubs.

Reid, D. H., Phillips, J. F., & Green, C. W. (1991). Teaching persons with profound multiple handicaps: A review of the effects of behavioral research. *Journal of Applied Behavior Analysis, 24,* 319–336.

Sailor, W., Gee, K., Goetz, L., & Graham, N. (1988). Progress in educating students with the most severe disabilities: Is there any? *Journal of the Association for Persons with Severe Handicaps, 13,* 87–99.

Saunders, M. D., Questad, K. A., Kedziorski, T. L., Boase, B. C., Patterson, E. A., & Cullinan, T. B. (2001). Unprompted mechanical switch use in individuals with severe multiple disabilities: An evaluation of the effects of body position. *Journal of Developmental and Physical Disabilities, 13,* 27–39.

Smalley, K. A., Certo, N. J., & Goetz, L. (1997). Effect of a staff training package on increasing community integration for people with severe disabilities. *Education and Training in Mental Retardation and Developmental Disabilities, 32,* 42–48.

Soifer, D. (2002, June 23). Special Education: Benefits, placements, funding and regulations are questionable at best. Lexington, KY: *Lexington Herald-Leader,* p. F2.

Stainback, W., & Stainback, S. (1983). A review of research on the educability of profoundly retarded persons. *Education and Training of the Mentally Retarded, 18,* 90–100.

Switzky, H. N., Haywood, H. C., & Rotatori, A. F. (1982). Who are the severely and profoundly mentally retarded? *Education and Training of the Mentally Retarded, 20,* 268–272.

Yu, D. C. T., Spevac, S., Hiebert, R., Martin, T. L., Goodman, R., Martin, T. G., Harapiak, S., & Martin, G. L. (2002). Happiness indices among persons with profound and severe disabilities during leisure and work activities: A comparison. *Education and Training in Mental Retardation and Developmental Disabilities, 37,* 421–426.

CHAPTER THREE

WORKING WITH FAMILIES OF CHILDREN WITH MODERATE AND SEVERE DISABILITIES:

Sources of Family Stress and Interventions

On completion of this chapter, the reader will meet the following objectives:

- Name the types of stressors that affect families of children with disabilities, and describe how stress can be manifested.
- Discuss characteristics of families of children with disabilities that have good strategies for coping with stress.
- List strategies and resources that can help families of children with disabilities cope with stress.
- Describe strategies for professionals who work with families of children with disabilities.

Families always have been faced with the necessity of coping with or adapting to the influence that a child with disabilities has on the family unit. In the past some families opted to keep their children within the home for the life span and found ways of coping with the stress that accompanied their decision. Others chose to institutionalize their children, thus alleviating stress by not having to deal with it on a daily basis. The trend today is to minimize institutional placements by providing support to families of children with disabilities that will enable them to keep their children within the home setting during the school years and enable them to transition their children to community placements during the adult years. This chapter will focus on the stressors that affect families of children with moderate and severe disabilities, the ways in which stress can be manifested, and the coping strategies and resources that can decrease stress.

Family intervention is a timely topic in the midst of changing factors within a modern society that affect families of today. Singer and Irvin (1991) noted a number of these factors that hold true in the new millennium:

1. Improved medical care has resulted in the survival of a larger number of infants with low birthweight who may have correlated developmental disabilities.
2. At a time when more infants with severe multiple disabilities are surviving, more mothers, who traditionally have been designated as caregivers, are joining the labor force.
3. Traditional social supports for families of children with disabilities are eroding with an increase in divorce, smaller extended families, and a mobile society where families do not settle in communities for long periods of time.
4. The trend toward single parenthood through choice, divorce, or circumstance results in the sole parent (most often the mother) carrying the double burden of child care and financial support.

5. At a time when more children are living in poverty, it is less likely that families will have health insurance to cover the costs associated with the treatment required by a child with multiple, intense, and ongoing medical needs.

6. A societal increase in drug addiction increases the likelihood of children born with birth defects or children born to families struggling with the problems associated with addiction.

7. An increase in homelessness affects the ability of families to obtain ongoing, coordinated services for their children.

8. There is an increase in family violence, and this may be exacerbated by the added stress related to caring for a child with disabilities.

It is clear that the factors that affect a large number of families in today's world can be compounded by the presence of a child with disabilities. Although this chapter will focus on parents and siblings, it is important to note that families may comprise a range of individuals, including grandparents or foster parents, who share caregiving responsibilities (Brown, Goodman, & Küpper, 2003).

Gallagher, Beckman, and Cross (1983) defined a stressor as "a crisis-provoking event or situation for which the family has little or no preparation," a "social stressor" as "any set of circumstances that requires change in the individual's ongoing life pattern," and stress as "the organism's response to the stressor, consisting of patterns of physiological and psychological reaction that are both immediate and delayed" (p. 11). Within the context of this chapter, a **family stressor** is the presence of a child with a moderate or severe disability, a **social stressor** is a circumstance affecting the family in relation to the child with a moderate or severe disability, and **family stress** is the family's reaction to the stressors that affect them. To put stress into perspective, complete Activity 3.1 before continuing.

ACTIVITY 3.1   Identifying Sources of Stress in Daily Life

Each of us has stressors in our daily lives. Think about the past week. What stressors can you identify? List these on a sheet of paper.

According to Singer and Irvin (1991), stressors can fall into several categories. Which stressors on your list have to do with a major life event? Have you recently been affected by a death, celebrated a milestone birthday, lost a job, encountered problems in personal relationships, or had a child?

Which stressors on your list involve daily hassles? Have you had a major exam, experienced car trouble, been given a deadline at work, engaged in an argument with a friend, or run short of cash?

If you are a parent, do you have stressors on your list associated with caregiving? Have you been dealing with the behavior of children in the "terrible two's" or teenagers with changing hormones, had an increase in household responsibilities (e.g., laundry or cooking), or had to adapt the weekly schedule to accommodate the activities of family members?

How many of your stressors were insignificant until they began to pile up over time? Have you had sleep interrupted for several nights, felt ill for several days, had several unexpected expenses arise, or had to cope with ongoing family problems?

Now identify stressors that might be associated with a child with disabilities. How might these stressors exacerbate the existing stress in your life?

Singer and Irvin (1991) identified four separate categories of stressors. The first category includes stressors associated with major life events beyond which people have little control (e.g., death, divorce, unemployment, illness), and the second category includes daily hassles that routinely cause stress (e.g., financial worries, work pressures, home and car repairs, housework). The presence of a child with a moderate or severe disability can add a third category of stressors associated with caregiving (e.g., adjusting schedules, providing nighttime care, lifting and transferring children with motor disabilities, changing and feeding over time, finding specialized transportation, managing problem behavior, dealing with the reactions of outsiders) and a fourth category of pile-up stressors that become significant only when they do not decrease over time (e.g., behavior problems, nighttime disturbances, a difference in the child's appearance, medical problems, trying to understand the child's efforts to communicate, and social isolation).

As you noted in Activity 3.1, all of us experience life-event stressors, daily hassles, and pile-up stressors. We can predict some of them, and others catch us by surprise. Families of children with moderate and severe disabilities experience the same stressors as the rest of society. However, they also are faced with additional stressors associated with caring for and living with a child with disabilities. Because some stressors are associated with a family's circumstances and others are associated with developmental events, it is possible for professionals to predict some of the sources of stress and some of the times when intervention may be helpful. The following sections identify stressors in the lives of families of children with moderate and severe disabilities.

STRESSORS AFFECTING FAMILIES OF CHILDREN WITH MODERATE AND SEVERE DISABILITIES

In reviewing the history of families and disabilities, Ferguson (2002) noted that 19th-century parents received the blame for their child's disability; thus, children often were placed in a residential setting away from their families. From 1920 to 1980, the focus shifted from blaming the family to blaming the child with a disability for the damage inflicted on the family. In the 1960s the focus in research on families and disabilities changed to the nature of parental reactions to the child with disabilities and the source of those reactions. This caused parents to be viewed as neurotic, dysfunctional, suffering, or powerless. Since 1980 the focus of research has shifted to models of stress and coping. The following sections detail some of the stressors identified in this body of research, most of which was conducted during the 1980s.

Stressors Occurring Across the Life Cycle

Some family and social stressors can occur at any point in the life cycle of a child with a moderate or severe disability. In 1983 Gallagher et al. identified a number of stressors reported in the professional literature. According to their research, factors influencing stress levels include socioeconomic status, IQ, verbal skills, morale, personality, past experiences, age, and occupation. In particular, lack of education, limited income, long working hours, depression, and illness are associated with higher levels of stress. Inclusion in community settings can serve as a social stressor, causing families to withdraw socially from embarrassment over their child. Inclusion in the school can be stressful in that this practice can be a daily reminder to families of the discrepancy between their child with a disability and his or her peers without disabilities and the social stigma that often accompanies a disability. In addition, concern over the child's social adjustment in the school and community and a corresponding lack of support services can serve as stressors.

In recent years Ferguson (2002) stated that family stress appears to be affected by the level of disability, the family structure, the behavior of the child, and the amount of income, with differences across ethnic and cultural groups. Based on a comparison of 110 families of children with and without mild to profound disabilities under the age of seven years, Dyson (1987) found that the families of children with disabilities scored higher on every item indicating stress. This included family problems, pessimism for the future, and negative feelings toward the behavior and physical characteristics of the child.

Bailey (1988b) identified four predictable times of crisis for families of children with disabilities that occur during the life cycle, as follows: (a) initial awareness of the condition, (b) determination of the educational placement, (c) recognition of issues regarding employment and the possibility of independent living after school, and (d) realization that aging parents can no longer care for a child. In addition, Bailey noted that stressors associated with a child with disabilities, such as obtaining services, transitioning to and from school, and experiencing medical crises, are added to normative events that cause stress, such as death, divorce, financial worries, and employment problems.

Stress and Developmental Milestones Wikler (1981) noted that parental stress increases as the discrepancy between the child's size and mental ability increases and, similar to Bailey et al. (1986), stated that there are critical periods where increased stress can be predicted. The first list is composed of times when there are discrepancies in expectations. This includes the age at which a child first walks, first talks, begins school, experiences the onset of puberty, and celebrates the 21st birthday. At these times parents are reminded of the differences in the abilities of their child and children without disabilities. The second list is composed of parent events. This includes the point when the parent receives the initial diagnosis of the disability, when the ability of a younger sibling surpasses that of an older sibling, when there are occasions of exacerbated health problems, when discussion of a placement outside of the home occurs, and when guardianship issues and plans for the future must be decided. Wikler also noted that parents often experience grief over the loss of the child of their fantasies on such occasions as birthdays, holidays, and sibling celebrations.

Stress and Gender There may be a difference in stress levels due to gender. While fathers tend to show more signs of depression, mothers and older sisters tend to be more at risk for stress due to added caregiving needs; some mothers who are employed, however, may experience less stress since work can be a respite from child care (Gallagher et al., 1983). In examining gender differences, Kazak (1986) concluded that fathers are often the recipients of financial stress while mothers have more caregiving stress. Again, mothers of children with disabilities often seek employment for respite in addition to financial reasons. Kazak also reported negative behaviors (e.g., irritability or withdrawal) in siblings of children with disabilities and stated that older sisters, in particular, may experience anxiety and restrictions from caregiving.

Stress and Marital Relationships The birth of a child with disabilities can be a positive or negative factor. According to Kazak (1986), greater marital stress occurs when a child with disabilities is the firstborn, is very young, has one sibling, or has a severe disability. Some parents, however, report marital satisfaction in spite of the tension of having a child with disabilities and even report that the child brought them closer.

Stress and Types of Disabilities Sometimes the type of disability or its severity is responsible for an increase in family stress. In comparing the stress levels in 22 mothers of children with autism or Down syndrome and 32 mothers of children without disabilities, Holroyd and McArthur (1976) found that autism resulted in higher levels of stress. Autism was associated with more disappointment in the child, more awareness and concern with dependency, more concern for the future, and more awareness of personality and behavior problems, while Down syndrome was associated with stress related to negative attitudes or child-care burdens.

McKinney and Peterson (1987) found higher scores of stress related to the severity of the disability in 67 mothers of children with developmental disabilities, ages 7 to 41 months, who were receiving special education services. In addition, Kazak (1986) reported greater levels of stress in families where the child was identified with mental retardation or behavior disorders. Again, increased caregiving or dealing with behaviors are stressors that affects some families.

Stressors Occurring at Specific Points in the Life Cycle

Some family stressors can be predicted in correlation to the age of the child with a moderate or severe disability. These predictable stressors begin at birth and continue throughout the life cycle.

Stress at Birth or Diagnosis The first predictable stressor occurs at the time a child with disabilities is first diagnosed. This may occur prior to birth, at birth, or at some point that follows (Smith, 2003). According to Donellan and Mirenda (1984), professionals can contribute to the initial stress experienced by a family during the period from birth to the diagnosis by initial denial of the existence of a disability, initial suppression of information about the disability, and disagreement with other professionals about the diagnosis. This encourages "shopping behavior" in parents, which can establish a lifelong pattern as they go from one professional to another in search of answers.

Stress During Infancy Whether or not parents are given a diagnosis, stress may be apparent during the infancy of a child with disabilities. After interviewing 31 mothers of infants with disabilities, Beckman (1983) found a high correlation between caregiving demands and the number of parent and family problems, with the highest degree of stress present when infants had greater caregiving demands, were less socially responsive, had more difficult temperaments, and had more repetitious behavior. In addition, single mothers experienced more stress than two-parent families.

Based on interviews with 30 couples with infants with disabilities and 30 couples with infants without disabilities, Waisbren (1980) compared family stress across Denmark and the United States. Although Denmark provided free services, financial support, cash subsidies, counseling, facilities, training, equipment, and medical care, there was little difference in the stress levels of parents in the two countries; all of the parents experienced similar levels of stress. Parents of children with disabilities, however, had more contact with doctors, experienced more negative feelings (e.g., anger, helplessness, rejection), and showed more concern for their children's appearance and lack of ability. Additional stressors included interactions with professionals, the inability to take a vacation, neglect of other children, inadequate home architecture, the need for special equipment, medical costs, and difficult health care needs.

Stress and Preschool Children   Because the preschool years are a time when most children without disabilities reach several developmental milestones, stress can be predicted at that time. The preschool years are the first time discrepancies in development may become apparent to parents. Stressful events during the preschool years include the age when the child with disabilities fails to walk, fails to acquire self-feeding skills, fails to talk, and fails to be toilet-trained while most children are acquiring these skills (Bailey, 1988b).

Stress and Older Children   As the child with disabilities grows older, stress may increase (Gallagher et al., 1983). After interviewing 60 mothers of older children with mental retardation who lived at home, Wikler (1986) identified five groups of responses across chronological ages and found that stress was highest during the transition to the onset of adolescence (11 to 15 years) and the onset of adulthood (20 to 21 years). This is not surprising since these are times when parents of children without disabilities also may experience an increase in stress. Again, stress for families of children with moderate to severe disabilities may be related to what the children cannot do (e.g., obtain a driver's license, go to college) as well as changes in caregiving responsibilities (e.g., shaving, caring for menstrual needs) as the child grows larger, experiences hormonal changes, and enters adulthood. These stressors occur at a time when parents are aging and beginning to worry about their ability to continue to care for their child in the future.

Manifestations of Stress in Families of Children with Disabilities

As described in the previous sections, some stressors can affect the families of children with moderate and severe disabilities throughout the life cycle, and some are predictable at specific points. Research from the 1980s showed that the stress resulting from social and family stressors can be manifested in several ways, including anxiety, anger, child abuse, decreased social mobility, depression, fatigue, financial difficulties, guilt, isolation, marital conflict and divorce, and even suicide (Gallagher et al., 1983).

The initial diagnosis of a disability is often accompanied by a range of emotions. These may include shock, denial, sadness, anger, anxiety, adaptation, and reorganization (Bailey, 1988b); shock, denial, disbelief, detachment, bereavement, bewilderment, guilt, disappointment, anger, lower self-esteem, resentment, aggression, loss, hopelessness, futility, loss of warmth, and detachment in relationships (Blacher, 1984); or denial, anger, fear, guilt, confusion, powerlessness, disappointment, and rejection (Smith, 2003). According to Blacher (1984), these emotions may be manifested through insomnia and loss of appetite. Following a period of mourning the loss of the child they expected, parents typically learn to accept the child who was born. This results in a period of acceptance, reconstruction, reorientation, and becoming advocates. The alternation of stress and acceptance tends to repeat itself throughout the child's life cycle.

According to Eden-Piercy, Blacher, and Eyman (1986) there are three specific categories of stress in the parents of young children with severe disabilities (e.g., spina bifida, autism, moderate and severe disabilities). These include (a) shock, despair, and guilt; (b) guilt, refusal, and denial; and (c) adjustment, recovery, and acceptance. The categories are not sequential and can be manifested at any point in the life cycle.

Suelzle and Keenan (1981) assessed family stress across the life cycle in 330 parents of children with severe disabilities ranging in age from birth to 21 years. They found that families with college degrees were less likely to contact doctors and that they were more likely to use dentists and babysitters. They also found that, while consultation with professionals increased over the life cycle, the use of support personnel decreased. The families also had less support for mainstreaming and experienced more difficulty coping as their children grew older. Unmet needs included transition services, respite care, and counseling.

COPING STRATEGIES IN FAMILIES OF CHILDREN WITH DISABILITIES

In the late 1980s, the focus of the research on family stress began to evolve from identifying stressors and the manifestions of stress to identifying strategies to enable families to better cope with stress. This research (Ferguson, 2002) has indicated adjustment and well-being to be similar across families with and without a child with a disability. An increasing number of parents of children with disabilities report benefits and positive outcomes as a result of their children. These include the development of coping skills, family harmony, spiritual growth or shared values, shared parenting roles, and communication. For example, Taunt and Hastings (2002) interviewed 47 parents (using face-to-face interviews and internet surveys) and found the positive impact of a child with disabilities on the family to include positive aspects of the child (e.g., happy disposition), change in life perspective (e.g., nothing taken for granted), increased sensitivity (e.g., more tolerance and patience), support from other families (e.g., sharing of information), and opportunities to learn (e.g., research). Taunt and Hastings also reported a positive impact on siblings (e.g., increased maturity) and increased sensitivity (e.g., tolerance and patience) in extended family members.

Recommended coping strategies for families have included (a) seeking assistance from other families, (b) talking openly with family members and significant others, (c) taking one day at a time, (d) becoming familiar with terminology associated with disabilities, (e) seeking accurate information, (f) failing to be intimidated by professionals, (g) being open with emotions, (h) finding ways to deal with emotions, (i) maintaining a positive outlook, (j) accessing programs for the child and the family, (k) tending to personal needs, (l) keeping normalcy in daily routines, and (m) joining support groups (Brown et al., 2003; Smith, 2003). In addition, research investigations have addressed the specific coping strategies that have been employed by families of children with moderate and severe disabilities. The following sections describe research investigations that have examined the characteristics of families who cope better than others and provide recommendations for professionals who work with families.

Family Factors That Influence the Ability to Cope

McKinney and Peterson (1987) found higher scores of stress in 67 mothers of children with developmental disabilities, ages 7 to 41 months, who were receiving special education services. While social support did not appear to make a difference in the ability of the mothers to cope, half reported that peer support was helpful and that spouse support lowered stress. In contrast, Waisbren (1980) reported that spouse support did not alleviate stress, but the support of parents or in-laws resulted in more positive feelings.

In analyzing 158 parents of children with disabilities, Friedrich, Wilturner, and Cohen (1985) found fewer problems in educated families, mothers who considered themselves capable, and those with social support. They also found that targeting multiple behaviors for intervention was more effective than targeting a single behavior.

In comparing 110 families of children under seven years of age with and without mild to profound disabilities, Dyson (1987) reported that the families of children with disabilities scored higher on every item indicating stress, including family problems, pessimism for the future, and negative feelings toward the behavior and physical characteristics of their children. The families of the children with disabilities, however, were more likely to emphasize child achievement, religious beliefs, family activities, and family rules of operation.

In a survey of 92 parents of children with severe disabilities who were enrolled in special education services, Lustig (2002) found that more **reframing** (i.e., the capability of the family to redefine stressful events in order to make them manageable) and less passivity were associated with higher levels of family adjustment. In interviewing 14 parents of children with disabilities, Scorgie, Wilgosh, and McDonald (1999) also identified reframing (e.g., accepting and valuing the child) as a coping strategy in addition to balancing personal roles and responsibilities (e.g., giving equal time to children, protecting health) and using resources (e.g., professionals). Scorgie et al. found that families who coped well with stress had identifiable personal attributes and characteristics that included personal traits (e.g., patience, positive outlook, determination, sense of humor, hopefulness), decision-making and problem-solving abilities (e.g., ability to identify creative solutions), and a strong philosophy of life and belief system (e.g., belief in personal choice, strong personal convictions).

Scorgie et al. also documented transformational experiences that occurred in families as they learned to cope. These included (a) personal transformations, such as learning to speak out, becoming more compassionate, or becoming stronger and more self-confident; (b) relational transformations, such as having wonderful people brought into their lives or gaining a new perspective on life; and (c) perspectival transformations, such as acquiring a more authentic view of life success, gaining more awareness of what is valuable and important in life, or learning to make the most of each day. They concluded that the transformational processes were due to image making (e.g., creating a new identity), meaning making (e.g., finding meaning or purpose in parenting), and choice making (e.g., gaining a perception of control).

Based on their research on support for the families of persons with severe disabilities, Singer and Irvin (1991) listed characteristics of families with good coping skills. These included (a) a sense of mastery over time, (b) participation in parent training, (c) advocacy, (d) stress management skills, (e) ability to live one day at a time, (f) assignment of meaning to difficulty, (g) child viewed with joy and pride, (h) rich sense of values, (i) assignment of a greater meaning to love, and (j) strengthening of the family. In addition, they listed coping strategies as including obtaining support from the family social network, obtaining support from the spouse, sharing caregiving responsibilities, problem solving, communicating without anger or depression, accessing community resources, and building parent-professional partnerships. Singer and Irvin further reported that parents of children with severe disabilities wish for increased support from the spouse and siblings, fiscal assistance for medical and household costs, in-home respite care, and access to generic community resources (e.g., recreational programming, transportation). They concluded that the major categories for reducing stress consist of (a) respite care, (b) child-focused education, (c) parent training, and (d) fiscal assistance.

Sandler and Mistretta (1998) analyzed the results of 50 questionnaires from parents of adults with mental disabilities who resided at home and attended adult workshops. Although 50% of the parents were bothered by the lifelong nature of their children's disabilities and were disappointed for their children, they stated several positive outcomes from their experiences. Of those questioned, 94% of the parents felt they had grown as parents; 90% felt they had increased in compassion, sympathy for others, flexibility, and tolerance and had decreased in selfishness; 84% had pride in their children with disabilities; and 75% felt fulfillment in their parental roles. In addition, 90% of the parents had developed coping strategies that included taking one day at a time, comparing their family situation favorably to another, giving attention to the positive, and having religious beliefs that sustained them.

In focusing on parents of adult children with mental disabilities, Lustig and Akey (1999) found three foci that emerged from 318 parents identified through the ARC (formerly the Association for Retarded Citizens) who responded to a survey. First, parents felt a need to increase the level of social support they received (e.g., support groups, resource centers, relatives). Second, parents stated a family sense of coherence where they viewed stressors as challenges rather than burdens. Third, parents stated the need for adaptability or flexibility in family structure, roles, and rules.

Beavers, Hampson, Hulgus, and Beavers (1986) examined factors in families who made healthy adaptations in coping with children with mental disabilities, ages 3 to 21 years of age. They found that healthy adaptation occurred when (a) the child with disabilities did not dominate the family system, (b) small gains in achievement were viewed as significant, (c) mothers were aware of embarrassment in siblings and worked to alleviate it, (d) parents made an effort to ensure that siblings in the family were not slighted, (e) there was an awareness of available possibilities, (f) there was an orientation to the present instead of the future, and (g) grandparents gave verbal support and did not show shame. It was also helpful when the family was involved in school and support groups. Other factors that appeared to result in positive outcomes included a clear diagnosis, information about the disability, and positive contact and responsiveness between family members.

Families who adopt children with disabilities may differ from those to whom children with disabilities are born because they make a conscious choice to bring the child into their families, knowing that there may be additional stress. Todis and Singer (1991) employed interviews and observations to examine stress management in six families who adopted children with disabilities. The target families had 3 to 29 children, with one to nine children within a family having some type of disability. As with nonadoptive families, sources of family stress included responding to medical crises, dealing with behavior problems, working with service providers, and having concerns for the future. The adoptive parents managed this stress through several strategies that included (a) household management, such as assigning chores or taking time away as an individual or a couple; (b) social support, such as having contact with other adoptive families or accessing church support; and (c) a positive focus, such as not experiencing guilt over a child's disability, maintaining a feeling of control over the problems of raising a child with a disability, or noting improvement in the child over time.

Example 3.1 describes the experience of a mother of a child with autism who was experiencing stress related to her child's disability. As you read through the example, note how she developed her own strategies to cope.

EXAMPLE 3.1	HOW A MOTHER OF A CHILD WITH AUTISM FOUND A WAY TO COPE WITH HER STRESS

Although Angie had family and friends to support her, she felt alone in dealing with the stress of having a child with autism (McLean, 2002). Her son, Lance, insisted on dressing in layer upon layer of clothing in 90-degree weather. He screamed around strangers. His father resorted to using duct tape to hold Lance's shoes together after returning 22 pairs of shoes to stores because he would not wear them. Angie felt that she could not reach her child. In her words, she "felt isolated. Anybody who has a typical child cannot understand what it's like" (p. E1). When Angie located a support group, she found that it gave her information but did not meet her emotional needs. That was when she decided to start her own group. She wanted more contact with other parents who were experiencing the same things she was.

During the first meeting of the support group she organized, Angie asked the other parents what they would like to discuss. The reply was "to sit back, have a cup of coffee, get away from the kids for a while, and just talk" (p. E3). The focus of the group became the personal aspects of raising their children. The support group of parents of children with autism provided an outlet for Angie's stress, and she stated that there is a need for similar groups in other communities based on their own cultures and challenges.

Resources That Enhance the Ability to Cope

Agosta and Melda (1995) reported that supports are often available for families of children with disabilities at both the state and local level. At the state level, for example, they found that Family Support Councils in New Hampshire designed and operated statewide family support programs, and a statewide council in West Virginia worked with the state to ensure family-centered programs, to develop a family support budget, and to establish procedures for administering family support programs. A number of states (e.g., Oregon, Colorado, West Virginia, Missouri, Utah, New Hampshire, Illinois) had family support programs at the local level. Typically, community service agencies had family representation on the board. Support services in Colorado included ongoing services, time-limited services, respite care (as needed), and a special reserve fund for emergencies. Through the provision of support services, Minnesota was able to reduce the number of children with disabilities living outside of the home from 830 to 291 and to increase the number of families served from 50 to 1,827 over a 10-year span. Agosta and Melda (1995) suggested that effective family support programs should enhance a sense of community, mobilize resources and support, emphasize shared responsibility and collaboration, protect family integrity, strengthen the family, and emphasize preferred human service practices.

Cole and Meyer (1989) surveyed 103 families and children with severe to profound disabilities regarding the factors that most influence keeping their children in the home rather than placing them in a residential or institutional setting. The results of the survey listed the following factors in the following order of importance: (a) spousal assistance, (b) coverage of medication and dental costs, (c) evening and weekend in-home respite, (d) extra funds for household help, (e) professional consultation for behavior problems, (f) a physician knowledgeable in severe disabilities, (g) special transportation to daily activities, (h) funds for special equipment, (i) out-of-home respite care, and (j) access to community recreation programs. Example 3.2 contrasts two mothers who made placement decisions for their children with profound disabilities.

EXAMPLE 3.2	**MAKING THE DECISION TO INSTITUTIONALIZE**

The current trend is to move away from out-of-home placements for children with disabilities by providing support to families who keep their children at home. In spite of this, out-of-home placements remain an option selected by a large number of families. The reasons vary.

Zachariah's mother (Kupfer, 1997) described herself as a family advocate in response to the anti-institutional bias in the United States. Zachariah had Canavan's disease (i.e., profound mental retardation, confinement to a wheelchair or a bed, nourishment through feeding tubes, severe scoliosis) and died in a residential setting at the age of 16 years. His mother attested to the fact that he had been loved by the child-care workers, the therapists, and the nurses who had cared for him. She also defended her view that home is not the best place for every child, stating that "Each family is different" (p. 20). Although she loved her son, Zachariah's mother asserted that placing him in a setting where his needs were met enabled her and her family to live a more "normal" life, that included marrying, holding a job, raising children, and going to college.

Jeremy's mother (see Examples 1.3 and 2.1 in Chapters 1 and 2), on the other hand, chose to keep her son in the home setting until he was in his 20s. Since Jeremy's characteristics were similar to those of Zachariah, he required a high degree of caregiving, and respite providers who were able to meet his needs were difficult to find. When he was young, Jeremy's family searched for a residential placement but could not find one they felt would provide the same degree of loving care he had been given in the home and still be close enough for the family to visit him on a regular basis.

Keeping Jeremy in the home was not easy. Someone had to be with him 24 hours each day, lift him in and out of his bed and adaptive equipment, administer medication for seizures, and care for his basic needs (e.g., feeding, toileting, dressing, grooming). When Jeremy's siblings had friends visit, his mother tried to be sensitive to the needs of her children by keeping Jeremy in his bedroom. When the school bus passed each day, she closed the curtain to keep from being reminded of the discrepancies between Jeremy and his peers. Family vacations required booking out-of-home respite services in advance. When asked if she felt she had made the right decision in keeping Jeremy in the home, his mother replied, "Yes. It brought our family closer."

Who is to say whether each of these families made the best choice? The right choice may not always be the same choice across families.

Ellis et al. (2002) also identified the self-reported needs of families of children with disabilities. In a survey of 91 families of children with developmental disabilities, ages 3 to 22 years, in a day or residential school program, they identified the top family needs as (a) information (e.g., future and present services, teaching and handling behavior, laws), (b) community services (e.g., leisure activities, respite), (c) support (e.g., time for self), (d) family functioning, (e) explaining child's disabilities to others, and (f) financial. Needs were greater when the child was younger, and needs decreased when the child was in a residential placement.

Professionals and Family Stress

Professionals can be a good resource for families of children with disabilities who have difficulty developing strategies for coping with stress. On the other hand, professionals can also contribute to family stress.

Professionals may have preconceived ideas about the families with whom they work. Donnellan and Mirenda (1984) pointed out that professionals may view ideal families as those who seek out help, understand the problems of their child, accept the disability, follow through on the advice of professionals, and make every effort possible to help their child progress. On the other hand, nonideal families ask questions, modify or reject professional advice, seek out services on their own, are not readily available to the professional, and fail to make efforts that will result in gains for their children. Without considering family dynamics, structure, and outside influences, professionals may make the assumption that nonideal families are not willing to work systematically with their children at home. Professionals may make dangerous assumptions in the absence of supporting data that include thinking that parents do not know what is best for or how to teach their child, need professionals to solve family problems, contribute to the child's problems, and put the child second to the needs of the family. Through initially denying that a problem exists, suppressing information, disagreeing with other professionals about the diagnosis, and giving out incomplete or inaccurate information that is not helpful, professionals may contribute to the "shopping behavior" mentioned in an earlier section, in which parents go from professional to professional, seeking information and solutions.

Donnellan and Mirenda identified best practices for professionals, with emphasis on working with families of children with autism and severe disabilities. Based on the **criterion of least dangerous assumption** that "in the absence of conclusive data, decisions should be based on the assumption which, if incorrect, will have the least dangerous effect on the student [and his/her family]" (p. 22), they suggested the following:

1. Interventions should be based on evidence that the disability (i.e., autism) is not caused by the parent or environment.
2. Historical misconceptions can have a negative impact on the family.
3. The weakness of the professional should not be inflicted on the family.
4. The criterion of least dangerous assumption should be applied to the family intervention.
5. Parents should be fully informed about a diagnosis.
6. Family problems require sensitivity.
7. Support services should be easily available.
8. The family should never be told that nothing can be done.

9. Families should be involved in intervention, to the extent possible.

10. The needs of the child are met through meeting the needs of the family.

11. Parents should be included on the educational team [and, according to federal law, must play an integral part].

12. Parents should have full access to information regarding their child's diagnosis and education.

Bailey (1988a) advocated the assessment of stress in families in order to provide family support and to evaluate family interventions. In addition, Bailey (1988b) stated that professionals should recognize that the assessment of stress can in itself be stressful and that stressors may occur and recur at any time; thus, professionals should identify stressor events, gather family information, determine family perceptions and resources, and discuss with the family the ways in which the professional can be most helpful. Bailey (1988b) also stated that professionals can alleviate some stress by following specific steps during the initial diagnosis of a disability. First, the pediatrician and a home health specialist should tell the parents of the diagnosis when they are together and holding their child in a private place. Second, information about the disability should be provided and the parents should be given time for questions, time to talk alone in private, and the phone number of the home health specialist for questions that arise later. Finally, a follow-up session should be conducted with the doctor and home health specialist.

According to Shapiro (1983), the most common error in professional intervention is overtreatment of the child and undertreatment of the family. Shapiro further stated that successful coping results in the acceptance of the child with a disability, developmental understanding, warm and secure family relationships, encouragement of self-help, initiative for therapy and rehabilitation, and professional trust. On the other hand, poor coping has negative outcomes for siblings (e.g., jealousy, negative social life and use of recreational time) and the child with disabilities (e.g., withdrawal, behavior problems, anxiety, depression, temper tantrums, enuresis, aggression). To facilitate coping, Shapiro suggested several strategies for professionals that included charting family—not individual—progress, changing staff attitudes toward families, gearing facilities (e.g., hospital, clinic) to family involvement, emphasizing the family unit in medical practices, and advocating insurance policies to ease the burden of preventative family treatment.

Reflecting more recent trends, Dunst (2002) stated that professionals should base family interventions on family centeredness. This includes (a) beliefs and practices that treat families with dignity and respect; (b) practices that are individualized, flexible, and responsive; (c) sharing of information that allows families to make informed decisions; (d) family choices regarding program practices and intervention options; (e) parent-professional collaboration and partnerships; and (f) provision and mobilization of resources and supports necessary for families to care for their own children (p. 189). Dunst noted that the preschool is more likely to be family centered than the elementary and high school program.

In summary, professionals can be a help instead of a hindrance when they approach the family in a positive manner, without making assumptions in the absence of data. Helping professionals are those who like the child with disabilities, are honest about what they do and do not know, have time for the family, reinforce parents for their efforts, allow parents to express their hopes and dreams, provide alternatives for the family, trust the parents' instincts about what is best for their child, promote hope, let parents express emotions, ask for parent opinions, say negative things in positive ways, help parents discover their strengths, connect parents with supports, and teach parents advocacy skills (Scorgie et al., 1999).

Empowerment of Families to Cope

The professional literature contains evidence that empowering families with intervention strategies to work with their child can reduce some of their stress. Reese and Serna (1986) suggested that, like children with disabilities, parents could benefit from an Individualized Education Program (IEP) that contains learning strategies to work with their child. (Indeed, this concept is used in early childhood special education with the practice of developing an Individual Family Support Plan [IFSP].) Goals and objectives would be for parents to acquire intervention skills that they can generalize across child behavior and across settings, as well as to ensure that skills learned in educational settings maintain over time. In this manner, parents can be valuable as "generalists" in the educational process.

Snell and Beckman-Brindley (1984) stated that family members can act as generalists in reducing inappropriate behavior and in teaching new skills (e.g., mobility, self-care, communication, academics). In addition to making families better equipped to cope with stress, involvement of the family socially validates target behaviors by providing evidence that targeted behaviors are valued in the real world). The child benefits by having more interventionists, such as parents, siblings, and extended family members, who are focused on programming. Family members who become generalists can apply behavioral principles and techniques to a variety of problems, thus increasing the outcomes of intervention.

Recent research has focused on empowering families by teaching them strategies to work with their children. For example, Tekin and Kircaali-Iftar (2002) found that three elementary-age students were reliable and effective in using systematic instructional procedures in teaching receptive picture identification to their younger siblings with moderate disabilities.

In another investigation, Reamer, Brady, and Hawkins (1998) taught two families of preschool children with disabilities to improve interactions with their children during self-care (e.g., dressing, brushing teeth, eating) and social (e.g., prompting siblings to play with toys together) tasks. The investigators videotaped the parents using model and verbal prompting in the home. After the parents watched the videotape, the investigators helped them rehearse correct procedures. As a result of watching the video of self-modeling, the parents increased the correct use of procedures and generalized the procedures across tasks and settings.

Clapham and Teller (1997) also reported effectiveness in using videotapes to work with parents. In their report teachers of children who were deaf and hard of hearing used videotapes to teach new manual signs and model speech development for parents in addition to using the videotapes to inform parents of homework and to communicate announcements and reminders. They found that the children liked being videotaped and the parents responded to the teachers with greater frequency.

Summary

It is clear that, while the presence of a child with disabilities can be a family stressor, there are a number of families who learn to cope and professionals who work with families can be either an additional stressor or a resource for coping. Based on the information you have read about family stress and intervention to this point, stop and consider the family case study described in Activity 3.2.

ACTIVITY 3.2   Identifying Stressors and Coping Strategies in Scotty's Family

A family-oriented newspaper detailed the story of Scotty, a child with Down syndrome, and the family who adopted him (Special needs adoption, 2001). The story serves as a case study in the ability of a family of a child with disabilities to cope with a number of stressors. As you continue to read, try to identify the stressors that occurred in the life of Scotty's family. When you finish, identify the characteristics and strategies that enabled the family to cope with each stressor.

THE STORY OF SCOTTY'S FAMILY

After two miscarriages, Cindy and Bill responded to an advertisement for special needs adoption. They took classes in special needs adoption and waited for the child they would adopt. After six months and one false alarm, they received a call that a child with Down syndrome was available.

They immediately left their small, rural town and drove to the city where the child waited, only to find that they had to meet with a social worker, a caseworker, and the foster mother before meeting their son. After learning about the child's background and medical history, they were more determined than ever to adopt the child. When they finally returned home with Scotty, there was a large celebration with their extended family.

Within two weeks of adopting Scotty, Cindy learned that she was pregnant. Just after Scotty's first birthday, Cindy gave birth to a son, putting two infants in her care.

At the age of two years, Scotty was diagnosed with leukemia. During a year of hospital treatments consisting of chemotherapy and radiation, Scotty's kidneys failed and he stopped breathing. Bill and Cindy reported that, after having a vision in which a man told them everything would be all right, Scotty went into remission. At the age of three, Scotty was able to return home.

Just after Cindy became pregnant with her third child, Bill was killed in an automobile accident. Although she felt like her world had collapsed, Cindy's parents kept her focused on her family. To help her with child care, Cindy's parents and sister moved into her house until her third child was born.

Although she never thought she would marry again, Cindy began dating a former classmate, Mike, who fell in love with her and her three children. Within six weeks, they married, adding Mike's daughter to their blended family. Five years later, Cindy and Mike became the parents of their own child.

During all of these events, Scotty thrived. He attended school in a district with an inclusive philosophy, going through graduation ceremonies for both middle and secondary school and attending an inclusive transition program housed at a local liberal arts college with a religious affiliation. As part of the transition program, he worked at a fast-food restaurant and a Goodwill store.

After being a full-time mother while her children were younger, Cindy became an instructional assistant in special education at a local elementary school. She stated that perspective is the key to a positive outlook, something she learned from seeing the world through Scotty's eyes.

WHAT FAMILIES OF CHILDREN WITH DISABILITIES WANT

Based on the information presented thus far, it is clear that a number of stressors affect families of children with disabilities and a number of strategies can be employed to support the families, thus decreasing some of the stress. The key to beginning to support families is to first listen to what they have to say. The following sections focus on what parents and siblings of children with moderate and severe disabilities want.

What Parents of Children with Disabilities Want

Sometimes listening to parents can be a difficult undertaking for professionals who are determined to implement current trends and best practices, such as in-home placement and inclusive school environments. For example, Bennett, Lee, and Lueke (1998) interviewed 18 parents of preschool children across disabilities and found that many desire more communication with professionals, while Soodak and Erwin (2000) interviewed 10 parents of preschool children with significant disabilities and found that they wanted assurance that their children will be protected and secure in inclusive school settings.

Westling (1996) reviewed 25 research investigations to determine what parents of students with moderate to severe disabilities want. Several categories emerged from his analysis. First, Westling found that parents wanted their children with disabilities to learn functional, chronologically age–appropriate skills across domains, even if they must partially participate. The most important skills listed across ages were (a) motor skills—age birth to 2 years, (b) communication and toileting skills—age 3 to 5 years, and (c) communication and self-care skills—age 6 to 12 years. Parents of school-age children also worried about their children's behavior, wanted information about the diagnosis and medical needs, wanted treatment in the home, wanted help with future needs, and needed babysitters. Parents of older children wanted social and recreation programs, behavior change techniques, communication training, and information about programs for the future. Parents of older children rated domestic skills, vocational skills, community skills, and leisure skills as important in that order. Parents of children with moderate disabilities were more concerned with functional academics, while parents of children with severe to profound disabilities were more concerned with friendships and social skills.

Second, Westling found that parents were concerned with where their children go to school. Parents of children in segregated placements feared inclusion more than those who had experience with it. While parents wanted their children to go to neighborhood schools, concerns in inclusive settings included the well-being of the child and the adequacy of teacher training.

Third, Westling found that parents of children with moderate and severe disabilities most often were satisfied with their children's participation in school, and parents with a higher socioeconomic status tended to be more involved. Most parents wanted information on academic and behavioral progress, and most were satisfied with the special education program, although they wanted their children to be more involved in general education. Reasons for less school involvement by some parents included cultural factors, language barriers, and problems in scheduling meetings.

Fourth, Westling found that parents were generally positive regarding special education services. A family focus was more likely during the early childhood years, with students with severe disabilities, or in home-based programs.

Fifth, in regard to social, medical, and community services, Westling found that parents of children with moderate and severe disabilities were desperate for more availability, better organization, and better coordination. Many had to battle for support services and became worn down in the process. Also, families sometimes found professionals to be condescending and not understanding of their needs. Some parents voiced that they were pushed to their economic limit.

Sixth, during the adult years of children with moderate and severe disabilities, Westling found that parents had few options and were placed on a waiting list for services. Those children who were placed out of the home tended to be older, have more severe disabilities and more behavior problems, come from a larger family, or have parents who were divorced or separated. Those children who remained in the home tended to have access to more services in the community and have more people to assist them. The greatest needs of parents of adult children with moderate and severe disabilities were residential information, respite care, recreational activities, and information on financial planning and guardianship.

Based on his research on what parents of children with moderate and severe disabilities want, Westling made the following recommendations:

1. Children with moderate and severe disabilities should have meaningful instruction.
2. The facilitation of social skills and friendships should be part of the curriculum.
3. Quality services and adequate support should be provided.
4. Children should have the opportunity to try inclusion.
5. Ways to participate in school activities should be provided.
6. Information should be available to parents in different formats.
7. Support should include respite, information about advocacy groups, and information about agencies.
8. Support should be provided to help with the stress of program entry.
9. Home-based services should be provided for infants and toddlers, and integrated services should be provided for preschool children.
10. Services should be coordinated during preschool to keep them from being a burden.
11. Parents should have the opportunity to help with planning.
12. Information and support should be provided during transition.
13. Parents should be assisted in dealing with community agencies.
14. Funding for home and community living for adults with moderate and severe disabilities should be increased.
15. Residential plans should be addressed during transition planning.
16. Parents should be given information about positive lifestyles and their child's potential. (Westling, 1996, p. 111)

What Siblings of Children with Disabilities Want

Sometimes the needs of siblings of children with moderate and severe disabilities are overlooked by parents and professionals. In the New York STEPPS program that works with siblings, Cramer et al. (1997) found that siblings of all ages have a number of questions regarding the child with disabilities. For example, siblings may question why a sister with disabilities goes to school, whether a sister with disabilities will frighten a boyfriend, who will be the guardian of a child with disabilities, or how the needs of an adult sibling's family can be balanced with the needs of an adult sibling with disabilities. Cramer et al. found that siblings wanted information on the child's disabilities, the opportunity to talk about their feelings, time to hear the experiences of other siblings, people with whom they could share their feelings, and ways to plan for the future. The STEPPS approach to working with siblings was to host a sibling day that involved stakeholders.

Lindsey and Stewart (1989) suggested that parents openly talk with siblings about a child's disability, teach siblings to deal with hostility and aggressions, allow siblings to be part of decision making, and role model an accepting attitude toward the child with a disability. Like Cramer et al., Lindsey and Stewart also suggested that a workshop for siblings could be helpful. A workshop might include an attitudes test, seminars on disabilities and ways to deal with emotions, speeches by famous persons who have siblings with disabilities, role playing, and a visit to a special education program.

How to Involve Families of Children with Disabilities

Although families have a great number of needs, it still can be a challenge to get them involved in the education of their children with disabilities. Each family is unique, and the strategy that gets one family involved may fail with another. The more opportunities that professionals can provide, the more likely families are to become involved in the educational process. Gallegos and Medina (1995) listed 21 ways to involve families that included such ideas as field trips, guest speakers, communal meals, home visits, telephone trees, newsletters, class calendars, respite care, resource libraries, and translators. Creativity in involving families mixed with caution in not overwhelming them can enable families to access valuable support.

Best Practices
Working with Families of Children with Moderate and Severe Disabilities

1. Be sensitive to the unique characteristics of the families of children with disabilities, recognizing that they are affected by stressors related to their children.
2. Understand that family stress can be manifested in a variety of ways, and be aware of times in the life cycle in which it can be predicted.
3. Empower families by providing support and resources that meet their individual needs and by arming them with strategies to work with their children.
4. Avoid using professional jargon and, in the absence of conclusive data, placing the blame on families for their children's problems.
5. Listen to families and provide them with honest information when they request it.

Conclusion

As shown through the sampling of professional literature described in this chapter, families of children with moderate and severe disabilities experience the same stressors as other families in addition to stressors attributed to the presence of a child with a disability. Some families have characteristics or resources that render them better able to cope, some families develop coping strategies on their own as time passes, and some families benefit from professional intervention. It is important to remember that, because a family is a complex and intertwined structure, a stressor that affects one member of the family affects all members. Family intervention is more than working with parents. Siblings and other extended family members intimately involved with the family need to be included.

An investigation by Heiman (2002) illustrates the information provided in this chapter and provides a ray of hope for families of children with moderate and severe disabilities. Heiman studied 32 parents of children with special needs in Israel to determine the factors in their past, present, and future in regard to their children, half of whom had moderate or severe cognitive disabilities, autism, or Down syndrome. Factors from the past included (a) suspicion of a disability and noting something different about their child by the age of four years, (b) initial negative emotional responses (e.g., depression, anger, shock, denial, fear, self-blame, guilt, sorrow, grief, confusion, despair, hostility, emotional breakdown), and (c) talking with family members (grandparents, sisters, brothers-in-law, other children) who reacted in positive, encouraging ways and expressed understanding, support, and love. Factors from the present included (a) coping difficulties and never-ending emotional and physical fatigue, social isolation, and lack of freedom; (b) medical concerns and stress related to illness; (c) worry about the impact of the disability on siblings, including the burden of future care; (d) the use of psychological services for the child, parents, or siblings; and (e) the replacement of negative feelings with positive feelings (e.g., love, joy, acceptance, satisfaction, strength) over time. Future factors included (a) concern about the child's inclusion in society (e.g., financial and physical independence), (b) concern with education and a profession for the child, and (c) concern for the child's welfare and security (although most had not taken any practical steps toward this). Heiman concluded that family resilience is due to (a) open discussions and consultations with family, friends, and professionals; (b) a positive bond between parents; and (c) continuous and intensive therapeutic and psychological support for family members.

Table 3.1 summarizes the stressors, manifestations of stress, and factors (i.e., coping strategies, resources) that enable families to cope that have been discussed in this

---

TABLE 3.1   *Stressors Affecting Families of Children with Moderate and Severe Disabilities, Manifestations of Family Stress, and Coping Strategies and Resources that May Decrease Stress.*

Family or Social Stressors

Aging of Caregivers	Employment Concerns	Level of Disability
Caregiving Responsibilities	Equipment Needs	Limited Income
Child's Behavior	Family Death	Long Working Hours
Child's Physical Characteristics	Family Divorce	Marital Conflict
Child Surpassed by Younger Sibling	Family Illness	Medical Concerns and Crises
	Family Problems	Obtaining Services
Community Inclusion	Guardianship	Onset of Adulthood
Concern for Future	Health Care Needs	Onset of Puberty
Death of Child	Illness	Social Isolation
Depression	Inability to Take Vacation	Social Stigma
Developmental Milestones	Inclusion in School and Community	Transitioning
Educational Placement	Initial Diagnosis	Type of Disability
Emotional and Physical Fatigue	Lack of Education	Unemployment
	Lack of Support Services	Working with Professionals
		Worry for Siblings

Manifestations of Stress

Aggression	Decreased Social Mobility	Emotional Breakdown
Anger	Denial	Emotional Problems in Child
Anxiety	Depression	Fatigue
Bereavement	Detachment	Fear
Bewilderment	Despair	Financial Difficulties
Child Abuse	Disappointment	Finding Purpose in Situation
Confusion	Disbelief	Futility

(continued)

TABLE 3.1 *(continued)*

Manifestations of Stress (*continued*)

Grief	Loss of Warmth	Self-Blame
Guilt	Lower Self-Esteem	Shock
Helplessness	Marital Problems	Shopping Behavior
Hopelessness	Neglect of Siblings	Sibling Jealousy
Hostility	Powerlessness	Sorrow
Insomnia	Rejection of Child	Suicide
Isolation	Resentment	
Loss of Appetite	Sadness	

Coping Strategies

Balancing Roles and Responsibilities	Developing Positive Personal Attributes	Maintaining Positive Outlook
Becoming an Advocate	Developing Problem-Solving Skills	Not Letting Child Dominate Family
Becoming Familiar with Terminology	Developing Stress Management Skills	Obtaining Grief Counseling
Being Open with Emotions		Orienting to Present
Creating a New Family Identity	Emphasizing Small Gains by Child	Reframing
		Refusing to Be Intimidated
Creating a Positive Bond Between Parents	Gaining Sense of Control over Life	Securing Spouse Support
		Seeking Continuous Therapeutic and Psychological Support for Family Member
Developing Awareness of and Tending to Sibling Problems	Increasing Family Adaptability	
Developing Awareness of Possibilities for Child	Increasing Family Flexibility	
	Keeping Normal Daily Routines	Sharing Caregiving Responsibilities
Developing Communication Skills	Living One Day at a Time	Talking with Supportive Family Members and Friends
Developing Decision-Making Skills	Maintaining a Child-Focused Education	Tending to Personal Needs

Family Resources

Choices in Interventions	Household Management Skill Training	Religious Beliefs and Affiliation
Community Access		
Community Services	Information about Disability	Respite Care
Consultation from Helpful Professionals	Knowledgeable Physician	Special Transportation
	Medical Insurance	Support from Extended Family
Fiscal Assistance	Parent-Professional Partnerships	
Foundations (e.g., Ronald McDonald House, Make a Wish Foundation)	Peer Support	Support from Friends and Community
Household Help	Psychological Services for Child and Family	Training in Skills to Work with Child

chapter. An awareness of family stress can contribute to the ability to predict potential stressors, recognize signs of stress, and develop appropriate interventions.

The performance-based assessment that follows this chapter presents a number of case studies in which stress is manifested in the families of children with moderate and severe disabilities and could be attributed to the unique set of stressors affecting each. Spending time thinking about each of these case studies will enable the reader to apply the information that has been covered in the chapter.

Questions for Review

1. Define the terms *stress* and *stressor* as they relate to families of children with disabilities.
2. List stressors that may be present in a family when a child has a disability.
3. What times of stress can be predicted within the life cycle?
4. What are some ways in which stress can be manifested in families?
5. Discuss the characteristics of families of children with disabilities who demonstrate the ability to cope with stress. What are some of the coping strategies that they employ?
6. Name several resources for families of children with disabilities that may be helpful to them in dealing with stress.
7. How can professionals contribute to family stress? How can they be helpful in alleviating stress?

Performance-Based Assessment

The following case studies provide examples of the unique stressors that may affect the families of children with moderate and severe disabilities. After reading through the case studies, select one. Then list the stressors influencing the family and develop a list of potential interventions.

1. Jenny is a 4-year-old female with severe disabilities. Due to hydrocephalus, she has paralysis on the right side. She cannot walk but gets around the room by scooting on the floor. She has good receptive language and a large expressive vocabulary; however, her speech is repetitive and often out of context. Jenny's mother is in and out of her life on a frequent basis, so Jenny lives with her grandmother, who is aging and suffers from chronic pain due to arthritis. Jenny's grandmother finds it easier to give in to Jenny's demands than to cope with her tantrums.

2. Randy is a 6-year-old male with autisticlike behaviors and a self-injurious behavior where he bites himself until he draws blood. He has caring parents who are concerned with his education and often check with his teacher to monitor his progress and address problems. The parents, however, both have jobs with long hours, so Randy must spend much of his time out of school with a babysitter.

3. Richard is a 13-year-old male with moderate mental retardation and poor expressive language skills. His parents were placed in special education classes when they were in school and have difficulty understanding educational

programming during IEP meetings. Their response to their child's inappropriate behavior at home is to use corporal punishment, and they do not understand why the school personnel do not do the same.

4. Tammy is a 16-year-old female with moderate mental retardation and severe epilepsy. She also is legally blind. When she entered puberty, her seizures increased in intensity and frequency. Her mother, however, refuses to give her medication due to religious beliefs.

5. Linda is a 21-year-old female with severe disabilities. She uses a wheelchair and has no expressive language or functional communication system. She lives at home with her elderly parents, who are having difficulty meeting her physical needs because she is overweight. Her education has not equipped her with independent living or employment skills, and her parents are concerned about her future.

References

Agosta, J., & Melda, K. (1995). Supporting families who provide care at home for children with disabilities. *Exceptional Children, 62,* 271–282.

Bailey, D. B. (1988a). Assessing family stress and needs. In D. B. Bailey & R. J. Simeonsson (Eds.), *Family Assessment in Early Intervention,* Columbus, OH: Merrill.

Bailey, D. B. (1988b). Assessing critical events. In D. B. Bailey & R. J. Simeonsson (Eds.), *Family Assessment in Early Intervention,* Columbus, OH: Merrill.

Bailey, D. B., Simeonsson, R. J., Winton, P. J., Huntington, G. S., Comfort, M., Isbell, P., O'Donnell, K., & Helm, J. (1986). Family-focused intervention: A functional model for planning, implementing, and evaluating individualized family services in early intervention. *Journal of the Division for Early Childhood, 10,* 156–171.

Beavers, J., Hampson, R. B., Hulgus, Y. F., & Beavers, W. R. (1986). Coping in families with a retarded child. *Family Process, 25,* 365–378.

Beckman, P. J. (1983). Influence of selected child characteristics on stress in families of handicapped infants. *American Journal of Mental Deficiency, 88,* 150–156.

Bennett, T., Lee, H., & Lueke, B. (1998). Expectations and concerns: What mothers and fathers say about inclusion. *Education and Training in Mental Retardation and Developmental Disabilities, 33,* 108–122.

Blacher, J. (1984). Sequential stages of parental adjustment to the birth of a child with handicaps: Fact or artifact? *Mental Retardation, 22,* 55–68.

Brown, C., Goodman, S., & Küpper, L. (2003). The unplanned journey: When you learn that your child has a disability. In Kupper, L. (Ed.), *Parenting a child with special needs* (3rd ed., pp. 7–16). Washington, DC: National Information Center for Children and Youth with Disabilities.

Clapham, J. A., & Teller, H. (1997). Using video to communicate with parents. *Rural Special Education Quarterly, 16*(2), 42–43.

Cole, D. A., & Meyer, L. H. (1989). Impact of needs and resources on family plans to seek out-of-home placement. *American Journal on Mental Retardation, 93,* 380–387.

Cramer, S., Erzkus, A., Mayweather, K., Pope, K., Roeder, J., & Tone, T. (1997). Connecting with siblings. *Teaching Exceptional Children, 30*(1), 46–51.

Donnellan, A. M., & Mirenda, P. L. (1984). Issues related to professional involvement with families of individuals with autism and other severe handicaps. *Journal of the Association for Persons with Severe Handicaps, 9,* 16–24.

Dunst, C. J. (2002). Family-centered practices: Birth through high school. *Journal of Special Education, 36,* 139–147.

Dyson, L. (1987). *Parent stress, family functioning, and social support in families of young handicapped children.* Paper presented at the National Early Childhood Conference on Children with Special Needs, Denver, CO, Nov. 1–3.

Eden-Piercy, G. V., Blacher, J. B., & Eyman, R. K. (1986). Exploring parents' reactions to their young child with severe handicaps. *Mental Retardation, 24,* 285–291.

Ellis, J. T., Luiselli, J. K., Amirault, D., Byrne, S., O'Malley-Cannon, B., Taras, M., Wolongevicz, J., & Sisson, R. W. (2002). Families of children with developmental disabilities: Assessment and comparison of self-reported needs in relation to situational variables. *Journal of Developmental and Physical Disabilities, 14,* 191–202.

Ferguson, P. M. (2002). A place in the family: An historical interpretation of research on parental reactions to having a child with a disability. *Journal of Special Education, 36,* 124–130.

Friedrich, W. N., Wilturner, L. T., & Cohen, D. S. (1985). Coping resources and parenting mentally retarded children. *American Journal of Mental Deficiency, 90,* 130–139.

Gallagher, J. J., Beckman, P., & Cross, A. H. (1983). Families of handicapped children: Sources of stress and its amelioration. *Exceptional Children, 50,* 10–19.

Gallegos, A. Y., & Medina, C. (1995). Twenty-one ways to involve families: A practical approach. *Rural Special Education Quarterly, 14*(3), 3–6.

Heiman, T. (2002). Parents of children with disabilities: Resilience, coping, and future expectations. *Journal of Developmental and Physical Disabilities, 14,* 159–171.

Holroyd, J., & McArthur, D. (1976). Mental retardation and stress on the parents: A contrast between Down's syndrome and childhood autism. *American Journal of Mental Deficiency, 80,* 431–436.

Kazak, A. E. (1986). Families with physically handicapped children: Social ecology and family systems. *Family Process, 22,* 265–281.

Kupfer, F. (1997, December 8). My turn: Home is not for everyone. *Newsweek,* p. 20.

Lindsey, J. D., & Stewart, D. A. (1989). The guardian minority: Siblings of children with mental retardation. *Education and Training in Mental Retardation and Developmental Disabilities, 24,* 291–296.

Lustig, D. C. (2002). Family coping in families with a child with a disability. *Education and Training in Mental Retardation and Developmental Disabilities, 37,* 14–22.

Lustig, D. C., & Akey, T. (1999). Adaptation in families with adult children with mental retardation: Impact of family strengths and appraisal. *Education and Training in Mental Retardation and Developmental Disabilities, 34,* 260–270.

McLean, T. (2002, October 2). *All alone no longer: Parents of autistic child form support group in Versailles. Lexington Herald-Leader,* p. E1.

McKinney, B., & Peterson, R. (1987). Predictors of stress in parents of developmentally disabled children. *Journal of Pediatric Psychology, 12,* 133–150.

Reamer, R. B., Brady, M. P., & Hawkins, J. (1998). The effects of video self-modeling on parents' interactions with children with developmental disabilities. *Education and Training in Mental Retardation and Developmental Disabilities, 33,* 131–143.

Reese, R. M., & Serna, L. (1986). Planning for generalization and maintenance in parent training: Parents need I.E.P.s too. *Mental Retardation, 24,* 87–92.

Special needs adoption (2001, December). Miracle workers. *Lexington Family: Central Kentucky's Parenting Magazine,* pp. 8–9.

Sandler, A. G., & Mistretta, L. A. (1998). Positive adaptation in parents of adults with disabilities. *Education and Training in Mental Retardation and Developmental Disabilities, 33,* 123–130.

Scorgie, K., Wilgosh, L., & McDonald, L. (1999). Transforming partnerships: Parent life management issues when a child has mental retardation. *Education and Training in Mental Retardation and Developmental Disabilities, 34,* 395–405.

Shapiro, J. (1983). Family reactions and coping strategies in response to the physically ill or handicapped child: A review. *Social Science Medicine, 17,* 913–931.

Singer, G. H. S., & Irvin, L. K. (1991). Supporting families of persons with severe disabilities. In L. H. Meyer, C. A. Peck, & L. Brown (Eds.), *Critical Issues in the Lives of People with Severe Disabilities* (pp. 271–312). Baltimore: Brookes.

Smith, P. M. (2003). You are not alone: For parents when they learn their child has a disability. In Küpper, L. (Ed.), *Parenting a child with special needs* (3rd ed., pp. 2–6). Washington, DC: National Information Center for Children and Youth with Disabilities.

Snell, M. E., & Beckman-Brindley, S. (1984). Family involvement in intervention with children having severe handicaps. *Journal of the Association for Persons with Severe Handicaps, 9,* 213–230.

Soodak, L. C., & Erwin, E. J. (2000). Valued member or tolerated participant: Parents' experiences in inclusive early childhood settings. *Journal of the Association for Persons with Severe Handicaps, 25,* 29–41.

Suelzle, M., & Keenan, V. (1981). Changes in family support networks over the life cycle of mentally retarded persons. *American Journal of Mental Deficiency, 86,* 267–274.

Taunt, H. M., & Hastings, R. P. (2002). Positive impact of children with developmental disabilities on their families: A preliminary study. *Education and Training in Mental Retardation and Developmental Disabilities, 37,* 410–420.

Tekin, E., & Kircaali-Iftar, G. (2002). Comparison of the effectiveness and efficiency of two response prompting procedures delivered by sibling tutors. *Education and Training in Mental Retardation and Developmental Disabilities, 37,* 283–299.

Todis, B., & Singer, G. (1991). Stress and stress management in families with adopted children who have severe disabilities. *Journal of the Association for Persons with Severe Handicaps, 16,* 3–13.

Waisbren, S. E. (1980). Parents' reactions after the birth of a developmentally disabled child. *American Journal of Mental Deficiency, 84,* 345–351.

Westling, D. L. (1996). What do parents of children with moderate and severe mental disabilities want? *Education and Training in Mental Retardation and Developmental Disabilities, 31,* 86–114.

Wikler, L. (1981). Chronic stresses of families of mentally retarded children. *Family Relations, 30,* 281–288.

Wikler, L. (1986). Periodic stresses of families of older mentally retarded children: An exploratory study. *American Journal of Mental Deficiency, 90,* 703–706.

CHAPTER FOUR

PROVIDING AN APPROPRIATE EDUCATION FOR STUDENTS WITH MODERATE AND SEVERE DISABILITIES:

A Foundation

On completion of this chapter, the reader will meet the following objectives:

- Explain the historical concepts that form the foundation of providing an appropriate education for students with moderate and severe disabilities, including the criterion of ultimate functioning, the least dangerous assumption, and the educational synthesizer.

- Describe the difference between multidisciplinary, interdisciplinary, and transdisciplinary models of service delivery.

- Design an appropriate school day for a student with moderate to severe disabilities.

- Discuss the evolution of practices in educating students with moderate and severe disabilities.

- Discuss the reluctance of some teachers to use research-based practices in their instruction.

The previous chapters have defined moderate and severe disabilities as a category, laid the foundation for including students with disabilities in educational settings regardless of the severity of the disability, and discussed some of the issues involved in working with families of children with moderate and severe disabilities with particular attention to providing strategies to cope with family stress. This chapter will begin a series of topics on providing an appropriate education for students with moderate and severe disabilities. In particular, this chapter will focus on the historical foundation that underlies an appropriate education. This includes the criterion of ultimate functioning, the role of the teacher as an educational synthesizer, and the criterion of the least dangerous assumption. In addition, this chapter will present various service delivery models with special emphasis on a transdisciplinary model, will provide an overview of an appropriate school day for a student with a moderate to severe disability, will address current shifts in special education practices, and will discuss ways of ensuring that students receive appropriate services. This will prepare the reader for the information on current practices that are in the chapters that follow.

CRITERION OF ULTIMATE FUNCTIONING

In 1976 Brown, Nietupski, and Hamre-Nietupski presented the term **criterion of ultimate functioning** in describing the goal of an education for each child with severe disabilities. In their words, "The criterion of ultimate functioning refers to the ever changing, expanding, localized and personalized cluster of factors that each person must possess in order to function as productively and independently as possible in socially, vocationally, and domestically integrated adult community environments"

(p. 8). Thus, the goal of education for children with disabilities is for them to become adults who function as independently as possible in least restrictive environments with their peers without disabilities. In order to assist students in reaching their full potential or in meeting the criterion of ultimate functioning, Brown et al. provided arguments for longitudinal programming, a least restrictive environment, heterogeneous grouping, a zero degree of inference strategy, early intervention, a transdisciplinary team approach, group instruction, distributed trials, and generalization strategies. These topics are introduced in the following sections. Later chapters will address the majority of each of these topics in further detail.

Longitudinal Programming

Students with moderate and severe disabilities need **longitudinal programming** to reach their full potential. Episodic programming occurs when students are taught isolated skills without planning for the future. With a longitudinal programming approach, teachers of young children talk with families about the future, and together, they select skills for instruction that a child will need in order to function as independently as possible in the next environment. This is a different concept from an episodic approach, where skills are taught in isolation with little thought given to their maintenance or generalization. In longitudinal programming the process of discussion and planning continues as a child moves from teacher to teacher or from grade to grade, with each teacher picking up instruction where the last teacher stopped. If a student with a moderate or severe disability does not master a skill needed for independent functioning during a unit of instruction or at a particular grade level, the teacher (with input from the child's team) assesses the student's progress to date, considers whether adaptations or modifications are needed, and continues instruction where it is feasible. This ongoing process results in a seamless transition to adulthood when the child exits from school services. (See Chapter 11 for a more detailed discussion of longitudinal transitioning.)

Least Restrictive Environment

Students with moderate and severe disabilities need to be included in environments with students without disabilities if they are to be expected to function in inclusive environments in adulthood. Using the **logic of homogeneity,** society sometimes errs in making the assumption that persons with disabilities are "better off with their own kind," where they can be served in groups by trained staff in segregated settings (e.g., self-contained classrooms or adult programs and workshops) or activities (e.g., leisure activities, such as art or sports, found in the community). Best practice, however, has shifted to a **logic of heterogeneity** based on research that students can learn from other students with different abilities and that students may fail to generalize skills across settings unless they are taught in heterogeneous settings. For example, students with moderate and severe disabilities often have difficulty acquiring language skills. Placed in an environment where there are few students who can serve as models, students are left without anyone to imitate and with few partners with whom they can practice the language skills they have been taught. In a heterogeneous environment, students have the opportunity to learn from role models and to practice the skills they are acquiring. (Note that full inclusion in general education will be discussed in depth in Chapter 7.)

Group Instruction

Although skills often are taught to students with moderate and severe disabilities in a one-to-one format, individualized instruction also can be presented in small groups (Collins, Gast, Ault, & Wolery, 1991). Effective instruction can be delivered to groups that are either homogeneous or heterogeneous, and a growing body of research on the acquisition of nontargeted information has shown that group instruction can be beneficial because students can learn from each other through observation (Collins, Hendricks, Fetko, & Land, 2002). Although this strategy will be explained in greater detail in Chapter 6, an example of observational learning can be found in Example 4.1.

EXAMPLE 4.1   Learning through Observation

To take advantage of the ability of students to learn through observing each other, Collins and Stinson (1994–1995) placed secondary students with moderate disabilities in dyads (i.e., groups of two) when they taught them to read and define key words found on the warning labels of household products. For example, Chet and Denise participated in instruction together. Chet's target words included *caution, harmful, precaution, swallowed, induce,* and *vomiting;* Denise's target words included *avoid, prolonged, irritant, contact, flush,* and *ingestion.* Each day, the teacher called the two students to a table where she used a progressive time delay procedure to teach the target words on flashcards. As she gave the students feedback on their responses, she defined the words ("Caution means a product can hurt you if you're not careful."). She then showed them the words as they would appear in context on the labels of potentially dangerous products and explained the phrases (e.g., "'Caution: First Aid' means to read what to do if you are hurt by a product."). She taught the words, two at a time, with twelve turns per student per instructional session. To facilitate attending, she called on students at random and praised students on the average of every three trials for paying attention (e.g., "I like the way you are watching and paying attention to each other."). The students mastered their target words in an average of 4.4 instructional sessions and were able to state most of the definitions. They also could identify and define at least 30% of each other's words by the end of instruction. This means that the teacher did not have to spend time teaching these words later and demonstrates the benefit of providing the opportunity for students to learn through observation.

Zero Degree of Inference

Third, a **zero degree of inference** should be practiced in working with students with moderate and severe disabilities. This means that teachers and others who work with students with moderate and severe disabilities should infer nothing. The practices of **community-based instruction** (described in Chapter 8) and a **functional curriculum** (described in Chapter 5) are two examples of zero degree of inference strategies. The practice of community-based instruction or **in vivo instruction** is based on the premise that students with moderate and severe disabilities may not generalize skills taught in classroom settings to the real world (see Collins, Stinson, & Land, 1993). Thus, instead of inferring that students will generalize, teachers should test students across environments to see if they can generalize the skills they have been taught; if not, instruction should take place in the natural environments where skills will be needed. An example that illustrates problems with generalization can be found in Example 4.2.

EXAMPLE 4.2 Problems in Generalizing Across Environments

In Example 4.1, Collins and Stinson (1994–1995) taught secondary students with moderate disabilities to read key words found on the warning labels of potentially dangerous products. Although the students quickly learned to read the words on flashcards and were exposed to the words as they would appear in context on the labels, they failed to generalize when they went to the grocery store and were asked to read the words on the labels of novel products.

Based on these results, Collins and Griffen (1996) altered their procedures in teaching elementary students with moderate disabilities to read and respond to key words on warning labels. Instead of teaching with flashcards, the teacher taught each target student to read words directly from the warning labels on a variety of potentially dangerous products using a constant time delay procedure. For example, the teacher taught Mickey to read the words *harmful, irritant,* and *swallowed* as they appeared on liquid bleach, liquid laundry detergent, and powdered laundry detergent. Instruction consisted of nine trials per session (three trials on each of the three products). In addition to facilitating generalization through the use of multiple examples of real products, the teacher also taught the student a safe response to the products by guiding him in walking away from the product within five seconds of reading the word on the label.

The outcome of Mickey's instruction was similar to the outcomes for the other target students. Although he learned to read the target words in four sessions, he did not reach criterion on performing the correct safe response to the product during classroom probe or test trials (i.e., safely reacting to the product when placed on a table or shelf) for 17 sessions. The instructional procedure proved to be effective when Mickey demonstrated that he had generalized the safe response to novel products (e.g., liquid disinfectant, oil furniture polish, spray insect repellent) placed in novel settings (e.g., school bathroom, hallway water fountain, office mailboxes, university table). This example shows the benefit of both planning and testing for generalization across settings and materials instead of inferring that generalization will occur.

The practice of teaching a functional curriculum began because students with moderate and severe disabilities may not acquire the life skills most children acquire unless those skills are specifically taught. For example, it is possible that a student with a moderate to severe disability who was taught a developmental or an academic curriculum could exit school being able to recite the alphabet without being able to read the words to select the appropriate restroom, to cross the street, or to exit a building in case of an emergency. In addition, a student may be able to count from one to one hundred without being able to give the correct number of dollars to make a simple purchase. Again, instead of inferring that students will acquire functional skills, students with moderate and severe disabilities should teach a curriculum that ensures they will have the life skills they need when they reach adulthood.

Early Intervention

Early intervention is important if students are to reach their full potential. The learning curve for students with moderate and severe disabilities tends to be more gradual than for students without disabilities or for students with mild disabilities. This means that students with moderate and severe disabilities can be expected to take longer to master fewer skills. In particular, those students with the most severe disabilities may master very few (if any) skills in a lifetime, even with intensive instruction. The earlier the educational process begins, the more time educators have to teach skills. Also, beginning instruction on basic life skills (e.g., feeding, walking, talking) at the same time most children are taught them is easier in inclusive settings than trying to teach those same skills after they have been mastered by same-age peers and the discrepancies between students with and without disabilities have increased. To demonstrate the importance of early education, a recent study of 296 children who were premature (i.e., born at 28 weeks and weighing an average of 2 pounds) revealed that those who received early services, such as speech therapy, showed improvement in mental ability (Tanner, 2003).

Distributed Trial Format

As will be described in greater detail in Chapter 6, there are three types of instructional trials: (a) **massed trial instruction,** in which one trial immediately follows another (e.g., one-to-one flash card instruction); (b) **spaced trial instruction,** in which there is a brief interval between trials (e.g., the teacher calls on another student in the group to respond before returning to the target student); and (c) **distributed trial instruction,** in which trials are interspersed at natural times throughout the day (e.g., reading words as they are naturally found on signs while in the community). While massed and spaced trials can be beneficial during the initial presentation of new tasks or during practice trials, distributed trials most closely reflect natural settings and the way in which students will need to generalize outside of the school setting in order to use the skills they have learned within the school setting. For ultimate functioning, educators should incorporate distributed trials into the school day, which gives students the opportunity to practice what they have been taught at times when skills are needed across settings and activities.

To illustrate the use of the various instructional trial formats, a teacher may teach community sight words using massed trials during one-to-one instruction or using spaced trials during small-group instruction. To ensure generalization, however, the teacher should also take the opportunity to teach these words as they naturally occur across settings and activities throughout the day. Specifically, the student could have instructional trials on reading the labels on restroom doors in the school during breaks and at various locations, such as the mall, a restaurant, or a grocery store during community-based instruction.

Generalization Strategies

The goal of education is to be able to apply or generalize what has been learned in future environments. However, it is common for students with moderate to severe disabilities to have difficulty generalizing across novel settings, persons, materials, or activities. Stokes and Baer (1977) and Stokes and Osnes (1986) presented several principles for facilitating generalization that will be covered in greater detail in later chapters. These principles can be applied during instruction in the following manner: (a) fading continuous feedback (e.g., praise) to a more natural schedule (e.g., intermittent praise), (b) teaching with multiple exemplars of materials (e.g., prices printed in various colors, sizes, and fonts), (c) using natural materials (e.g., real money instead of play money), (d) teaching in natural environments (e.g., teaching the use of money while making purchases in the community instead of teaching money skills with worksheets), and (e) using natural cues and reinforcers during instruction that the student is likely to encounter across settings (e.g., verbally stating prices and saying "thank you" as a store clerk would do).

Transdisciplinary Approach

There are three team models for providing services to students with moderate and severe disabilities (Dunn, 1991): (1) multidisciplinary, (2) interdisciplinary, and (3) transdisciplinary. In a **multidisciplinary team model,** a range of professionals work individually to provide assessment and intervention from each of their own perspectives. There is rare contact between the team members who work in isolation to teach various skills needed by the student. In an **interdisciplinary team model,** several professionals assess and plan together to provide programming but, again, may work in isolation to teach skills. In a **transdisciplinary team model,** several professionals, using **role release,** determine as a group who will conduct assessment activities and teach skills from their various disciplines within the context of activities in natural environments. For ultimate functioning, the transdisciplinary model is more likely to yield the best assessment results and result in optimal programming for skill acquisition. This model is more fully described in the section on the educational synthesizer later in this chapter.

Summary of the Criterion of Ultimate Functioning

It is apparent that there are many pieces to putting together an educational program that will result in students with moderate and severe disabilities reaching the criterion of ultimate functioning. Based on Brown et al. (1976), Activity 4.1 presents the questions instructors should ask before teaching skills to students with moderate and severe disabilities if they want their students to reach their full potential.

ACTIVITY 4.1   Criterion of Ultimate Functioning

Select an educational activity that you think should be taught to a student at the particular age level in which you are interested. It may be a developmental (e.g., motor, self-care, language) or academic (e.g., math, reading, writing) task. Once you have selected the activity, ask yourself each of the following questions regarding the participation of students with moderate to severe disabilities:

- Why do the activity?
- Is the activity necessary to prepare students with moderate to severe disabilities for ultimate functioning?

- Could students with moderate and severe disabilities function as adults without the skill taught in the activity?
- Is there a different activity that will allow more rapid or efficient acquisition of the skill taught in the activity?
- Will the activity impede ultimate functioning in the community setting?
- Are the skill, materials, tasks, and criteria similar to those that will be found in adult life?

Once you complete this task, compare and discuss your responses with another person.

EDUCATIONAL SYNTHESIZER

In another foundational piece, Bricker (1976) introduced the concept of the **educational synthesizer,** changing the role of teachers of students with moderate and severe disabilities. According to Bricker (1976), the educational synthesizer is "any interventionalist who (a) seeks appropriate information or techniques from professionals in other disciplines, (b) applies such information or techniques to develop effective intervention strategies, and (c) implements such strategies in order to remediate problems (e.g., insuring special diets for children with allergies, monitoring seizure activity) or to facilitate the acquisition of new skills (e.g., implementing muscle relaxing activities or special language training procedures)" (p. 88). In addition to the special education teacher and the student's family members, a number of professionals may be on the team serving a student with moderate to severe disabilities. The team members may come from disciplines that include general education, medicine, mobility and orientation, nutrition, occupational therapy, physical therapy, psychology, rehabilitation counseling, social work, and speech/language pathology. Trained in the skills to acquire, organize, evaluate, and implement input from other disciplines, the teacher of a student with moderate to severe disabilities, in collaboration with the student's family, would determine a child's needs, consult with professionals, create a program for the student based on their input, and monitor the effectiveness of the intervention. The professional would serve as a consultant rather than a direct service provider, resulting in more frequent and consistent delivery of services within routine, functional activities. Using this model, work through Activity 4.2.

ACTIVITY 4.2   The Educational Synthesizer

Create a list of professionals that may be involved with a student with a moderate to severe disability at the age level in which you are interested. Using the activity you selected in Activity 4.1, list the information you would seek from each of the professionals before teaching the skills in the activity. For example, a physical therapist might provide information on positioning the student for the activity.

The transdisciplinary approach is compatible with the concept of the educational synthesizer. In this model the teacher works with professionals to compile information, create programming, and evaluate progress. However, using the practices of arena assessment and role release, various members of the team may be responsible for implementing the program. An **arena assessment** occurs when the professionals on the team provide input to the individual working directly with the student in order to identify the student's instructional needs. The assessor is the person (e.g., teacher, parent) who typically can get the optimal performance from the student. In the practice of role release, professionals work on a consultant basis to train and monitor the person who will be working with a student in the skills that person will need to conduct the intervention.

In describing the transdisciplinary team approach, Downing and Bailey (1990) stressed integration of skill instruction into the functional program. According to Downing and Bailey, a transdisciplinary approach has three characteristics. First, the model is family centered, with family members serving as part of the team. Second, the model involves collaborative consultation in the sharing of information, strategies, and techniques, using role release instead of pull-out services. Third, the model integrates service delivery with services blended across activities and no one having sole responsibility for working on a single skill.

While the transdisciplinary provision of services may be implemented in a segregated setting, Dunn (1991) described how related services could be integrated into the general education setting as well. According to Dunn, there are four models of integration. In **peer integration** students with and without disabilities are placed together. In **functional integration** therapeutic strategies are applied in life environments. In **practice integration** collaboration occurs between therapists and teachers to meet students' needs. Finally, **comprehensive integration** combines all three models. In integrated programming (a) goals and objectives are formed with input from all team members; (b) each team member contributes knowledge; and (c) team members design assessment, intervention, data-collection, and supervision strategies as a group.

Dunn noted that different models of service provision can be appropriate. The therapist may be responsible in a **direct therapy model** when others cannot safely carry out procedures. The therapist also would be responsible in a **monitoring therapy model,** where the therapist develops strategies for a student then trains others to carry them out under the therapist's supervision. The trainee, however, would be responsible in a **consultation therapy model,** where the therapist initially trains another person then withdraws. This could occur as (a) a **case consultation** for a single student (e.g., behavioral specialist performs one-time consultation for single student and writes behavioral recommendations), (b) a **colleague consultation** for a trainee (e.g., a teacher enrolls in a behavioral training workshop conducted by a behavioral specialist on safe physical management), or (c) a **system consultation** for a school or agency (e.g., a school district contracts with a behavioral specialist to provide an in-service seminar on positive behavioral support).

According to Dunn, there are several factors to be considered in selecting an appropriate model. These include (a) the potential for functional improvement, (b) the expertise of professionals in the educational environment, and (c) the age of the student.

Giangreco (1990) surveyed 58 parents of school-age children with severe disabilities as well as 100 special education teachers, 71 communication specialists, 46 occupational therapists, and 37 physical therapists regarding their roles in collaborative efforts. All ranked adaptation (e.g., materials, curriculum) as the top related service delivery role for students with severe disabilities. This was followed by functional skill instruction. Most rated the educational program as the criteria used to make related service decisions.

To illustrate a transdisciplinary model integrated in the general education setting, Downing and Bailey (1990) contrasted a traditional model to a transdisciplinary model in describing the typical school day of Jerri, a 13-year-old student with a moderate to severe disability (she had cerebral palsy, visual impairment, and severe mental retardation; used wheelchair and palmar grasp; did not respond to verbal directions; and communicated by looking, reaching, and grabbing). In the traditional model, Jerri's day took place in segregated settings, such as the resource room, the speech room, a separate table in the cafeteria, and the vision impairment office, with isolated instruction during nonfunctional activities (e.g., isolated physical therapy exercises; activities of putting together a large-piece puzzle, putting clothespins in a jar, sorting poker chips in cups, identifying animal sounds, identifying prepositions). Staff helped her to perform self-care skills and pushed her from place to place in her wheelchair. She was stimulated by lights in a dark room and received weight-bearing physical therapy in a stander while she worked with Legos and colored pictures and was stimulated by a vibrator. Her program was conducted by the teacher, an aide, or a specialist.

In contrast, when the trandisciplinary model was implemented, Jerri's day consisted of natural activities with embedded skill instruction monitored by specialists and supported by peers without disabilities and technology in age-appropriate activities (e.g., music class, language arts class, art class) in general education settings. This was supplemented by simulations of functional activities in the resource room. Jerri was "put through" self-care tasks instead of having the tasks done for her, and she participated in community-based instruction with a small group that included peers without disabilities.

Example 4.3 shows another example of a day that was created for a student with a moderate to severe disability using a transdisciplinary model. In this example the consultants and teacher acted as educational synthesizers to create an appropriate school program for the student.

EXAMPLE 4.3   EXAMPLE OF NED'S DAY

In Example 1.3 you were introduced to Ned, an adolescent with Down syndrome and a moderate to severe mental disability, and read how a consultation revealed his strengths and abilities (Collins, Schuster, & Grisham-Brown, 2002). Prior to the consultation, Ned's day consisted of staying home with a babysitter although he was 12 years old and his same-age peers were in school. He was not permitted to attend school during regular operating hours due to aggressive behaviors (e.g., hitting, spitting). When his peers ended their school day and went home, Ned's mother brought him from home to begin his school day. He was met by his teacher and an instructional assistant, who quickly put him through a semblance of instruction that consisted of doing whatever Ned wanted to do (e.g., listen to music, tear up paper, play games on the computer) in order to avoid his behavioral tantrums. After an hour of refusing to participate in any meaningful instruction, his teacher typically walked him to a local fast-food restaurant and bought him something to eat before he went home.

After working with the consultants over a semester, Ned's day looked quite different. As his teacher systematically implemented a series of recommended changes, Ned's day evolved to include (a) riding the bus to school with his peers without disabilities, (b) being reinforced on an average of every 10 minutes for having appropriate behavior across settings and teachers, (c) using a picture schedule that alternated between easy and difficult tasks and provided good choices, (d) receiving systematic instruction on functional skills from various staff members, (e) participating in several classes with same-age peers without disabilities, (f) eating lunch with those peers in the cafeteria, (g) doing jobs throughout the school (e.g., watering plants), (h) using a combination of manual signing with a communication board, and (i) going on community-based instruction in the company of a peer without disabilities. A system of natural supports was created in which a number of persons took responsibility for implementing Ned's educational program. When Ned completed middle school, he walked across the stage with his peers in a recognition ceremony before transitioning to the secondary school. For this student, an inappropriate day evolved into an appropriate one.

Demchak, Alden, Bergin, Ting, and Lacey (1995) asserted that there are specific indicators to consider in evaluating the effectiveness of a transdisciplinary program for a student with moderate or severe disabilities as follows. First, the team should include members from all relevant disciplines; family members; classroom personnel; and if appropriate, the student. Second, assessment should be conducted within the context of routine activities in the natural environment with parent involvement and the sharing of results with all team members, and the IEP goals and objectives should be based on assessment results, developed as a team, and written as embedded activities in functional, age-appropriate activities. Third, sufficient time should be devoted to the delivery of related services in a collaborative format in age-appropriate activities in the natural environment and to regular team meetings to exchange information and evaluate adaptations. Fourth, training for role release should be provided to personnel and family members by a qualified person in a systematic and data-based fashion. Fifth, ongoing monitoring using an appropriate data collection system should be reviewed regularly by the team. Finally, team meetings should be held on a regular basis with minutes kept and copies distributed to team members.

Summary of the Educational Synthesizer

Bricker (1976) laid the foundation for the teacher's role in working with related service delivery personnel within a transdisciplinary model. This model is more relevant than ever with the advent of full inclusion for students with moderate and severe disabilities. Today's special education teacher often assumes the intermediary role of gathering information from a broad array of service providers then collaborating with general educators on ways to ensure that students receive an appropriate education.

THE CRITERION OF LEAST DANGEROUS ASSUMPTION

The criterion of least dangerous assumption was introduced in Chapter 3 in regard to working with families. This concept, as described by Donnellan (1984), can be applied to a much broader frame of reference. To review, the criterion of least dangerous assumption states that "in the absence of conclusive data, educational decisions should be based on assumptions which, if incorrect, will have the least dangerous effect on the student" (Donnellan, 1984, p. 142). Although Donnellan based her comments on her work with children with autism, the criterion of least dangerous assumption can be applied to most of the principles, many of which already have been introduced in this chapter, that are fundamental to teaching students with moderate and severe disabilities. These are overviewed in the following paragraphs. In reading through the arguments that follow, bear in mind that there always are exceptions to the rule (e.g., students who are too easily distracted for group instruction and learn best in a one-to-one setting), but exceptions should be driven by data.

Integration with Peers without Disabilities

As mentioned earlier, the logic of heterogeneity promotes the concept that people are better served in segregated settings. Yet research tells us that students with moderate and severe disabilities benefit from exposure to students without disabilities. Students without disabilities are role models for behaviors that students with moderate and severe disabilities work to acquire (e.g., language, social, academic, self-care) and can be partners in practicing skills and facilitating generalization. Thus, if there are no data to tell us that specific students will benefit from segregation, then it is less dangerous to assume that they will benefit from integrated settings.

Heterogeneous Grouping

As with integrated settings, there are data that have shown that students with moderate and severe disabilities can benefit from instruction in heterogeneous groups. While data also support one-to-one instruction, heterogeneous group instruction is more likely to result in more efficient learning as students acquire information taught to other students through observation (Collins et al., 2002). In addition, group instruction allows students to practice social skills (e.g., taking turns) that will benefit them across settings. Thus, if there are no data to tell us that students need to be taught in a one-to-one format or in a homogeneous setting, then it is less dangerous to teach students in heterogeneous groups.

Natural Materials and Settings

There are many commercial materials available that teach life skills, and these often are used in classroom settings. For example, direct instruction may include play money and flashcards of survival words to teach community skills in classroom settings. Although some students with moderate and severe disabilities may generalize across materials and settings what they learn through classroom instruction with commercial materials, Example 4.4 illustrates that there are data that show that many do not generalize unless taught with real materials (e.g., real money and actual examples of signs using survival words), and many do not generalize until they are taught skills as they naturally occur in activities (e.g., shopping in a store or crossing a street) in community settings. Thus, if there are no data to tell us that specific students can generalize from artificial materials or from classroom instruction, then it is less dangerous to teach with natural materials in the natural settings where skills are needed.

**EXAMPLE 4.4 TEACHING WITH REAL MATERIALS
IN NATURAL SETTINGS**

Collins et al. (1993) conducted instruction with four elementary and with four secondary students with moderate disabilities in a research investigation that illustrates the difficulties students have in generalizing to natural settings. During classroom instruction, the teachers simulated an outdoor setting by marking off a street with masking tape on the classroom floor and by placing a box with a slit for a quarter beside a disconnected telephone. During in vivo (real-world) instruction, the teacher taught students using multiple examples of community streets and public pay telephones. The resulting data across the two groups were mixed when the investigator tested students on a novel street and a novel public pay telephone.

Some students mastered and generalized the skill from the classroom simulation, while others failed to master the skill until taught in a natural setting with real materials. Based on the results of this investigation, the least dangerous assumption would be to train all students in the natural settings with real materials unless there are data to show that they can generalize from classroom simulations with artificial materials.

Natural Cues and Consequences

Instruction of students with moderate and severe disabilities often includes artificial cues, such as teacher directions and artificial consequences or reinforcers, such as candy, tokens, or points, that are not found across settings. While these may be needed for initial instruction on tasks, they seldom are found in the environments where students will need to perform the skills they have been taught. Data show that artificial cues and consequences can be paired with natural cues (e.g., written directions for filling out forms, price displayed on cash register or ticket) and natural consequences (e.g., praise, money) and that schedules for delivering consequences can be thinned to reflect the natural settings (e.g., intermittent praise, payment at the end of a set period of time). Thus, if there are no data to show that students will generalize skills taught with artificial cues and consequences, then strategies should be used to teach with those that are more natural and reflect the environments where skills will be needed.

Instructional Arrangements

Some schools make the mistake of assigning a specific teacher or instructional assistant to a single student. Even if the student and the instructor are in inclusive classrooms with students without disabilities, instruction for the student is the responsibility of the assigned person on a one-to-one basis. Yet there are data that show that students taught in this kind of instructional arrangement may not generalize the skills they have been taught to other persons (e.g., parent, employer) or to larger settings with persons without disabilities (e.g., neighborhood, employment site). Thus, if there are no data to show that a student with a moderate to severe disability needs one-to-one instruction from a specific person, then the student should be taught by various persons throughout the day (e.g., general education teacher, instructional assistant, special education teacher, therapist) and should be included in groups of various sizes and with types of students that reflect natural proportions.

Zero Degree of Inference

As noted earlier, one should never infer that a student has learned a skill just because it was taught. Practicing a zero degree of inference philosophy, teachers of students with moderate and severe disabilities should infer nothing and should test everything to ensure that students have learned skills that they can generalize across materials, settings, and persons. If there are no data to show that students can generalize all they have been taught, then teachers should conduct probe or test trials across natural environments to make certain.

Age-Appropriate Curriculum

In a developmental approach, students are taught through a readiness model, based on the idea that certain prerequisite skills must be mastered before students can move on to other skills. Students with moderate to severe disabilities, however, may never be ready to move on. As will be described in Chapter 5, continuing to work on skills long after their peers have mastered them can prevent students with moderate and severe disabilities from being able to take part in environments with same-age peers. Data show that modifications and adaptations can enable students with moderate to severe disabilities to access environments that include same-age peers without disabilities. Thus, unless there are data to show that students with moderate and severe disabilities cannot benefit from a functional approach to teaching an age-appropriate curriculum, then they should be exposed to an age-appropriate curriculum through a functional approach (e.g., teaching those skills that are most useful through adaptations and modifications).

Data-Based Decision Making

Sometimes the labels placed on students cause their abilities to be underestimated. As noted in Chapter 1, labels such as mental retardation, autism, and Down syndrome may cause instructors to form lower expectations for a student than they have the capability of attaining. Basing instructional decisions on data collected on each individual student's ability to learn allows the instructor to individualize instruction regardless of a student's label. Thus, unless there are data to substantiate a student's prognosis, then it is less dangerous to assume that all children can learn and to continue to search for an appropriate instructional technology.

Parents

As stated in Chapter 3, it can be easy to blame parents (or other family members) when their children do not learn. Parents can be convenient scapegoats for a student who is challenging. Yet many parents are as perplexed as instructors in finding the best strategy for working with a child. Thus, unless there are data to show that the parents are factors that negatively influence their child's ability to learn, then it is less dangerous to accept parents as equal partners in the educational process and to proceed as if it is the school program that needs to be changed to best work with the child.

Summary of the Criterion of Least Dangerous Assumption

Donnellan (1984) set the standard for decision making in working with students with moderate and severe disabilities that continues to be an underlying foundation for special education today. Teachers who use the criterion of least dangerous assumption in making decisions will err on the side of caution in developing appropriate programming for their students. This is preferable to making the wrong decision in the absence of conclusive data.

SHIFTS IN PRACTICES FOR STUDENTS WITH MODERATE AND SEVERE DISABILITIES

The previous sections in this chapter have focused on the early foundations laid for educational practices with students with moderate and severe disabilities. To provide an appropriate education for a student with a moderate to severe disability, it is clear that practitioners must know what to teach, where to teach, and how to teach, based on the principles presented in this chapter. In 1997 Browder updated these principles when she addressed the changing aspects of an appropriate education. According to Browder, there is a current shift in best practices in the following areas: (a) functional curriculum, (b) general education settings, (c) technology, (d) embedded instruction, (e) inclusion, and (f) teacher research. These current shifts are described in the following sections.

What to Teach

Because they facilitate independence, the acquisition of life skills are crucial if persons with moderate and severe disabilities are to have access to least restrictive environments. As will be described in detail in Chapter 5, life skills are functional skills that are immediately useful in a person's life. Their presentation is not limited by failure to master prerequisite skills, as would be the case in a developmental approach. Ecological assessment of a student's environment helps to identify priority skills for mastery. For example, a student who needs to cook can bypass prerequisite skills of reading or measuring through using adaptations, such as picture recipes or premeasured ingredients. An ecological assessment conducted in collaboration with members of the student's family would reveal the types of cooking appropriate in the student's home environment (e.g., stove top versus microwave) as well as student and family preferences and cultural differences (e.g., ethnic recipes). With the increasing focus on delivering functional skill instruction in general education environments, the challenge is to determine how to teach functional skills within a general education curriculum consisting of academic skills. Indeed, this challenge has been renewed with the current legal mandate that all children have access to general education core content and will be explored in depth in later chapters.

Where to Teach

As demonstrated through a discussion of the transdisciplinary team approach in this chapter, professionals and family members must work together to determine where instruction will take place and by whom it will be delivered. Research data support the conclusion that a number of students with moderate and severe disabilities will not generalize unless taught with natural materials in natural environments. Again, the increasing focus on inclusion in the general education setting and access to a general education curriculum provides a challenge for meeting the needs of students with moderate and severe disabilities with the outcome that students will be able to apply or generalize what they have learned across current and future natural environments. The challenge is to find a way to balance the need for community-based instruction with the need for interaction with peers without disabilities in general education settings.

How to Teach

There is a large body of research that shows that direct, systematic instruction is the most effective and efficient way to teach skills to students with moderate and severe disabilities (Wolery & Schuster, 1997). Researchers have collected data to show that a number of errorless instructional strategies (e.g., response prompting strategies to be described in Chapter 6) have social validity. That is, the strategies are acceptable to relevant members of society (e.g., parents, teachers) and result in attainment of goals valued by society (e.g., functional academics, self-care, language). While there is evidence that these strategies can be embedded within general education settings (see Collins, Branson, Hall, & Rankin, 2001) and that students without disabilities also can benefit from errorless instructional strategies (e.g., Fickel, Schuster, & Collins, 1998), the challenge is to continue to identify the strategies that work best in teaching various skills across students with a variety of disabilities.

Future Research

Browder (1997) identified several areas where continued research to benefit students with severe disabilities is warranted. These areas also apply to students with moderate disabilities. First, researchers need to determine how to plan appropriate educational programming for students with moderate and severe disabilities as best practices shift from a developmental approach to a functional approach and from teaching in community settings to teaching in general education settings. Second, researchers need to determine ways to use assistive technology to allow students with limited communication skills to indicate preferences in regard to their educational programs. Third, researchers need to determine, with input from families, how to balance the instruction of academics, social skills, and life skills and how to provide services (e.g., therapy) within a general education curriculum. Fourth, researchers need to determine how to adapt effective instructional and behavioral methods to support students in inclusive settings. Finally, researchers need to find the best research methods available (e.g., single-subject research, group quantitative research, qualitative research) to answer research questions in partnership with teachers.

It is important to note that research should not be the sole responsibility of persons who work in higher education or at research institutes. Teachers need to be trained in research skills that they can apply to situations in their own classrooms. Having the skills to determine best practices in the field is a valuable tool in providing an appropriate education for all students.

DOCUMENTING THAT STUDENTS WITH MODERATE AND SEVERE DISABILITIES RECEIVE AN APPROPRIATE EDUCATION

Documentation of an appropriate education can occur both prior to and following program implementation. To be most effective, documentation should be an ongoing, formative process.

In regard to initial assessment, Giangreco, Edelman, Dennis, and Cloninger (1995) documented that appropriate initial assessment can lead to appropriate programming. For example, COACH (Choosing Options and Accommodations for Children) (Giangreco, Cloninger, & Iverson, 1993) is an assessment instrument based on six underlying assumptions (valued life outcomes, family involvement in planning, collaborative teamwork, coordinated planning, problem-solving, and service-based special education) and five valued life outcomes (safe, stable home environment; access to a variety of settings and meaningful activities; social network of meaningful relationships; personal choice and control; and safety/health). The COACH assessment has three parts: (a) family prioritization interview, (b) definition of educational program components, and (c) educational program components in inclusive settings.

When Giangreco et al. (1995) interviewed 72 parents, teachers, and service-delivery personnel involved with children with deaf/blindness, they found that using COACH (a) caused team members to think differently and focus on student priorities, (b) resulted in educational program components being referenced to valued life outcomes, (c) resulted in a smaller number of IEP goals with each based on family input, (d) resulted in more favorable relationships between family and professionals, and (e) provided more life outcome opportunities for students.

In compliance with No Child Left Behind, most states are generating minimal standards to be met by students without disabilities that require postprogram assessment. For example, Kentucky has developed a Program of Studies with a Core Content and Academic Expectations, Virginia has developed Standards of Learning, and Maryland has developed Learner Outcomes and Core Learner Goals. It is often unreasonable for students with moderate and severe disabilities, however, to be placed in a diploma track where mastery of these standards is mandatory. Kleinert and his colleagues have written numerous articles about alternate assessment for students with moderate and severe disabilities (see Kleinert, Green, Hurte, Clayton, & Oetinger, 2002; Kleinert, Haig, Kearns, & Kennedy, 2000). They maintain that the core curriculum for general education can be adapted to meet the needs of students with moderate and severe disabilities. In their work in Kentucky, they have demonstrated how an alternate portfolio requirement for students without moderate and severe disabilities can be adapted to document appropriate programming for students.

Kleinert et al. (2000) demonstrated how they identified the critical function of each of Kentucky's academic expectations to assess students with moderate and severe disabilities. For example, the critical function of "Students use research tools to locate sources of information and ideas relevant to a problem" is "Requests assistance" (p. 59). In compiling alternate portfolios, teachers of students with moderate and severe disabilities must work with each student in documenting how they learn the critical function through sustained interactions with peers without disabilities across multiple school and community settings using natural supports (e.g., peer tutors, assistive technology). Like the portfolios of students without moderate and severe disabilities, alternate portfolios are rated at the levels of novice, apprentice, proficient, or distinguished. The overall score of each alternate portfolio is rated as if the student had received the score in all of the areas of assessment completed by peers without moderate and severe disabilities. Typically, alternate portfolios that reflect best practices receive higher scores. Thus, the scores reflect the implementation of appropriate programming rather than student progress, with the logic being that appropriate programming ultimately leads to optimal student progress.

Best Practices
Providing an Appropriate Education for Students with Moderate and Severe Disabilities

1. Apply the criterion of ultimate functioning and the least dangerous assumption when making educational decisions for students with moderate and severe disabilities.
2. View the teacher's role as that of an educational synthesizer who is responsible for gathering information from a variety of sources (e.g., parents, professionals) to create an appropriate educational program.

3. Using a transdisciplinary team model, use an arena assessment in working with professionals and families to gather information for programming.

4. Using a transdisciplinary team model, practice role release in implementing educational programming.

Conclusion

This chapter highlighted basic principles that constitute the historical foundation for teaching students with moderate and severe disabilities. Most have been recognized as good practices for more than 25 years. It is puzzling, then, that some school programs continue to fail to meet the needs of students with moderate and severe disabilities. Heward (2003) addressed this paradox when he identified the "faulty notions about teaching and learning that hinder the effectiveness of special education" (p. 186). He based his assertions on four basic assumptions that include (1) the right of students to an effective education, (2) the premise that instruction should be individualized, (3) the presence of a research base in special education, and (4) the reluctance of special educators to use research-based practices.

Why do some students with moderate and severe disabilities fail to receive an appropriate education? In spite of a substantial research base that has developed over the years, Heward asserted that special educators continue to adhere to a number of worst practices for students with disabilities, such as discovery learning activities, trial and error instructional procedures, low expectations, slow pacing, and inconsistent application of learning theories, instead of using best practices, such as direct instruction to teach predetermined objectives, devoting time to drill and practice, using data to measure performance, and providing feedback to enable students to correct errors. Heward warned that creativity can be detrimental when it is contrary to best practices. To improve special education, Heward recommended that teachers (a) view their job as a profession and return to sound research-based instruction; (b) practice data-based decision making in their instruction; and (c) tend to alternate variables that can influence the effectiveness of instruction by evaluating the time allotted to instruction, instructional materials, the frequency of opportunities to respond, and the types of feedback following responses.

The chapters of this text thus far have identified who falls into the category of moderate and severe disabilities, a rationale as to why they should receive an education, and the variables that affect their families. This chapter reviewed the historical principles that set the foundation for providing an appropriate education for students with moderate and severe disabilities. The following chapters will focus on current best practices by exploring what to teach, as well as how and where to deliver instruction. Before proceeding to those chapters, however, stop and review the concepts presented in this chapter and complete the performance-based assessment that follows.

Questions for Review

1. In your own words, explain each of the following principles that constitute a historical foundation for providing an education for students with moderate to severe disabilities: (a) the criterion of ultimate functioning, (b) the least dangerous assumption, and (c) the educational synthesizer.

2. How does a transdisciplinary model differ from a multidisciplinary or an interdisciplinary model of service delivery?

3. What would an appropriate school day for a student with moderate or severe disabilities contain? Describe a school day from arrival to dismissal.

4. According to Heward (2003), some teachers are reluctant to use research-based practices in their instruction. Why?

Performance-Based Assessment

This chapter presented three team models for service delivery with a particular emphasis on the transdisciplinary model. Describe how you would apply a transdisciplinary model by answering the following questions.

1. Who might be part of the team?

2. How would assessment be conducted?

3. How would the IEP be written?

4. Where would instruction take place?

5. Where would related services be delivered?

6. Who would deliver instruction?

7. Who would deliver related services?

8. Who would monitor student progress?

References

Brown, L., Nietupski, J., & Hamre-Nietupski, S. (1976). The criterion of ultimate functioning. In M. A. Thomas, Ed. *Hey! Don't forget about me!* Reston, VA: The Council for Exceptional Children.

Bricker, D. (1976). The educational synthesizer. In M. A. Thomas, Ed. *Hey! Don't forget about me!* Reston, VA: The Council for Exceptional Children.

Browder, D. M. (1997). Educating students with severe disabilities: Enhancing the conversation between research and practice. *The Journal of Special Education, 31,* 137–144.

Collins, B. C., Branson, T. A., Hall, M., & Rankin, S. W. (2001). Teaching secondary students with moderate disabilities in an inclusive academic classroom setting. *Journal of Developmental and Physical Disabilities, 13,* 41–59.

Collins, B. C., Gast, D. L., Ault, M. J., & Wolery, M. (1991). Small group instruction: Guidelines for teachers of students with moderate to severe handicaps. *Education and Training in Mental Retardation, 26,* 18–32.

Collins, B. C., & Griffen, A. K. (1996). Teaching students with moderate disabilities to make safe responses to product warning labels. *Education and Treatment of Children, 19,* 30–45.

Collins, B. C., Hendricks, T. B., Fetko, K., & Land, L. (2002). Student-2-student learning in inclusive classrooms. *Teaching Exceptional Children, 34*(4), 56–61.

Collins, B. C., Schuster, J. W., & Grisham-Brown, J. (2002). *Success story: Ned.* Unpublished manuscript.

Collins, B. C., & Stinson, D. M. (1994–1995). Teaching generalized reading of product warning labels to adolescents with mental disabilities through the use of key words. *Exceptionality, 5,* 163–181.

Collins, B. C., Stinson, D. M., & Land, L. (1993). A comparison of in vivo and simulation prior to in vivo instruction in teaching generalized safety skills. *Education and Training in Mental Retardation, 28,* 128–142.

Demchak, M. A., Alden, P., Bergin, C., Ting, S., & Lacey, S. (1995). Evaluating transdisciplinary teaming for students with disabilities. *Rural Special Education Quarterly, 14*(1), 24–32.

Donnellan, A. M. (1984). The criterion of the least dangerous assumption. *Behavior Disorders, 9,* 141–150.

Downing, J., & Bailey, B. R. (1990). Sharing the responsibility: Using a transdisciplinary team approach to enhance the learning of students with severe disabilities. *Journal of Educational and Psychological Consultation, 1*(3), 259–278.

Dunn, W. (1991). Integrated related services. In L. H. Meyer, C. A. Peck, & L. Brown (Eds.), *Critical Issues in the Lives of People with Severe Disabilities* (pp. 353–377). Baltimore: Brookes.

Fickel, K. M., Schuster, J. W., & Collins, B. C. (1998). Teaching different tasks using different stimuli in a heterogeneous small group. *Journal of Behavioral Education, 8,* 219–244.

Giangreco, M. F. (1990). Making related service decisions for students with severe disabilities: Roles, criteria, and authority. *Journal of the Association for Persons with Severe Handicaps, 15,* 22–31.

Giangreco, M. F., Cloninger, C. J., & Iverson, V. S. (1993). *Choosing Options and Accommodations for Children: A guide to planning inclusive education.* Baltimore: Brookes.

Giangreco, M. F., Edelman, S. W., Dennis, R. E., & Cloninger, C. J. (1995). Use and impact of COACH with students who are deaf-blind. *Journal of the Association for Persons with Severe Handicaps, 20,* 121–135.

Heward, W. L. (2003). Ten faulty notions about teaching and learning that hinder the effectiveness of special education. *Journal of Special Education, 36,* 186–205.

Kleinert, H., Green, P., Hurte, M., Clayton, J., & Oetinger, C. (2002). Creating and using meaningful alternate assessment. *Teaching Exceptional Children, 34*(4), 40–47.

Kleinert, H. L., Haig, J., Kearns, J. F., & Kennedy, S. (2000). Alternate assessments: Lessons learned and roads to be taken. *Exceptional Children, 67,* 51–66.

Stokes, T. F., & Baer, D. M. (1977). An implicit technology of generalization. *Journal of Applied Behavior Analysis, 10,* 349–367.

Stokes, T. F., & Osnes, P. G. (1986). Programming the generalization of children's social behavior. In P. S. Strain, M. J. Guralnick, & H. M. Walker (Eds.). *Children's social behavior: Development, assessment, and modification* (pp. 407–443). Orlando, FL: Academic Press.

Tanner, L. (2003, February 12). Preemie study shows IQ advances. *Lexington Herald-Leader,* p. A3.

Wolery, M., & Schuster, J. W. (1997). Instructional methods with students who have significant disabilities. *The Journal of Special Education, 31,* 61–79.

PART TWO

Creating Appropriate Programming for Persons with Moderate and Severe Disabilities

CHAPTER FIVE

IDENTIFYING FUNCTIONAL AND AGE-APPROPRIATE SKILLS:

A Curriculum for Students with Moderate and Severe Disabilities

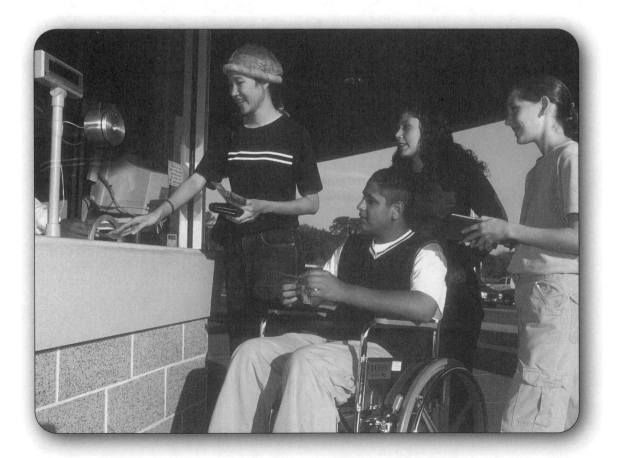

On completion of this chapter, the reader will meet the following objectives:

- State a rationale for teaching a functional- and chronological-age-appropriate curriculum to students with moderate and severe disabilities.
- List the sources of data that can be used to develop an individualized curriculum for a student with a moderate to severe disability.
- Describe the sequence of steps to be followed in conducting an ecological inventory.
- State the principle of partial participation and tell how it can be applied in selecting adaptations for students with moderate and severe disabilities.
- Describe how a functional curriculum can be taught within an inclusive program.

Chapter 4 of this text laid the foundation for providing an appropriate education for students with moderate and severe disabilities. In spite of this foundation, some students with moderate and severe disabilities receive an inappropriate education. In some cases teachers focus solely on caregiving needs when students are capable of more. In others teachers target skills for instruction based on the student's mental age instead of the chronological age (i.e., developmental approach).

In pivotal position papers that formed a foundation for teaching functional skills and including students, Brown et al. (1979) and Baumgart et al. (1982) addressed the issue of inappropriate education when they described the poor excuses teachers give for providing unacceptable programs. These excuses included (a) "the MA-CA discrepancy hypothesis," in which skills for older students are selected based on their mental ages rather than their chronological ages; (b) "the earlier stage hypothesis," in which prerequisite skills that hold little meaning in the student's life are selected from developmental scales for younger children; (c) "the 'not ready' hypothesis," in which skills are not taught until the child has the ability to perform them independently; and (d) "the artificial-approximation hypothesis," in which only semblances of skills are taught out of context. To illustrate how special education for students with moderate and severe disabilities has changed in the subsequent decades, an example of an early teacher preparation program in moderate and severe disabilities based on a developmental model is described in Example 5.1.

EXAMPLE 5.1   AN EXAMPLE OF AN EARLY TEACHER PREPARATION PROGRAM

In 2001 Collins and Schuster described the evolution of the field of special education for students with moderate and severe disabilities from a personal perspective. In doing so, they described an undergraduate program in "trainable mental retardation" in the 1970s as including a course in kindergarten methodology. The rationale was that a kindergarten curriculum would be appropriate for students with moderate and severe disabilities, regardless of their chronological age. The 1972 text that was used in the program contained the following sections that were considered best practices at the time:

1. A diagram showing how to set up a self-contained classroom
2. A daily schedule that included circle time with artificial materials (e.g., mannequin to dress for the weather), skills (e.g., cutting, pasting, coloring), and concepts (e.g., big, little) taught in isolation lunch in the classroom, and naptime on cots
3. Prescriptive teaching that had older students role playing to preschool music (e.g., taking train to zoo) and learning to rhyme words in Dr. Seuss stories
4. Units of instruction, such as the circus and the five senses, intended for older students that typically are taught to elementary school students.

During the teacher preparation program, practice and student teaching took place in a segregated school for children with disabilities, ages 5 through 21 years. Although the authors described feelings of enthusiasm and competence as they exited the program, they concluded that it is an irony that, as teacher educators thirty years later, they still visit classrooms in which the model has not changed.

The problem with the hypotheses described by Brown et al. and Baumgart et al. are that they result in programming that is based on a developmental or *bottom-up* approach to instruction. This is appropriate for young children, with or without disabilities, since all children begin life working on the same skills (e.g., crawling then walking, babbling then talking). A point arrives in the education of children with significant developmental delays or diagnosed moderate or severe disabilities, however, in which the discrepancy between what they can do and what their peers can do widens to the point that the children with delays and disabilities are left behind to work on skills they have not yet mastered while children without disabilities proceed to work on higher-level skills. The result is functional exclusion.

DEFINING A FUNCTIONAL APPROACH

Functional skills are skills that are meaningful and immediately useful in a child's life across settings. According to Brown et al. (1979), functional skills are those "that are frequently demanded in natural domestic, vocational, and community environments" (p. 83). In other words, functional skills are identified from natural environments and specifically those in which students with moderate and severe disabilities will be expected to function. Unlike a **bottom-up** or **developmental approach** in which students work on skills in a predetermined sequence that is typical of the development of children without disabilities, a **functional approach** to developing a curriculum is a top-down approach, in which the teacher surveys the skills that are needed in a child's current and future environments and provides instruction on those skills, regardless of whether the child has mastered prerequisite skills. Both Brown et al. (1979) and Baumgart et al. (1982) noted that, in addition to teaching functional skills, the curricula of students with moderate and severe disabilities should be chronological-age appropriate as well, with skills taught across a variety of school and nonschool environments. Not only are chronological-age-appropriate skills more likely to be useful, but their instruction also is less stigmatizing to the student.

TABLE 5.1 *Developmental vs. Functional Skills (based on Lewis, 1997, TASH Newsletter, 23(3), 19, with permission from TASH).*

Developmental Skills Daryl Can Do	Functional Skills Daryl Cannot Do
Put 100 pegs in board in less than 10 minutes	Put quarters in vending machine
Touch body parts on command	Blow nose
Work Big Bird puzzle and color Easter Bunny	Use radio or record player
Fold paper in halves and quarters	Fold clothes
Sort blocks by color	Sort white clothing from colored from washing
Roll clay snake	Roll bread dough
String beads in alternating pattern	Lace shoes
Sing alphabet and identify letters in upper case	Read labels on community restrooms
Place weather symbol on correct day on calendar	Determine when to wear raincoat or hat
Identify 100 Peabody Picture Cards by pointing	Order hamburger by pointing
Walk balance beam	Walk up steps in gym at basketball game
Count to 100	Determine how many dollars to pay waitress in restaurant
Put cups in, under, beside, and behind box	Find trash can and empty trash into it in restaurant
Play "Duck, Duck, Goose" in circle	Play age-appropriate game

In 1987 Lewis wrote a piece for the *TASH Newsletter* that demonstrated the importance of a chronological-age-appropriate functional skill approach for students with moderate and severe disabilities. As shown in Table 5.1, he contrasted the skills that Daryl, an 18-year-old male with a moderate to severe disability, could and could not do based on having received 12 years of education with a developmental approach. In 1997 the *TASH Newsletter* reprinted this piece as one of a collection of pieces recognized as being the most significant in the history of the organization. This recognition showed that a functional approach is still valued today.

Determining chronological-age-appropriate skills requires the teacher to determine both the form and the function of skills. The **form** of a skill is the way in which the skill is performed (i.e., the way the skill looks). The **function** of a skill is its outcome (i.e., what the skill accomplishes). As Brown et al. (1979) noted, sometimes the form of a skill that is appropriate for a younger child is inappropriate for an older student. It is then up to the teacher to determine the function of the skill and a way in which the function of the skill can be accomplished in a form that is age appropriate. For example, a very young child typically crosses a room by scooting or crawling. It is inappropriate, however, for an older student to cross a room in this manner; most students walk across a room. The function of ambulation is to get from one point to another as independently as possible. If a student cannot perform this function in the way it is performed by most peers of the same age, the teacher must find another acceptable form to teach the student. Thus, the teacher may teach the student to walk with the assistance of another person, to use a walker, or to propel a wheelchair. All of these modes of ambulation require adaptations that are age appropriate. More will be presented on adaptations later in this chapter. In the meantime, check your understanding of the concepts of form and function by completing Activity 5.1.

Activity 5.1   Distinguishing Between Form and Function

All skills have a form and a function. This is evident in the area of communication. List several functions of communication (e.g., making a request). When you finish your list, select one of the functions and make a list of various forms in which that function can be accomplished (e.g., verbal speech). Are some forms more appropriate at specific ages? Do some forms require adaptations?

When Hamre-Nietupski, Nietupski, and Strathe (1992) surveyed the parents of 192 children with moderate and severe disabilities in Iowa, they found that the parents valued a functional skill approach. Specifically, parents of children with moderate disabilities ranked functional life skills before academic skills and friendship/social relationships; parents of children with severe or profound disabilities ranked functional life skills immediately after friendship/social relationships and before academic skills. Hamre-Nietupski et al. reasoned that parents of children with moderate disabilities may be more optimistic about their children's ability to acquire skills and function independently than are parents of children with more severe disabilities.

The remainder of this chapter will focus on ways to determine functional skills in planning an appropriate curriculum for students with moderate and severe disabilities, ways in which functional skills can be adapted when students cannot perform them independently, and ways to mesh a functional curriculum with the core content of an academic general education curriculum.

Identifying a Functional Curriculum

A curriculum that focuses on functional skills must be individualized. What is functional (e.g., useful and meaningful) for one student may not be functional for another. For example, a teacher may teach students who come from families who wash dishes in an electric dishwasher, wash dishes by hand, or never wash dishes because they use disposable paper products or eat in restaurants. In this example the function of cleaning up after eating is accomplished through different forms. It is important to know the form that is immediately relevant to each student before teaching the skill; it also is important to know what forms might be needed in each student's future environments.

Compiling Data to Plan a Functional Curriculum

To determine an individualized functional curriculum for a student with a moderate or severe disability, the teacher needs to draw from various sources of data. In a text on assessment, Browder (1987) suggested gathering data from previous records (e.g., medical reports, therapy evaluations), an ecological inventory of relevant environments, surveys and checklists of related skills (e.g., motor, communication), and an adaptive behavior scale (e.g., Vineland-II). These sources are still valid today. In addition, a family survey (e.g., COACH) and published functional curricula (e.g., Syracuse) can yield important information for selecting skills for instruction. With the advent of No Child Left Behind, it also is crucial that functional skills be linked to the core content of the general education curriculum, especially in math, reading, and science, since it is likely that students with moderate and severe disabilities will be assessed in these areas even if they fall within the 1% of the school population eligible for alternate assessment (Browder et al., 2004). Table 5.2 lists sources of data for planning a functional curriculum and provides examples of each source. In addition, the following sections describe each of these sources.

TABLE 5.2 *Sources of Data for Planning a Functional Curriculum for Students with Moderate and Severe Disabilities.*

SOURCES OF DATA PLANNING A FUNCTIONAL CURRICULUM

Method	Examples
Previous educational and medical records	Medical reports
	Therapy evaluations
	Cumulative educational records
Ecological inventory of skills needed in current and future environments	Community domain
	Domestic domain
	Educational domain
	Recreation/leisure domain
	Vocational domain
Assessments of related skills	Communication/language skills
	Fine and gross motor skills
	Assistive technology devices
Adaptive behavior scales	*Adaptive Behavior Scale* (Lambert, Nihira, & Leland, 1981)
	Vineland-II Adaptive Behavior Scale (Sparrow, Cicchetti, & Balla, 2005).
Family surveys	*Impact* (Neel & Billingsley, 1989)
	Choosing Options and Accommodations for Children (COACH) (Giangreco, Cloninger, & Iverson, 1993)
Published functional curricula	*The Syracuse Community-Referenced Curriculum Guide* (Ford et al., 1989)
	The Activities Catalog (Wilcox & Bellamy, 1987)
	Volume One of *A Functional Curriculum for Teaching Students with Disabilities* (Bender, Valletutti, & Baglin, 1996)
	Volume Two of *A Functional Curriculum for Teaching Students with Disabilities* (Valletutti, Bender, & Sims-Tucker, 1996)
General education core content	National and state standards and core content

Previous Records   The previous records of a student can provide a wealth of information if they can be read with the intention of locating information and not as a way of making predeterminations that may prove limiting. For example, medical records may provide information on the way functional skills are taught, such as taking precautions that a child's seizures are not exacerbated by certain activities or environmental conditions. Educational records may reveal functional skills that have not yet been mastered. Therapy evaluations may provide clues for positioning a child when teaching a functional skill as well as therapy objectives that can be embedded in a functional curriculum.

Ecological Inventory   In 1979 Brown et al. described the steps of an **ecological inventory** as a means of determining a functional curriculum. The ecological inventory is a valuable assessment tool in that it provides a way to identify the individual skills across students that are needed to perform the functions in their daily lives, as well as in the future.

The first step of the ecological inventory is to identify the major curricular domains. Brown et al. divided these into the four major life areas of (a) domestic, (b) community, (c) recreation/leisure, and (d) educational or vocational (depending on the age of the student).

The second step is to identify the current environment and future environments of the student in each domain. For example, a student's current domestic environment may be the family home (e.g., house, apartment, mobile home). The future environment may be the home of a relative, a supported apartment, a group home, or an institution.

Once each environment has been identified, the third step is to divide environments into subenvironments. For example, a student's home may have a living area, a kitchen, two bedrooms, a bathroom, and a patio.

The fourth step is to determine the activities that take place in each subenvironment. This yields information about the student's lifestyle. For example, some students may eat meals around a table in a dining room, some may eat on stools at a counter in the kitchen, and some may eat from a tray in the living area in front of the television set.

After the activities in each subenvironment have been identified, the fifth step is to identify the skills needed to perform each activity. These may include skills from the more traditional curricular domains of academics, communication, motor, self-care, and social.

It is clear that the ecological inventory could result in a large document. To keep the results manageable and useful, it may be helpful to focus on those activities that the family determines are most important in the child's present lifestyle (e.g., living at home) and those that will be most important for the child to transition to the next environment (e.g., living in a supported-living apartment). Example 5.2 describes an example of an ecological inventory conducted in a student's home (i.e., domestic) environment. Activity 5.2 provides an opportunity for you to test your skills by completing an ecological inventory of a school (i.e., educational) environment.

EXAMPLE 5.2   **AN ECOLOGICAL INVENTORY OF A STUDENT'S HOME ENVIRONMENT**

As described in Chapter 4, a school consultation resulted in an appropriate educational program for Ned, an adolescent male with Down syndrome (Collins, Schuster, & Grisham-Brown, 2002). As suggested in this chapter, the consultants used various sources of data to determine Ned's curriculum. One source of data came from a visit to Ned's home, in which one of the consultants walked through the rooms of the house with Ned's mother and discussed what took place in each room and which skills his mother considered important for Ned to perform. The following chart is based on that activity.

Domain: Domestic

Current Environment: Ranch-style house in rural area

Subenvironment 1: Kitchen
Activity 1: Preparing meals on electric stove, in oven, and in microwave
Skills: cognitive (following recipe, measuring, setting timer), motor (opening packages, stirring, working appliances)
Activity 2: Eating meals "family style" at round table
Skills: motor (passing dishes), self-care (eating/drinking), communication (indicating desires)
Activity 3: Cleaning up after meals using electric dishwasher
Skills: motor (carrying dishes from table to counter, rinsing, loading dishwasher), cognitive (setting dial)

Subenvironment 2: Living Room
Activity 1: Watching television programs and movies on videocassette player
Skills: motor (working switches, inserting tape), cognitive (locating channel, reading switch labels)
Activity 2: Playing games on computer using joystick and keyboard
Skills: motor (using joystick and keyboard), cognitive (following directions)

Subenvironmnet 3: Bedroom
Activity 1: Dressing and undressing (e.g., jeans, T-shirts, socks, lace-up tennis shoes
Skills: motor (manipulating fasteners, including zipper, snaps, and laces), self-care (putting on/taking off), communication (indicating choice)
Activity 2: Playing with and putting away toys (e.g., cassette tape player, picture books, miniature cars)
Skills: motor (manipulating objects and switches), cognitive (following along in book as tape reads, sorting objects)
Activity 3: Sleeping in twin-size bed with sheet, quilt, and spread
Skills: motor (making bed)

Subenvironment 4: Bathroom
Activity 1: Bathing in tub
Skills: motor (manipulating knobs and stopper), self-care (washing self with bar of soap and washcloth, drying with towel)
Activity 2: Taking care of personal toileting needs
Skills: motor (manipulating fasteners, flushing), self-care (cleaning self)
Activity 3: Brushing teeth using toothpaste in tube
Skills: motor (squeezing toothpaste, turning knobs), self-care (brushing teeth, rinsing)

Based on the preceding chart, the consultant's visit yielded two types of important information in selecting functional skills for Ned's curriculum. First, the ecological inventory provided data about the activities that took place in Ned's home and the skills he would use to participate in those activities. For example, Ned's family cooked on an electric stove with an oven underneath as well as in a microwave; they ate "family style," passing serving dishes and filling plates at a round table; and they used an electric dishwasher to clean up after meals. Based on this information, the classroom teacher purchased a microwave oven to begin teaching Ned to prepare snacks each afternoon.

Second, the consultant was able to gather data about Ned's ability to perform the various activities by task-analyzing them and using them as a checklist for identifying skills that should be priorities for instruction. For example, Ned's performance across several activities showed that he had difficulty with fine motor skills. Instead of teaching these in isolation or nonfunctional activities, such as putting beans in a jar, the teacher determined that fine motor skills could be taught in the context of manipulating fasteners during toileting, manipulating knobs on faucets during handwashing, and manipulating switches during recreational skills (e.g., playing a videotape or audiotape).

ACTIVITY 5.2   Constructing an Ecological Inventory

To assess your skills at developing an ecological inventory, walk through a school and survey the settings frequented by students. Select three settings (e.g., art or music rooms, cafeteria, general education classroom, gymnasium, playground, restroom, school office) and construct a chart in a format like the one that follows.

Domain: Educational
Environment: School

Subenvironment 1:	Subenvironment 2:	Subenvironment 3:
Activity 1:	Activity 1:	Activity 1:
Skills:	Skills:	Skills:
Activity 2:	Activity 2:	Activity 2:
Skills:	Skills:	Skills:
Activity 3:	Activity 3:	Activity 3:
Skills:	Skills:	Skills:

Although the purpose of the ecological inventory is to determine an individualized functional curriculum for a student, the teacher may find that some of the same activities occur across students. For example, the majority of the students may come from families that frequent restaurants in the local community. Compiling a list of the restaurants (e.g., fast food, buffet style, sit down) and the activities performed in each (e.g., ordering at the counter or from a table menu, paying at the counter or paying a table check) over time can be compiled in a curriculum catalog. The **curriculum catalog** is a large document that contains task-analyzed activities across domains, environments, and subenvironments that can be used as a reference in collecting assessment data and writing instructional programs for functional skills across students.

Related Skills   Although related service delivery personnel may perform detailed assessments, it also can be useful for teachers to gather assessment data on related skills. For example, Mar and Sall (1999) described how profiles of expressive communication skills can be used to assess the functional communication skills of students with severe cognitive disabilities. Their method of data collection consisted of observing students for 30 to 60 minutes doing activities in natural environments (e.g., lunch in the cafeteria, recess on the playground, group instruction in the classroom) as well as engaging students in 30-minute one-to-one interactions during designated activities (e.g., playing a game, drawing a picture). During these sessions, the assessor can record the types of expressive communication used by the student (e.g., basic reflexes, physical actions, gestures, vocalizations, manual signs, oral speech, augmented communication). In addition, the assessor can note the use of symbols, intentionality, reciprocity, and complexity. According to Mar and Sall, this type of information can help teachers interpret the ways students communicate, and this information can be used to formulate meaningful goals.

It also can be advantageous for specialists to involve family and educational personnel in the assessment of related skills. For example, an expert in assistive technology may want input from other relevant people in the student's natural environments. If assistive technology, such as a communication device, will be used with a child, Parette and Brotherson (1996) recommended that a comprehensive assistive technology assessment be conducted that focuses on the child (e.g., needs, capabilities), the family (e.g., perceptions, resources, preferences), the technology (e.g., demands), and the service system (e.g., limitations, resources). The process would include discussions using friendly terminology and collection of baseline data across domains.

Adaptive Behavior Scales   Several adaptive behavior scales have been developed over the years. In most cases these consist of checklists that can be filled out through observation (e.g., watch the student eat a meal in lunch setting), interview (e.g., ask a family member if the student must be fed), or direct testing (e.g., provide food and ask the student to eat it). While the school psychologist may use these instruments during formal assessments, the instruments are simple for teachers to use and can provide specific data about skills that may be appropriate targets for instruction. Samples of adaptive behavior scales that may be used by teachers include the *Adaptive Behavior Scale* (Lambert, Nihira, & Leland, 1981) and the *Vineland-II Adaptive Behavior Scale* (Sparrow, Cicchetti, & Balla, 2005).

Family Survey   Some assessment data can be gathered from family members within a structured format. For example, Neel and Billingsley (1989) developed *Impact* as a means of determining a functional curriculum for students with moderate and severe disabilities. Using a variety of forms, family members are interviewed about a number of items that include their personal information, where the child spends his or her time (e.g., community, recreation), what the child does with his or her time (e.g., independently and with family at and away from home), what the child likes, how the child communicates, how the child handles change, and what the child can do independently (e.g., prepare snacks, perform personal-care routines). Family members and teachers collaborate in compiling a list of the child's environments (e.g., restaurants, houses of worship, shopping malls); forms of communication; and preferences for activities, people, and foods. The outcome of these interviews is an IEP that focuses on functional skills.

As described in Chapter 4, Giangreco, Cloninger, and Iverson (1993) also had a goal of an IEP that focuses on functional skills when they developed COACH (Choosing Options and Accommodations for Children). Through family member interviews, the teacher gathers data leading to five valued life outcomes: (a) safe, stable home environment; (b) access to a variety of settings and meaningful activities; (c) social network of meaningful relationships; (d) personal choice and control; and (e) safety/health. The result is a functional program that is embedded within inclusive settings.

Published Functional Curricula Over the years several available curricula have been published that are excellent sources for identifying functional skills that are age appropriate. These can be especially helpful when a teacher has worked with family members and team members in identifying functions that need to be performed in a student's environments but is having difficulty identifying chronological-age-appropriate forms. *The Syracuse Community-Referenced Curriculum Guide* (Ford et al., 1989) contains charts that pair specific functions with appropriate forms at the kindergarten (age 5), elementary (primary [ages 6 to 8]/intermediate [ages 9 to 11]), middle school (ages 12 to 14), high school (ages 15 to 18), and transition (ages 19 to 21) levels across domains. For example, the function of food preparation would begin as preparing simple snacks, pouring drinks, serving peers, and cleaning up one's own place at the kindergarten level and would progress to planning a menu for self, family, or roommates; preparing the entire meal; serving others; cleaning up (e.g., doing dishes); storing leftovers; and making a weekly grocery list at the transition level.

The Activities Catalog (Wilcox & Bellamy, 1987) lists functional activities for youth and adults across the domains of leisure, personal management, and work. For example, food activities include the following: (a) using a fast-food restaurant, (b) using a sit-down restaurant, (c) using a cafeteria, (d) using vending machines, (e) using a snack shop or canteen, (f) using street vendors, (g) buying groceries, (h) storing groceries, (i) setting the table, (j) planning meals, and (k) preparing meals. Each of these activities is further broken down into component skills. For example, preparing meals includes selecting a menu or recipe, gathering necessary equipment and ingredients, following a recipe or instructions, serving the meal, eating, and cleaning up.

Volume one of *A Functional Curriculum for Teaching Students with Disabilities* (Bender et al., 1996) lists activities for teachers and family members to use in teaching self-care, motor skills, household management, and living skills at the infant to preschool, primary, and secondary levels. For example, a goal of preparing food would consist of objectives for (a) opening and closing packages, (b) using can and bottle openers, (c) using kitchen utensils, (d) preparing snacks or meals with or without cooking appliances, (e) setting the table, (f) washing and drying dishes, and (g) storing leftover food. The student might learn to use a toaster for preparing waffles, bread, or bagels at the primary level and to use a skillet to fry bacon and eggs at the secondary level. At both levels family members would follow through at home with activities for cooking on the stove (e.g., boiling water for macaroni) and in the oven (e.g., baking frozen pie).

Volume Two of *A Functional Curriculum for Teaching Students with Disabilities* (Valletutti et al., 1996) follows a similar format in listing skills for teaching functional academics (i.e., reading, writing, math). An objective for functional reading of container labels would have a teacher focus on saying the names of packaged items to preschoolers, having elementary students identify names on containers in a class store, taking intermediate students to a grocery store to read labels of containers on shelves, and sending a secondary student to the grocery store to shop for the class from a handwritten list. In a similar vein, family members would show their preschoolers package labels as they prepare meals, have elementary students assist them in locating items on shopping trips, have intermediate students help compile weekly shopping lists, and send secondary students on independent shopping trips to the grocery store.

General Education Core Content   In addition to identifying appropriate functional skills, educators need to be aware of the academic core content required of students in the general education curriculum, especially in the areas of math, reading, and science. For example, Browder et al. (2004) listed a functional skill with a clear link to language arts as the recognition of survival words and a functional skill with a clear link to math as identifying differences in temperature. By being aware of state and national standards, teachers can identify functional skills that can be taught within the general education curricula as part of the state's alternate assessment process. An example of a functional math skill linked to state and national standards (Collins, Kleinert, & Land, 2006) can be found in Example 5.3.

EXAMPLE 5.3   A LESSON PLAN MESHING FUNCTIONAL SKILL INSTRUCTION WITH GENERAL EDUCATION CORE CONTENT

The following example from Collins, Kleinert, and Land (2006) demonstrates how a functional math skill of telling time can be linked to national (National Council of Teachers of Mathematics, n.d.) and state (Kentucky Department of Education, 2004) standards.

NCMT Number and Operations Standard	Understand numbers, ways of representing numbers, relationships among numbers, and number systems.
↓	
NCMT Expectation	Develop a sense of whole numbers and represent and use them in flexible ways.
↓	
Kentucky Core Content Skills	Students will read, write, count, and model whole numbers, 0–20, developing place value for ones and tens (M-P-NC-7).
↓	
Long-Term Instructional Goal	The student will "use clock time on the hour and half-hour to comment on the time, estimate time needs, and solve real-life problems" (Ford et al., 1989, p. 149).
↓	
Long-Term Instructional Objective	When presented with a variety of time-pieces throughout the day, the student will match the time shown on the timepiece to the clock picture beside activities on her daily schedule.
↓	
Short-Term Instructional Objectives	When presented with a picture of a clock face and an analog timepiece that represents time to the hour, the student will match the timepiece to the correct clock picture with 100% accuracy for five days.

Summarizing Information and Prioritizing Skills

Once target skills are identified, the instructional team needs to meet and share information for program planning. Allinder and Siegel (1999) stated that there are two ways to summarize assessment data. A traditional summary provides the basic information found in most assessment reports, including the student's name, date of birth, placement, date(s) of evaluation, and test results from instruments (e.g., developmental or norm-referenced measures) and techniques (e.g., ecological inventory or family interviews). A profile summary also provides the student's name, date of birth, and placement; however, instead of stating test results, a profile summary presents outcomes that can be used to influence instruction. This information includes the student's history, strengths, weaknesses, and successes.

In a hypothetical example, Allinder and Siegel (1999) described 10-year-old Brad using both a traditional summary (i.e., scores from PIAT, Brigance, WISC III, PPVT-R, Vineland) and a profile summary (i.e., reads and writes at first-grade level, works hard on assignments with redirection for short periods of time, uses intelligible speech to socialize, performs age-appropriate daily living skills). Based on feedback from 54 students seeking teacher certification, they concluded that a traditional summary conveys information needed for identification, but a profile summary facilitates better communication between staff and family members, provides appropriate information for peers without disabilities, and describes the student in a more well-rounded way.

It is clear that, after compiling data from a variety of sources, a large number of functional skills can emerge as targets for instruction for a single student. After sharing information, the next step for the instructional team is to prioritize these skills. They can do this by asking a number of questions:

1. Are there certain skills that emerge as important across data sources or across domains?
2. Is the skill valued by the family?
3. Will the skill provide immediate access to less restrictive age-appropriate environments?
4. Is the skill crucial for transitioning to the next environment?
5. Is the skill crucial for a child's safety?

In other words, will teaching the skill help the child meet the criterion of ultimate functioning (Brown, Nietupski, & Hamre-Nietupski, 1976) as described in Chapter 4?

To illustrate why dressing might be targeted as a functional activity for a child with a moderate or severe disability, consider how each of the above questions would be answered. First, the ability to dress oneself may have been identified in several environments during the ecological inventory, including the home (e.g., dressing in the morning, undressing at night), the school (e.g., changing into a uniform for gym class, putting on a paint smock for art activities), the place of employment (e.g., putting on a uniform to work in a restaurant), and the recreational center (e.g., changing into exercise clothes or a swimsuit at the YMCA). Further assessment data from adaptive behavior scales and related service assessments may have shown a need to work on fine motor skills that can be embedded in dressing and undressing activities.

Second, the primary caregiver may have indicated that the ability of the child to independently dress would save valuable time in the mornings when family members are in a hurry to meet timelines. Third, a child with dressing skills may be more likely to be included with peers without disabilities who are going on a camping trip; an adolescent with dressing skills would be able to quickly change into a uniform and, thus, be more likely to obtain competitive employment in a factory. Fourth, dressing skills may be required for students transitioning to physical education classes in secondary school or for older youths who are transitioning to supported living in an apartment. Finally, being able to keep shoelaces tied can prevent a child from tripping during play or while crossing the street and being able to put on protective equipment (e.g., safety goggles, hard-toed shoes) can help ensure job safety for a youth who mows lawns. It should be noted that dressing skills could be linked also to state core content for becoming a more self-sufficient person. Activity 5.3 allows you to practice prioritizing skills in a similar manner.

ACTIVITY 5.3   Prioritizing Functional Skills for Instruction

In Activity 5.2 you identified several functions and forms of communication. Select one of those functions, and provide a rationale as to why that skill should be targeted for instruction. Is it important across environments? Could it have been identified by related service personnel? Would it be valued by family members? Why?

Will it provide access to less restrictive age-appropriate environments? If so, give an example. Is it crucial for transitioning? If so, in what capacity? Is it crucial for ensuring the safety of the child? If so, how? Finally, can the skill be linked to the state core content?

Writing an IEP with a Focus on Functional Skills

Once skills from various data sources have been prioritized for instruction, the next task is to develop the IEP. In doing so, the team will determine if the function or the form is more important.

As previously demonstrated, dressing may be a functional activity for a student with a moderate or severe disability. If the goal is to independently dress, this may take different forms that may include adaptations to accomplish the outcome. For example, a student can bypass the need to manipulate fasteners by putting on T-shirts instead of shirts with buttons, putting on pullover windshirts instead of jackets that zip, putting on jogging pants with elastic waists instead of pants that zip and snap, or putting on athletic shoes with Velcro straps or zippers instead of shoelaces. An appropriate objective focusing on function would be as follows:

> When presented with clothing without fasteners (e.g., T-shirt, jogging pants, pullover windshirt, socks, and/or shoes with Velcro straps), Ned will be able to independently dress himself with 100% accuracy for five consecutive days across the following activities: dressing for school in the home, dressing for gym class in the school, dressing for recreational activities at the YMCA, and dressing for bed in the home.

On the other hand, the team may decide that the form is more important because it will allow the student to work on embedded fine motor skills within the context of dressing and to be able to wear a wider variety of age-appropriate clothing options (e.g., shoes that lace, pants that zip, shirts that button). In this case an appropriate objective would be:

> When getting dressed across activities (e.g., dressing for school in the home, gym class in the school, recreational activities at the YMCA, bedtime in the home), Ned will be able to manipulate buttons, zippers, snaps, and laces on his clothing with 100% accuracy for five out of five opportunities each.

To practice writing objectives focused on function and form, complete Activity 5.4.

ACTIVITY 5.4   Writing Objective for Function and Form

In Activity 5.2 you identified functions and forms found in communication. Select one form and write an objective that shows how that form could be targeted across activities. When you are finished, select one function and demonstrate through an objective how that function could be accomplished using a number of forms.

IDENTIFYING ADAPTATIONS IN A FUNCTIONAL SKILL APPROACH

The examples and activities this chapter has provided show that it is sometimes necessary for a child with a moderate or severe disability to rely on adaptations to perform functions when the child cannot use the forms typically used by same-age peers without disabilities (e.g., using Velcro straps or zippers to fasten shoes in place of tying shoelaces). In 1982 Baumgart et al. used the **principle of partial participation** as a term to describe the use of adaptations to facilitate the ability of students with disabilities to perform functions through various forms. In their words, "The principle of partial participation is essentially an affirmation that all [students with severe disabilities] can acquire many skills that will allow them to function, at least in part, in a wide variety of least restrictive school and nonschool environments and activities" (p. 19). According to Baumgart et al., practicing the principle of partial participation prevents a child from being excluded or succumbing to discriminatory practices while causing the child to have more value in the eyes of others.

The crux of the principle of partial participation is that a child does not have to be able to perform a skill independently in order to engage in the same activities as peers without disabilities. Instead, adaptations can be used that will enable the child to perform the function of the skill through a different form. Baumgart et al. described an individualized adaptation as "one that is personalized and enables a particular student to participate at least partially in a chronological age appropriate and functional activity" (p. 20). Adaptations may consist of (a) materials or devices, such as a communication device; (b) personal assistance, such as someone to push a wheelchair; (c) adapted skill sequences, such as sitting on the commode before removing pants; (d) adapted rules, such as decreasing the physical size of a playing field; and (e) social/attitudinal adaptations, such as allowing an athlete to compete on a team using a prosthetic device.

Baumgart et al. proposed a sequence of steps for selecting an appropriate adaptation. The first step is to inventory persons without disabilities to document how they complete a specific activity. This can be done by constructing a **task analysis** (i.e., a list of the steps that comprise the chained task) based on the person's performance. The next step is to conduct a discrepancy analysis to determine the specific skills of the task analysis that a person with disabilities cannot perform. The third step is to establish reasonable expectations as to the steps that the person with disabilities will be likely to acquire and not acquire through instruction. The instructional team then generates hypotheses for adaptations to be used to complete those steps identified as being difficult (or impossible) to acquire. Subsequently, the team begins the process of testing which of the possible adaptations that were generated are most feasible or appear to work best. Once these steps are completed, the team selects the final adaptation and begins teaching the skill using that adaptation.

This process can be illustrated by returning to the example of independent dressing. By the time they exit primary school, most children can fasten a belt. A task analysis of fastening a belt can be compiled by collecting data on the kind of belt most often worn by most elementary students of the same gender and watching a student without disabilities fasten that type of belt. A discrepancy analysis is conducted by asking the target student with disabilities to put on the same type of belt. This will yield information on the steps the student can perform or is likely to learn and the steps where the students may continue to encounter difficulty. For example, the student may be able to put the belt through the pant loops independently, be able to insert the end of the belt through the buckle with minimal guidance, be unable to fasten the belt by pressing the metal notch through a corresponding hole, and be able to finish the process of inserting the end of the belt through the remainder of the buckle with minimal guidance. From this analysis, the teacher may determine that the student can acquire all of the steps except fastening the buckle. Through brainstorming with the team, the following hypotheses for adaptations are generated: (a) wearing pants that do not require a belt, (b) fastening a cloth belt that catches on metal teeth instead of a leather belt with notches, (c) fastening a belt with a larger buckle, (d) fastening a belt with a buckle that hooks into a notch and does not have to be threaded, or (e) wearing suspenders that can be fastened to the pants prior to dressing then slipped over the shoulders. Because the student is transitioning to a secondary school where a school uniform of khaki trousers with a belt will be required and, because the student can complete most of the steps with minimal assistance, the team decides to investigate different types of buckles that will be easier to fasten and finds a cloth belt with teeth that is still fashionable when worn with khaki slacks.

This example also illustrates some of the cautions for selecting adaptations that Baumgart et al. listed. First, the team considered the *appropriateness and effectiveness* of the belt for the target setting. Second, the team realized that *adaptations may change over time*, making stretch sweatpants appropriate for elementary school, belts appropriate for high school, and suspenders under a suit jacket possibly appropriate for a future employment setting. *Overdependency was discouraged* by finding an adaptation the student could use independently. The type of belt buckle was *individualized* for the particular student, and *the environment was selected prior to the selection of the adaptation.* Finally, as the team made plans for instruction, they planned to collect data *to reevaluate the need for the adaptation over time.* To practice selecting adaptations, complete Activity 5.5.

ACTIVITY 5.5   Selecting Adaptations

In previous activities in this chapter, you gave thought to appropriate forms and functions of communication. Assuming that you are working with a student with a moderate to severe disability who currently is not capable of producing intelligible verbal speech, brainstorm the types of adaptations you might consider. Consider adaptations that do and do not require technology. What are the advantages and disadvantages of each based on the environments in which the child may need to communicate? Are there factors that should be considered in terms of cost, durability, and portability? Could the adaptation be stigmatizing to the student?

In 1991 Ferguson and Baumgart revisited the concept of the principle of partial participation and discussed error patterns often employed in applying this principle. The first was **passive participation,** in which students with disabilities are physically placed in natural environments but are given only the opportunity to watch peers engage in activities instead of being allowed to actively participate in them. For example, a student in a music class would only listen as others performed.

The second error pattern was **myopic participation,** in which the teacher narrowly focuses on one or a few perspectives of the curriculum and does not allow the student to take advantage of the full range of instructional opportunities. For example, a teacher may have a student practice only pushing a cart in a grocery store instead of selecting and purchasing items or practice using a can opener in preparing a snack instead of preparing a meal and cleaning up afterwards.

The third error pattern was **piecemeal participation,** in which a student participates in some activities on an irregular basis. For example, a student might be included in a general education social studies class with peers three days a week and pulled out to go to therapy conducted in isolation at the same time two days per week.

Finally, the fourth error pattern was **missed participation,** in which the time and effort the student must put in to performing activities independently causes the student to miss being included in a larger number of activities. For example, a student who slowly propels a wheelchair between classes in a large secondary school may miss part of each class throughout the day.

Ferguson and Baumgart (1991) noted that the principle of participation had been misused as a means of socially including students with disabilities at the cost of instruction. Adaptations are not meant to be permanent but, instead, should be a way of allowing a child to participate while instruction is continuing. Thus, adaptations should be evaluated on a continual basis to determine if they still are necessary or if they need to be changed. To avoid the errors associated with the principle of participation, Ferguson and Baumgart made four recommendations. First, teachers should promote active partial participation over passive partial participation. This can be achieved by having students practice a repertoire of behaviors across a number of environments and teaching skills in an embedded context and may enhance the student's physical condition and social status. Second, teachers should attend to multiple perspectives to avoid myopic participation. This is facilitated by using family- and community-referenced assessment strategies (e.g., ecological inventory, family interviews) and maintaining data on progress and outcomes. Third, teachers can avoid piecemeal participation by obtaining information from a wide range of sources to develop the curriculum (as has been discussed in this chapter). This can be done through a team approach to (a) assessment, (b) program development, (c) instruction, and (d) evaluation. Fourth, teachers can avoid missed participation by working toward a goal of interdependence. This is accomplished through assistance (e.g., natural support from peers) to maintain a functional lifestyle.

MESHING A FUNCTIONAL CURRICULUM WITH THE CORE CONTENT OF A GENERAL EDUCATION CURRICULUM

In recent years the field of special education has moved toward a philosophy of inclusion for all students regardless of ability. With an emphasis on making adaptations to include students with moderate and severe disabilities in instruction on the core content of the general education curriculum, it sometimes seems as if a functional approach has gone by the wayside. In a commentary Sandler (1999) noted that students with severe disabilities who were included in general education classes were spending significantly more time engaged in academic activities than in those who would be considered functional and were having more objectives written on their IEPs based on an academic rather than a functional approach. Just as Lewis (1987) made the point that a continued developmental approach puts a child with a moderate to severe disability at risk for being able to sing the alphabet without being able to read labels on a restroom door, an inappropriately designed inclusion program puts a child with a moderate to severe disability at risk for being able to state letter sounds from a general education language arts lesson or being able to read isolated vocabulary words from a general education science unit (e.g., photosynthesis) without being able to identify labels on a restroom door.

Chesley and Calaluce (1997) addressed the lack of balance between inclusion and functional skills when they noted that the general education curriculum does not contain a focus on functional and vocational skills that students with moderate and severe disabilities need to prepare them for future environments. To make their point, they cited an example of parents of a student with a moderate to severe disability who petitioned a school district for an out-of-state residential placement for their child during the final year of secondary school because the general education placement, which their child had been in for 10 years (and for which they had advocated), had not taught their child the skills necessary to function in the real world. Although Chesley and Calaluce agreed that students with disabilities should be educated to the extent possible with their peers without disabilities, they concluded that general education teachers do not have the time or knowledge to teach the functional skills that students need.

Billingsley and Albertson (1999) also asserted that a focus on inclusion in general education was jeopardizing functional skill instruction to prepare students for natural environments and noted that the professional literature was showing a decrease in articles focusing on the instruction of functional skills. They proposed a solution in which teachers identify natural opportunities throughout the school day to teach functional skills (e.g., lunch in the cafeteria, general education field trips) and general education teachers adapt their curriculum to focus on meaningful skills (e.g., teaching word problems in math that focus on real needs for application). Still, they concluded that there are some functional skills that cannot readily be taught within a general education context (e.g., doing laundry, purchasing clothing); thus, general education classes may need to be supplemented with community-based instruction. To make community-based instruction more appropriate, Billingsley and Albertson suggested that (a) special educators and general educators implement joint activity-based or service learning projects in the community, (b) community-based instruction be scheduled around secondary general education classes, and (c) off-campus community-based instruction programs be implemented for 18- to 21- year-old students when their same-age peers have graduated from high school.

Although later chapters will focus on how and where to teach functional skills, the following sections briefly describe how functional and general education curricula can be meshed across age levels.

School Approaches

Field, LeRoy, and Rivera (1994) asserted that functional skills are important for students both with and without disabilities. Thus, they proposed that the following activities take place to embed key functional activities in the general education curriculum. First, general education teachers should receive training to understand the needs of students with disabilities, the special education curriculum, instructional strategies, and collaboration between home and school. In addition, special education teachers should receive training to understand the general education curriculum, the learning needs of children without disabilities, general education expectations, instructional methods, and communication between home and school.

Second, extensive and thorough collaborative planning is needed in which the team adopts the philosophy that everyone is responsible for every child; gathers information and meets to plan for individual students; and continues to meet to share information, refine goals, and develop instructional strategies. Third, there must be strong, ongoing support during implementation to ensure that students with disabilities engage in social relationships with their peers, develop a circle of friends, and engage in cooperative learning. In addition, instructional support in the general education classroom should provide options for students with disabilities that include the following: (a) learning through a different format, (b) learning less of the same content, (c) learning a streamlined sequence of the content, (d) learning through partial participation, (e) learning the same skill with different materials, (f) learning a different skill with the same materials, (g) learning different skills within the same activity, and (h) learning embedded skills. Finally, both home and school collaboration and support are needed.

Helmke, Havekost, Patton, and Polloway (1994) described a top-down model for developing courses for students with disabilities that focused on functional skills. Their model was based on an approach used with secondary students in Dubuque, Iowa, and paralleled the ecological inventory model. According to Helmke et al., the team would (a) identify adult domains (i.e., areas of adult functioning), (b) identify major life domains (i.e., events encountered in everyday life), (c) identify specific life skills (i.e., competencies to perform life demands), and (d) organize instruction (e.g., curriculum).

To develop this type of functional approach, Helmke et al. suggested a process that included several steps. The curriculum would be developed by a curriculum development committee, and priorities would be based on a survey of students who have exited the program and a survey of the professional literature. In addition, a specific course would be developed by matching life demands and life skills to a subject area, establishing a course description, identifying outcomes for the course, writing a course guide, and evaluating the course as it was taught.

In applying the model to teaching functional skills to students with moderate and severe disabilities, an adult domain for a student might be an employment setting and a major life demand might be following a checklist of job responsibilities. The specific life skills would be reading the schedule, performing the responsibilities, checking off completed tasks, and taking a break. The curriculum would be organized by selecting inclusive academic classes in which these skills can be embedded and organizing instruction within that setting. Specifically, a student could enroll in a biology class that focuses on growing plants in a greenhouse. After reading through the words found on the daily schedule (e.g., water, fertilize) with a teacher, instructional assistant, or peer, the student would have a daily checklist (written or picture) to follow in watering and fertilizing the plants, checking the temperature, and rotating the plants for proper sunlight. As each of these tasks was completed, the student would check them off on the list, and at the end of class, the student would be able to take a 10-minute break before going to the next class.

Best Practices
Functional and Age-Appropriate Skills

1. In selecting target skills to teach to students with moderate and severe disabilities, use a functional approach that relies on data collected from multiple sources, including previous records, an ecological inventory, surveys and checklists of related skills, and an adaptive behavior scale, with attention to linking these skills to general education core content.

2. Practice the principle of participation by including students with moderate and severe disabilities in functional activities through the use of appropriate adaptations.

3. Select adaptations that enhance the student's ability to actively participate in age-appropriate activities with peers without disabilities.

4. When including students with moderate and severe disabilities in general education settings, embed functional skills within the academic curriculum and plan community-based activities for all students.

Conclusion

In addressing the compatibility of a functional approach and an inclusive model of education, Clark (1994) posed a series of questions that have been addressed throughout this chapter and which provide a good review of this chapter's content. To review, try to answer each of these questions as they are presented in Activity 5.6 before reading through the following paragraphs.

ACTIVITY 5.6 Understanding a Functional Curricular Approach

The following questions were posed by Clark in 1994. Being able to answer these questions demonstrates an understanding of functional curricular approach. Based on what you have read in this chapter, answer each of the questions and then check your answers by reading the conclusion of Chapter Five.

1. What is a functional curricular approach?
2. How do you determine what is functional knowledge or a functional skill?
3. When do you start a functional curriculum?
4. Who needs a functional curriculum?
5. How do a functional curriculum and a traditional curriculum relate to one another?
6. How can school develop a functional curricular approach and promote inclusive education?

In review, a functional curricular approach focuses on instruction in life skills or those skills that are immediately useful to a student with a moderate to severe disability or will be useful in the student's future. Functional skills are individually determined for each child through gathering several sources of data that include previous records, an ecological inventory, surveys and checklists of related skills, and an adaptive behavior scale. Clark (1994) suggested that functional skills also be determined by asking if the content of a child's placement is meeting the child's needs, if the content focus allows knowledge and skills to function independently, if the family agrees that the content is important for the child's current and future needs, if the content is appropriate to the child's chronological age, and if there are consequences if the students fails to learn content and skills in the current placement. A functional curricular approach should begin for a child with a moderate to severe disability when the child enters school or a discrepancy of skills of two or more years exists in relation to same-age peers without disabilities. Although all children can benefit from a functional approach, it is crucial for students with moderate and severe disabilities if they are to function as independently as possible in least restrictive environments. A functional curriculum and a traditional curriculum relate to each other in that functional skills can be embedded within a more traditional, academic approach; this approach is beneficial because it leads to skills that are likely to generalize across settings with peers without disabilities. Schools can promote a functional approach within an inclusive education by presenting individualized instruction for students within the general education setting, advocating for community-based instruction for all students, and adopting a transdisciplinary approach for planning and instruction with family members and general educators on the team.

In 1991 Baumgart and Ferguson discussed the skills that teachers would need to meet the needs of students with moderate and severe disabilities during the following decade that still can be considered best practice today. Their description of best-practice content as activity based, community referenced, and comprehensive would include functional skills taught through functional activities. The processes used to teach functional content would focus on team collaboration with related services; substantive family involvement for generalization; negotiation to balance what is idealistic (e.g., functional knowledge) with what is realistic (e.g., functional skills); and instructional effectiveness evaluated by formative data collected during acquisition, generalization, and maintenance. With this approach, the outcome for students with moderate and severe disabilities would be community participation with social support networks and, perhaps most important, "ordinariness and invisibility" (Baumgart & Ferguson, 1991, p. 325) where students with moderate and severe disabilities fit in with their peers instead of standing out in the crowd as noticeable and different.

This chapter has established the importance of a functional skill approach in designing a curriculum for students with moderate and severe disabilities. The following chapters will describe instructional techniques for teaching a functional curriculum and how instruction can take place in inclusive school and community settings. Before continuing to these chapters, stop and check your understanding of the content of this chapter by completing the performance-based assessment that follows.

Questions for Review

1. Why do students with moderate and severe disabilities need to learn functional skills? Why should the skills they are taught be chronological-age appropriate?

2. What sources of data should be considered in developing a functional curriculum? From what types of assessments would these sources of data be derived?

3. List and describe the steps to be followed in conducting an ecological inventory.

4. What is the principle of partial participation, and how is it applied in identifying adaptations for students with moderate and severe disabilities?

5. How can a functional curriculum be embedded within the core content of an inclusive general education setting?

Performance-Based Assessment

You are part of a transition team that will be facilitating the transition of a student with a moderate to severe disability to supported community living. Describe how you will conduct an ecological inventory of the future community domain before developing the student's IEP and transition plan. Describe where and how you might embed functional skills needed for future environments within the core content of the secondary school curriculum.

References

Allinder, R. M., & Siegel, E. (1999). "Who is Brad?" Preservice teacher's perceptions of summarizing assessment information about a student with moderate disabilities. *Education and Training in Mental Retardation and Developmental Disabilities, 34,* 157–169.

Baumgart, D., Brown, L., Pumpian, I., Nisbet, J., Ford, A., Sweet, M., Messina, R., & Schroeder, J. (1982). Principle of partial participation and individualized adaptations in educational programs for severely handicapped students. *Journal of the Association for Persons with Severe Handicaps, 7,* 17–27.

Baumgart, D., & Ferguson, D. L. (1991). Personnel preparation: Directions for the next decade. In L. H. Meyer, C. A. Peck, & L. Brown (Eds.), *Critical Issues in the Lives of People with Severe Disabilities* (pp. 313–352). Baltimore: Brookes.

Bender, M., Valletutti, P. J., & Baglin, C. A. (1996). *A functional curriculum for teaching students with disabilities: Self-care, motor skills, household management, and living skills.* Austin, TX: Pro-Ed.

Billingsley, F. F., & Albertson, L. R. (1999). Finding a future for functional skills. *Journal of the Association for Persons with Severe Handicaps, 24,* 298–302.

Browder, D. M. (1987). *Assessment of individuals with severe handicaps.* Baltimore: Brookes.

Browder, D., Spooner, F., Ahlgrim-Delzell, L., Flowers, C., Algozzine, B., and Karvonen, M. (2004). A content analysis of the curricular philosophies reflected in states' alternate assessment performance indicators. *Research and Practice for Persons with Severe Disabilities, 28,* 165–181.

Brown, L., Branston, M. B., Hamre-Nietupski, S., Pumpian, I., Certo, N., & Gruenwald, L. (1979). A strategy for developing chronological-age-appropriate and functional curricular content for severely handicapped adolescents and young adults. *The Journal of Special Education, 13,* 81–90.

Brown, L., Nietupski, J., & Hamre-Nietupski, S. (1976). The criterion of ultimate functioning. In M. A. Thomas, Ed. *Hey! Don't forget about me!* Reston, VA: The Council for Exceptional Children.

Chesley, G. M., & Calaluce, P. D. (1997). The deception of inclusion. *Mental Retardation, 35,* 488–490.

Clark, G. M. (1994). Is a functional curriculum approach compatible with an inclusive education model? *Teaching Exceptional Children, 26,* 36–39.

Collins, B. C., Kleinert, H., & Land, L. (2006). Addressing math standards and functional math. In D. M. Browder & F. Spooner (Eds.) *Teaching language arts, math, and science to students with significant cognitive disabilities.* Baltimore: Brookes.

Collins, B. C., & Schuster, J. W. (2001). Some thoughts on the history of rural special education: A first hand account. *Rural Special Education Quarterly, 20*(1/2), 22–29.

Collins, B. C., Schuster, J. W., & Grisham-Brown, J. (2002). *Success story: Ned.* Unpublished manuscript.

Ferguson, D. L., & Baumgart, D. (1991). Partial participation revisited. *Journal of the Association for Persons with Severe Handicaps, 16,* 218–227.

Field, S., LeRoy, B., & Rivera, S. (1994). Meeting functional curriculum needs in middle school general education classrooms. *Teaching Exceptional Children, 26,* 40–43.

Ford, A., Schnorr, R., Meyer, L., Davern, L., Black, J., & Dempsey, P. (1989). *The Syracuse community-referenced curriculum guide for students with moderate and severe disabilities.* Baltimore: Brookes.

Giangreco, M. F., Cloninger, C. J., & Iverson, V. S. (1993). *Choosing Options and Accommodations for Children: A guide to planning inclusive education.* Baltimore: Brookes.

Hamre-Nietupski, S., Nietupski, J., & Strathe, M. (1992). Functional life skills, academic skills, and friendship/social relationship development: What do parents of students with moderate/severe/profound disabilities value? *Journal of the Association for Persons with Severe Handicaps, 17,* 53–58.

Helmke, L. M., Havekost, D. M., Patton, J. R., & Polloway, E. A. (1994). Life skills programming: Development of a high school science course. *Teaching Exceptional Children, 26,* 49–53.

Kentucky Department of Education (2004). *Program of studies: Primary mathematics.* Retrieved June 17, 2005, from www.education.ky.gov/KDE/Instructional+Resources/Curriculum+Documents+and+Resources/Program+of+Studies/Primary+Mathematics+−+Program+of+Studies.htm.

Lambert, N., Nihira, K., & Leland, H. (1981). *Adaptive Behavior Scale-School.* Austin, TX: Pro-Ed.

Lewis, P. (1987). A case for teaching functional skills. *TASH Newsletter, 23*(3), 19.

Mar, H. H., & Sall, N. (1999). Profiles of the expressive communication skills of children and adolescents with severe cognitive disabilities. *Education and Training in Mental Retardation and Developmental Disabilities, 34,* 77–89.

National Council of Teachers of Mathematics (n.d.). *Overview of principles and standards for school mathematics.* Retrieved June 8, 2004 from http://www.ntcm.org/standards/principles.htm.

Neel, R. S., & Billingsley, F. F. (1989). Impact: A functional curriculum handbook for students with moderate to severe disabilities. Baltimore: Brookes.

Parette, H. P., & Brotherson, M. J. (1996). Family participation in assistive technology assessment for young children with mental retardation and developmental disabilities. *Education and Training in Mental Retardation and Developmental Disabilities, 31,* 29–43.

Sandler, A. G. (1999). Continued commentaries on inclusion: Short-changed in the name of socialization? Acquisition of functional skills by students with severe disabilities. *Mental Retardation, 37,* 148–150.

Sparrow, S. S., Cicchetti, D. V., & Balla, D. A., (2005). *Vineland Adaptive Behavior Scales* (2nd ed.). Circle Pines, MN: American Guidance Service.

Valletutti, P. J., Bender, M., & Sims-Tucker, B. (1996). *A functional curriculum for teaching students with disabilities: Functional academics.* Austin, TX: Pro-Ed.

Wilcox, B. & Bellamy, G. T. (1987*). The activities catalog: An alternative curriculum for youth and adults with severe disabilities.* Baltimore: Brookes.

CHAPTER SIX

TEACHING STUDENTS WITH MODERATE AND SEVERE DISABILITIES:

Systematic Instruction

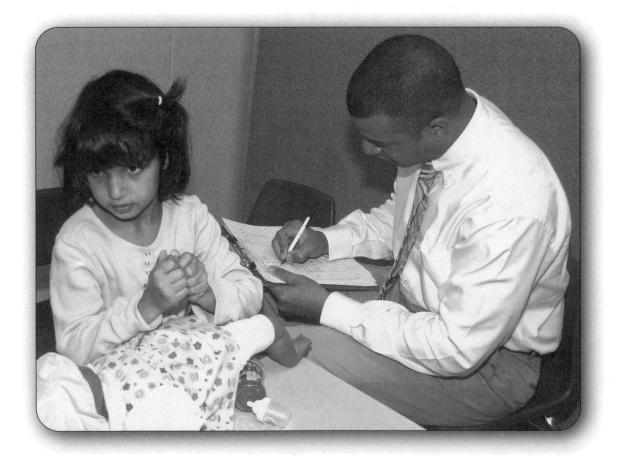

On completion of this chapter, the reader will meet the following objectives:

- State a rationale for using systematic instructional procedures.
- Describe the difference between antecedent- and response-prompting procedures.
- Demonstrate the ability to use a response-prompting procedure to teach a functional skill.
- Describe strategies to increase the efficiency of systematic instruction.
- Tell how the use of systematic instruction can facilitate appropriate behavior.
- Describe how systematic instruction of functional skills can be embedded in inclusive settings and activities.

Research in the field of special education has evolved to include a rich array of systematic instructional strategies that are both effective and efficient. Data show they result in the acquisition of skills and that students learn skills in fewer sessions, in less time, with less teacher effort, and with fewer errors than with less systematic procedures. According to Wolery, Bailey, and Sugai (1988), systematic instruction is based on **applied behavior analysis.** This means that it is (a) applied—used to teaching meaningful or functional skills, (b) behavioral—teaches skills that can be observed and measured, (c) analytic—based on data to show that the procedures are responsible for the acquisition of skills, (d) technological—clearly described and replicable, (e) conceptually systematic—based on behavioral principles, (f) effective—results in desired changes in behavior, and (g) generalizable—results in skills that transfer to novel settings, persons, and materials (Stokes & Baer, 1977).

The principles of applied behavior analysis are based on a large of body of research that includes systematic instruction (e.g., Martella, Nelson, & Marchand-Martella, 2003; White & Haring, 1980). The basic principle of applied behavior analysis is that every **behavior** *(B)* is preceded by an **antecedent** *(A)* and followed by a **consequence** *(C)* as shown in the following formula:

$$A \rightarrow B \rightarrow C$$

When applying this principle to learning, the antecedent is synonymous with the **stimulus** *(S)* and the behavior is synonymous with the **response** *(R)*. The stimulus (e.g., task direction) sets the stage for the response to occur and the consequence acts either as a **reinforcer** by increasing the likelihood that the response will recur or as a **punisher** by decreasing the likelihood that the response will recur. The model then would look like this:

$$S \rightarrow R \rightarrow C$$

The goal of education is to increase meaningful behaviors. To do this, **prompts** can be inserted either during or immediately following the delivery of the stimulus (Wolery, Ault, & Doyle, 1992). Prompts are events that are added to instruction to increase the likelihood of a correct response and to decrease the probability of making errors, particularly if they are **controlling prompts** (i.e., prompts that ensure that a correct response will occur).

The preceding chapter provided the basis for selecting skills for instruction. This chapter will describe how to teach those skills through the systematic implementation of prompting procedures and will provide specific examples from the professional literature. The chapters that follow will describe how to embed systematic instruction of functional skills in both inclusive educational and community settings.

SYSTEMATIC INSTRUCTION

In 1981 Liberty, Haring, and Martin described several variables that are beneficial in teaching skills to students with severe disabilities. In particular, they noted that the cues, materials, settings, prompts, instructional formats (e.g., chaining versus total task performance), and consequences should be selected with care; that instruction should be applied in a systematic manner; and that, in addition to **acquisition** (i.e., initial learning), strategies should be used that will facilitate **fluency** (i.e., how well a response is performed), **generalization** (i.e., the application of a response in the real world), and **maintenance** (i.e., the occurrence of a response of over time).

In 1984 Wolery and Gast discussed the effective and efficient transfer of **stimulus control** through the implementation of (a) stimulus manipulation procedures that included stimulus shaping and fading and (b) response-prompting strategies that included graduated guidance, most-to-least prompting, system of least prompts, and time delay. Although their writing focused on early childhood special education, they concluded with recommendations for instructors and researchers based on the research at that time that could be applied across age levels of students.

In 1997 Wolery and Schuster updated the work of previous authors by making research-based recommendations for instructional methods to be used with students having significant disabilities. Their discussion centered on the motivation to learn, as well as on instructional strategies, settings, and formats (e.g., small-group instruction). Wolery and Schuster added simultaneous prompting to the list of response-prompting strategies and built a case for including the systematic delivery of nontargeted information in instruction as a way of increasing instructional efficiency.

The remaining information in this chapter is meant to provide an overview of the technology of systematic instruction as it applies to students with moderate and severe disabilities based on the professional literature (e.g., Liberty et al., 1981; Wolery & Gast, 1984; Wolery & Schuster, 1997), including the research of the author and her colleagues. Readers who want to apply these procedures will find additional information, such as ways to collect data and ways to graph and analyze results, in other texts where the sole focus is instructional methodology.

Before instruction begins, the instructor should make basic decisions regarding format so instructional trials will be presented in a manner that is predictable to the student. Several of the variables to be predetermined are the format for teaching chained tasks, the format for delivering instructional trials, the use of cues in securing attention, and the procedures for delivering consequences following correct and incorrect responses. Each of these variables is discussed in the sections that follow.

Discrete and Chained Tasks

When selecting target skills for instruction, two types of behaviors can be identified (Wolery et al., 1988): (a) discrete behaviors and (b) chained behaviors. **Discrete behaviors** are those responses that have a definite beginning and ending and can be recorded as either occurring or not occurring. In other words, discrete behaviors consist of a single step. Examples include reading a sight word, activating an electronic switch, pointing to an object, or selecting a coin. **Chained behaviors** are a series of discrete responses that are linked together in a sequential fashion to result in a single skill. Examples include buttoning a shirt, writing a sentence, making a purchase, or preparing a snack. The steps of the chain can be identified through creating a task analysis of the component steps (i.e., list each step of the task in the sequence in which it should occur). Data would be collected on each step of the task as it is performed, and criterion would not be reached until a student could perform each step of the task with a specified degree of accuracy.

Depending on the functioning level of the student, some tasks can be recorded either as a discrete behavior or as a chained behavior. For example, a student without a disability might write a complete sentence as a single behavior. A student with a mild disability might write an entire word of the sentence as a single step. A student with a moderate disability might form a single letter as a step in writing a word. A student with a severe disability might have the formation of a single letter broken down into the smaller steps, such as (a) making a vertical stroke down, (b) making a horizontal stroke from left to right beginning at the top of the vertical line, (c) making a horizontal stroke from left to right beginning at the middle of the vertical line, and (d) making a horizontal line from left to right beginning at the bottom of the vertical line to form the letter *E*. Work through Activity 6.1 to demonstrate understanding of this concept.

ACTIVITY 6.1   Identifying Discrete and Chained Tasks

To demonstrate your understanding of the difference between discrete and chained behaviors, sort the following tasks as to those that are discrete (i.e., single step) and those that are chained (i.e., multiple steps):

Making a bed	Filling out a check	Making juice	Starting a videotape
Crossing a street	Eating a bite of food	Drawing a circle	Combing hair
Reading a stop sign	Grasping a door knob	Matching capitol to state	Zipping a jacket
Tying a shoe	Mailing a letter		

Are there any tasks that could be viewed as either discrete or chained? Which ones? Why? Now select one of those tasks that might be recorded as a single step for a student without a disability and write it for a student with a significant disability. How many steps does it have?

There are three formats for teaching chained tasks (Wolery et al., 1988): (a) forward chaining, (b) backward chaining, and (c) total task presentation. In **forward chaining** the student receives instruction on the first step of the task and must reach criterion on that step before proceeding to the second step. Instruction occurs in a forward fashion, teaching one step to criterion at a time, until the task is mastered. In **backward chaining** the student receives instruction on the last step of the chain after the instructor has performed the preceding steps. When the student reaches criterion on this step, instruction occurs on the preceding step and, again, proceeds in a backward fashion, teaching one step at a time, until the task is mastered. In **total task presentation,** the student is given the opportunity to perform every single step of the chain during every single trial and receives instruction only on those steps where it is needed, until mastery of the entire skill is demonstrated. Since all steps are taught at once, this may increase the length of the instructional session but can decrease the number of sessions to criterion. Liberty et al. (1981) recommended total task instruction in teaching chained tasks to students with disabilities since this format allows students to complete steps they previously have acquired.

Massed, Spaced, and Distributed Trials

Each episode of instruction on a discrete behavior or step is considered a **trial.** Trials can be massed or spaced within a single instructional session, or they can be distributed throughout the day (Wolery et al., 1988).

Massed trial instruction occurs when the instructor delivers repeated instruction on a single behavior, one trial immediately following another, as demonstrated in the following visual where X equals a trial on the target behavior:

XXXXXXXXXXXX

Spaced trial instruction occurs when the instructor delivers instruction on a single behavior then allows the student to have a break before delivering another trial. During the break, the instructor may call on another student to perform the same behavior or a different behavior, as would be the case in group instruction. The student has the opportunity to think about the behavior or to observe others receiving instruction before again being asked to make a response, as demonstrated in the following visual:

X X X X X X

Distributed trial instruction occurs when the instructor delivers instruction on a target behavior throughout the day, preferably when the behavior can be embedded within the natural context of an ongoing activity. Between trials the student has the opportunity to engage in other activities and to receive instruction on other behaviors, as depicted in the following visual where X represents the target skill and Y represents other skills:

X Y X Y X Y

Each of the formats of instructional trial delivery can be used within the course of a day. For example, massed trials can be used for acquisition of a new skill or for building fluency in one-to-one instruction, such as the presentation of functional sight words taught with flash cards presented by a peer tutor during language arts class. Spaced trials, such as those conducted by the instructor during group instruction, facilitate maintenance by allowing the students to practice reading the words with peers from a text or as projected on a screen. Distributed trials conducted throughout the day in places where the words are found in natural settings (e.g., menus, signage, scoreboards, directions) facilitate generalization by having the student apply what has been taught. Example 6.1 shows how massed, spaced, and distributed trials all can be used in the instruction that a single student receives.

EXAMPLE 6.1 USING MASSED, SPACED, AND DISTRIBUTED TRIALS

Example 5.2 reviewed the ecological assessment conducted for Ned, a middle school student with Down syndrome. Based on the skills selected as a result of that assessment, the consultants designed a school day for Ned that consisted of various instructional trial formats on Ned's target skills (e.g., manipulating fasteners, communicating greetings and needs, preparing a snack, making purchases with dollars and coins, providing personal information) (Collins, Schuster, & Grisham-Brown, 2004).

For example, Ned received massed trials of one-to-one instruction on identifying coins and using the next dollar strategy each morning. In the afternoon Ned received spaced trials on purchasing during small-group instruction on grocery shopping with peers, in which students selected and paid for grocery items placed on a shelf during simulations in the life skills classroom. Throughout the day Ned had opportunities to use this skill during distributed trials in which he selected coins to purchase a drink from a vending machine in the school, used the next dollar strategy to pay for his lunch in the cafeteria with his peers, used the next dollar strategy to purchase real grocery items with a peer for a snack he would prepare for the class, and selected coins to play a video game after grocery shopping.

Attentional Cues

Before learning can take place, it is necessary for the student to be focused on the stimulus (e.g., making eye contact, listening). This can be accomplished through the delivery of general or specific **attentional cues** (Wolery et al., 1992). For some students, **general attentional cues** (e.g., calling the student by name, stating "Look") are sufficient to focus the student on the task at hand. For other students, **specific attentional cues** are necessary to ensure the student is ready to learn. Specific cues require the student to demonstrate, in some fashion, the readiness to learn. For example, the instructor may require the student to respond to, "Are you ready?" by nodding the head and saying, "Yes." If this still is not sufficient, the instructor may ensure the student's attention is focused by asking the student to perform an indicator related to the stimulus, such as having the student's finger point to or trace the letters of a word before asking the student to read the word. Using the formula presented previously, attentional cues (*AC*) would be inserted as follows:

$$AC \rightarrow S \rightarrow R \rightarrow C$$

Prompts

Prompts are events that are added to instruction to increase the likelihood that the student will make the correct response (Wolery et al., 1992). In most cases they are not permanent but are faded as a student learns to perform a response independently over time. Prompts may consist of (but are not limited to) pictures, words, videos, verbal models or directions, gestures, physical models, or physical guidance.

There are several types of prompts. **Antecedent prompts** typically consist of modifications to or placement of instructional materials. (These will be discussed in a later section of this chapter.) **Antecedent-prompting procedures** use prompts (*P*) to modify the stimulus as shown in the following formula:

$$S/P \rightarrow R \rightarrow C$$

On the other hand, **response-prompting procedures** insert a prompt between the stimulus and the response as follows:

$$S(P) \rightarrow R \rightarrow C$$

Response prompts typically consist of actions performed by the instructor, such as presenting a verbal model of the correct response or providing verbal directions, providing a gesture that indicates the correct response, physically modeling the correct response, or physically guiding the student through the correct response. (Specific response-prompting strategies will be described in later sections of this chapter.)

Both antecedent- and response-prompting procedures are considered near errorless because they typically result in 20% errors or less (Wolery et al., 1992). This is advantageous because performing the correct response results in the opportunity for the instructor to follow the behavior with a reinforcer (e.g., praise, points, smiley faces) instead of a punisher (e.g., error correction, reprimand, failure to acknowledge the response). In addition, prompting correct responses allows students to perform correct responses until they no longer need assistance rather than ingraining the performance of incorrect responses. Using prompting strategies systematically allows a student to anticipate what is expected and what will occur during the instructional session, increasing the pace of instruction and decreasing behavioral problems. Also, the systematic application of prompting strategies allows the instructor to collect data on a routine basis and to make instructional decisions (e.g., make modifications, change procedures, change consequences) based on an analysis of whether or not the student is making progress. This results in learning and provides the teacher with accountability for the progress of the student. As learning results, prompts are faded, transferring stimulus control from the prompt to the antecedent/stimulus over time. Once prompts are faded, reinforcers also are faded to facilitate maintenance in a world in which reinforcers may occur only on an intermittent basis.

Consequences

Liberty et al. (1981) noted the importance of planning consequences as a part of systematic instruction. As stated earlier, consequences either increase or decrease the likelihood that a student will repeat a response. Thus, when the student responds correctly to a stimulus, the instructor should provide a reinforcer (*Rf*), as shown in the following formula:

$$S \rightarrow R \rightarrow Rf$$

For some students, this can be a natural reinforcer, such as a smile, a pat on the back, general praise (e.g., "Good," "Nice job"), or descriptive praise (e.g., "I like the way you wrote your name," "Yes, that word is 'stop'"). Other students may require a more tangible and immediate reinforcer (e.g., a small edible, time to engage in a preferred activity). The delivery of these types of **secondary reinforcers** can be delayed by allowing them to accumulate until the end of the session or by delivering a token that can be traded later for preferred reinforcers. Regardless of the type of individualized reinforcer that is selected, it should be delivered consistently after each trial during acquisition of a new behavior. Once criterion is met, the reinforcer should be thinned to a less frequent schedule of delivery to facilitate maintenance of the skill across natural environments where, as noted earlier, reinforcers may not be available or may not be delivered consistently.

When the student makes an incorrect response, the instructor has three options: (a) model the correct response for the student, (b) have the student correct the error before proceeding, or (c) ignore the error and proceed to the next trial. Modeling the response and correcting the error have the advantage of decreasing the probability that the student will repeat the error in the future. Each of these options are preferable to punishing the response (e.g., reprimanding the student, removing a reinforcer) because they respond to errors in a positive manner. Delivering consequences for incorrect responses (i.e., model [M], error correction [EC], ignore) can be demonstrated by the following formulas:

$$S \rightarrow R \rightarrow M \text{ and/or } EC$$

or

$$S \rightarrow R, S$$

Shaping

Reinforcement also can be used in **shaping** correct responses over time (Wolery et al., 1988). This typically occurs when the target behavior is too complex or difficult for initial learning. Thus, the instructor reinforces the student for making an approximation of the response. Over time, the response must more closely mirror the target response before it is reinforced. For example, a child learns verbal language through a shaping process. The child initially is reinforced for babbling (e.g., receives a hug, receives food, receives attention). Over time, the child's utterances begin to sound more like real words (e.g., "ba-ba" for bottle, "ma-ma" for Mommy, "da-da" for Daddy), so babbling is no longer reinforced. Eventually, the child's utterances become intelligible words (e.g., "bottle," "Mommy," "Daddy"), so less intelligible speech is no longer reinforced. In addition to communication, the shaping process can be applied to a number of other tasks (e.g., motor, social).

SPECIFIC PROMPTING STRATEGIES

Once the basic framework for instruction is in place, the instructor can determine the type of individualized prompting procedure that will be used facilitate learning. Although error correction can be used in a systematic fashion (Wright & Schuster, 1994), it has the disadvantage of allowing students to make errors before receiving a prompt, thus decreasing the likelihood that they will receive reinforcement. As previously noted, the addition of prompts allows students to make fewer errors, thus increasing the likelihood that they will receive reinforcement. For this reason, antecedent- and response-prompting procedures are considered near-errorless procedures. The following sections describe both antecedent- and response-prompting procedures.

Antecedent-Prompting Procedures

As previously noted, antecedent- (or stimulus-) prompting procedures typically involve manipulation of the instructional materials. Wolery and Gast (1984) described two specific antecedent-prompting procedures: (a) stimulus shaping and (b) stimulus fading.

In **stimulus shaping** the instructional materials highlight a relevant feature to facilitate the success of the student. For example, the instructor may teach shapes by asking a student to make an easy discrimination by selecting a circle from a choice of a circle and a rectangle. Through a series of trials, the circle would remain constant, but the rectangle would slowly transform into an oval as the corners became more rounded. After numerous trials in which the discrimination between the two shapes became more difficult over time, the student would be able to select a circle from a choice of a circle and an oval. The relevant feature would be highlighted in that the difference between a circle and an oval is the length and not the lack of corners.

In **stimulus fading** the instructional materials highlight an irrelevant feature to facilitate the success of the student. For example, the instructor may teach the student to read the word "red" by initially showing the word printed in the color red. Over a series of trials, the color would fade across letters then within the final letter until the word was no longer printed in color. The irrelevant feature would be highlighted in that the letters R–E–D always spell red, regardless of the color in which the word is printed.

These strategies can be combined through **superimposition** (i.e., slowly shaping a relevant feature as an irrelevant feature is faded). For example, the instructional materials would begin with the face of a boy. As the relevant feature of the word *boy* slowly takes shape around the boy's eyes and ear, the irrelevant feature of the boy's face fades until only the letters B-O-Y appear.

Instructors will find commercial print-based and computer-based materials available that employ these techniques, saving them the time and effort of constructing materials. Wolery and Gast (1984), however, recommended that instructors consider using response-prompting procedures over antecedent-prompting procedures. This is congruent with the **principle of parsimony** (Etzel & LeBlanc, 1979): if two procedures are equally effective, use the one that is simpler to implement.

Response-Prompting Procedures

In their text on response-prompting strategies, Wolery et al. (1992) identified those strategies found in the professional literature that effectively teach students with disabilities. These included the graduated guidance, most-to-least prompting, system of least prompts, constant time delay, progressive time delay, antecedent-prompt-and-test, and antecedent-prompt-and-fade instructional strategies. In their review of instructional strategies for students with significant disabilities, Wolery and Schuster (1997) dropped the antecedent-prompt-and-fade strategy and noted a growing literature base on the simultaneous-prompting strategy as a specific form of the antecedent-prompt-and-test instructional strategy. Taking into consideration those strategies most likely to be found as examples for teaching functional skills in the professional literature since 1990, the following sections of this chapter will describe these response-prompting procedures: (a) graduate guidance, (b) most-to-least prompting, (c) system of least prompts, (d) time delay (constant and progressive), and (e) simultaneous prompting. In addition, the following sections will illustrate each procedure by describing examples of their application from the professional literature, where the procedures have been demonstrated to be effective through the use of single-subject research designs (Horner et al., 2005). The trial sequence for each of these procedures can be found in Table 6.1.

TABLE 6.1	*Comparison of the Steps of Systematic Response-Prompting Procedures.*

Steps of Systematic Response-Prompting Strategies

Graduated Guidance	Most-to-Least Prompting	System of Least Prompts	Time Delay (Constant/Progressive)	Simultaneous Prompting
Secure attention	Secure attention	Secure attention	Secure attention	Secure attention
↓	↓	↓	↓	↓
Deliver task direction	Deliver task direction	Deliver task direction	Deliver task direction	Deliver task direction
↓	↓	↓	↓	↓
Physically shadow student, providing physical prompts as needed	Prompt with most intrusive prompt until criterion met; systematically fade to less intrusive prompt over time	If no independent response during response interval, prompt with least intrusive prompt needed from set prompt hierarchy	Immediately prompt during initial session(s); wait for a set delay interval before delivering controlling prompt during subsequent sessions	Conduct probe trial(s); follow with training trials in which controlling prompt is delivered immediately
↓	↓	↓	↓	↓
Deliver consequences	Deliver consequences	Deliver consequences	Deliver consequences	Deliver consequences

Graduated Guidance   **Graduated guidance** is an instructional strategy that is useful when a student requires a physical prompt to perform a correct response. The instructor provides the amount of physical guidance necessary to ensure that the student performs the correct response then fades the intensity of the prompt over time. One way is to shadow the student's movements, only providing assistance as needed. Think of a parent helping a child learn self-feeding skills for the first time. The parent allows the child to pick up the spoon then guides the child through scooping food into the bowl of the spoon. The parent then follows the child's movement closely, ready to steady the child's hand until the food is in the child's mouth. Formative data are recorded on correct unprompted and prompted responses to monitor progress to criterion.

As described in Example 2.2 earlier in this text, Collins, Gast, Wolery, Holcombe, and Leatherby (1991) taught two preschool children with severe to profound multiple disabilities to use a spoon and cup. When the children failed to meet criterion on a specific step (e.g., scooping with spoon, tilting the cup), the instructor used graduated guidance on those steps by initially providing hand-over-hand guidance and systematically fading the prompt by proximity (e.g., full guidance of hand to nudge of elbow) over time. Although graduated guidance is a simple procedure to perform, instructors should reserve it for those cases where other procedures are not effective because it is physically intrusive and because physically shadowing can be stigmatizing by making a student appear helpless and dependent.

Most-to-Least Prompting   **Most-to-least prompting** is another instructional strategy that is effective for students who require a great deal of assistance when learning a new task. Instead of relying on a single prompt, the instructor uses prompts from a hierarchy in which prompts are ordered from the most intrusive to the least intrusive. The instructor might begin with physical guidance (the most intrusive prompt) for several sessions then proceed to partial physical guidance for several sessions, a model prompt for several sessions, and a verbal prompt for several sessions before the student is given the opportunity to perform the response independently. When to change the level of prompt can be based on the judgment of the instructor or, more systematically, based on periodic probes to see if the student is ready to move to less assistance. Formative data are recorded on correct responses with each level of prompting until the student reaches criterion at the independent level.

The most-to-least prompting procedure is flexible in that if the student moves to a new prompt level that fails to consistently control the response, the instructor can revert to the previous level, based on the data. Even if the student cannot follow a verbal prompt at the onset of instruction, pairing a verbal prompt with the prompts at more intrusive levels of the hierarchy can result in the student responding to verbal prompts by the time that level is introduced. The obvious drawback to this procedure is that it takes a good deal of time to move through the prompt hierarchy; however, the procedure can be effective with a student who requires a high degree of assistance during initial instruction.

Miller and Test (1989) taught laundry skills (using a washer and dryer) to four secondary school students with moderate disabilities using two procedures, one of which was most-to-least prompting. When students performed a step incorrectly, the instructor used a direct verbal prompt plus physical assistance, the most intrusive prompt, from a hierarchy of prompts, to assist the student in performing the step correctly. Over time, the most intrusive prompt faded to direct verbal plus gesture then to direct verbal only. Although the most-to-least prompting procedure was not as efficient as the other procedure used (i.e., time delay), all of the students learned to perform the task and maintained the skill over time.

System of Least Prompts   Although the **system of least prompts** (i.e., least-to-most prompting) procedure also uses a prompt hierarchy, it differs from the most-to-least prompting procedure in that the instructor has the opportunity to use each prompt of the hierarchy during each instructional trial. The instructor begins by providing the opportunity for the student to respond independently. If this does not occur after a preset response interval (e.g., three to five seconds), the instructor delivers the least intrusive prompt from the hierarchy (e.g., verbal prompt) then again waits the same response interval for the student to respond. Instruction proceeds in this manner with the instructor delivering increasingly intrusive prompts from the hierarchy (e.g., gesture, model, and physical prompts) until the student responds correctly. Formative data are recorded on the type of prompt necessary to perform a correct response until the student reaches criterion at the independent level.

Collins, Epstein, Reiss, and Lowe (2001) recommended simplifying the description of the system of least prompts instructional strategy for noneducators as telling the child what to do, then showing the child what to do, and finally helping the child do the task. Thus, the system of least prompts procedure is a simple strategy to implement. In addition, it has the advantage of allowing the student to be independent when possible and only providing the amount of assistance the student needs on difficult steps.

Collins, Hall, and Branson (1997) selected the system of least prompts procedure to teach four leisure skills (i.e., selecting a television program, watching a videotape, playing a computer game, playing a card game) to four students with moderate disabilities because it was a natural procedure to use within the context of the selected activities. For example, in playing cards with peers, it is natural to wait for a player to draw a card before telling the player to take a turn. If the player does not know what to do, it is natural to show the player how the game should proceed (e.g., "Watch. You draw a card") before providing physical assistance to draw a card. The obvious drawback to the procedure is that sessions can become lengthy if a student needs a great deal of assistance and must work through the entire prompt hierarchy on most trials.

Time Delay The time delay procedure is based on the premise that it is more parsimonious to provide only one type of prompt per trial. In other words, there is one prompt level for the instructor to remember and to deliver if the student cannot perform the response independently. This prompt is the controlling prompt because it ensures a correct response from the student. It does not have to be intrusive, however, since some students can perform skills with less intrusive prompts, such as a verbal or physical model. While the previous procedures faded prompts by intensity, the time delay procedure fades prompts over a dimension of time. During initial instructional trials, the instructor operates on the assumption that the student cannot perform the response; thus, the instructor immediately delivers the controlling prompt following the stimulus to respond (i.e., zero-second delay interval). When the student demonstrates the ability to perform a correct response following the prompt (typically one or two sessions), the instructor has two options: (a) a progressive time delay or (b) a constant time delay. Regardless of the option, formative data are recorded on whether the student performed a correct response before or after the prompt until the student reaches criterion without a prompt.

In the **progressive time delay** procedure, the instructor increases the delay interval by small increments of time across trials or sessions. For example, the instructor might increase the interval from one second to two seconds then to three seconds for one session each before holding the delay interval constant for all subsequent sessions. This option is appropriate for students who have not learned to wait for a prompt to be delivered when they do not know how to respond correctly.

In the **constant time delay** procedure, the instructor immediately increases the delay interval for all subsequent sessions to a number of seconds that would be considered acceptable for fluency. If students have the ability to wait for a prompt when they do not know how to perform a correct response, this procedure is more parsimonious because the instructor only has to remember a set number of seconds for the delay interval across sessions. Regardless of which option is selected, the time delay procedure allows the student to slowly transfer stimulus control from the prompt (i.e., responding correctly after the prompt) to the stimulus (i.e., responding correctly before the prompt).

The progressive and constant time delay procedures have been used in teaching both discrete and chained tasks. For example, Collins and Stinson (1994–1995) used a progressive time delay procedure to teach four secondary students with moderate and severe disabilities the discrete skill of reading safety words found on product warning labels, and Collins, Stinson, and Land (1993) used a progressive time delay procedure to teach the chained safety tasks of crossing a street to use a public pay telephone to four secondary school and four elementary school students with moderate to severe disabilities. Likewise, Cromer, Schuster, Collins, and Grisham-Brown (1998) used a constant time delay procedure to teach three middle school students with moderate and severe disabilities the discrete task of reading sight words on critical information on medical prescription containers, and Fiscus, Schuster, Morse, and Collins (2002) used a constant time delay procedure to teach three food-preparation skills to four elementary school students with moderate and severe disabilities.

Simultaneous Prompting   **Simultaneous prompting** is a systematic form of the antecedent-prompt-and-test procedure and grew out of the research showing that many students taught with the time delay procedures transfer stimulus control from the prompt to the stimulus in a minimal number of sessions. The logic is that if students learn so quickly after receiving trials with prompt delivery after a zero-second delay interval, it is more parsimonious to continue with zero-delay trials until criterion is reached. To identify the point at which the transfer of stimulus control (i.e., learning) takes place, probe trials are conducted prior to each instructional session to see if the student can demonstrate mastery of the skill. If the student can perform the task, instruction stops; if the student cannot perform the task, zero-delay instructional trials continue. As with the time delay procedure, the simultaneous-prompting procedure also uses a single controlling prompt. Since probe trial data are the only data recorded, the procedure is less time consuming for the instructor. In addition, it is necessary to collect formative data on whether or not the student performs the correct response during probe trials only until the student reaches criterion.

Although relatively new in the professional literature, the simultaneous-prompting procedure has been used effectively with both discrete and chained tasks across levels of age and ability. For example, Singleton, Schuster, Morse, and Collins (1999) taught four secondary school students with moderate and severe disabilities to read grocery words from flash cards with both the antecedent-prompt-and-test procedure (i.e., probe trial immediately following zero-delay instructional sessions) and the simultaneous-prompting procedure (i.e., probe trial immediately prior to zero-delay instructional sessions). While the students acquired the skill in fewer trials with the antecedent-prompt-and-test procedure, they exhibited better maintenance with the simultaneous-prompting procedure. Examples of chained tasks taught with the simultaneous-prompting procedure include handwashing with elementary school students with moderate and severe disabilities (Parrott, Schuster, Collins & Gassaway, 2000), unlocking keyed locks with secondary school students with moderate and severe disabilities (Fetko, Schuster, Harley, & Collins, 1999), and assembling boxes with adults with moderate and severe disabilities (Maciag, Schuster, Collins, & Cooper, 2000).

Naturalistic Teaching   There are four **naturalistic teaching strategies** (i.e., **milieu teaching strategies**) (Kaiser, 2000). These procedures are systematically implemented in ongoing activities to teach language skills. In addition, each of the procedures is child directed, relying on child interest in communicating to initiate an instructional trial.

The first strategy, **modeling,** teaches the acquisition of language skills through the instructor modeling followed by a response interval in which the child can imitate the instructor (e.g., instructor says, "Ball," when child looks at ball). The second procedure, **mand-model,** is used to teach fluency with words in the child's repertoire. In this procedure the instructor first provides a mand when the child fails to use a target word; if the child does not respond within a set response interval, the instructor models and again waits for the child to imitate the model (e.g., "Tell me what you want" followed by "Ball"). The third procedure, **incidental teaching,** is used to expand the child's existing repertoire by modeling an expanded version of what the child says (e.g., "Yes, that is a ball; tell me *red* ball"). The fourth procedure, **naturalistic time delay,** is similar to the time delay procedure described earlier and is used to facilitate the child's ability to initiate known words within functional activities. In this procedure the instructor inserts a delay interval within an ongoing activity and waits for the child to initiate communication before delivering a model prompt (e.g., game of catch interrupted for five seconds before instructor says, "Tell me, 'play ball'"). In each of the naturalistic procedures, formative data are collected on the student's use of targeted responses.

Although the naturalistic procedures were developed with preschool children with language delays, they have been used effectively also with older students with moderate to severe disabilities. Hemmeter, Ault, Collins, and Meyer (1996) used the a mand-model procedure and incidental teaching to teach targeted verbal language skills to four elementary school students with moderate and severe disabilities within the context of play time, and Miller, Collins, and Hemmeter (2002) used a naturalistic time delay procedure to teach targeted manual signing to three nonverbal secondary school students with moderate and severe disabilities within the context of school activities (e.g., lunch in the cafeteria).

Summary

In summary, instructors who use systematic instruction have a number of strategies from which to choose, and each is based on research conducted over time that has shown the procedures to be effective in teaching functional skills to students with disabilities. Example 6.2 shows how the instructor can use various procedures to teach a number of skills within the context of a single day. After reading this example, test your understanding of systematic instruction by completing Activity 6.2.

EXAMPLE 6.2   USING SYSTEMATIC INSTRUCTION

Example 6.1 showed how the school day of Ned, a middle school student with a moderate disability and Down syndrome, received instruction in various formats throughout the day (Collins et al., 2004). Based on the task, Ned also received instruction using various procedures.

For example, the instructor used a system-of-least-prompts procedure to teach Ned to manipulate fasteners during the day, when he needed to put on and remove his jacket (e.g., community-based instruction, playground). The instructor first secured his attention by calling his name. When eye contact was established, the instructor gave the task direction, "Zip your jacket." The instructor then waited three seconds for Ned to begin the first step. If he could not do this correctly, the instructor delivered a prompt from the hierarchy, beginning with a verbal direction, proceeding to a model, then using physical guidance, as needed. Whenever Ned made a correct response, he received praise; whenever he started to make an error, the instructor interrupted him by delivering the next prompt from the hierarchy.

In another example the instructor used a constant time delay procedure to teach Ned to identify coins. Whether in one-to-one instruction when making a purchase or in small-group instruction with his peers, the instructor delivered an attentional cue of saying his name and gave the task direction (e.g., "Show me quarter"). On the first day of instruction, the instructor immediately pointed to the quarter so Ned could imitate the model. On all subsequent days, the instructor waited three seconds for Ned to respond before prompting him by pointing to the quarter. When Ned initiated the response before the prompt or correctly imitated the model, he received praise. When he made an error, the instructor placed his finger on the quarter and said, "No, that is the quarter."

In a final example, the instructor used a naturalistic time delay with a mand-model procedure to encourage Ned to use the manual sign for "more." When they played ball in the gym or on the playground, the instructor interrupted the game and waited for him to initiate the sign for "more." If he failed to do this, the instructor said, "Tell me what you want." If he still failed to make the sign, she modeled the sign for him to imitate. Whenever he made the sign for "more," he received praise and the natural reinforcer of continuing the game.

ACTIVITY 6.2   Using Systematic Instruction

Example 6.2 provided three examples of systematic instruction for Ned. In addition to the examples provided, Ned received systematic instruction on using the next dollar strategy and providing personal information. To test your understanding of systematic instruction, describe how you would use a simultaneous-prompting procedure to teach one of these skills to Ned.

STRENGTHENING SYSTEMATIC INSTRUCTION

Increasing Efficiency

In addition to a large body of evidence to support the **effectiveness** of response-prompting procedures (i.e., that the procedures result in the acquisition of skills), there also are a number of research investigations in which variables have been added to the format of systematic instruction to increase the **efficiency** of the procedures (i.e., that the procedures compare better to others in terms of learning) (Wolery et al., 1992). These efficiency variables include programming for generalization, teaching in a small-group format, adding nontargeted information, and using technology.

Programming for Generalization   Teaching single and/or poor examples (i.e., exemplars) within a specific context can be termed *teach and hope*. For example, the instructor teaches the skill to criterion with an artificial material (e.g., flash card or play money) or limits instruction to the classroom setting and hopes the student will generalize to other materials or settings. If the student does not generalize, instruction must continue with a new material or in a new setting. This can be viewed as an inefficient way to teach.

Billingsley, Burgess, Lynch, and Matlock (1991) recommended beginning to plan for generalization when writing instructional objectives, and Liberty, Haring, White, and Billingsley (1988) suggested decision rules for analyzing data as instruction proceeds to see if students are generalizing. As discussed in Chapter 4, there are strategies that can be employed during instruction to facilitate generalization (Stokes &

Baer, 1977; Stokes & Osnes, 1986), thus increasing the efficiency of instruction. One strategy is to teach with materials that would be found in the natural settings. For example, Collins, Branson, and Hall (1995) used a constant time delay procedure to teach four secondary school students with moderate and severe disabilities to read key cooking words directly from the labels of real food products; the students generalized the skill to cooking activities using novel products.

Another strategy to facilitate generalization is in vivo instruction (i.e., teaching in the natural setting where the skill will be needed). When this is not possible, instructors can teach with good classroom **simulations** using **community-referenced** materials (i.e., those that would be found in the natural setting). Collins et al. (1993) use a progressive time delay procedure to teach four elementary school students and four secondary school students with moderate and severe disabilities to cross streets and use a public pay telephone and found that some of the students learned the skills when taught in the community, while others learned the skills when taught in classroom simulations. All of the students generalized to novel settings and materials.

When planning for generalization, it is important also to consider both stimulus and response generalization (Wolery et al., 1988). In **stimulus generalization** the student performs a single type of behavior in response to a class of stimuli. To facilitate stimulus generalization, the instructor should teach across **multiple exemplars** of materials, persons, and settings, as depicted in the following formula:

$$S1/S2/S3 \rightarrow R \rightarrow C$$

This helps students build concepts (e.g., C-A-U-T-I-O-N spells "caution" whether it is written in red or blue letters, whether it is written in large or small letters, and whether it is on a box or a bottle). In teaching four secondary school students with moderate and severe disabilities to clean tables, Smith, Collins, Schuster, and Kleinert (1999) used a system-of-least-prompts procedure with multiple exemplars of cloths, buckets, tables, and settings; the students generalized to novel materials and tables in a novel setting.

To facilitate stimulus generalization across persons, multiple instructors should conduct instruction. Paraprofessionals (Grisham-Brown, Schuster, Hemmeter, & Collins, 2000), peer tutors (Collins et al., 1995), parents (Mobayed, Collins, Strangis, Schuster, & Hemmeter, 2000), and related service delivery personnel (Roark, Collins, Hemmeter, & Kleinert, 2002) have demonstrated that they can reliably implement systematic instructional strategies. Also, when compared to the instructor, peers can be as effective in their delivery of instruction (Miracle, Collins, Schuster, & Grisham-Brown, 2001). When instructors have used a constant time delay procedure with multiple exemplars of persons as confederates delivering multiple exemplars of stimuli in role playing, adults with moderate and severe disabilities have generalized a response to novel lures from novel "strangers" in novel settings (Collins, Schuster, & Nelson, 1992) and secondary school students with moderate and severe disabilities have generalized a response to novel types of peer pressure applied in novel settings (Collins, Hall, Rankin, & Branson, 1999).

Finally, teaching across multiple exemplars of settings can also facilitate stimulus generalization. When Branham, Collins, Schuster, and Kleinert (1999) used a constant time delay procedure to teach community skills to three secondary school students with moderate and severe disabilities across two exemplars each of streets, banks, and post offices, the students generalized to novel exemplars in the community.

In teaching with multiple exemplars of materials, the instructor can employ as few as two types of stimuli that may or may not sample the range of exemplars. Teaching in **general case** is an even stronger means of facilitating generalization because the instructor employs examples with all of the variations that may be found across settings. Day and Horner (1986) demonstrated a good example of general case instruction in an investigation in which the use of a single exemplar of shirt (i.e., T-shirt with crew neck and short sleeves, medium fit, light fabric) during instruction resulted in a male with a moderate to severe disability having limited ability to dress himself. When he was taught with exemplars that sampled the range (i.e., eight exemplars with variations across shirt type, neckline, sleeve length, fit, and fabric), he was able to dress himself in any pullover shirt with which he was presented.

In **response generalization** the student performs a class of behaviors in response to a single stimulus. To facilitate response generalization, the instructor should reinforce numerous acceptable responses, as depicted in the following formula:

$$S \rightarrow R1/R2/R3 \rightarrow C$$

For example, the response to the task direction, "Show me fifty cents," could consist of the student handing the instructor a half-dollar, two quarters, or five dimes. Regardless of the response given, the student would receive praise from the instructor and, even better, a natural reinforcer if allowed to make a purchase (e.g., snack or drink from vending machine).

In summary, teachers can employ strategies to facilitate both stimulus and response generalization, thus making instruction more efficient. The only way to tell if generalization occurs, however, is to conduct test (i.e., probe) trials with novel exemplars in novel settings.

Teaching in a Small-Group Format Because Individualized Educational Programs (IEPs) guide the instruction of students with moderate to severe disabilities, it is a common practice to conclude that students with moderate and severe disabilities should be taught in a one-to-one format. There is evidence, however, to show that small-group instruction (two to six students) can be a more efficient way to teach (Wolery et al., 1992). One of the benefits for instructors is that it takes less time to teach several students at once, thus increasing the amount of instruction that can be delivered in a day. In addition, behavior problems are decreased since there is less down time for students and because teachers can use behavioral strategies with small groups that facilitate appropriate behavior (e.g., using vicarious reinforcement, calling on students in random order, having students reinforce each other's performance).

There are learning benefits for students as well. First, students have the opportunity to practice social skills, such as taking turns. Second, students benefit because observational learning can occur. When the same task is taught to everyone in the group, students learn in fewer trials because they have the opportunity to learn by watching each other. When different tasks are taught to students in the group, students tend to learn at least some of the tasks, discrete or chained, that are targeted for other students in the group, whether or not the tasks are related.

As an example of the observational learning of discrete related tasks, Palmer, Collins, and Schuster (1999) used a simultaneous-prompting procedure to teach receptive manual sign identification to three adults with moderate and severe disabilities. Each of the adults learned their own targeted signs and at least some of the signs targeted for the other students. As an example of the observational learning of discrete unrelated tasks, Fickel, Schuster, and Collins (1998) used a simultaneous-prompting procedure to teach different tasks (i.e., manual signs, simple addition, states on a map, and flags of foreign countries) to a heterogeneous group of middle school students that included a mild disability, a moderate disability, a severe disability, and no disability. Three of the students (e.g., those with a mild, moderate, or no disability) learned part or all of the tasks taught to the other students.

To demonstrate the observational learning of chained tasks in a small-group format, Stonecipher, Schuster, Collins, and Grisham-Brown (1999) used a constant time delay procedure to teach four elementary school students with moderate and severe disabilities to wrap gifts. Although each student completed only one-fourth of the task during instructional sessions, each of the students learned how to complete the entire task.

In 1984 Reid and Favell concluded that small-group instruction was an effective practice for students with severe disabilities, based on the limited evidence at the time. In 1991 Collins, Gast, Ault, and Wolery created guidelines for small-group instruction based on a growing body of research. They stated that instructors who conduct small-group instruction with students with disabilities should consider several variables in planning instructional sessions.

First, they should consider the variables of group composition: (a) size (i.e., up to seven members), (b) homogeneous or heterogeneous grouping (i.e., variance in age or ability), (c) same or different task taught to group members, (d) entry criteria to be a group member (e.g., appropriate social behavior), (e) group arrangement (i.e., intrasequential—one-to-one instruction to each member, intersequential—cooperative tasks, tandem—gradual increase of group size over time, or group instruction supplemented by one-to-one instruction), and (f) criteria for conducting instructional sessions (e.g., number present). Second, instructors should plan instructional procedures to include the following: (a) instructional strategy, (b) attentional cue (i.e., general or specific), (c) presentation of stimulus (i.e., predictable or random), (d) presentation of trial (i.e., massed, spaced, or distributed), (e) target response (i.e., choral or individual), (f) consequences (e.g., reinforcers, corrective feedback), and (g) criterion (i.e., individual or group). Third, instructors should determine how learning will be measured: (a) effectiveness (e.g., formative or summative data), (b) efficiency (e.g., time or number of sessions to criterion), (c) method of summarizing data (e.g., graph, table), and (d) generalization and maintenance. Finally, instructors need to plan how to manage group behavior, such as using group contingencies (i.e., independent contingency—student reinforced based on individual criteria, dependent contingency—group reinforced based on behavior of target student, or interdependent contingency—group reinforced based on group criterion).

Adding Nontargeted Information   As previously stated, students can acquire **nontargeted information** (information that students learn in addition to skills targeted for instruction) through **observational learning,** making group instruction a more efficient way to teach. In addition, students can learn nontargeted information when it is placed as **instructive feedback** (*IF*) in a systematic fashion within the instructional trial sequence (Collins, Hendricks, Fetko, & Land, 2002).

There are three places where instructive feedback can be inserted within an instructional trial. The first is in the antecencent or stimulus as depicted in the following formula:

$$S/IF \rightarrow R \rightarrow C$$

For example, Roark et al. (2002) inserted manual signs in the task direction when they used a constant time delay procedure to teach four elementary school students with moderate and severe disabilities to receptively identify food products. The students learned at least some of the manual signs.

A second place where instructive feedback can be inserted in the instructional trial is within the prompt hierarchy as depicted in the following formula:

$$S \rightarrow P1/IF, \ P2/IF, \ P3/IF \rightarrow R \rightarrow C$$

For example, Jones and Collins (1997) inserted nutrition and safety facts when delivering prompts with a system-of-least-prompts procedure to teach four women with moderate and severe disabilities to cook with a microwave. The women learned all the facts.

A third place where instructive feedback can be inserted is within the consequence, as depicted in the following formula:

$$S \rightarrow R \rightarrow C/IF$$

For example, Wolery, Schuster, and Collins (2000) used a constant time delay procedure to teach four secondary school students with mild and moderate disabilities to read functional sight words. When the instructor praised correct responses, he inserted instructive feedback by showing the students sight words targeted for future instruction. When the instructor later taught these words, instructional time was diminished due to previous exposure.

Students with moderate and severe disabilities can learn nontargeted information also when it is systematically embedded within activities in the absence of instructional trials. For example, Collins et al. (2002) had peers systematically deliver nontargeted information to elementary and secondary school students with moderate and severe disabilities during inclusive classes, and Collins, Hall, Branson, and Holder (1999) had general education teachers systematically deliver nontargeted information to two secondary school students with moderate and severe disabilities in inclusive classes. In both of these examples, the students with moderate and severe disabilities learned nontargeted information that was both related and unrelated to the class in which they were included (e.g., related grammar rules and unrelated government facts delivered in language arts activities).

Using Technology   A final way to increase the efficiency of instruction is to use technology (Collins, 2003). Technology can be used to involve a student in instructional trials when the instructor is busy elsewhere in the classroom. In addition, technology can allow a student to independently perform tasks in less restrictive environments whether or not an instructor is present. Three examples of technology that have been used effectively with students with moderate and severe disabilities include (a) audiotapes, (b) videotapes, and (c) computers.

Mitchell, Schuster, Collins, and Gassaway (2000) taught three middle school students with moderate and severe disabilities to perform vocational tasks (i.e., cleaning mirror, sink, and toilet) by following directions on audiotapes while wearing headphones. After the students demonstrated mastery of the tasks, the teacher faded the audiotape by omitting steps from the new tapes.

Norman, Collins, and Schuster (2001) taught three elementary school students with moderate and severe disabilities to perform self-care tasks (i.e., cleaning sunglasses, putting on wristwatch, zipping jacket) by modeling videotapes of the tasks. The tape was based on a constant time delay procedure in which the students were prompted by the video when they could not perform a step of the task.

Finally, Mechling, Gast, and Langone (2002) taught four students with moderate disabilities to shop for groceries by using streaming video of simulations across three grocery stores on a computer. Using a system-of-least-prompts procedure, the instructor prompted the students, as needed, to locate items on the grocery list and to touch corresponding aisle signs and items on the computer screen.

Facilitating Inclusion

In 1997 Brown, McDonnell, and Billingsley questioned the compatibility of systematic instruction to inclusive settings and asserted that the time had come to investigate new paradigms. Yet there is limited evidence that systematic procedures can be effective within the context of inclusive settings. Although inclusion will be discussed in depth in Chapter 7, there are several strategies that will be mentioned here to demonstrate how this can occur.

The **individualized curriculum sequencing model** was developed around the concept of using distributed trials to teach functional skills within natural contexts, such as daily routines. Bambara, Warren, and Komisar (1988) demonstrated this model in using the system-of-least-prompts procedure to teach functional skills to two preschool students with severe developmental delays. Specifically, the teachers taught (a) matching to sample during group play, lunch, and grooming (generalized to music group and free play); (b) manually signing "more" during group play, art group, and one-to-one play with the teacher (generalized to diapering and transitions); (c) recognizing name during group play, snack, and group theme activities (generalized to departure and group game); and (d) reaching and touching during group play, art group, and lunch (generalized to gym game and cooking).

More recently, Grisham-Brown et al. (2000) demonstrated how several response-prompting strategies (i.e., constant time delay, most-to-least prompting, simultaneous prompting, system of least prompts), could be used to embed the teaching of functional skills to four preschool students with significant disabilities. After learning the response-prompting strategies, paraprofessionals embedded instruction on the following skills: (a) following directions for spatial concepts and expressing needs or desires during diapering, (b) activating a switch and grasping small objects during group circle time, (c) indicating need to get up and removing shirt during group art activity, and (d) activating switch and indicating choices during arrival and rest time. All of the students made progress on the targeted skills.

Gee, Graham, Sailor, and Goetz (1995) also implemented systematic instruction embedded within activities in teaching functional skills to four elementary school students with severe multiple disabilities. In two cases the instruction occurred in inclusive activities with peers without disabilities using either an antecedent-prompt-and-fade procedure or a time delay procedure at a critical moment of the activity as follows: (a) maintaining head up, using right arm to move items to right side, holding on to grasped items, and maintaining right arm and hand at right edge of tray while selling ice cream on the playground with peers without disabilities and (b) passing game pieces, maintaining visual fixation to complete visual-motor game components, verbalizing turns, and requesting with pictures while playing games with peers without disabilities.

As an example of how functional skills can be taught to older students in an inclusive setting, Collins, Branson, Hall, and Rankin (2001) used a system of least prompts to teach three secondary school students with moderate and severe disabilities to write personal letters within an advanced English class. The students with moderate and severe disabilities wrote letters to people on various topics (e.g., fan letter to television star) as part of their alternate assessment portfolios while peers without disabilities worked on their entries for their writing assessment portfolios. The original plan was for the general education teacher to circulate around the classroom and prompt the students from the prompt hierarchy whenever they raised their hands for help. When this resulted in a high amount of downtime for the students with moderate to severe disabilities, a peer tutor was assigned to assist the students in writing the body of the letter (e.g., spelling), leaving the general education teacher responsible for delivering the initial direction to write the letter and delivering the feedback upon completion of the letter. All of the students learned to write and punctuate the date, the greeting, the body, and the closing of a personal letter.

Another strategy that can be effective in inclusive settings is allowing partial participation (Baumgart et al., 1982). (For an in-depth discussion of this principle, refer back to Chapter 5.) Using this strategy, the student does not have to participate in all aspects of an activity to be included. For example, a student with significant disabilities may activate an electronic switch during an elementary music class to play a tape to which the rest of the class can sing, or a student with significant disabilities in a secondary school drama class might press a button on a communication device to recite a line in a play with peers without disabilities.

In 1992 York, Doyle, and Kronberg presented guidelines for embedding a functional curriculum within an inclusive setting. Citing the work of Giangreco, Cloninger, and Iverson (1992), they noted that there are different options for teaching functional skills within inclusive classrooms. The first option is for students with and without disabilities to participate in the same activities (e.g., all students working on basic addition facts). The second option is for the instructor to teach multilevel activities (e.g., students without disabilities working on adding with regrouping while students with moderate and severe disabilities (MSD) working on basic addition facts). The third option is to teach with one curriculum overlapping another within the same activity (e.g., students without disabilities working on applied addition problems with money in simulation while students with moderate to severe disabilities practice motor skills of grasping and releasing money). The final option is for the student to engage in alternate activities (e.g., typical students working on applied math problems on worksheets while students with moderate and severe disabilities practice next dollar strategy with real money in a one-to-one or small-group format). Regardless of the option selected by the instructional team, systematic instruction can be implemented by the instructor (e.g., general education teacher, special education teacher, paraprofessional, peer tutor).

Increasing Appropriate Behavior

There are several reasons that systematic instruction may facilitate appropriate behavior. For example, making fewer errors results in less frustration for the student, as well as the delivery of more reinforcers. Teaching within a small group (particularly heterogeneous groups) can provide students with appropriate role models while providing the instructor with an opportunity to teach social skills and to vicariously reinforce those in the group who have appropriate behavior.

Wolery and Schuster (1997) stated that there are additional variables that can be added to systematic instruction to facilitate student motivation to learn. One strategy is to add choice and preferences. For example, the instructor can offer the student two appropriate choices (e.g., "It's time to do math now. Would you prefer to work problems in your workbook with a calculator or to practice next dollar strategy with money first?"). A second strategy, as already discussed, is to teach at an appropriate level with a focus on skills that are functional or can be readily applied across natural settings. A third strategy is to teach at a quick pace, as would be the case with response-prompting strategies that use only one prompt level (e.g., constant time delay, progressive time delay, simultaneous prompting), minimizing the length of time that the student who cannot perform a correct response must wait to be prompted. A fourth variable is to be systematic in delivery, regardless of the procedure, so students know what to expect. A final strategy is to deliver contingent and individualized reinforcement, with a continuous schedule of reinforcement delivered during acquisition or initial learning of a task.

To check understanding of the variables to increase efficiency discussed in this and the previous sections, take time to work through Activity 6.3.

ACTIVITY 6.3   Making Systematic Instruction Efficient

In Example 6.2 you designed instruction for teaching a skill (i.e., next dollar strategy or personal information) for Ned, a middle school student with a moderate disability. Now add variables to the instruction you designed to make it more efficient. For example, consider ways you might add nontargeted information or ways that might facilitate generalization.

DATA-BASED INSTRUCTION

Regardless of the instructional strategy or the context in which it is implemented, data should guide instructional decisions. One strategy may work better than another for a particular student, and if that is the case, the data will show that to the instructor, provided that data are collected, graphed, and analyzed on a frequent and consistent basis. The decisions made in each of the examples of systematic instruction cited in this chapter were guided by the data. For example, Collins et al. (1993) added an adaptation (i.e., a written telephone number students carried in their pockets) for elementary students who had difficulty making telephone calls from public pay telephones; Collins et al. (1991) changed the procedure (i.e., constant time delay to graduated guidance), added massed trials, and used differential reinforcement (i.e., praised unprompted correct responses only) when a student had difficulty learning to scoop with a spoon; Norman et al. (2001) pulled a student out of a small group for one-to-one supplemental instruction when he had trouble with a self-care task; and Collins et al. (2001) added a peer tutor to deliver prompts to students writing personal letters when the general education teacher needed assistance.

When planning systematic instruction, the instructor is wise to set data decision rules in advance, such as changing to an easier level of a skill when there is no progress after two weeks of instruction or adding a different reinforcer when performance is erratic for two weeks. This increases the instructor's accountability and facilitates the student's learning.

Best Practices
Systematic Instruction

1. Carefully plan systematic instruction with response-prompting strategies using appropriate attentional cues, prompts, and consequences.
2. Balance one-to-one instruction with small-group interaction to facilitate social skills and observational learning.

3. Increase the efficiency of instruction by programming for generalization with multiple exemplars of real materials, instructors, and settings and by adding nontargeted information as instructive feedback.

4. Use systematic instruction in inclusive settings by embedding trials of functional skill instruction within ongoing activities and routines.

Conclusion

This chapter has focused on the use of systematic instructional strategies to teach functional skills whether in a one-to-one format or in small-group instruction, whether in isolation or within the context of ongoing activities and natural routines, and whether in special education, general education, or community settings. The following chapters will expand on this topic by further elaborating on the delivery of functional skill instruction in inclusive school and community settings. Before continuing, however, check your understanding of systematic instruction by completing the performance-based assessment at the end of this chapter.

(The author has focused on her research with colleagues at the University of Kentucky on the use of systematic response-prompting strategies to teach functional skills to students with moderate and severe disabilities in providing examples throughout this chapter. For further examples, the research of Drs. Diane M. Browder, David L. Gast, John W. Schuster, Mark Wolery, and their colleagues also provide a wealth of information on this topic.)

Questions for Review

1. Why is it desirable to use systematic instructional procedures to teach skills to students with moderate and severe disabilities?

2. Differentiate among forward chaining, backward chaining, and total task instruction.

3. Differentiate among massed, spaced, and total task instruction.

4. What is the difference between antecedent-prompting and response-prompting procedures?

5. Briefly describe the differences among the following response prompting procedures: (a) graduate guidance, (b) most-to-least prompting, (c) system of least prompts, (d) time delay, and (e) simultaneous prompting.

6. What is the difference between effectiveness and efficiency? What are some variables that can increase efficiency?

7. How can generalization be systematically addressed during instruction?

8. Describe how the systematic use of response-prompting procedures can be employed in inclusive settings.

Performance-Based Assessment

To practice designing and delivering systematic instruction, look around the room where you are reading this for functional tasks that you might teach. Ideas include stapling paper together or removing staples, reading personal information from an identification card, writing a check, punching holes in paper with a hole puncher, cutting paper with scissors, inserting and playing an audiocassette or compact disc, or starting a computer program.

First, plan the instruction using a response-prompting procedure. Include attentional cues, task directions, task analyses, prompts, and consequences. Next, add variables to increase the efficiency of instruction. Consider instructional materials, settings, and instructors, as well as the addition of nontargeted information. When you have finished designing the instruction, practice delivering the instruction you have designed to a peer.

References

Bambara, L. M., Warren, S. F., & Komisar, S. (1988). The individualized curriculum sequencing model: Effects on skill acquisition and generalization. *Journal of the Association for Persons with Severe Handicaps, 13,* 8–19.

Baumgart, D., Brown, L., Pumpian, I., Nisbet, J., Ford, A., Sweet, M., Messina, R., & Schroeder, J. (1982). Principle of partial participation and individualized adaptations in educational programs for severely handicapped students. *Journal of the Association for Persons with Severe Handicaps, 7,* 17–27.

Billingsley, F. F., Burgess, D., Lynch. V. W., & Matlock, B. L. (1991). Toward generalized outcomes: Considerations and guidelines for writing instructional objectives. *Education and Training in Mental Retardation, 26,* 351–360.

Branham, R., Collins, B. C., Schuster, J. W., & Kleinert, H. (1999). Teaching community skills to students with moderate disabilities: Comparing combined techniques of classroom simulation, videotape modeling, and community-based instruction. *Education and Training in Mental Retardation and Developmental Disabilities, 34,* 170–181.

Brown, F., McDonnell, J., & Billingsley, F. F., (1997). Responses to Wolery and Schuster. *Journal of Special Education, 31,* 80–83.

Collins, B. C. (2003). Using video strategies to teach functional skills to students with moderate to severe disabilities. 2003 Conference Proceedings of the American Council for Rural Special Education. Utah: ACRES.

Collins, B. C., Branson, T. A., & Hall, M. (1995). Teaching generalized reading of cooking product labels to adolescents with mental disabilities through the use of key words taught by peer tutors. *Education and Training in Mental Retardation and Developmental Disabilities, 30,* 65–75.

Collins, B. C., Branson, T. A., Hall, M., & Rankin, S. W. (2001). Teaching secondary students with moderate disabilities in an inclusive academic classroom setting. *Journal of Developmental and Physical Disabilities, 13,* 41–59.

Collins, B. C., Epstein, A., Reiss, T., & Lowe, V. (2001). Including children with mental disabilities in the religious community. *Teaching Exceptional Children, 33,* 52–58.

Collins, B. C., Gast, D. L., Ault, M. J., & Wolery, M. (1991). Small group instruction: Guidelines for teachers of students with moderate to severe handicaps. *Education and Training in Mental Retardation, 26,* 18–32.

Collins, B. C., Gast, D. L., Wolery, M., Holcombe, A., & Leatherby, J. (1991). Using constant time delay to teach self-feeding to young students with severe/profound handicaps: Evidence of limited effectiveness. *Journal of Developmental and Physical Disabilities, 3,* 157–179.

Collins, B.C., Hall, M., & Branson, T. A. (1997). Teaching leisure skills to adolescents with moderate disabilities. *Exceptional Children, 63,* 499–512.

Collins, B. C., Hall, M., Branson, T., & Holder, M. (1999 [published in 2001]). Acquisition of related and nonrelated nontargeted information presented by a teacher within an inclusive setting. *Journal of Behavioral Education, 9,* 223–237.

Collins, B. C., Hall, M., Rankin, S. W., & Branson, T. A. (1999). Just say "No!" and walk away: Teaching students with mental disabilities to resist peer pressure. *Teaching Exceptional Children, 31,* 48–52.

Collins, B. C., Hendricks, T. B., Fetko,. K., & Land, L. (2002). Student-2-student learning in inclusive classrooms. *Teaching Exceptional Children, 34*(4), 56–61.

Collins, B. C., Schuster, J. W., & Grisham-Brown, J. (2004). *Success story: Ned.* Unpublished manuscript.

Collins, B. C., Schuster, J. W., & Nelson, C. M. (1992). Teaching a generalized response to the lures of strangers to adults with severe handicaps. *Exceptionality, 3,* 67–80.

Collins, B. C., & Stinson, D. M. (1994–1995). Teaching generalized reading of product warning labels to adolescents with mental disabilities through the use of key words. *Exceptionality, 5,* 163–181.

Collins, B. C., Stinson, D. M., & Land, L. (1993). A comparison of in vivo and simulation prior to in vivo instruction in teaching generalized safety skills. *Education and Training in Mental Retardation, 28,* 128–142.

Cromer, K., Schuster, J. W., Collins, B. C., & Grisham-Brown, J. (1998). Teaching information on medical prescriptions using two instructive feedback schedules. *Journal of Behavioral Education, 8,* 37–61.

Day, H. M., & Horner, R. H. (1986). Response variation and the generalization of a dressing skill: Comparison of single instance and general-case instruction. *Applied Research in Mental Retardation, 7,* 189–202.

Etzel, B. C., & LeBlanc, J. M. (1979). The simplest treatment alternative: The law of parsimony applied to choosing appropriate instructional control and errorless learning procedures for the difficult-to-teach child. *Journal of Autism and Developmental Disorders, 9,* 361–382.

Fetko, K. S., Schuster, J. W., Harley, D. A., & Collins, B. C. (1999). Using simultaneous prompting to teach a chained vocational task to young adults with severe intellectual disabilities. *Education and Training in Mental Retardation and Developmental Disabilities, 34,* 318–329.

Fickel, K. M., Schuster, J. W., & Collins, B. C. (1998). Teaching different tasks using different stimuli in a heterogeneous small group. *Journal of Behavioral Education, 8*(2), 219–244.

Fiscus, R., Schuster, J. W., Morse, T., & Collins, B. C. (2002). Teaching elementary students with cognitive disabilities food preparation skills while embedding instructive feedback in the prompt and consequence event. *Education and Training in Mental Retardation and Developmental Disabilities, 37,* 55–69.

Gee, K., Graham, N., Sailor, W., & Goetz, L. (1995). Use of integrated, general education, and community settings as primary contexts for skill instruction for students with severe, multiple disabilities. *Behavior Modification, 19,* 33–58.

Giangrego, M. F., Cloninger, C. J., & Iverson, V. S. (1992). *Choosing options and accommodations for children (COACH): A guide to planning inclusive education.* Baltimore: Brookes.

Grisham-Brown, J., Schuster, J. W., Hemmeter, M. L., & Collins, B. C. (2000 [published in 2001]). Using an embedding strategy to teach preschoolers with significant disabilities. *Journal of Behavioral Education, 10,* 139–162.

Hemmeter, M. L., Ault, M. J., Collins, B. C., & Meyer. S. (1996). The effects of teacher-implemented language instruction within free-time activities. *Education and Training in Mental Retardation and Developmental Disabilities, 31,* 203–212.

Horner, R. H., Carr, E. G., Halle, J., McGee, G., Odom, S., & Wolery, M. (2005). The use of single-subject research to identify evidence-based practice in special education. *Exceptional Children, 71,* 165–179.

Jones, G. Y., & Collins, B. C. (1997). Teaching microwave skills to adults with disabilities: Acquisition of nutrition and safety facts presented as non-targeted information. *Journal of Physical and Developmental Disabilities, 9,* 59–78.

Kaiser, A. P. (2000). Teaching functional communication skills. In M. E. Snell & F. Brown (Eds.), *Instruction of students with severe disabilities* (5th ed.). Upper Saddle River, NJ: Merrill/Prentice-Hall.

Liberty, K. A., Haring, N. G., & Martin, M. M. (1981). Teaching new skills to the severely handicapped. *Journal of the Association for Persons with Severe Handicaps, 6,* 5–13.

Liberty, K. A., Haring, N. G., White, O. R., & Billingsley, F. (1988). A technology for the future: Decision rules for generalization. *Education and Training in Mental Retardation, 23,* 315–326

Maciag, K. G., Schuster, J. W., Collins, B. C., & Cooper, J. T. (2000). Training adults with moderate and severe mental retardation in a vocational skill using a simultaneous prompting procedure. *Education and Training in Mental Retardation and Developmental Disabilities, 35,* 306–316.

Martella, R. C., Nelson, J. R., & Marchand-Martella, N. E. (2003). *Managing disruptive behaviors in the schools.* Boston: Allyn & Bacon.

Mechling, L. C., Gast, D. L., & Langone, J. (2002). Computer-based video instruction to teach persons with moderate intellectual disabilities to read grocery aisle signs and locate items. *The Journal of Special Education, 35,* 224–240.

Miller, C., Collins, B. C., & Hemmeter, M. L. (2002). Using a naturalistic time delay procedure to teach nonverbal adolescents with moderate to severe mental disabilities to spontaneously initiate manual signs. *Journal of Physical and Developmental Disabilities, 14,* 247–261.

Miller, U. C., & Test, D. W. (1989). A comparison of constant time delay and most-to-least prompting in teaching laundry skills to students with moderate retardation. *Education and Training in Mental Retardation, 24,* 363–370.

Miracle, S. A., Collins, B. C., Schuster, J. W., & Grisham-Brown, J. (2001). Peer- versus teacher-delivered instruction: Effects on acquisition and maintenance. *Education and Training in Mental Retardation and Developmental Disabilities, 36,* 375–385.

Mitchell, R. J., Schuster, J. W., Collins, B.C., & Gassaway, L. J. (2000). Teaching vocational skills with a faded auditory prompting system. *Education and Training in Mental Retardation and Developmental Disabilities, 35,* 415–427.

Mobayed, K. L., Collins, B. C., Strangis, D., Schuster, J. W., & Hemmeter, M. L. (2000). Teaching parents to employ mand-model procedures to teach their children requesting. *Journal of Early Intervention, 23,* 165–179.

Norman, J. M., Collins, B. C., & Schuster, J. W. (2001). Using video prompting and modeling to teach self-help skills to elementary students with mental disabilities in a small group. *Journal of Special Education Technology, 16,* 5–18.

Palmer, T., Collins, B. C., & Schuster, J. W. (1999). The use of a simultaneous prompting procedure to teach receptive manual sign identification to adults with disabilities. *Journal of Developmental and Physical Disabilities, 11,* 179–191.

Parrott, K. A., Schuster, J. W., Collins, B. C., & Gassaway, L. J. (2000 [published in 2001]). Simultaneous prompting and instructive feedback when teaching young children with moderate and severe mental retardation. *Journal of Behavioral Education, 10,* 3–19.

Reid, D. H., & Favell, J. E. (1984). Group instruction with persons who have severe disabilities: A critical review. *Journal of the Association for Persons with Severe Handicaps, 9,* 167–177.

Roark, T. J., Collins, B. C., Hemmeter, M. L., & Kleinert, H. (2002). Including manual signing as non-targeted information when teaching receptive identification of packaged food items. *Journal of Behavioral Education. 11,* 19–38.

Singleton, D. K., Schuster, J. W., Morse, T. E., & Collins, B. C. (1999). A comparison of antecedent prompt and test and simultaneous prompting procedures in teaching grocery sight words to adolescents with mental retardation. *Education and Training in Mental Retardation and Developmental Disabilities, 34,* 182–199.

Smith, R. L., Collins, B. C., Schuster, J. W., & Kleinert, H. (1999). Teaching table cleaning skills to secondary students with moderate/severe disabilities: Facilitating observational learning during instructional downtime. *Education and Training in Mental Retardation and Developmental Disabilities, 34,* 342–353.

Stokes, T. F., & Baer, D. M. (1977). An implicit technology of generalization. *Journal of Applied Behavior Analysis, 10,* 349–367.

Stokes, T. F., & Osnes, P. G. (1986). Programming the generalization of children's social behavior. In P. S. Strain, M. J. Guralnick, & H. J. Walker (Eds.), *Children's social behavior: Development, assessment, and modification* (pp. 407–443). Orlando, FL: Academic Press.

Stonecipher, E. L., Schuster, J. W., Collins, B. C., & Grisham-Brown, J. (1999). Teaching gift wrapping skills in a quadruple instructional arrangement using constant time delay. *Journal of Developmental and Physical Disabilities, 11,* 139–158.

Taylor, P., Collins, B. C., Schuster, J. W., & Kleinert, H. (2002). Teaching laundry skills to high school students with disabilities: Generalization of targeted skills and nontargeted information. *Education and Training in Mental Retardation and Developmental Disabilities, 37,* 172–183.

White, O. R., & Haring, N. G. (1980). *Exceptional teaching* (2nd ed.). Columbus, OH: Charles E. Merrill.

Wolery, M., Ault, M. J., & Doyle, P. M. (1992). *Teaching students with moderate to severe disabilities: Use of response prompting strategies.* New York: Longman.

Wolery, M., Bailey, D. B., & Sugai, G. M. (1988). *Effective teaching: Principles and procedures of applied behavior analysis with exceptional students.* Boston: Allyn & Bacon.

Wolery, M., & Gast, D. L. (1984). Effective and efficient procedures for the transfer of stimulus control. *Topics in Early Childhood Special Education, 4,* 52–77.

Wolery, M., & Schuster, J. W. (1997). Instructional methods with students who have significant disabilities. *Journal of Special Education, 31,* 61–79.

Wolery, T. D., Schuster, J. W., & Collins, B. C. (2000 [published in 2001]). Effects of future learning of presenting non-target stimuli in antecedent and consequent conditions. *Journal of Behavioral Education, 10,* 77–94.

Wright, C., & Schuster, J. W. (1994). Accepting specific versus functional student responses when training chained tasks. *Education and Training in Mental Retardation and Developmental Disabilities, 29,* 43–56.

York, J., Doyle, M. B., & Kronberg, R. (1992). A curriculum development process for inclusive classrooms. *Focus on Exceptional Children, 25,* 1–16.

CHAPTER SEVEN

TEACHING STUDENTS WITH MODERATE AND SEVERE DISABILITIES IN SCHOOL SETTINGS:

Inclusion and Collaboration

On completion of this chapter, the reader will meet the following objectives:

- Provide definitions contrasting integration and inclusion.
- Differentiate among physical, social, and instructional integration.
- List benefits for students with moderate and severe disabilities that can be derived from inclusion.
- Identify challenging aspects to implementing an inclusive program for students with moderate and severe disabilities.
- Discuss strategies that can be employed to facilitate the successful inclusion of students with moderate and severe disabilities.

Previous chapters have discussed who falls into the category of moderate and severe disabilities, what should be taught in their curriculum, and how instruction should be delivered. This chapter will focus on where instruction should occur by addressing the topic of inclusion. Collaboration also will be addressed since general and special educators must work together when serving students in inclusive settings. Although this chapter will address inclusion as an instructional setting, it should be noted that persons with moderate and severe disabilities should be included also in the community environments where they live, work, and socialize. It is more likely that persons with moderate and severe disabilities will transition to inclusive settings as adults if they are in inclusive settings during their school years. In providing a foundation for inclusion, this chapter will clarify terminology, discuss the philosophy behind inclusion, highlight the issues involved in making inclusion successful, provide a sampling of the research on the topic to date, and offer suggestions for strategies to facilitate inclusion in the school setting. To identify some of the issues involved in inclusion, work through Activity 7.1 before proceeding further in this chapter.

ACTIVITY 7.1   Identifying the Issues Involved in Inclusion

Three newspaper articles on recreational activities highlight some of the issues involved in inclusion. Read through the following descriptions of the articles then answer the questions that follow.

ARTICLE ONE

The first article appeared as a feature on the cover page of a newspaper section on "Living Well" (Isaacs, 2002). The picture showed thirteen individuals that appeared to range in age from early elementary school through adulthood who were dressed in matching sweatshirts and were in a huddle with their hands pressed together in camaraderie. The picture caption identified the group as a cheerleading squad of people with disabilities, some of which could be identified in the picture (e.g., Down syndrome). Other pictures in the article showed the same individuals dressed in matching uniforms at a regional competition for cheerleaders with disabilities and included one picture where female members of the squad representing a variety of ages and physiques formed a human pyramid with visible assistance from adult volunteers. The accompanying article provided details about the group, including the following information. The co-ed group ranged in ages from 9 to 31 years, trained year round, and was one of the few groups for participants with disabilities to train in a cheerleading center for persons without disabilities. The group had performed exhibitions at competitions for cheerleaders without disabilities across the nation (e.g., Florida, Georgia) and cheered for special events (e.g., university gymnastic events). The group was affiliated with a Special Olympics cheerleading squad, and its members also competed in other Special Olympics sports. Throughout the article parents and coaches described how meaningful it was for them to watch the cheerleading squad perform and how much the members of the squad enjoyed the activity.

ARTICLE TWO

The second article appeared on the cover of the "Lifestyle for Young Readers" section of a newspaper (Jackson, 2002). The picture accompanying the article showed a young female adolescent with Down syndrome dressed in a cheerleading uniform and suspended in the air by four teenage cheerleaders wearing the same uniform. The caption gave the names of those in the picture, but neither the caption nor the title of the article mentioned that anyone had a disability. The article described how the young lady suspended in the air was a new special education student in high school who enjoyed watching the cheerleaders practice. Most of the article described how the high school was making major efforts to include students with disabilities in classes and activities and noted that the administration had placed the young lady in the picture on the cheerleading squad based on her interest instead of having her go through the usual cheerleading tryouts. The response from the school was described as understanding and embracing.

ARTICLE THREE

The third article appeared as a feature on the cover page of a newspaper's "Communities" section (Corbett, 2003). The article focused on a new school football

team, and the largest picture in the article showed two teenage males in football uniforms holding up their hands to indicate "number one" at a pep rally. It was obvious that one of the young men had Down syndrome, but no mention of his disability was made in the picture caption or in the article. Instead, the caption identified the young man as the team manager, and the article focused on the success of a first-time football team.

Questions

As you compare and contrast these three articles, consider the following questions:

1. In what ways do each of the articles show persons with disabilities being included in recreational activities?

2. Does the segregated squad give its members opportunities they would not otherwise have? Is a squad made up of members with disabilities stigmatizing? What are the benefits to its members and their parents? Should there be an age limit on who can participate on a recreational team?

3. Should tryouts be waived to include persons with disabilities on an inclusive squad? Is it stigmatizing for a person with disabilities to appear as a "mascot" to their same-age peers? What would happen if all of the students in the school with moderate and severe disabilities showed an interest in cheering? Would they all be placed on the squad? Should students who do not possess competitive athletic skills be included as part of the team in competitions?

4. Is the role of manager a good compromise for a student who is interested in a sport but may not have the talent, ability, or physical vitality to participate on the team? Why or why not?

5. How are persons with disabilities portrayed by the media in each of the articles? Which of the articles is most appealing to you? Why?

6. Wolf Wolfensberger (1995) has criticized the Special Olympics for hurting the image of persons with disabilities and reinforcing stereotypes by having children compete with adults, having "escort huggers," and trivializing competition in an era in which we are striving for normalization for persons with disabilities. Reflect on this as you brainstorm a model for including persons with disabilities in normalized recreational activities.

EVOLUTION OF TERMINOLOGY AND PLACEMENT SETTINGS

Since de-institutionalization began, the practice of including persons with disabilities in educational settings and the community has evolved, and new terminology has been introduced to describe practices. The following sections define terms and describe the evolution of practices.

Terminology

Terminology has evolved in conjunction with practices. When services began to be offered within community educational settings rather than in institutions, the term **mainstreaming** gained favor as a way to describe the physical placement of persons with disabilities in settings with persons without disabilities. Brady, McDougall, and Dennis (1989) stated that there are three characteristics to note when placing a person with disabilities in a least restrictive environment: "(a) physical space integration, (b) social integration, and (c) instructional integration" (p. 43). Although Cook (2001) defined inclusion as "the physical placement of students with disabilities in general education classrooms" (p. 203), physical placement alone may not ensure social or instructional integration, much less inclusion. It is possible for **physical integration** (i.e., placement of students with disabilities in the same setting as students without disabilities) to occur and students with disabilities still experience **functional exclusion** (i.e., lack of interaction and involvement in a setting). As described in later sections in this chapter, planning must take place and strategies must be implemented if **social integration** (i.e., meaningful interactions among students with and without disabilities) and **instructional integration** (i.e., involvement of students with disabilities in the same lesson as their peers without disabilities) are to occur.

Hamre-Nietupski et al. (1999) defined the **neighborhood school** (i.e., local school, home school) as "the one a student would attend if he/she did not require special services" (p. 235). Janney and Snell (1997) defined *integration* as occurring when students attend general education schools other than their neighborhood schools and that **partial integration** or **full integration** can occur in those school settings, based on the amount of time students spend in general education classes. They also defined **inclusion** as occurring when students are fully integrated into general education classes in their neighborhood schools, although educators often use *inclusion* as a term to describe the provision of partial services in general education settings. Because they considered inclusion to be an embracing term for full-time placement in the general education setting, Janney and Snell did not further define partial inclusion.

When Freeman and Alkin (2000) conducted a literature review on the integration and inclusion of students with mental retardation over a 40-year span (1957 to 1997), they also noted that there was a difference between integration and inclusion. Freeman and Alkin defined *inclusion* as a full-time placement in general education and *integration* as a partial placement in general education but did not specify that the setting needed to be a neighborhood school.

In a survey of experts on inclusion (i.e., authors who have written on the topic in texts and referred journals), Jackson, Ryndak, and Billingsley (2000) found some variance in how those individuals defined *inclusion*. Components of definitions from the experts included placement in the typical natural setting, all students being placed together for instruction and learning, the provision of supports and modifications, a sense of belonging, and provision of collaborative integrated services. Some of the experts also noted that inclusion is a philosophy in which general and special education services are meshed in a unified system.

In reporting national data on inclusion, McLeskey, Henry, and Hodges (1999) defined several placement options for students with disabilities in accordance with those used by the U.S. Department of Education in *Reports to Congress* during 1991 and 1997. The options were based on the percent of time students received special education and related services outside of the general education classroom during the school day as follows: (a) general education—less than 21% in segregated class, (b) resource room—from 21% to 60% in segregated class, (c) separate class—more than 60% in segregated class, and (d) separate school—more than 50% in segregated school. Again, these definitions did not specify if general education, resource rooms, or separate classes had to be within the neighborhood school. In addition, the definition of *inclusion* in general education allowed students to spend some time each day in a segregated class.

This chapter will use *inclusion* to refer to general education class placement in the neighborhood school for students with moderate and severe disabilities (i.e., students listed on the role of the general education classroom teacher and considered to be part of the general education class) with the understanding that a minimal amount of time may be spent outside of the general education class setting (e.g., resource room, community-based instruction). In addition, the chapter will use *integration* to describe efforts to involve peers without disabilities in settings in the neighborhood school outside of the general education class (e.g., peer tutoring in resource room, peer buddy in community-based instruction).

Placement Settings

The practice of inclusion has evolved over several decades, beginning with deinstitutionalization in the 1960s. At one time segregated services were considered to be best practice. Persons with mental disabilities were placed in institutional settings where they could receive specialized services that were not available in their home communities. As time passed, communities began to offer services (e.g., segregated schools or classes, sheltered workshops and group homes), so children with moderate and severe disabilities could remain with or near their families in their home communities. In 1989 Larson and Lakin reviewed 15 data-based reports on deinstitutionalization that documented the benefits of community placements for persons with mental retardation. Among the desired outcomes were increases in adaptive behavior, self-care, domestic skills, and positive behaviors, as well as reductions in problem behavior. The authors maintained that these outcomes resulted in positive changes in the lifestyle that included health and safety, social relationships, recreation and leisure, and quality of life.

In 1983 Brown et al. laid a foundation for inclusion. They stated that it was not enough to educate persons with severe disabilities in segregated community schools or centralized segregated classes within general education schools and built a case for educating students with severe disabilities in chronological-age-appropriate schools that they would attend if they did not have disabilities. Their logical arguments included the following premises. First, any skill that can be taught in a segregated school can be taught in a regular school, including skills taught by related service delivery personnel (e.g., speech and language). More specifically, related services could be enhanced in a regular school (e.g., models for language and social skills, communication partners, activities for embedding motor skills). Next, the school setting should reflect the real world by adhering to the **principle of natural proportions;** in other words, the percentage of persons with disabilities in school settings should be no greater than would occur naturally in the typical community. For example, 1% of the population would be expected to have a severe disability. From a legal standpoint, students are entitled to a free and appropriate public education in the least restrictive environment, and for most, segregation is restrictive. From a social standpoint, sustained interactions with persons without disabilities are necessary for friendships to form, and friendships can be a form of natural support once students transition from school. Finally, the education program should be individualized (as stated by the team on the Individualized Education Program [IEP]) and tailored to the unique characteristics of the student; thus, a "one size fits all" segregated setting is not appropriate for all students.

Brown et al. continued their position paper by highlighting the benefits of education in chronological-age-appropriate regular schools for students with severe disabilities. First, they stated that accessibility is increased when students attend the schools closest to their homes, making it possible for them to (a) participate in more instruction (instead of spending time devoted to transportation), (b) form friendships that carry over in their neighborhoods after school hours, (c) engage in instruction and related services in nonschool environments within their communities, (d) participate in extracurricular school activities, and (e) have their parents more involved.

Second, the authors argued that maximal participation is enhanced in inclusive settings because peers can be used to decrease noninstructional downtime. Third, they addressed factors related to cost by arguing that placing students in regular home schools cuts costs associated with duplication (e.g., administrative and custodial staff) and better uses existing resources (e.g., cafeteria, gymnasium, athletic field) to their full potential. Fourth, the authors stated there are beneficial social and psychological effects that occur when students with disabilities have role models for such things as age-appropriate dress, and this builds self-esteem while increasing the likelihood of social acceptance. Fifth, the authors noted that related services are enhanced in regular school settings because students have opportunities to use skills they are taught (e.g., language) in natural environments. Sixth, they listed benefits to students without disabilities that included a decrease in social stigma for being perceived as different, formation of positive attitudes in students who will someday be service providers and parents, and the tendency for students without disabilities to put their own problems in perspective when they get to know others with greater challenges (e.g., a temporary skin blemish in relation to a permanent physical disability). Finally, Brown et al. identified a benefit to students with disabilities as the ability to have interactions with those who would not be available in a segregated environment.

As a result of the advocacy efforts of parents and professionals, best practice in special education for students with moderate and severe disabilities has evolved to include education in neighborhood schools, with inclusion in general education classes with students without disabilities. In 1988 Taylor described the evolution of the continuum of educational placements for persons with moderate and severe disabilities when he contrasted a traditional continuum of services to a newer, more acceptable community-based continuum. Table 7.1 is adapted from Taylor (1988) and allows the reader to see this contrast in educational settings.

Based on data from the *Annual Report to Congress* for the years 1988–89 to 1994–95, McLeskey, Henry, and Hodges (1998) found an increase in the number of

TABLE 7.1 *Comparison of Traditional and Community-Based Educational Continuums (based with permission on Taylor, 1988).*

Educational Continuums

Traditional		Community-Based
Hospital or Public Institution	Most Restrictive	Self-Contained Special Class in Regular School
Residential School Homebound Instruction		Self-Contained Special Class with Integration in Extracurricular Activities
Special School		
Special Class in Regular School		
Part-Time Special Class		Part-Time Special Class
Regular Class with Resource Room		Regular Class with Resource Room or Special Assistance
Full-Time Regular Class	Least Restrictive	Full-Time Regular Class

students being educated in general education classrooms and a decrease in the number being served in resource settings. For example, they stated that almost half of the students in a typical school attend general education classes for the majority of the day. They explained this trend by noting that a large number of students with mild disabilities have been moved from resource rooms to general education settings and that there has been an increase in the number of students identified as having learning disabilities since the 1980s.

In a further analysis of the same data, McLeskey, Henry, and Hodges (1999) also reported a trend toward serving students in less restrictive settings across categories of disabilities. In particular, they noted fewer placements in separate schools with the exception of placement for students with visual impairments, deafblindness, multiple disabilities, and serious emotional disturbances. They also noted that, even though progress has been made in moving students with mental retardation and deafblindness out of separate schools, those groups still had a small number of placements in general education classrooms when compared to other groups of disabilities.

In an analysis of the data from the 1994–95 *Reports to Congress,* McLeskey and Henry (1999) found that the placement of students with disabilities differs drastically across the United States, with the most restrictive practices found in Washington, D.C.; New Jersey; New York; and New Mexico and the least restrictive practices found in Vermont, North Dakota, Idaho, and South Dakota. To illustrate the dilemma this causes, McLeskey and Henry noted that a student in Pennsylvania was four times more likely to be placed in a separate class than a student in Minnesota. McLeskey and Henry concluded that, although many professionals agree that general education classrooms may not be appropriate for all students with disabilities, more progress is needed toward placing students in less restrictive settings. Example 7.1 presents some observations on rural services for students with moderate and severe disabilities that illustrates the trends identified by McLeskey et al. (1999) and the issues raised by McLeskey and Henry (1999).

EXAMPLE 7.1 INCLUSION OF STUDENTS WITH MODERATE AND SEVERE DISABILITIES IN RURAL SCHOOL SETTINGS

Writing from a personal historical perspective, Collins and Schuster (2001) shared their experiences as rural teachers and their observations of rural teacher educators across four decades. After describing the evolution of options for including students with moderate and severe disabilities in rural settings across the decades, they stated that the rural districts of Kentucky in which they currently prepare teachers continue to be plagued by a scarcity of teachers with special education certification, resulting in a continuum of models being implemented.

With the dawning of a new century, they noted that the type of services available for students with moderate and severe disabilities remains diverse across rural school districts. A few districts have adopted a full inclusion model with students placed in their neighborhood schools and spending the entire day in general education classes with special education services. A few districts continue to operate segregated classes with students with moderate and severe disabilities clustered in designated schools, most often based on the availability of a certified teacher. The majority of schools fall somewhere in the middle of the continuum, with special education classes in neighborhood schools where students participate in selected general education classes or activities for part of the school day.

While the public segregated school model has been abandoned, the inclusive general education model has not yet been embraced. The reasons are varied. Some teachers are not willing to change, while others embrace new practices. Some teachers struggle with lack of support from administrators and general education teachers, while others are given the support they need for inclusion to be successful. Most teachers try to balance the need for functional skill training and community-based instruction with the need for inclusion and instruction on core content in general education classes, finding ways to mesh the two. With the challenge of finding a sufficient number of certified teachers and the challenge of changing ingrained attitudes, it is clear that the implementation of inclusive services in rural districts is a continuing process.

The Law and Inclusion

Brady et al. (1989) stated that five issues have arisen in court cases on inclusion. First, the educational setting must be appropriate, and the courts have stressed the least restrictive environment as being more appropriate over parents' requests for more restrictive placements. Second, in regard to exportability of services, the court has ruled that segregated facilities are inappropriate if services can be feasibly provided in integrated settings. Third, students with disabilities need opportunities for growth, and segregated settings do not provide students with severe disabilities with the appropriate role models they need to imitate the behavior of others. Fourth, the individual needs of the students have priority over district preferences for service delivery. Fifth, schools have the alternative of complying with integration by placing classrooms for students with disabilities within general education settings, using reverse integration by placing students without disabilities in previously segregated settings, or recruiting volunteers without disabilities to work with students with disabilities. The court has ruled that segregated settings can be used only when (a) there are no available alternatives (e.g., the parent would be reimbursed for taking child with deafness to another district that has a teacher certified in deaf education), (b) the student characteristics preclude integration (e.g., child is a danger to self or others), or (c) the severity of the disability precludes integration (e.g., child's disability, such as a serious medical condition, so severe that child cannot benefit).

After analysis of the Individuals with Disabilities Education Act (IDEA) and regulations relating to the least restrictive environment, Yell (1995) concluded that the law supports a continuum of placements for students with disabilities and that students with disabilities should be served in general education settings only when inclusion is appropriate to the students' educational and social needs. Yell also described standards (e.g., Daniel R. R. Test) that have been used by courts to determine compliance with the least restrictive environment. These have included (a) whether the student with disabilities can derive educational and nonacademic benefits in inclusive settings through the use of supplementary aids and services, (b) if the presence of the students with disabilities will have a detrimental effect on the general education environment and the education of other students, and (c) the cost of mainstreaming the student with disabilities. After reviewing court decisions in a number of cases (e.g., *Daniel R. R. v. State Board of Education*, 1989; *Greer v. Race City School District*, 1991; *Oberti v. Board of Education of Clementon School District*, 1993; *Sacramento City Unified School District v. Rachel H.*, 1994), Yell concluded that placement should be based on each child's needs, schools must make efforts to keep students in integrated settings, a continuum of placements should be available in school districts, the student's peers without disabilities should be considered, students should be integrated to the maximum extent possible, and schools must be able to provide proof to substantiate their placement decisions. To gain insight on some of the issues involved in making inclusive placements, work through Activity 7.2.

Activity 7.2   Working with Inclusion Placement Issues

A number of issues can arise in placing students with moderate and severe disabilities in inclusive settings, especially in rural settings where there may be a lack of certified personnel to provide support. In the following case, pretend you are a due process officer who must determine the most appropriate placement for Brandon, a 6-year-old male with Down syndrome who lives in a rural county. Although he has limited expressive verbal skills, Brandon has good receptive language and the potential for learning a variety of skills. His disruptive behavior (noncompliance, severe tantrums) and his limited attention span (three to five minutes) are perceived as barriers to inclusion. At the time of the hearing, Brandon had a successful experience in an inclusive preschool.

His parents were not satisfied, however, when he began elementary school and was placed in a partially integrated placement (i.e., non-neighborhood school with partial participation in general education classes) in a school with the only certified special education teacher in the county. Thus, they have chosen for him to receive homebound services until the county agrees to put him in an inclusive placement (i.e., full general education placement in his neighborhood school). A two-day trial in a kindergarten in the desired setting was considered a failure by the staff in that school because of the classroom disruption Brandon caused.

To make your decision, consider the information obtained from each of the following witnesses.

County (Non-neighborhood School) Personnel

County school principal. She is willing to have Brandon attend her school and to make accommodations necessary for a fully integrated placement.

Teacher certified in moderate and severe disabilities in county school. He is willing to provide consultative services for a fully integrated placement.

Kindergarten teacher with dual certification (special and general education) in county school. She is willing to have Brandon integrated into her class although he is a year older than the other students.

Neighborhood School Personnel

Neighborhood school principal. He cannot find a certified special education teacher available to provide support for Brandon in his school.

General education primary teacher in neighborhood school. She does not want Brandon in her class due to disruptive behavioral issues that were present during the trial period in her classroom.

Instructional assistant. She was unable to control Brandon's behavior during the two-day trial in the inclusive primary setting and wants more behavioral support if he returns.

School District Personnel

School psychologist. He is willing to work with staff in either setting on a behavioral program for Brandon.

Special education director. She is willing to hire consultative services to set up an integrated program for Brandon in either setting.

Speech therapist, physical therapist, and homebound teacher (no certification). They are displeased with Brandon's progress in the homebound setting and are anxious for Brandon to be served in any school setting. What would you suggest?

BENEFITS OF INCLUSION

Many authors have reviewed the professional literature on the benefits of inclusive practices for persons with moderate and severe disabilities. For example, Freeman and Alkin (2000) identified higher academic gains reported for students with moderate and severe disabilities in general education settings. In reviewing the preschool literature on inclusion, Diamond, Hestenes, and O'Connor (1994) stated that the benefits for young children include higher levels of play and social interactions as well as gains in language, cognitive, and motor skills when compared to self-contained settings. Although preschool students with disabilities are less likely to participate in play with peers without disabilities, they are more likely to initiate play and communicate with their peers in inclusive settings. Diamond et al. also noted that children without disabilities make the same gains in inclusive programs that they would make in noninclusive programs while becoming more accepting of human differences and the needs of others.

In reviewing the research on inclusion of students with severe disabilities across four professional journals, Hunt and Goetz (1997) found similar results in that the presence and participation of students with severe disabilities in inclusive settings does not detract from the academic achievement of peers without disabilities. Hunt and Goetz also concluded that students with severe disabilities can achieve positive academic and learning outcomes; students with severe disabilities gain acceptance, interactions, and friendships; and students without disabilities experience positive outcomes.

The studies presented as examples in the following sections were conducted by researchers in the area of inclusion and further substantiate the benefits described by Freeman and Alkin (2000), Diamond et al. (1994), and Hunt and Goetz (1997). Note that the studies are grouped by the research methodology. While surveys and interviews provide insight into the perceptions of respondents (e.g., how people feel about practices or think the outcomes are), observational data provide stronger evidence that outcomes actually occur (e.g., increase in social or academic skills).

Benefits Reported in Surveys and Interviews

Researchers have surveyed and interviewed parents, general education teachers, and special education teachers in an effort to identify their perception of the benefits derived from inclusion. While these respondents have stated clear inclusion benefits, they also have noted problems that have occurred during implementation.

Benefits Identified by Family Members In 1998 Palmer, Borthwick-Duffy, Widaman, and Best surveyed parents of students with significant disabilities and mental retardation regarding their perceptions of inclusion. They found that the perceptions of parents are influenced by the individual characteristics of the child, the needs they perceive in the child, and the child's placement history. Parents who placed a higher value on socialization as an outcome were more willing to place their children in inclusive settings, while parents who placed a higher value on a functional curriculum were more apprehensive about inclusion and preferred the individualized attention and shelter they believed to be provided in a special education classroom. In another analysis of survey data from parents, Palmer, Fuller, Arora, and Nelson (2001) stated that parents with positive perceptions of inclusion believed their children would experience improvement in academic and functional skills and that general education students would benefit by becoming more sensitive after seeing how others deal with adversity.

While Seery, Davis, and Johnson (2000) found similar results from interviews of parents of preschool children with mental retardation, autism, blindness, or behavior disorders and the staff in an inclusive preschool program, they also found a discrepancy between the two groups of respondents. While the benefits of inclusion were listed as both social and cognitive, the parents were stronger than staff in the belief that their children received social benefits from inclusion although they voiced concerns over safety, adequate resources, and staff ratio. When asked if all preschool programs should be inclusive, more parents responded with an unconditional "yes" while more staff responded with a conditional "yes."

Benefits Identified by Teachers Across a school year, Hamre-Nietupski et al. (1999) interviewed three general education and three special education teachers regarding two elementary and two middle school students with moderate and severe disabilities who were included in their rural neighborhood schools for the first time. Based on the interviews, they found that the teachers were pleased with the students' progress in at least one area of performance, and as a result, they increased their expectations for the students. The teachers also reported positive experiences that included (a) increased interactions, acceptance, and support for the students with moderate and severe disabilities; (b) increased acceptance, knowledge, understanding, tolerance, and patience in their peers; and (c) a feeling of reward in the teachers as they watched the students with moderate and severe disabilities making progress and being accepted.

York, Vandercook, MacDonald, Heise-Neff, and Caughey (1992) obtained responses from 11 general education teachers and 7 special education teachers of students with moderate and severe disabilities regarding their experiences with inclusion in two middle schools. The general educators reported that, for the most part, the students with moderate and severe disabilities were involved in the same activities as their classmates, although some parallel activities occurred. The special education teachers stated that they became involved in inclusion to give their students more interactions with students without disabilities and the opportunity to learn more skills. Although developing strategies and schedules were difficult, both general and special education teachers stated that the best aspect of inclusion was acceptance by peers and that this resulted in social interactions and friendships outside of class. The classmates without disabilities affirmed this by stating that inclusion was a good idea, with positive benefits for the students with moderate and severe disabilities (e.g., more social talk, happiness, appropriate behavior, cooperation, responsibility, confidence, and independence) and their peers without disabilities (e.g., learning about disabilities).

Benefits Reported from Observational Data

Researchers have reported increases in both academic and social skills, validating the result of studies conducted through surveys and interviews. A sample of these follow.

Acquisition of Academic Skills   A series of studies by Collins and her colleagues provide evidence of the acquisition of academic skills in general education settings. In the first investigation (Collins, Branson, Hall, & Rankin, 2001), three secondary school students with moderate and severe disabilities learned to write letters in a general education composition class. Although the original plan was for the English teacher to provide instruction to the target students using a system-of-least-prompts procedure, data showed that this was inefficient since the students were spending long periods waiting for her to have time to provide prompts as she circulated around the room. Thus, instruction was modified to have the English teacher provide initial directions for writing the letter (e.g., "Today, you are going to write a fan letter to a television star.") and feedback on the completed letter (e.g., "You did a good job starting sentences with capital letters, but you need to remember to end sentences with a period."), while a peer tutor provided immediate prompts as the student worked on the letter.

In the second investigation (Collins, Hendricks, Fetko, & Land, 2002), a student teacher in special education first worked with secondary school peers in a general education social studies class to deliver facts (e.g., state capitol) to two students with moderate and severe disabilities and later with elementary school peers in a general education language arts class to deliver information (e.g., names of foods in pictures) to two students with moderate and severe disabilities. In both classes the peers received cards each day to prompt them to share the facts or information on the cards with the students with moderate and severe disabilities, and the students acquired this over time. In the third investigation (Collins, Hall, Branson, & Holder, 1999), two secondary school students with moderate and severe disabilities who were placed in separate advanced English classes acquired information (grammar rules, community information) systematically delivered at intermittent intervals by their general education teachers each day as they worked on written entries for their alternate assessment portfolios.

In each of the three investigations, the special education teachers were responsible for daily data collection and graphing. Either the teachers or the peers in the general education settings assumed the responsibility for systematically delivering either target skills or nontarget information.

Increase in Social Skills   Kennedy, Shukla, and Fryxell (1997) conducted observations to compare the social interactions and friendships of middle school students with severe disabilities in a general education setting and a self-contained special education setting. The general education setting provided the most benefits in that the students with disabilities interacted more frequently and had more social contacts with peers without disabilities, as well as larger networks of friendships and more durable relationships with peers without disabilities.

Benefits Reported from Longitudinal Studies

Some researchers have followed students with moderate and severe disabilities over a period of time in an effort to identify the benefits they derived from inclusion. In a case study, Ryndak, Morrison, and Sommerstein (1999) followed the progress of a 15-year-old female with a moderate to severe disability who moved from a placement in a self-contained program with integration in a single class and pull-out services to a general education placement with a resource class and integrated speech services. During her junior year, she began community-based instruction, and at the age of 20, she received service in an inclusive college program with a focus on functional skill instruction in natural settings with consultation services from special education. Examples of her work and anecdotal data showed that the young woman's literacy skills, intelligible speech, and appropriate behavior increased following placement in inclusive general education settings.

Staub, Spaulding, Peck, Gallucci, and Schwartz (1996) conducted a longitudinal study of four middle school students with moderate and severe disabilities who were included in general education and found inclusion to be facilitated by (a) building a philosophy through a task force, (b) having leadership to provide support, and (c) training student aides to serve in the roles of monitor, helper, friend, and teacher. They found that there were benefits for the students with moderate and severe disabilities that included increased independence, social and academic growth, opportunities for socialization with peers without disabilities, and positive behavioral changes, as well as benefits for the student aides that included a larger social network, acknowledgment from faculty, increased responsibility, and more appreciation for others.

CHALLENGING ASPECTS OF INCLUSION

While the data appear to show benefits of inclusion for students with moderate and severe disabilities (e.g., gains in academic and social skills), students without disabilities (e.g., gains in knowledge and positive attitudes), and teachers (e.g., collaboration with colleagues), numerous researchers have identified a number of challenging aspects to the successful implementation of inclusion. For example, Mamlin (1999) described the failure of inclusion at an elementary school and identified contributing factors as the unwillingness to make the restructuring decisions necessary for inclusion and a resistance to change.

In a review of 25 studies on integration and inclusion from 1957 to 1997, Freeman and Alkin (2000) concluded that the time in general education does not equal more acceptance from their peers for children with mental retardation. Although children with mental retardation who were fully included appeared to make higher academic gains and be more socially competent than their peers in segregated settings, their overall social status did not improve. The authors posed the question, "Does inclusion work?" and responded by stating "Partially—for academics and social competence, especially at the younger age groups, but not for social acceptance" (p. 15). They also concluded that full inclusion is better than partial inclusion for students with disabilities, especially if they are young. Further challenging aspects of inclusion identified through surveys of parents and teachers are described in the following sections.

Challenging Aspects Identified Through Surveys and Interviews

Just as researchers have surveyed and interviewed parents and teachers to identify their perceptions of the benefits of inclusion, they have used the same methodology also to identify their perceptions of the challenges. Again, it is important to note that data on perceptions can be strengthened by observational data.

Challenging Aspects Identified by Parents   When Palmer et al. (2001) surveyed parents of children with severe disabilities, they found that half had a positive perception of inclusion. Those who were not supportive of inclusion identified factors such as the child's medical needs, sensory impairments, lack of self-help skills, lack of language, or presence of a physical condition (e.g., seizures, cerebral palsy). Because of these factors, they believed that (a) inclusion would burden general education teachers and negatively impact general education students; (b) the child required care and attention not possible in general education settings; (c) the child's need for functional skill instruction could not be met in academic settings with a focus on a core curriculum; (d) the child would be neglected, mistreated, harmed, or ridiculed by peers; and (e) specially trained personnel and special services would not be available in general education settings. In Example 7.2 the author describes similar challenging aspects that parents identified during interviews in Kentucky.

EXAMPLE 7.2   CHALLENGING ASPECTS IDENTIFIED BY PARENTS IN KENTUCKY

In 1991 the three remaining segregated schools for students with moderate and severe disabilities across the state of Kentucky were being closed, and many of the parents of the students were vocal and visible in the media as they voiced their opposition to moving their children to integrated school settings (e.g., Warren, 1991). This created the opportunity for parents in the three schools to be interviewed prior to the end of the school year and the closing of the schools. As described by Collins (1995), a group of the parents consented to be interviewed on their predictions as to whether or not their children would be mistreated, isolated, or lose services in the new setting. One year later the parents again were contacted to see if their predictions had come true during the first year of integration. Ironically, those parents who had been most vocal in fighting the practice of integration in the media refused to participate in the interviews.

When the interview data from the two sets of interviews were compared and analyzed, the perceptions of the majority of parents appeared to have changed in a positive way. Although many voiced fears and concerns prior to integration, most parents during postintegration interviews stated that their children (a) did not suffer verbal or physical abuse, harmful practices, or resentment from others; (b) made friends and had access to extracurricular activities; and (c) retained most related services. In spite of this, there were individual accounts of problems, such as being placed in overcrowded substandard segregated classrooms and not having interactions with peers without disabilities (e.g., peer tutoring or peer buddies). The author concluded that the success of integration was dependent on the quality of the program.

Challenging Aspects Identified by Teachers and Staff   In surveys of general and special educators at the state and national levels, Werts, Wolery, Snyder, and Caldwell (1996) identified barriers to successful inclusion as being (a) lack of training, time, and administrative support and (b) the inability to meet students' needs. In a survey of teachers certified in moderate and severe disabilities in Iowa, Agran, Alper, and Wehmeyer (2002) found that, although most participated in general education on a frequent basis, there were problems that included (a) few efforts to provide access to the curriculum, (b) lack of involvement in planning activities, (c) lack of a district plan to involve students in general education, and (d) confusion over student evaluation based on the general education curriculum or the IEP. In addition, the teachers identified specific barriers as resistance from general education and administrators, the challenging behaviors of students with moderate and severe disabilities, and the reliance on primary support from instructional assistants. When Pearman, Huang, and Mellblom (1997) surveyed staff in a Colorado district, the respondents voiced concern over such items as having the time to plan and meet the needs of all students, having the training to work with all students, and having additional paperwork.

Challenging Aspects Identified Through Interviews

Researchers have identified challenging aspects of inclusion through interviewing both teachers and students. In the examples described below, the interviews used social nominations to identify attitudes and practices.

Teacher Attitudes   Cook (2001) found that confronting the attitudes of teachers can be a challenge when he asked 70 general education teachers of inclusive classes across six elementary schools to nominate those students for whom they felt (a) attachment (i.e., find it a pleasure to teach, deliver more praise and less criticism—the student they would keep as a student for the joy of it), (b) concern (i.e., believe they can make a difference between the student's success and failure, deliver more praise, ask more questions—the student to whom they devote more time), (c) indifference (i.e., overlook the student or have brief, infrequent interactions—the student they would be least prepared to discuss), and (d) rejection (i.e., have given up on the student, provide little feedback, deliver more criticism, give fewer turns—the student they would like to have removed from the class). The results showed that the teachers had more attachment to students with obvious disabilities and were more likely to reject those with hidden disabilities.

Student Attitudes   Student attitudes can be just as problematic as teacher attitudes. When Cook and Semmel (1999) had elementary school students in two California districts nominate their first and second choices of students they would like to play or work with and report the students they actually played with each day, they found that students with severe disabilities were better accepted in nonheterogeneous classes (i.e., students similar in abilities and ethnicity) than in heterogeneous classes (i.e., students with more diversity in terms of abilities and ethnicity). In addition, those students most often rejected were the ones with atypical behavior, causing the authors to conclude that students with more obvious disabilities are better accepted because peers have decreased expectations of those students. Even this type of acceptance may not be desirable due to students viewing peers with severe disabilities as "mascots" that they need to parent.

Challenging Aspects Identified Through Observations

As stated earlier, observations help substantiate perceptions and practices. In the following examples, the researchers investigated social and instructional challenges through observation.

Lack of Social Acceptance   Observations seem to provide support for the challenging attitudes of students identified through interviews. In addition to interviewing caregivers and teachers, Wolfberg et al. (1999) conducted observations of 10 children with disabilities (e.g., autism, mental retardation) and their peers in six preschools across geographic regions and found that a peer culture exists that may cause children with disabilities to be excluded by their peers without disabilities. For example, peers without disabilities may exhibit apathy and indifference by ignoring children with disabilities, overlook social cues from children with disabilities that keep them from being included in activities, have conflicts over having to share with children they do not perceive as friends, or congregate in cliques that exclude children who are different.

Hall and McGregor (2000) found similar attitudinal challenges when they conducted playground observations of the social behaviors (e.g., smiling and laughing, talking to others, sharing, showing affection) of three male students with moderate and severe disabilities in kindergarten and again in the upper elementary grades. The authors also collected data from peer nominations and interviews regarding friendships. They found that the time the students with moderate and severe disabilities spent alone increased as they grew older and that they talked to others less frequently. In addition, reciprocal nominations as friends decreased over time, and the peers who considered a child with a moderate or severe disability as a friend tended to have an association outside of the school settings (e.g., a family connection). Finally, students with moderate and severe disabilities did not tend to gravitate to same-gender friendships over time, as did their peers without disabilities.

Instructional Format   Several studies have documented the type of instruction delivered in inclusive general education settings, and many have found that it is not always conducive to learning by students with moderate and severe disabilities. For example, Logan and Keefe (1997) compared data from inclusive general education classrooms and segregated special education classrooms in elementary schools, with each data group containing 15 students with moderate to profound disabilities. They found that both groups received more instruction focusing on academics than functional skills and that the students included in general education classrooms received twice as much one-to-one instruction as students in segregated classrooms. In both settings, the target students had similar levels of engagement (36% to 38%), and the teachers used high rates of whole group instruction.

Over a five-month period, McDonnell, Thorson, and McQuivey (1998) conducted weekly observations of six elementary school students with moderate to profound disabilities who were included in general education classes in a neighborhood school for two subjects per day. They found that the general education teachers, who were the primary instructors, used whole class instruction more than 50% of the time. The students with disabilities had high rates of academic responding during one-to-one and small-group instruction but tended to be engaged in different instructional tasks during whole class instruction.

When McDonnell, Thorson, and McQuivey (2000) compared the observational data of six elementary school students with moderate and severe disabilities and six peers without disabilities in the same general education class across four elementary schools, they found that the students with moderate and severe disabilities were more likely to have instruction focused on them than were their peers without disabilities. Again, peers received more whole class instruction and students with severe disabilities received more one-to-one instruction, with the students with severe disabilities being more likely to receive instruction from a paraprofessional or a peer than from the general education teacher.

Helmstetter, Curry, Brennan, and Sampson-Saul (1998) observed nine elementary school students with severe and profound disabilities who were included in general education for an hour each day. They found distinct differences between general and special education classrooms. In the general education classroom, the general education teacher or peers delivered instruction—the teacher used more whole group instruction, while peers delivered one-to-one instruction—the focus was on academic skills, and students with disabilities spent more time in passive engagement (e.g., watching the instructor). In the special education classroom, the special education teacher or assistants delivered instruction, the instructors used more one-to-one instruction, the focus was across domains (e.g., academic, language, motor, self-help), and students with disabilities spent more time in active engagement (e.g., responding to the instructor). Although there was a great deal of time spent waiting for instruction and a number of missed opportunities to embed instruction in daily activities in the special education setting, total engagement was higher in that setting than in general education.

Logan and Malone (1998) collected data in four schools where a special education teacher or paraprofessional taught with a general education teacher in several classes that included four to six students with moderate and severe disabilities. They found that the students with moderate and severe disabilities in these settings spent the majority of their time in academic activities, general education teachers tended to use whole group instruction, the general education teacher conducted instruction more than half of the time, and prompting data were not recorded. In addition, the students with moderate and severe disabilities were the least engaged during whole group instruction, although the students with moderate disabilities were more engaged in academic instruction and worked more independently than the students with severe or profound disabilities.

Challenging Aspects Identified Through Longitudinal Studies

Several studies have identified challenges in inclusion of students with moderate and severe disabilities over time. The following examples highlight various age levels.

Mills, Cole, Jenkins, and Dale (1998) examined the progress of preschool students over three years who were randomly assigned to three types of classrooms: (a) special education students only, (b) integrated special education classrooms, and (c) inclusive general education classrooms. While all of the students benefited from some level of inclusion, students with milder disabilities seemed to reap the greatest benefits from an integrated placement, and students with more severe disabilities seemed to benefit as much from an inclusive placement as from a segregated placement.

Tapasak and Walther-Thomas (1999) described the first year of an inclusion program in an urban elementary school that included students with moderate and multiple disabilities. In the school model, each class had two coteachers (one general education and one special education). Prior to beginning the program, teachers attended a three-day workshop. After the school year began, the speech/language pathologist and inclusion specialist provided weekly social skills and communication instruction for the students while the teacher spent time in planning. At the end of the year, the primary school students fared better than older students in terms of self-esteem and feelings of competence. The teachers recommended that other schools implementing inclusion prepare professionals and provide ongoing classroom support, place a value on peer relationships and interactions, make social skills a priority, and pay attention to progress monitoring and reporting.

Hamre-Nietupski et al. (1999) maintained that rural schools may have unique problems in implementing inclusion due to lack of resources (e.g., university support, grant funding) available to large urban school districts; yet rural schools reflect the majority of American schools. Thus, the authors conducted a study of three small rural neighborhood schools in Iowa (two elementary and one middle school) to see how each successfully implemented inclusion for students with moderate and severe disabilities. To obtain data, they interviewed three general education and three special education teachers at points throughout the initial school year and found the following: (a) teachers needed advance preparation to transition the students to general education neighborhood schools, (b) teachers increased their expectations of the students with moderate and severe disabilities after observing at least one area in which performance increased, (c) there were positive results (e.g., acceptance, support) from interactions between the students with moderate and severe disabilities and their peers, and (d) teachers had positive experiences as they observed the students with moderate and severe disabilities making progress and being accepted. When listing the challenging aspects of implementing inclusion in rural neighborhood schools, the teachers identified (a) the process of making adaptations, (b) the need for someone with expertise in inclusion as a resource to consult with teachers, (c) continuing resistance to including students with moderate and severe disabilities in the neighborhood schools, and (d) the need for training and more information.

FACILITATING SUCCESSFUL INCLUSION OF STUDENTS WITH MODERATE AND SEVERE DISABILITIES

It should be evident that successful inclusion does not just happen. While there are benefits to be derived from inclusion, schools must go beyond the physical placement of students to ensure that social and instructional integration occurs.

Factors That Have Been Identified in Successful Inclusion

Numerous authors have listed factors that contribute to the successful inclusion of students with moderate and severe disabilities based on their work in the field. According to Hamre-Nietupski et al. (1999), the critical elements of successful inclusion are a shared vision, administrative commitment and support, staff preparation and training, time for communication and collaboration among staff, a structured planning process, ongoing direct service and consultative support and resources, and support of peers without disabilities.

Hunt and Goetz (1997) identified essential factors from a review of the professional literature for including students with severe disabilities as including the need for parental involvement, collaboration among personnel, and curricular adaptations. As mentioned earlier in this chapter, a survey of experts in inclusion for students with moderate and severe disabilities (i.e., those who had authored journal articles or books on the topic between 1990 and 1996) for their views on the topic resulted in a list of useful practices: (a) the promotion of inclusive values; (b) collaboration between general and special educators; (c) collaboration between educators and related service providers; (d) family involvement, (e) choosing and planning what to teach; (f) scheduling, coordinating, and delivering inclusive services within schools; (g) assessing and reporting student progress on an ongoing basis; (h) using instructional strategies; and (i) supporting students with challenging behaviors (Jackson et al., 2000).

Researchers have identified a number of factors that contribute to successful inclusion based on surveys, interviews, and observations involving those in the field. For example, an analysis of the survey results of teachers involved in the implementation of inclusion across 120 schools in New York City from 1994 through 2003 revealed that 74% felt that teachers must have positive attitudes (e.g., being dedicated to ensuring that all students learn) for successful inclusion to occur (Weiner, 2003). In an survey of teachers (elementary through secondary school) in school districts in Georgia, the factors that contributed to the success of inclusive placements of students with moderate and severe disabilities consisted of the (a) willingness of general education teachers to accept and work with the student, (b) characteristics (e.g., medical needs, arousal state) of the student being placed, (c) learning opportunities to work on objectives in the placement, (d) instructional format of the general education setting, (e) support for inclusion from administration and personnel, and (f) ability of the special education teacher to make adaptations to the curriculum (Brozovic, Stafford, Alberto, & Taber, 2000). In a final example, a state and national survey of general and special educators, resulted in recommendations for help from additional classroom personnel, assistance from a multidisciplinary team, and training if inclusion is to be successful (Werts et al., 1996).

The observation of two secondary school students, one with mild disabilities and one with moderate disabilities, who were fully integrated in general education for the first time and interviews with their teachers revealed two variables that led to their successful experiences (Dore, Dion, Wagner, & Brunet, 2002). The first variable was the adaptation of materials by a part-time teacher who faded over time after initially accompanying the students to class. The second variable was the use of strategies to improve social interaction, such as treating the students the same as general education students, demanding that respect be shown toward the students by their peers, permitting peer tutoring during general education classes, and seating students in "lively" corners of the classroom. Most of the teachers were satisfied with the experience, and the student with a moderate disability made more gains than the student with a mild disability.

Salisbury and McGregor (2002) focused on the type of administrative support needed for successful inclusion when they described the characteristics of five principals from inclusive schools. They found that these principals were (a) self-directed and not afraid to take risks or say "no," (b) interested in relationships and willing to "go the extra mile," (c) accessible and willing to "get their hands dirty," (d) reflective with a strong sense of direction, (e) collaborative with shared leadership with their staff, and (f) intentional with purposive hiring to lessen friction before making changes.

Strategies That May Be Helpful in Implementing Inclusion

In addition to identifying the factors that appear to result in successful inclusion, the professional literature also contains strategies that are recommended to increase the likelihood that the physical inclusion of students with moderate and severe disabilities will result in social and instructional inclusion that is beneficial for those students. These are discussed in the following sections.

Incentives for Teachers to Participate in Inclusion   When Pearman, Huang, and Mellblom (1997) surveyed staff in a Colorado district, they identified a number of incentives that would encourage inclusion. These included (a) staff training in working with all students, (b) funding for time and staff (especially in elementary school settings), (c) rewards for teachers, (d) site-based ability to choose staff and have flexibility in the school budget, (e) a reduction in program paperwork, (f) the ability to disaggregate testing results, (g) assistance in assessment, (h) more equipment, and (i) instruction with less emphasis on standardized testing.

Implementation of Inclusion in Phases Over Time   Wisniewski and Alper (1994) suggested implementing the inclusion process in three phases that include (a) developing community to overcome attitudinal barriers, (b) assessing school and community resources to show that it is more cost effective to serve students in neighborhood schools, and (c) reviewing strategies suggested for inclusion (e.g., team teaching, consultant teachers, flexible grouping, cooperative learning, peer tutors, special friends, assistive technology).

Clarification of Responsibilities   Federico, Herrold, and Venn (1999) suggested developing a checklist for implementing inclusion that clarifies the process. Their example included the (a) general responsibilities of those involved (e.g., teachers, administration, parents), (b) specific professional responsibilities (e.g., monitoring IEPs), (c) team member responsibilities (e.g., attending in-services), (d) teacher-student interactions (e.g., making adaptations), (e) fundamental responsibilities (e.g., maintaining sense of humor), and (f) end-of-year responsibilities (e.g., assigning grades).

Recognition of Geographic Needs   After conducting interviews with rural teachers who were implementing inclusion, Hamre-Nietupski et al. (1999) noted that (a) rural practitioners need information on best practices, (b) leadership from state departments of education need to assist rural districts, (c) expertise in including students with severe disabilities is needed, and (d) university programs need to focus on assisting distant rural programs as well as local urban districts. Zeph (1991) identified six options for including students with severe disabilities in general education classes in rural districts. These included (a) team teaching—general and special education teachers in equal roles during same lesson, (b) parallel teaching—general and special education teachers in equal roles during separate lessons,

(c) regular classroom-based tutorials—special education teacher assisting students with disabilities in general education, (d) separate tutorials with a regular classroom base—special education teacher offering assistance in resource room, (e) regular classroom placement with support services—special education staff in general education, (f) regular classroom placement with a dual-certified teacher—single teacher certified in both general and special education serving all students in same setting.

Peer Tutors or Peer Buddies   Peer tutors are those students who engage in an instructional relationship with other students, while peer buddies are those students who interact and provide support for other students on a social level. Both roles can be useful in an inclusive setting. As an example of a peer tutoring program, Gilberts, Agran, Hughes, and Wehmeyer (2001) used middle school students without disabilities to teach five of their peers with severe disabilities to self-monitor "classroom survival skills" (i.e., going to class and taking a seat when the bell rings, greeting the teacher and other students, asking and answering questions, recording classwork in a planner) in the general education classroom. As an example of a peer buddy program, Hughes et al. (1999) described a one-credit course in a Tennessee secondary school in which students without disabilities learned to facilitate the inclusion of their peers with severe disabilities in various activities that included classes, recreation, clubs, lunch, shopping, and community events.

The use of peer tutoring and peer buddy programs can have unexpected outcomes. Collins (2002) described a series of investigations she conducted with colleagues employing peer tutors and peer buddies to facilitate learning by students with moderate disabilities. One of the co-investigators in a number of these studies was an English teacher who, prior to the first investigation, had no experience with students with disabilities. In Example 7.3 this general education teacher describes how her involvement in the investigations that used her students without disabilities in peer roles changed her attitude and the practices in her classroom over time.

EXAMPLE 7.3   MESSAGE ON INCLUSION FROM A GENERAL EDUCATION TEACHER

NO! I thought as I smiled and said aloud, "Yes, I'd love to." A university professor had just asked me if I would like to take part in a research project involving students in regular education classes acting as peer tutors for students with disabilities. I was resistant to the idea, thinking that I had no idea how to work with students with disabilities and that the students in my classroom would be condescending and rude. I agreed to the idea because I needed to stretch my learning and because I had always been ashamed of my fear of students with disabilities. I didn't know what to say or do and feared hurting feelings or making a fool of myself.

Keeping that NO! silent has turned out to be one of my best educational decisions. That first research project produced more real learning than any textbook I might have used. Students wrote personal experience essays, poems, plays, and informative essays for people who had misconceptions about the nature of teenagers—with and without disabilities. I learned to have faith in myself and, more important, in high school students and their humanity.

That "yes" turned into two collaborative classes I have requested to teach every year for nine years now. Resistance became professional and personal rejuvenation.
Terri A. Branson, English teacher

Team Collaboration Collaboration can be across schools as well as across disciplines. Hunt, Doering, Hirose-Hatae, Maier, and Goetz (2001) described how an experienced collaborative inclusion team met with another inclusion team from a neighboring district to help develop "Unified Plans of Support" for including students with disabilities. Some of the team members were administrators, general and special educators, classroom assistants, and parents, and the plans included educational supports (e.g., adaptations, curricular and instructional modifications, peers) and social supports (e.g., buddy systems, circles of support, interactive media, social facilitation). Once the support plans were in place, students' engagement, student-initiated interactions, the use of adaptations, and academic skills increased.

Responsiveness to the Needs of All Students In a responsive classroom, teachers see students as individuals and strive to meet the needs of each. According to Winterman and Sapona (2002), a social curriculum is as important as an academic curriculum since cognitive growth occurs through social interactions.

Modification of General Education Lessons Instead of teaching alternate lessons in the general education setting, it is possible to involve students with moderate and severe disabilities in thematic units of study by modifying the lesson plans. Stainback and Stainback (1992) presented three examples of modified lessons for students with severe disabilities. In the first, a third-grade student worked on using items that were hot or cold while other students worked on Fahrenheit and Celsius within the context of a science unit on temperature. In the second, a secondary school student worked on drawing a mural while other students worked on assignments involving reading, discussing, and writing within the context of an American history unit on the Civil War. In the third, a middle school student listened to a tape and prepared a picture book while other students worked on assignments involving reading and discussion within the context of an English class unit on courage.

Inclusive Instructional Strategies As noted earlier in the chapter, one of the challenges in inclusion is the tendency of general education teachers to focus on academic whole group instruction that is focused on a core curriculum instead of the needs of the individual child. McDonnell (1998) addressed the issue of instruction when he described a number of instructional strategies that can be employed to teach students with severe disabilities in general education settings. Some of the strategies he suggested included (a) designing lessons to ensure engagement and success that include systematic presentation of concepts and immediate feedback on performance, (b) using heterogeneous small groups to teach specific skills, (c) using cooperative learning to encourage social skills, (d) using peer tutors, (e) using parallel instruction (i.e., instruction for students with disabilities separate from instruction delivered to other students), (f) using naturalistic teaching strategies during ongoing activities, and (g) conducting distributed instructional trials throughout the day. For example, telling time can be taught in an elementary school classroom with timepieces during learning center time.

Functional Skill Instruction Provided in the General Education Setting A number of the research investigations discussed thus far in this chapter noted that general education classrooms tend to focus on academic skills and use whole group instruction. Chapter 5 of this text discussed the need for functional skill instruction. Hamre-Nietupski, McDonald, and Nietupski (1992) stated that it is possible to teach functional skills within the general education setting by (a) using peers to teach functional skills, (b) providing functional skill instruction during class "down time" or while students without disabilities are completing academic work (e.g., writing essays or working math problems), or (c) removing the student with moderate to severe disabilities from the classroom for a brief period of time to work on functional skills (e.g., delivering school newspapers, dusting library shelves, watering office plants).

Collins, Kleinert, and Land (2006) provided sample lesson plans of how functional math skills for students with moderate and severe disabilities can be tied to national and stated standards and core content (see Example 5.3 in Chapter 5) and taught within an inclusive setting. For example, the teacher would use a constant time delay procedure (see Chapter 6) to teach a student with moderate to severe disabilities to match a set timepiece to the correct time written on one of two cards. When the student performed the response correctly, the teacher would provide praise and state an example of what occurs at that targeted time of day. To facilitate generalization, the teacher would have the student match the time on a timepiece to the times shown on the daily schedule throughout the day.

Peer Inclusion in Community-Based Instruction This text has noted the importance of community-based instruction because students with moderate and severe disabilities may fail to generalize across community settings, materials, or persons. Hamre-Nietupski et al. (1992) provided two options for teaching community skills to students who are placed in an inclusive setting. The first is to bring the community into the classroom through simulations or the use of community-referenced materials (e.g., making grocery lists and computing prices from newspaper ads). The second is to include peers without disabilities in community-based instruction (e.g., shopping for science project materials). These strategies will be discussed further in Chapter 8.

Creative Staff Assistance in General Education Settings When inclusion is implemented, students with moderate and severe disabilities should be placed in the same grade in which they would be if they did not have a disability. In addition, they should be placed in classes in natural proportions and not clustered together. This means that the students will be spread over a number of classrooms, making it difficult for the special education teacher to serve them all on a frequent basis. According to Nietupski et al. (1992), there are several ways to for the teacher to schedule the necessary staff coverage. These include (a) having special education staff (e.g., classroom assistants, related service delivery personnel) and volunteers (e.g., parents, students conducting service projects) assist in the general education setting, (b) empowering the general education teacher to work with students with moderate and severe disabilities by sharing strategies and providing information, and (c) reducing class size when a student with a moderate or severe disability is included so the general education teacher has more time to work with all students.

It should be noted that the practice of assigning one-to-one assistants for students with disabilities who are placed in general educations settings should be implemented with caution since this practice may have undesirable effects, such as creating an atmosphere where the student is viewed as being more dependent than is the actual case, where the general education teacher defers sole responsibility for the student with the disability to the assistant, or where peers without disabilities are reluctant to interact freely with the student. In cases where an assistant is assigned to a student with a disability, a collaborative model should be implemented in which all classroom staff share responsibility for all students, regardless of whether or not there is a disability.

Social Integration Promotion Within the School Setting As mentioned throughout this chapter, physical integration does not mean that social integration will occur. Hamre-Nietupski et al. (1992) discussed several strategies that can be helpful in facilitating social integration. The first strategy is to place students in neighborhood schools so they will be attending classes with students they know from neighborhood interactions outside of school and where their parents can be involved in school functions without commuting. The second is to conduct school-based sessions on differences and similarities in all people. The third is to develop a "Circle of Friends" program. The fourth is to include parents and their children with moderate and severe disabilities in school activities (e.g., sports teams, clubs, plays). The final strategy is to encourage parents to provide their children with moderate and severe disabilities with age-appropriate clothing, haircuts, and accessories that will help them "fit in" and be more accepted.

Family Feedback on Inclusion Practices One of the best ways to monitor the success of inclusion is to measure the satisfaction of families. Salend and Duhaney (2002) suggested that teachers conduct family interviews regarding their views of their child's educational program, the communication they have with school personnel, and the policies of the school and district. In addition, teachers may want to provide parents with a survey form that covers these issues and can be filled out in minimal time by rating their agreement or disagreement with the quality of their child's program.

Extension of Inclusion Beyond the School Setting Inclusive practices should not be confined to the educational setting Including students with disabilities in community activities provides a network of support that is available to students when school is not in session and once the student transitions to the adult world. As noted earlier in Activity 7.1, there are ways to make extracurricular sports activities more inclusive. For example, Collins, Epstein, Reiss, and Lowe (2001) suggested that the religious community is one of the segments of the community where children should be included without question. Thus, they provided suggestions for inclusive strategies to be used by volunteers who may not have backgrounds in working with children with moderate and severe disabilities, mild disabilities, or sensory impairments, such as using a hands-on approach and cooperative learning. Strategies to facilitate inclusion also can be shared with volunteers in other community activities, such as scouting or recreational groups.

Advocacy Activities That Promote Inclusion When garnering support for an inclusive program, organized advocacy activities can lead to systemic changes. In 1988 Hamre-Nietupski et al. (1988) provided a list of suggestions for involving parents as advocates that can be applied to other interested stakeholders as well. The authors suggested that interested persons (e.g., family members, educators) form an advocacy group that meets on a regular basis to concentrate on a small number of specific goals they wish to accomplish. In order to better educate the public, the members should become better informed themselves through such sources as the ARC and TASH, two well-known and influential advocacy groups for persons with moderate and severe disabilities. When ready, they should work to effect change through contacts and presentations from the local to the national level, through meetings with the media and school officials, and through participating on school committees and in organizations. Finally, advocates should be educated on the law and should work to ensure that the law is carried out in IEP conferences and placement meetings.

Best Practices
Inclusion and Collaboration

1. To increase the success of inclusion, devote time to planning prior to implementation.
2. Do not assume that social integration will occur because physical integration has taken place.
3. Balance the need for social interactions with the need for functional skill instruction.
4. Address functional skills through embedding systematic instruction within general education academic instruction on core content, conducting parallel instruction within the general education setting, and using peer tutors.

Conclusion

This chapter has addressed the topic of the educational placement of students with moderate and severe disabilities by addressing the topic of inclusion. Research has shown that, while there are benefits to be derived from inclusion, the practice is confronted with a number of challenges that must be met if students with moderate and severe disabilities are to reap the potential benefits. Physical placement in inclusive settings is the first step. Social integration in which students with moderate and severe disabilities form friendships and make gains in language and social skills through modeling others is the second step. The third step is more difficult. If students with moderate and severe disabilities are to achieve the outcome of community inclusion when they transition to adulthood, they must acquire and generalize the functional skills they will need in the future. Thus, one of the greatest challenges of inclusion is finding ways to ensure that systematic functional skill instruction is embedded in the core content of the general education curriculum. Stainback and Stainback (1992) stated that "there is more to life than learning only to make a sandwich or sweep a floor" (p. 29); yet the ability to perform these functional tasks makes a person less dependent on others to complete the tasks and increases the likelihood that the person can live in a less restrictive environment as an adult.

Heward (2003) asserted that students with disabilities have a right to an effective education that is individualized and built on a research base. Much of the research that supports inclusion is based on gains in social skills and language. The research showing us how to embed systematic functional skill instruction in inclusive settings remains in its infancy, and the need continues for researchers to validate practices for meeting individual needs of students with moderate and severe disabilities in inclusive settings. In addressing where students with disabilities should receive an education, Zigmond (2003) stated that those in the field of special education have been asking the wrong questions. According to Zigmond, those in the field should stop asking, "What is the best place?" and begin asking which placements are "best for whom?" and "best for what?" In that way, the field can return to identifying individualized models of delivery over a philosophy of "one best place" (p. 196–197).

The research presented in this chapter has shown that placement alone does not ensure inclusion and that making inclusion work takes a great deal of planning and the implementation of a number of strategies to increase the likelihood of success. The strategies that were suggested at the end of this chapter are but a few examples of those that others are finding useful as they strive to provide appropriate inclusive settings. For further strategies, readers should consult texts that have a specific focus on inclusion. In considering the benefits and challenges of inclusion and the recommendations for implementation, take time to complete the performance-based assessment at the end of this chapter by contrasting examples of appropriate and inappropriate inclusion practices.

Questions for Review

1. What is the difference between integration and inclusion?
2. What are the differences among physical, social, and instructional integration?
3. List five benefits students with moderate and severe disabilities can derive from inclusion.
4. List five challenging aspects that may be problematic in implementing an inclusive program for students with moderate and severe disabilities.
5. Describe five strategies that can facilitate the successful implementation of inclusion of students with moderate and severe disabilities.

Performance-Based Assessment

The following examples come from observations in general education classrooms in which teachers are implementing inclusion. Select and contrast either the elementary school or secondary school examples. State why one example is better than the other, and tell how practices could be changed in the less appropriate example.

Elementary School Example One

Toby is a male elementary school student with multiple severe disabilities who is included in a language arts class. He is nonverbal and communicates through eye blinks. In addition, he has minimal motor movements and requires assistance in propelling his wheelchair from one setting to another. Toby is supported by a classroom assistant who circulates and assists the general education teacher with the entire class. During the weekly spelling bee, the peers on Toby's team provide natural support by giving him options for spelling the word correctly when it is his turn by watching to see which word he indicates has the correct spelling by blinking his eyes. When he gets the correct word, his classmates cheer just as they do when other teammates answer correctly.

Elementary School Example Two

The classroom assistant in Ms. Arnold's room accompanies four students with moderate and severe disabilities to their general education science class. In the class, the general education teacher teaches measurement through a hands-on activity using cooperative groups of four students to a table. The students with moderate and severe disabilities sit together at one of the tables where the assistant can assist them in pouring as they determine how many ounces of water it takes to fill various containers. At the end of the lesson, a representative from each table writes the results on a blackboard chart.

Secondary School Example One

Courtney and Erin are two students with moderate and severe disabilities who attend a chemistry class each day with their special education teacher. The two females sit in the back row of the class. While the general education teacher lectures, the special education teacher takes notes for the students. When their peers without disabilities work on written assignments, the special education teacher quizzes the students with moderate and severe disabilities on chemistry terms and formulas.

Secondary School Example Two

Jon is a student with a moderate disability and Down syndrome who attends a calculus class with support from an assistant. While the general education teacher and the special education assistant circulate about the room, the students work on probability in cooperative groups by rolling dice and using formulas to see how many roles it takes to get various combinations. Jon works on fine motor skills by rolling the dice and works on functional math skills by counting the number of dots on the dice for his team.

References

Agran, M., Alper, S., & Wehmeyer, M. (2002). Access to the general curriculum for students with significant disabilities: What it means to teachers. *Education and Training in Mental Retardation and Developmental Disabilities, 37,* 123–133.

Brady, M. P., McDougall, D., & Dennis, H. F. (1989). The schools, the courts, and the integration of students with severe handicaps. *The Journal of Special Education, 23,* 43–58.

Brown, L. Ford, A., Nisbet, J., Sweet, M., Donnellan, A., & Gruenwald, L. (1983). Opportunities available when severely handicapped students attend chronological age appropriate regular schools. *Journal of the Association for Persons with Severe Handicaps, 8,* 16–24.

Brozovic, S. A., Stafford, A. M., Alberto, P. A., & Taber, T. A. (2000). Variables considered by teachers of students with moderate and severe disabilities when making placement decisions. *Journal of Developmental and Physical Disabilities, 12,* 131–144.

Collins, B. C. (1995). The integration of students with severe or profound disabilities from segregated schools into regular public schools: An analysis of changes in parent perceptions. *Journal of Developmental and Physical Disabilities, 7,* 51–65.

Collins, B. C. (2002). Using peers to facilitate learning by students with moderate disables. *The Behavior Analyst Today, 3,* 329–341.

Collins, B. C., Branson, T. A., Hall, M., & Rankin, S. W. (2001). Teaching secondary students with moderate disabilities in an inclusive academic classroom setting. *Journal of Developmental and Physical Disabilities, 13,* 41–59.

Collins, B. C., Epstein, A., Reiss, T., & Lowe, V. (2001). Including children with mental retardation in the religious community. *Teaching Exceptional Children, 33*(5), 52–58.

Collins, B. C., Hall, M., Branson, T. A., & Holder, M. (1999). Acquisition of related and unrelated factual information deliver by a teacher within an inclusive setting. *Journal of Behavioral Education, 9,* 223–237.

Collins, B. C., Hendricks, T. B., Fetko, K., & Land, L. (2002). Student-2-student learning in inclusive classrooms. *Teaching Exceptional Children, 34*(4), 56–61.

Collins, B. C., Kleinert, H., & Land, L. (2006). Addressing math standards and functional math. In D. M. Browder & F. Spooner (Eds.), *Teaching language arts, math, and science to students with significant cognitive disabilities.* Brookes.

Collins, B. C., & Schuster, J. W. (2001). Some thoughts on the history of rural special education: A first hand account. *Rural Special Education Quarterly, 20*(1), 22–29.

Cook, B. G. (2001). A comparison of teachers' attitudes toward their included students with mild and severe disabilities. *The Journal of Special Education, 34,* 203–213.

Cook, B. G., & Semmel, M. I. (1999). Peer acceptance of included students with disabilities as a function of severity of disability and classroom composition. *The Journal of Special Education, 33,* 50–61.

Corbett, J. (2003). Play's the thing: Bracken County is proud of its new team. *Lexington Herald-Leader,* p. E1.

Diamond, K. E., Hestenes, L. L., & O'Connor, C. E. (1994). Integrating young children with disabilities in preschool: Problems and promise. *Young Children, 49,* 68–75.

Dore, R., Dion, E., Wagner, S., & Brunet, J. (2002). High school inclusion of adolescents with mental retardation: A multiple case study. *Education and Training in Mental Retardation and Developmental Disabilities, 37,* 253–261.

Federico, M. A., Herrold, W. G., & Venn, J. (1999). Helpful tips for successful inclusion: A checklist for educators. *Teaching Exceptional Children, 32*(1), 76–82.

Freeman, S. F. N., & Alkin, M. C. (2000). Academic and social attainments of children with mental retardation in general education and special education settings. *Remedial and Special Education, 21,* 3–18.

Gilberts, G. H., Agran, M., Hughes, C., Wehmeyer, M. (2001). The effects of peer delivered self-monitoring strategies on the participation of students with severe disabilities in general education classrooms. *Journal of the Association for Persons with Severe Handicaps, 26,* 25–36.

Hall, L. J., & McGregor, J. A. (2000). A follow-up study of the peer relationships of children with disabilities in an inclusive school. *Journal of Special Education, 34,* 114–126.

Hamre-Nietupski, S., Dvorsky, S., McKee, A., Nietupski, J., Cook, J., & Costanza, C. (1999). Going home: General and special education teachers' perspectives as students with moderate/severe disabilities return to rural neighborhood schools. *Education and Training in Mental Retardation and Developmental Disabilities, 34,* 235–259.

Hamre-Nietupski, S., Krajewski, L., Nietupski, J., Ostercamp, D., Sensor, K., & Opheim, B. (1988). Parent/professional partnerships in advocacy: Developing integrated options within resistive systems. *Journal of the Association for Persons with Severe Handicaps, 13,* 251–259.

Hamre-Nietupski, S., McDonald, J., & Nietupski, J. (1992). Integrating elementary students with multiple disabilities into supported regular classes: Challenges and solutions. *Teaching Exceptional Children, 24*(3), 6–9.

Helmstetter, E., Curry, C. A., Brennan, M., & Sampson-Saul, M. (1998). Comparison of general and special education classrooms of students with severe disabilities. *Education and Training in Mental Retardation and Developmental Disabilities, 33,* 216–227.

Heward, W. L. (2003). Ten faulty notions about teaching and learning that hinder the effectiveness of special education. *The Journal of Special Education, 36,* 186–205.

Hughes, C., Guth, C., Hall, S., Presley, J., Dye, M., & Byers, C. (1999). "They are my best friends": Peer buddies promote inclusion in high school. *Teaching Exceptional Children, 31,* 32–37.

Hunt, P., Doering, K., Hirose-Hatae, A., Maier, J., & Goetz, L. (2001). Across-program collaboration to support students with and without disabilities in a general education classroom. *Journal of the Association for Persons with Severe Handicaps, 26,* 240–256.

Hunt, P., & Goetz, L. (1997). Research on inclusive educational programs, practices, and outcomes for students with severe disabilities. *Journal of Special Education, 31,* 3–29.

Isaacs, B. (2002, January 22). Leading the way in cheerleading. Lexington, KY: *Lexington Herald-Leader,* pp. 1, 8–9.

Jackson, M. (2002, January 7). Cheerleaders have new reason to shout. Chattanooga, TN: *Chattanooga Times Free Press,* p. D1.

Jackson, L., Ryndak, D. L., & Billingsley, F. (2000). Useful practices in inclusive education: A preliminary view of what experts in moderate to severe disabilities are saying. *Journal of the Association for Persons with Severe Handicaps, 25,* 129–141.

Janney, R. E., & Snell, M. E. (1997). How teachers include students with moderate and severe disabilities in elementary classes: The means and meaning of inclusion. *The Journal of the Association for Persons with Severe Handicaps, 22,* 159–169.

Kennedy, C. H., Shukla, S., & Fryxell, D. (1997). Comparing the effects of educational placement on the social relationships of intermediate school students with severe disabilities. *Exceptional Children, 64,* 31–47.

Larson, S. A., & Lakin, K. C. (1989). Deinstitutionalization of persons with mental retardation: Behavioral outcomes. *Journal of the Association for Persons with Severe Handicaps, 14,* 324–332.

Logan, K. R., & Keefe, K. R. (1997). A comparison of instructional context, teacher behavior, and engaged behavior for students with severe disabilities in general education and self-contained elementary classrooms. *Journal of the Association for Persons with Severe Handicaps, 22,* 16–27.

Logan, K. R., & Malone, D. M. (1998). Instructional contexts for students with moderate, severe, and profound intellectual disabilities in general education elementary classrooms. *Education and Training in Mental Retardation and Developmental Disabilities, 33,* 62–75.

Mamlin, N. (1999). Despite best intentions: When inclusion fails. *The Journal of Special Education, 33,* 36–49.

McDonnell, J. (1998). Instruction for students with severe disabilities in general education settings. *Education and Training in Mental Retardation and Developmental Disabilities, 33,* 199–215.

McDonnell, J., Thorson, N., & McQuivey, C. (1998). The instructional characteristics of inclusive classes for elementary students with severe disabilities: An exploratory study. *Journal of Behavioral Education, 8,* 415–438.

McDonnell, J., Thorson, N., & McQuivey, C. (2000). Comparison of the instructional contexts of students with severe disabilities and their peers in general education classes. *Journal of the Association for Persons with Severe Handicaps, 25,* 54–58.

McLeskey, J., & Henry, D. (1999). Inclusion: What progress is being made across states? *Teaching Exceptional Children, 31*(5), 60–64.

McLeskey, J., Henry, D., & Hodges, D. (1998). Inclusion: Where is it happening? *Teaching Exceptional Children, 31*(2), 4–10.

McLeskey, J., Henry, D., & Hodges, D. (1999). Inclusion: What progress is being made across disability categories? *Teaching Exceptional Children, 33*(5), 56–62.

Mills, P. E., Cole, K. N., Jenkins, J. R., & Dale, P. S. (1998). Effects of differing levels of inclusion on preschoolers with disabilities. *Exceptional Children, 65,* 79–90.

Palmer, D. S., Borthwick-Duffy, S. A., Widaman, K., & Best, S. J. (1998). Influences on parent perceptions of inclusive practices for their children with mental retardation. *American Journal on Mental Retardation, 103,* 272–287.

Palmer, D. S., Fuller, K., Arora, T., & Nelson, M. (2001). Taking sides: Parent views on inclusion for their children with severe disabilities. *Exceptional Children, 67,* 467–484.

Pearman, E. L., Huang, A., and Mellblom, C. I. (1997). The inclusion of all students: Concerns and incentives of educators. *Education and Training in Mental Retardation and Developmental Disabilities, 32,* 11–20.

Ryndak, D. L., Morrison, A. P., & Sommerstein, L. (1999). Literacy before and after inclusion in general education settings: A case study. *Journal of the Association for Persons with Severe Handicaps, 24,* 5–22.

Salend, S. J., & Duhaney, L. M. G. (2002). What do families have to say about inclusion? How to pay attention and get results. *Teaching Exceptional Children, 35*(1), 62–66.

Salisbury, C. L., & McGregor, G. (2002). The administrative climate and context of inclusive elementary schools. *Exceptional Children, 68,* 259–274.

Seery, M. E., Davis, P. M., & Johnson, L. J. (2000). Seeing eye-to-eye: Are parents and professionals in agreement about the benefits of preschool inclusion? *Remedial and Special Education, 21,* 268–278.

Stainback, S., & Stainback, W. (1992). Including students with severe disabilities in the regular classroom curriculum. *Preventing School Failure, 37*(1), 26–30.

Staub, D., Spaulding, M., Peck, C. A., Gallucci, C., & Schwartz, I. S. (1996). Using nondisabled peers to support the inclusion of students with disabilities at the junior high school level. *Journal of the Association for Persons with Severe Handicaps, 21,* 194–205.

Tapasak, R. C., & Walther-Thomas, C. S., (1999). Evaluation of a first-year inclusion program: Student perceptions and classroom performance. *Remedial and Special Education, 20,* 216–225.

Taylor, S. J. (1988). Caught in the continuum: A critical analysis of the principle of the least restrictive environment. *Journal of the Association for Persons with Severe Handicaps, 13,* 41–53.

Warren, J. (1991, January 27). Parents doubt care as good elsewhere. *Lexington Herald-Leader,* p. C1, 4.

Weiner, H. M. (2003). Professional development in the context of the classroom. *Teaching Exceptional Children, 35*(6), 12–18.

Werts, M. G., Wolery, M., Snyder, E. D., & Caldwell, N. K. (1996). Teachers' perceptions of the supports critical to the success of inclusion programs. *Journal of the Association for Persons with Severe Handicaps, 21,* 9–21.

Winterman, K. G., & Sapona, R. H. (2002). Everyone's included: Supporting young children with autism spectrum disorders in a responsive classroom learning environment. *Teaching Exceptional Children, 35,* 30–35.

Wisniewski, L., & Alper, S. (1994). Including students with severe disabilities in general education settings. *Remedial and Special Education, 15,* 4–13.

Wolfberg, P. J., Zercher, C., Lieber, J., Capell, K., Matias, S., Hanson, M., & Odom, S. L. (1999). "Can I play with you?" Peer culture in inclusive preschool programs. *Journal of the Association for Persons with Severe Handicaps, 24,* 69–84.

Wolfensberger, W. (1995). Of "normalization," lifestyles, the Special Olympics, deinstitutionalization, mainstreaming, integration, and cabbages and kings. *Mental Retardation, 33,* 128–131.

Yell, M. L. (1995). Least restrictive environment, inclusion, and students with disabilities: A legal analysis. *Journal of Special Education, 28,* 389–404.

York, J., Vandercook, T., MacDonald, C., Heise-Neff, C., & Caughey, E. (1992). Feedback about integrating middle-school students with severe disabilities in general education classes. *Exceptional Children, 58*(3), 244–258.

Zeph, L. A. (1991). Considering regular classroom options for students with severe disabilities in rural settings. *Rural Special Education Quarterly, 10*(4), 5–9.

Zigmond, N. (2003). Where should students with disabilities receive special education services? Is one place better than another? *Journal of Special Education, 37,* 193–199.

CHAPTER EIGHT

TEACHING STUDENTS WITH MODERATE AND SEVERE DISABILITIES IN COMMUNITY SETTINGS:
Community-Based Instruction

On completion of this chapter, the reader will meet the following objectives:

- Define in vivo and simulated instruction.
- Differentiate between consecutive and concurrent instruction as they relate to community-based instruction.
- Provide guidelines for both community-based and simulated instruction.
- Discuss the amount of time that students should spend engaged in community-based instruction by age level.
- Describe ways to embed related services and inclusive interactions in community-based instruction.

Chapter 7 examined the practice of using inclusive general education settings for delivering systematic instruction to students with moderate and severe disabilities. This chapter will examine the practice of delivering systematic instruction to students with moderate and severe disabilities in community settings, a practice known as community-based instruction.

In recent years, the practice of community-based instruction has drawn criticism as being inappropriate for the chronological age of children with disabilities who attend school since their peers without disabilities are in school on weekdays and because leaving the school grounds causes students to miss opportunities to be included with their same-age peers without disabilities (Browder, 1997). Based on the opinions of 65 special educators who taught students with mental retardation across age levels and responded to a survey conducted in Utah, Agran, Snow, and Swaner (1999) argued that there are benefits to both school inclusion and community-based instruction and that the two do not have to be mutually exclusive. The majority of the special educators stated that their students had opportunities to interact with peers without disabilities during community-based instruction and that the benefits of community-based instruction (e.g., opportunity to perform skills across natural environments, preparation for postschool environments, increase in opportunities to make choices) gave support for the practice.

Brown et al. (1983) set the historical foundation for community-based instruction as an acceptable standard practice in the education of students with moderate and severe disabilities when they argued for nonschool instruction for students with severe disabilities. In providing a basis for their arguments, Brown et al. traced the progression of services for students with severe disabilities over time as shown in Figure 8.1. When setting criterion for where instruction should be provided, Brown et al. stated that teachers should consider the number and complexity of skills that

FIGURE 8.1

Progression of Services for Students with Severe Disabilities (Brown et al., 1983).

No schools

↓

Segregated private schools

↓

Regular chronological-age-inappropriate schools

↓

Regular chronological-age-appropriate schools with natural proportions

↓

Regular chronological-age-appropriate schools with natural proportions and nonschool instruction in the natural environment

a student can acquire; the number of instructional trials and amount of time that a student needs to perform skills at a meaningful criteria; and the ability of a student to maintain, generalize, and synthesize skills that are acquired, noting that each of these variables may be problematic for students with severe disabilities.

McDonnell, Hardman, Hightower, Keifer-O'Donnell, and Drew (1993) provided data to substantiate the case that Brown et al. (1983) built for community-based instruction. When McDonnell et al. examined the progress of 34 secondary school students with moderate and severe disabilities who participated in community-based instruction, they found that the students made significant gains in the categories of social and communication skills, personal living, and community living on the Scales of Independent Behavior. In addition, the amount of community-based instruction the students received was not affected by their IQ, mobility skills, or behavior problems. Although the amount of community-based instruction students received appeared to be a better predictor of their adaptive behavior than other characteristics, even students with the most severe disabilities and profound mental retardation appeared to benefit from the practice.

Cook (2002) noted that community-based instruction is best practiced in teaching the skills needed for successful transitioning and argued against the perception that only students with the most severe disabilities can benefit from the practice. Cook also noted that many students with mild to moderate mental retardation do not participate in community-based instruction because they are included in classes with an academic focus and asserted that these students could benefit from community-based instruction since it is associated with positive transitions to employment settings. Based on the rating of 173 pre-service and in-service special education teachers to the vocational outcomes of hypothetical case studies, Cook warned that the outcome of an emphasis on inclusion in academic classes could result in less attention placed on successful transitions to community-based work.

When determining the individual programs of students with disabilities, Brown et al. (1983) stated that there are four settings where instruction can be delivered. In the first option, instruction takes place in the school only. This is convenient, safe, and less costly. In the second option, **consecutive instruction** occurs in which students first acquire skills in the school setting then go into the community to practice them. This is not ideal since valuable time is lost for those students who fail to generalize and must be retaught to perform skills in the natural environment. In the third option, **concurrent instruction** occurs in which students receive instruction across school and community settings. This allows students to participate in inclusive classes and still receive the benefits of participating in community-based instruction. In the final option, instruction occurs in nonschool settings only. This is ideal for those over the age of 18 since their same-age peers have transitioned from school to the community and because the years of 18 to 21 can be used to focus on those skills that will be needed for a successful transition to adult living and work.

Stokes and Baer (1977) labeled school and consecutive options as "train and hope" since instructors are relying on the assumption that students will generalize from school to community environments. With concurrent and nonschool options, the data provide evidence that generalization is occurring. Sailor et al. (1986) agreed with the assertion that community-based instruction becomes more important as the student grows older and provided a model in which community-based instruction would increase from 10% of the time for preschool students with moderate to severe disabilities to 85% of the time for students in the transition years of 8 to 21. Likewise, classroom instruction would decrease from 65% of the time for preschool students to 0% for students in the transition years. This model is illustrated by the bar graph in Figure 8.2.

The remainder of this chapter will focus on two practices: (a) community-based instruction and (b) school-based simulation. As already stated, community-based instruction, or in vivo instruction, is the practice of teaching functional skills in meaningful natural environments, as identified through the ecological inventory approach described in Chapter 4. Simulation, or **community-referenced instruction,** is the practice of teaching functional skills in classroom or school settings using realistic cues and materials that reflect the natural environment where the skills will be needed. The sections that follow will provide guidelines for community-based instruction and school-based simulation with data based on examples from the research base. In addition, the final sections in this chapter will address the practice of integrating related services and inclusive activities with peers without disabilities in community-based instruction.

FIGURE 8.2

Community-Based Instruction by Age Groups (Sailor et al., 1986).

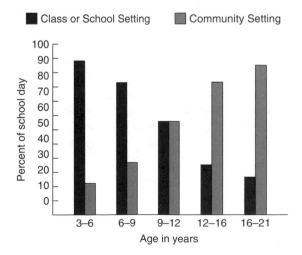

COMMUNITY-BASED INSTRUCTION

The practice of community-based instruction is based on the least dangerous assumption that it is better to ensure that students will be able to use functional skills in natural settings than to infer that generalization will occur following classroom instruction. The following sections provide guidelines for conducting community-based instruction, considerations for working with community sites, and examples from the professional literature to illustrate ways in which instruction can be delivered.

Guidelines for the Delivery of Community-Based Instruction

Sailor et al. (1986) listed four categories of constraints in the implementation of community-based instruction. The first category included constraints that are administrative and logistical, such as liability and insurance, unions, transportation, staff ratio, and cost. The second category included constraints that are related to parental concerns, such as community safety and social stigma. The third category included constraints that are related to the student with moderate to severe disabilities, such as the type and degree of the student's disability. Finally, the fourth category included constraints that are related to the teacher, such as training and philosophy. As noted earlier, a new constraint identified in recent years can be added to this list. This is the constraint of inclusive education (e.g., Hamre-Nieuptski, McDonald, & Nietupski, 1992). Example 8.l lists some creative ways in which educators have dealt with these constraints.

EXAMPLE 8.1 **OVERCOMING CONSTRAINTS TO COMMUNITY-BASED INSTRUCTION**

Sometimes there are constraints to the practice of community-based instruction, such as the distance to community sites from rural schools. The following sections contain strategies for overcoming these constraints based on the experiences of the author and her associates (e.g., Collins & Schuster, 2001).

Transportation

Sometimes it can be difficult to access transportation to community-based sites. If a bus is available, the teacher or an assistant may become licensed as a bus driver, allowing flexibility as to when, where, and how often community-based instruction can occur. Some districts have allowed teachers to drive school-owned cars that are insured or to take public transportation, such as buses or taxis. If a bus is not available or funding for travel is limited, community-based instruction can take place at sites that are within walking distance of the school. For example, it may be possible to walk to a service station or convenience store to practice purchasing skills, to walk to a local church to practice vocational skills, or to walk to a home to practice domestic skills.

Staff Ratio

Although large buses may be used to transport students for purposes of liability, current best practice is for students to participate in community-based instruction in small groups. Teachers may be able to leave staff behind to work with students in the school setting while they accompany two to three students on community-based instruction. Under ideal conditions, peer tutors or peer buddies participate as well. When there are not enough staff or peers for an acceptable ratio, volunteers from the community, parents, or related service personnel (e.g., speech/language pathologist) also can assist students during community-based instruction. When it is necessary to go as a large group, an effort should be made to divide into small groups within the community (e.g., only one or two students per business site).

Cost

Although the cost of community-based instruction should be absorbed by the school district if it is on the student's IEP, teachers can gain administrative support by helping to meet the cost. In some cases family members are willing to contribute toward the cost of making purchases, such as having their child purchase items they need in their home (e.g., groceries). School and civic organizations may fund community-based instruction as a service project, or teachers can request that school fundraising events (e.g., Fall Festival) earmark a percentage of dollars for community-based instruction. In some instances teachers finance community-based instruction by making purchases for others (e.g., shopping for teachers or school projects) or by making purchases that can be resold on the school grounds (e.g., bottled water). When funding is limited, a viable option is to simulate activities in the community, such as locating items on shelves then replacing them.

Family Concerns

Family concerns for safety can be alleviated by ensuring that there is an adequate student/staff ratio on all outings. One teacher (who also happened to be a former nurse) developed what she called a "community-based instruction kit" by filling a briefcase with permission forms, student medical information and medications, first-aid supplies, and emergency phone numbers with a cellular phone. The issue of stigma can be countered by accompanying students one to one or in small groups that include students without disabilities. Data collection materials and artificial reinforcers can be minimized. Also, teachers can avoid settings at peak hours when large crowds can be anticipated.

Student Factors

Although the Americans with Disabilities Act has mandated that community settings should be accessible to persons regardless of disability, some student factors, such as severe behavior disorders or medical conditions, cause businesses to perceive the presence of students with disabilities as disruptive. To establish good working relations with businesses, teachers can talk with businesses in advance to discuss potential problems and times when businesses might be less crowded. An example of good public relations occurred when a teacher who had several students who were deaf and used manual signing to communicate provided local businesses in advance with a book of manual signs that the student were likely to use in making requests and purchases.

Teacher Training and Philosophy

When a district makes the commitment to offer community-based instruction for students, it is useful to establish policies in writing. In addition to administrators and special education staff, the involvement of general education teachers can lead to the implementation of inclusive activities, and the involvement of related services can lead to the embedding of related skills. Once the planning is complete, training for those who will be going into the community to conduct instruction is beneficial.

Implementation of Community-Based Instruction

Several authors have addressed the issues involved in making community-based instruction a successful practice. In 1986 Snell and Browder elaborated on several of these issues. First, community-based instruction should rely on an assessment of each student's environments through an ecological inventory (as described in Chapter 5). Through this process, it may become evident that appropriate community sites vary across students. For example, one student's family may eat out in fast-food restaurants, another in buffet-style cafeterias, and another in restaurants with waiters and menus. The skills for ordering and purchasing food vary across each of these settings, making it unlikely that a student would generalize skills learned in one setting to the other.

Once settings are identified, appropriate instruction must be designed, with attention to the factors discussed in Chapter 5. These include creating task analyses, determining task presentation (e.g., forward or backward chaining, total task presentation) and trial presentation (e.g., massed, spaced, distributed) and selecting prompting strategies (e.g., constant time delay, system of least prompts) and reinforcement procedures. In conducting community-based instruction, Snell and Browder (1986) recommended that teachers (a) determine how skills will be selected, (b) ensure that target skills are valid (e.g., valued by the student, the family, and the community), (c) task analyze skills as they will be performed in the natural environment, (d) determine a sequence for trial presentation, (e) develop an instructional procedure (e.g., prompting, reinforcement, error correction), (f) create a data-collection system and schedule for monitoring skills in the community, (g) identify collateral behaviors that can be measured (e.g., communication, appropriate behavior, motor skills), (h) implement data-based instruction in target settings over time, and (i) demonstrate generalization through probes or tests in novel (untrained) settings.

Collins (2003) asserted that there might be challenges associated with the implementation of community-based instruction in rural settings that are not present in urban or suburban communities. Based on examples of community-based instruction implemented with students with disabilities across age levels in rural settings that have been reported in the professional literature, she recommended that rural teachers (a) assess families to determine skills that are valued in their communities, (b) take advantage of local resources (e.g., country stores or churches), (c) involve peers without disabilities as community tutors, (d) supplement infrequent community-based instruction with frequent classroom simulations, and (e) use systematic data-based procedures to determine student progress.

In addition to considering the guidelines for community-based instruction offered in the professional literature, it also is useful for teachers to work with administrators in their districts to establish policies that may vary across communities based on their unique characteristics. An example of guidelines for community-based instruction developed by teachers in a Kentucky school district can be found in Example 8.2.

EXAMPLE 8.2	GUIDELINES FOR COMMUNITY-BASED INSTRUCTION DEVELOPED BY TEACHERS IN A KENTUCKY SCHOOL DISTRICT

A group of teachers of students with moderate and severe disabilities in a Kentucky school district wrote a manual for community-based instruction based on best practices (Miracle, McNabb-Kuebler, Hardy, Pinto, & Davis, n.d.). The manual contained (a) a rationale for community-based instruction; (b) guidelines for conducting community-based instruction; (c) policies for transportation, staffing, and the inclusion of same-age peers without disabilities; (d) emergency and safety procedures; (e) parent permission and communication forms; (f) sample data sheets for instruction, and (g) an ecological inventory of the community. The manual set parameters for community-based instruction that included limiting the practice to groups of three to four students in age-appropriate settings. The teachers recommended that community-based instruction (with peers without disabilities) take place once per week during elementary school, twice per week during middle school, and four to five times per week during secondary school. While appropriate instruction for younger students would center on community, recreation/leisure, and personal management skills, community-based instruction for older students would expand to include vocational and domestic skills. Finally, the manual stated that the presence of a certified teacher was required during community-based instruction, but an instructional assistant could remain in the school setting to conduct instruction with students not participating in community-based instruction.

Working with Community Sites

In planning community-based instruction, it is important to consider that instruction is taking place in nonschool settings where it will be observed by members of the community and has the potential to be disruptive to business. Thus, it is necessary to be sensitive to the reaction of those who work in community settings and the members of the community who frequent their businesses. To determine the preferences of community members for community-based instruction that takes place in their establishments, Aveno, Renzaglia, and Lively (1987) surveyed the staff and management of 74 community training sites that included retail business, religious, health, recreation, education, social service, and restaurant settings. Of these, almost half refused to allow on-site training. Those that did not object to community-based instruction on the premises had definite preferences that included prearranging the day and time of community-based instruction and using training materials (e.g., clipboards, timers), adaptive aids, on-site simulations, and reinforcers (e.g., beverages, money, food) only as necessary. The respondents did not state preferences as to group size or trainer/student ratio. Training for staff employed at the site would be allowed depending on availability during business hours. The use of devices for mobility or communication were not a problem. The respondents anticipated that the presence of community-based instruction would have a positive effect on patrons, but they stressed that all facility rules and policies would apply during community-based instruction. Based on an analysis of the responses, Aveno et al. recommended that community-based instruction sessions be arranged with sites in advance, that sessions be kept to 45 minutes or less, that the staff/student ratio be one on two, and that instructional materials be as inconspicuous as possible.

In a later investigation, Wolfe (1994) evaluated the social acceptability of community-based instruction techniques to 178 individuals from four groups: (a) business students, (b) employers and employees of fast-food establishments, (c) job coaches, and (d) sheltered workshop staff. Based on their ratings of tapes, there were differences of opinions across the groups as to the acceptability of procedures. In general, however, consequent techniques (e.g., reinforcing with money or tokens, punishing with timeout) were less acceptable than antecedent (e.g., picture or model prompting) and data collection (e.g., using stopwatches and data sheets) techniques. In addition, positive techniques (e.g., praise) rated higher than negative techniques (e.g., overcorrection). Based on an analysis of the responses, Wolfe recommended that instructors use more positive techniques than negative techniques in community settings and that they limit the use of physical prompts.

Examples of Community-Based Instruction from the Professional Literature

The following examples illustrate how community-based instruction has been used to teach functional skills to students with moderate and severe disabilities. In each of the examples, the recipients of instruction were either secondary school students or adults in programs for persons with disabilities. In each case the authors addressed research questions pertaining to the generalization of functional skills. These research questions often involved the use of multiple exemplars or general case instruction to facilitate generalization. As described in Chapter 5, the use of multiple exemplars (e.g., materials, instructors, settings, cues) helps students learn that the same response may be appropriate across a variety of stimuli (i.e., stimulus generalization). When general case (i.e., selecting examples that sample the range of potential stimuli) is used as a method for selecting instructional exemplars, students can learn to apply a single response to an entire class of stimuli.

Using Community-Based Instruction to Teach Functional Skills   In an illustration of the way in which community-based instruction can be used to teach functional skills, Everington and Stevenson (1994) described a service project implemented during community-based instruction that resulted in the acquisition of a number of skills for secondary school students with multiple disabilities. In this example the students provided services for "Grandma," a 97-year-old woman in a nursing home, during scheduled blocks lasting two and one-half hours and occurring two to three times per week. Through completing activities for Grandma that included shopping, watering plants, straightening the room, adjusting the bedding, tidying the bathroom, and assisting with the lunch tray, the students met IEP objectives that included sitting on furniture, moving without breaking items, behaving appropriately at meals, and conversing with others.

Several investigations have focused on the use of multiple exemplars or general case to teach skills in a more systematic fashion during community-based instruction. In teaching across a variety of restaurants, Cooper and Browder (1998) embedded the skill of choice making through touching, pointing, or moving toward an object during instruction of the skills needed to eat in a restaurant. Using a constant time delay procedure, they prompted three adults with severe disabilities through making choices of doors, foods, sweeteners, condiments, eating materials, and tables across a variety of restaurants. The adults showed an increase in their ability to make choices as well as in acquisition of the task analyses. In a second example using multiple settings, Gumpel and Nativ-Ari-Am (2001) used general case to teach four secondary school students with visual impairments and cognitive disabilities (i.e., learning disability or moderate mental disability) to purchase items in grocery stores. Community-based instruction took place across eight training stores that sampled the range of characteristics. Students learned to perform the steps of task analyses using either audiotaped instructions or cards with enlarged printed cues.

During daily community-based instruction, Collins, Schuster, and Nelson (1992) used multiple settings (e.g., businesses, parks, libraries, malls, apartments) as well as multiple exemplars of stimuli (i.e., male or female persons varying in age and physical characteristics providing various lures) to teach three adults with severe disabilities to respond to the lures of strangers. Varying the settings, strangers, and lures on a daily basis, the instructor conducted in vivo instruction using a constant time delay procedure to teach a safe response (say "no" and walk away at least five feet within five seconds) following daily probes for generalization. Although the adults met criterion during instruction, there were mixed results in generalizing to a novel stranger with a novel lure in a novel setting, reflecting the difficulty in teaching a generalized safe response to strangers to adults with a history of complying with the requests of strangers (e.g., therapists, social workers).

Using Community-Based Instruction to Probe for Generalization of Skills Taught in the Classroom
In several examples, instructors have taught functional skills in school settings and used community-based instruction as an opportunity to determine if classroom instruction was generalizing to community settings. In each of the following examples, the instructors taught the target skills in the school settings using the same materials that would be found in community settings.

In the first example, Smith, Collins, Schuster, and Kleinert (1999) used a system-of-least-prompts procedure with multiple exemplars of materials (e.g., cleaning cloths, buckets, and tables that varied in color) to teach four secondary school students with moderate and severe disabilities to clean tables in the classroom setting. In addition to generalizing across school settings (e.g., school cafeteria, teachers' lounge), the students demonstrated generalization to a church setting during community-based instruction.

In a similar example, Taylor, Collins, Schuster, and Kleinert (2002) used a system-of-least-prompts procedure with multiple exemplars of materials (e.g., three brands of laundry detergent and fabric softener sheets) to teach four secondary school students with moderate and severe disabilities to perform laundry skills (i.e., washing and drying clothing) in the family living area of the classroom. The students were able to later perform the skills across two community laundromats during community-based instruction. In addition, the students generalized the ability to read the words on the laundry products and appliances that had been presented as nontargeted information during instruction.

In a third example, Sprague and Horner (1984) investigated the use of general case exemplars when they taught six secondary school students with moderate and severe disabilities to make purchases from vending machines in the school and during community-based instruction in community recreational facilities, a hospital lobby, a laundromat, and the lunchroom of a public service building. Probe sessions for generalization occurred on 10 untrained vending machines. The students showed minimal generalization when taught with a single vending machine near their class-room or when taught with three exemplars that had similar characteristics. General-ization showed a marked increase, however, when the students received instruction on three vending machines that sampled the range of characteristics.

Summary

To summarize, the rationale behind community-based instruction is that students with moderate and severe disabilities may fail to generalize to community settings the skills they are taught in classroom settings. By learning skills in the settings in which they will be needed, students learn to attend to natural cues, practice with natural materials, and receive natural consequences following their actions. While the amount of community-based instruction should increase as students grow older, teaching full time in the community is desirable during the transition years of 18 to 21 years when peers without disabilities have transitioned from school to the com-munity. When the frequency of community-based instruction must be limited, teach-ers should teach community skills with multiple exemplars of natural materials in the school setting and use community-based instruction as an opportunity to assess gen-eralization to the community environment. To further examine the issues involved in designing community-based instruction, complete Activity 8.1.

ACTIVITY 8.1   Designing Community-Based Instruction

Select a functional skill that a student with a moderate or severe disability might need to perform in a com-munity setting. Tell how you will provide instruction on that skill in the community. List the setting(s) and the materials that will be used. If multiple exemplars will be used, specify what they will be. Describe the instructional procedure. Tell how often community-based instruction will occur and any considerations that should be given in determining the community setting.

COMMUNITY-REFERENCED SIMULATED INSTRUCTION

Although the previous section provided evidence that community-based instruction is a beneficial practice for students with moderate and severe disabilities, there are reasons that a teacher may not take students into the community for instruction. First, the constraints of transportation, cost, staffing, safety, or geographic location may limit access to the community as frequently as desired. Second, students placed in inclusive settings may be involved in school activities that do not leave time for community-based instruction. Third, school policy may dictate that younger students receive less community-based instruction than older students. Finally, the character-istics of individual students (e.g., medical conditions, behavior problems) may limit the amount of community-based instruction in which they can participate. In these cases, teachers may want to facilitate generalization of functional skills to the com-munity by conducting community-referenced instruction. This is instruction con-ducted in realistic simulations in the classroom or school setting that is referenced to the community. While this does not replace the need for community-based instruc-tion to determine if generalization has occurred, teaching through simulations can

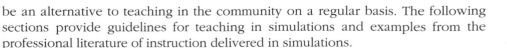

be an alternative to teaching in the community on a regular basis. The following sections provide guidelines for teaching in simulations and examples from the professional literature of instruction delivered in simulations.

Guidelines for the Delivery of Instruction in Simulations

Nietupski, Hamre-Nietupski, Clancy, and Veerhusen (1986) proposed teaching in simulation as an adjunct to community-based instruction or in vivo instruction. Noting that instruction in simulation should not be considered prerequisite to community-based instruction, they advocated for concurrent instruction in the classroom and the community in accordance with the model described by Brown et al. (1983). To deliver instruction in simulation, Nietupski et al. offered several guidelines.

First, the teacher should conduct an inventory of the community to determine the possible range of stimuli to which students will be required to respond, as well as the possible acceptable response variations students may perform. This fits in with the ecological inventory approach described in Chapter 5. For example, parents may tell the teacher that they eat most often at two fast-food restaurants in the community. In visiting the restaurants, the teacher notes that a student placing an order may hear, "May I take your order, please?" or "Would you like a double burger with a large order of fries today?" In responding, the student may have the option of placing a verbal order or pointing to pictures on a laminated menu.

Second, Nietupski et al. stated that classroom simulations should vary to provide a sufficient range of training exemplars. Based on the previous example, the teacher could set up a simulated fast-food counter in the classroom. The student would stand to place an order. The instructor would vary the stimulus for the student to respond across instructional sessions by providing various verbal cues and showing pictures from different menus.

Third, Nietupski et al. recommended using community performance data to modify simulations. In this case the teacher would observe students during community-based instruction and record data on a task analysis to determine if the students were able to generalize from classroom simulations to the community. The data would reveal those steps that were problematic. On analysis of the errors, the teacher would adjust the classroom simulation to better reflect the community site. For example, the teacher might note that the cashier stated, "Four ninety-five" instead of "Four dollars and ninety-five cents," causing the student to have difficulty counting out the correct number of dollars using a next dollar strategy. Thus, the classroom simulation would change to use this cue, and the teacher would show the student how to cue into the number(s) to the left of the decimal point on the cash register as well.

Fourth, Nietupski et al. suggested that classroom simulations be used to provide intensified practice on problem areas. Following through on the fast-food example, it would be discourteous to hold up the crowd of patrons in line to order during lunch hour while a student struggled with counting out the correct number of dollars to pay. As soon it became obvious that the student counted out the wrong number of the dollars, the teacher could terminate the trial in the real world and pay the amount for the student. On returning to the classroom, the teacher could then intensify instruction on paying for food by conducting massed trials on using the next dollar strategy during classroom simulations.

Finally, Nietupski et al. recommended scheduling simulations to allow for sufficient community-based instruction (e.g., minimum of once per week) and providing simulations in close temporal proximity to in vivo instruction. For example, immediately prior to leaving the school to participate in community-based instruction, the teacher could talk with the student about where they will be eating, what the menu choices will be, and how much they will cost. This would be followed by a brief session with the student to practice ordering and paying before leaving for the restaurant.

Examples of Simulations from the Professional Literature

The guidelines offered by Nietupski et al. (1986) for using simulation as an adjunct to community-based instruction are apparent in the following examples from the professional literature. In some cases the investigators taught across both school and community settings, then used novel settings to probe for generalization (i.e., concurrent instruction), and in some cases the investigators used community-based instruction to probe or test for generalization of skills taught through classroom simulations (i.e., consecutive instruction).

Using Classroom Simulation with Concurrent Community-Based Instruction to Teach Functional Skills
Morse and Schuster (2000) illustrated concurrent instruction in classroom simulation and the community when they taught 10 elementary school students with moderate disabilities to shop for groceries. The teacher delivered classroom simulations three times per week that consisted of using a storyboard lesson to sequence photographs of the steps involved in shopping for groceries and a constant time delay procedure. Community-based instruction occurred twice per week in which students received additional trials with a constant time delay procedure as they performed the steps of the task analysis. Those students who reached criterion by the end of the investigation were able to generalize the shopping skills to a novel grocery store during community-based instruction.

In an example with older students, Branham, Collins, Schuster, and Kleinert (1999) illustrated three variations of community-based instruction available to classroom teachers when they taught three community skills (mailing a letter, cashing a check, crossing a street) to three secondary school students with moderate disabilities. In the investigation the students each learned a skill using one of three formats: (a) community-based instruction plus classroom simulation, (b) community-based instruction plus classroom videotape modeling, and (c) community-based instruction plus classroom simulation and videotape modeling. Since the students attended a rural school, the teacher wanted to limit the time and expense of transportation to and from community sites. Thus, students either practiced the tasks with the assistance of peers without disabilities during classroom simulations or viewed the tasks in the classroom as they were performed by peers without disabilities on videotape. Regardless of the format, the instructor employed a constant time delay procedure. In addition to acquiring the tasks with each format, the students generalized each to a novel community setting.

Using Classroom Simulation with Consecutive Community-Based Instruction to Probe for Generalization
If access to the community is limited, instructors may wish to use community-based instruction as an opportunity to ensure that generalization has occurred. When the classroom is the primary setting for instruction, it is important to plan simulations to reflect the community as realistically as possible. For example, Mechling, Gast, and Langone (2002) used computer-based video instruction to teach four students (elementary through secondary school) with moderate disabilities to shop for groceries. In creating the video, the investigators taped stimuli

(e.g., aisle signs, shelf locations, grocery items) across three grocery stores. They then conducted classroom simulations in which they used a system of least prompts to teach the students to touch the correct stimuli on the computer screen. When taken to a novel grocery store during community-based instruction, the students were able to shop for the target items.

Frederick-Dugan, Test, and Varn (1991) also used simulation to teach purchasing skills. In their investigation, they taught purchasing skills to two secondary school students using a calculator and real price tags during simulations in the library. During weekly community-based instruction, the students received probes for generalization with untrained items in a department store until they reached criterion and demonstrated generalization to untrained items in a novel store.

Summary

It is possible for students to generalize skills taught in classroom simulations if instruction is referenced to the community by using realistic cues, task analyses, and materials. Community-based instruction, however, is still necessary to validate that generalization has occurred. Even when community-based instruction and simulation are used concurrently, novel exemplars of settings should be used to validate that generalization has occurred. To further examine the issues involved in designing effective simulations, complete Activity 8.2.

ACTIVITY 8.2   Designing Simulations

Return to the functional skill you selected in Activity 8.1, and describe how you would teach that same skill in classroom simulations. List the cues, materials, and reinforcers that will be used. If multiple exemplars will be used, specify what they will be. Describe the instructional procedure. Tell if you will conduct instruction concurrently across school and community settings or you will use community-based instruction to probe for generalization. List any additional considerations that should be given to school and community settings (e.g., involvement of peers).

COMPARISON OF COMMUNITY-BASED INSTRUCTION AND SIMULATION

A number of research investigations have focused on comparing the acquisition of functional skills taught in classroom simulations to the acquisition of functional skills taught in the community. A sample of these investigations are discussed in this section.

In the first example, Cuvo and Klatt (1992) found that simulations were as effective as community-based instruction in teaching three adolescents with mild and moderate disabilities to read community signs (e.g., *We're closed, Employees only*). The instructor used a constant time delay procedure across three formats: (a) flashcards of signs in the classroom, (b) videotape of signs in the community that was shown in the classroom, and (c) real signs during community-based instruction. Regardless of format, the students learned to read the signs. In addition, the students generalized the words taught from flashcards and videotape to the community.

Neef, Lensbower, Hockersmith, DePalma, and Gray (1990) also compared simulations to community-based instruction, but the simulations were not as realistic.

The instructor used a model-lead-test procedure to teach four adults with moderate and severe disabilities to do laundry (i.e., use a washer and dryer). During classroom simulations, the participants learned the tasks on a single example of appliances that were constructed of cardboard, styrofoam, and spare parts. During community-based instruction, the participants learned the tasks on a variety of appliances that sampled the range of examples (i.e., general case). The participants increased their ability to perform the tasks during both simulations and community-based instruction. Although instruction in simulations cost half as much, the investigators recommended using simulation as an adjunct to community-based instruction; they also concluded that the use of general case teaching exemplars is more important than the instructional setting.

When Gast, Collins, Wolery, and Jones (1993) used multiple exemplars of strangers and lures during classroom simulations to teach preschool children with developmental delays to respond to the lures of strangers, they found that the children failed to generalize to community settings during daily community-based instruction. When they moved simulated instruction to the community, the children were able to generalize the target response (say "no" and walk away five feet within five seconds). Based on this study, the investigators questioned whether classroom simulations served a purpose in practicing the response prior to instruction in the community.

Collins, Stinson, and Land (1993) addressed this question when they taught elementary and secondary school students with moderate disabilities to cross the street and use a public pay telephone. Some of the students received instruction in classroom simulations prior to instruction in the community, while others received instruction in the community only. During probes for generalization conducted in the community, it became apparent that some children were able to generalize when taught only in classroom simulations and some were not. Thus, the authors recommended that teachers who use classroom simulations conduct concurrent probes in the community for generalization to determine that it is taking place and that they change to instruction in the community when generalization does not occur.

In a final example, Bates, Cuvo, Miner, and Korabek (2001) compared classroom simulation to community-based instruction in teaching 20 young adults with mild disabilities and 20 young adults with moderate disabilities to perform a variety of functional tasks (grocery, laundry, restaurant, and janitorial skills). During classroom simulation, the instructor taught with photographs of an adult performing the tasks in the community. During community-based instruction, the instructor taught in a single setting and assessed generalization in two other settings. Regardless of the instructional setting, both groups showed an increase in skill performance from pretests to post tests. While community-based instruction was the optimal setting for both groups, the students with mild disabilities made more progress during simulation than the students with moderate disabilities made. Based on the results, the authors stated that, although it is not as strong a strategy as community-based instruction, teachers should consider using classroom simulation because (a) it is easier to conduct massed trials within a single session, (b) it is less expensive, (c) it is less dangerous or risky, (d) it is less stigmatizing, and (e) it is less disruptive to school schedules. Bates et al. also stressed that community-based instruction is an effective technology that should be merged with the philosophy of inclusion by involving peers without disabilities.

INTEGRATING COMMUNITY-BASED INSTRUCTION

Chapter 4 stressed the importance of a transdisciplinary approach in which related services are embedded in instruction, and Chapter 7 addressed the benefits of inclusive activities with peers without disabilities. The integration of community-based instruction with related services and inclusive activities is discussed in this section.

Integrating Related Services with Community-Based Instruction

Rainforth and York (1987) used the term *integrated therapy* to describe the practice of embedding related services in community-based instruction. The rationale is that students with moderate and severe disabilities learn to use the skills taught by related services (e.g., communication, motor skills) in a functional manner when they are embedded within functional activities. Thus, Rainforth and York recommended that these skills be embedded in community-based instruction. To do this, they suggested several guidelines.

First, the teacher should conduct an inventory of the community environment to determine the skills that will be needed in target activities. For example, students who shop for groceries need the gross motor skills to propel a grocery cart down aisles without bumping into shelves and displays, the fine motor skills to retrieve items for the cart, and the communication skills to ask for assistance when something is out of reach or cannot be located. Second, the student should be assessed in the natural environment to determine skills that can and cannot be performed on the task analysis of the activity. Third, the instructional team should develop instructional objectives for the students based on the results of the assessment. Fourth, the instructional team should develop an instructional program to teach the student to perform the activity, taking into account cues, task directions, instructional prompting procedures, reinforcers, and adaptations (e.g., picture shopping list, communication device). Fifth, the instructor who will be responsible for community-based instruction should be selected. This may be the teacher, an instructional assistant, a related service provider, or a peer tutor. Sixth, the team members should exchange information to ensure that appropriate techniques are used to teach the embedded skills (e.g., mand-model procedure to teach use of communication devices, switch used to propel wheelchair). Last, the instructor should share data from community-based instruction with the team members so progress can be evaluated and procedures can be modified, as necessary.

Integrating Inclusive Activities with Community-Based Instruction

In addressing the meshing of community-based instruction with inclusion, Beck, Broers, Hogue, Shipstead, and Knowlton (1994) posed the question, "Will I need it when I'm 21?" (p. 44) as a factor to determine the curriculum for students with moderate and severe disabilities. Beck et al. then offered the term *community-based integrated instruction* to describe the involvement of students from both general and special education in community-based instruction. Beck et al. stated that one of the benefits to be derived from a community-based integrated instruction model is the positive interaction that occurs between peers with and without disabilities and that the success of a community-based integrated instruction model is dependent on administrative support. Thus, Beck et al. recommended that administrators take the leadership for encouraging the involvement of students with and without disabilities in community-based integrated instruction. In doing this, administrators can provide staff development on the importance of functional skills and how they relate to the general education curriculum, provide time for collaborative planning between general and special educators, garner parent and community support by creating awareness of the benefits, and give recognition to those who participate. It should be noted that, in addition to promoting social interactions, community-based integrated instruction should be based on appropriate objectives for all participating students. An example can be found in Example 8.3.

EXAMPLE 8.3 **INTEGRATING COMMUNITY-BASED INSTRUCTION BY INCLUDING PEERS WITHOUT DISABILITIES**

There are several references in this text to Ned, a middle school student with a moderate to severe disability (Collins, Schuster, & Grisham-Brown, 2002). One of the recommendations for Ned's new educational program was for community-based instruction to occur at least twice each week, preferably in a small-group format. As Ned began to interact with peers without disabilities in the general education classes and school activities he attended, he formed a friendship with another male student who often challenged his teacher with his behavior. The teacher struck a deal with the student that he could be a peer tutor for Ned if his behavior improved. As the special education and general education teacher collaborated, a plan evolved in which the student would accompany Ned on community-based instruction contingent on appropriate behavior in the classroom.

The program was an immediate success, and Ned's friend turned out to be an excellent peer tutor. During community-based instruction in restaurants and stores, the student prompted Ned to perform target tasks (e.g., pay for purchases, order from menu), provided feedback for responses (e.g., praise, modeling of correct response), and collected data. The student also modeled appropriate behavior for Ned, thus reinforcing his own appropriate behavior.

Best Practices
Community-Based Instruction

1. To ensure generalization of functional community skills, either teach them in the community during regularly scheduled instruction or use community outings to test for generalization of skills taught during simulations in the classroom.

2. Increase the amount of community-based instruction as students grow older, using programs that are completely community-based by the time students enter the transition years.

3. When community-based instruction cannot be conducted as frequently as desired, use realistic classroom simulations as an adjunct to community-based instruction.

4. Increase the number of skills taught in the community by embedding related skills (e.g., communication, motor) and using a transdisciplinary team approach.

5. Increase the opportunity for interactions with peers without disabilities by including them in community-based instruction as peer buddies who also have instructional goals for the outing or as peer tutors who assist with instruction.

Conclusion

The practice of community-based instruction is based on the logic of the least dangerous assumptions (Donnellan, 1984) that teaching in the natural environment where a student will need to be able to perform a skill ensures that the student will be able do so. In other words, community-based instruction facilitates generalization for students with moderate and severe disabilities who may not generalize across settings, materials, or cues when they are taught in the classroom setting. There also is a research base that shows that skills taught in good simulations using materials and cues referenced to the community sometimes can result in generalization, causing simulation to be an effective adjunct to community-based instruction when trips to the community must be limited; however, probes for generalization in the community are needed to establish that the skills taught during classroom simulations have been generalized. In addition, the research shows that the use of multiple exemplars or general case instruction in both classroom simulations and community-based instruction can facilitate generalization to novel exemplars.

With the practice of inclusion becoming more prevalent, some advocates for inclusion have argued that community-based instruction and inclusion are mutually exclusive or that community-based instruction should not take place until students are older (e.g., 18 to 21 years) and their peers without disabilities have transitioned from school to community settings. Collins (2003), however, argued that community-based instruction can be appropriate across age levels and offered the following examples from the professional literature.

During the preschool years, instructors can incorporate community-based instruction in inclusive activities, such as using daily walks around the block to teach an appropriate response to strangers (e.g., Gast et al., 1993). In elementary school, students can learn functional skills, such as safely crossing the street, in settings immediately adjacent to the school during natural times, such as arrival or dismissal from school or during short breaks for transition during the day (e.g., Collins et al., 1993). In secondary school, students can practice skills with peers without disabilities during daily classroom simulations or during frequent community outings as part of a life skills class that employs peer tutors without disabilities, and instructional time can be increased by adding instructional videotape of the skills as they are performed in the community (e.g., Branham et al., 1999). Finally, programs that are completely community based can be offered to students who are in the transition years of 18 to 21 through a collaborative effort, such as creating a base of operations at a local college campus where students can practice functional skills, attend classes with peers without disabilities, engage in employment opportunities, and spend time in the community practicing the skills the students will need in adulthood (e.g., Hall, Kleinert, & Kearns, 2000). In short, as students grow older, the time spent in the community and the intensity of instruction in that setting should increase.

In summary, community-based instruction remains a critical component in ensuring that students with moderate and severe disabilities will have the skills they need to transition to least restrictive settings as adults. When community-based instruction cannot be conducted on a regular basis, classroom simulations can be a viable adjunct. To strengthen the practice of community-based instruction, related services and inclusive activities with peers without disabilities can be incorporated. To illustrate an understanding of community-referenced simulations and community-based instruction, work through the performance-based assessment at the end of this chapter.

Questions for Review

1. What is the difference between community-based instruction and community-referenced instruction?

2. What is the rationale behind involving students with moderate and severe disabilities in community-based instruction?

3. What is the difference between consecutive and concurrent instruction in regard to community-based instruction?

4. List four guidelines each for conducting community-based instruction and classroom simulations.

5. In what way would community-based instruction change as students grow older? Why?

6. How can related services (e.g., speech therapy) be embedded in community-based instruction?

7. How can community-based instruction be made more inclusive?

Performance-Based Assessment

Sometimes community-based instruction does not go as planned. After analyzing one of the scenarios below, tell what could have been done to avoid the problems that were encountered. In addition, tell how the staff should have followed up in the community and planned for future instruction.

Example One: Elementary School

The teacher in this scenario planned a community-based instruction trip to a new restaurant in advance by sending a note to the students' parents requesting their permission and a set amount of money that would be needed. In addition, the teacher selected the skills to be taught or monitored in the setting. The bus arrived on time and transported the entire class to the restaurant along with the teacher, classroom assistants, and several peers without disabilities. The characteristics of the children varied in terms of severity of disability and the level of self-help, mobility, and communication skills. When the class arrived, the restaurant was at the peak of the lunch hour, although a few empty tables were scattered across the room. The teacher explained to the hostess that the staff would prefer to be seated at the available tables with one adult and one or two children per table. Instead, the hostess insisted that the class sit as a group in a separate dining room where they would not disturb other diners, defeating the teacher's goal of community integration. Once the class was situated, a waitress took the orders of each student. Ordering was slow because some of the students were not familiar with the items on the menu and needed help selecting foods that they might like. Because the restaurant was crowded, the food was late in arriving, creating a situation in which inappropriate behaviors began to escalate. Although behavior improved when the food arrived, some of the entrées were not to the liking of the students. In addition, the teacher found the objective for each student to pay individually for his or her meal was curtailed when the waitress brought the bill and explained that the restaurant did not issue individual bills for large parties. During the outing, the staff did not have the opportunity to work on many of the objectives that had been planned, and the outing ended with tension between the restaurant and classroom staff.

Example Two: Secondary School

The teacher of a class of secondary school students with severe multiple disabilities and severe behavior problems arranged for the students to participate in community-based instruction in small groups of two or three several times per week. A bus transported the students with their teacher and classroom assistant. Both had experience with safe physical management techniques for behavioral crisis intervention. A morning trip to a local grocery store began well enough, with the students walking the aisles and selecting items from the shelves using a picture list. Then a shopper pushed a cart between a student and the item he was selecting from the shelf. Lacking the verbal skills to voice his agitation, the student rammed the woman's grocery cart into the shelves, knocking over the cans displayed on them. When the assistant tried to intervene, the student went on a rampage, knocking over displays, and had to be physically restrained on the floor while the teacher called for assistance. Once the staff got the student to the bus, the student's behavior had escalated to the point that he broke a bus window, injuring his hand. The incident ended with the student receiving medical attention and being sent home.

References

Agran, M., Snow, K., & Swaner, J. (1999). A survey of secondary level teachers' opinions on community-based instruction and inclusive education. *Journal of the Association for Persons with Severe Handicaps, 24,* 58–62.

Aveno, A., Renzaglia, A., & Lively, C. (1987). Surveying community training sites to insure that instructional decisions accommodate the site as well as the trainees. *Education and Training in Mental Retardation, 22,* 167–175.

Bates, P. E., Cuvo, T., Miner, C. A., & Korabek, C. A. (2001). Simulated and community-based instruction involving persons with mild and moderate mental retardation. *Research in Developmental Disabilities, 22,* 95–115.

Beck, J., Broers, J., Hogue, E., Shipstead, J., & Knowlton, E. (1994). Strategies for functional community-based instruction and inclusion for children with mental retardation. *Teaching Exceptional Children, 26*(2), 44–48.

Branham, R. S., Collins, B. C., Schuster, J. W., & Kleinert, H. (1999). Teaching community skills to students with moderate disabilities: Comparing combined techniques of classroom simulation, videotape modeling, and community-based instruction. *Education and Training in Mental Retardation and Developmental Disabilities, 34,* 170–181.

Browder, D. M. (1997). Educating students with severe disabilities: Enhancing the conversation between research and practice. *The Journal of Special Education, 31,* 137–144.

Brown, L., Nisbet, J., Ford, A., Sweet, M., Shiraga, B., York, J., & Loomis, R. (1983). The critical need for nonschool instruction in educational programs for severely handicapped students. *Journal of the Association for Persons with Severe Handicaps, 8,* 71–77.

Collins, B. C. (2003). Meeting the challenge of conducting community-based instruction in rural settings. *Rural Special Education Quarterly, 22*(2), 31–35.

Collins, B. C., & Schuster, J. W. (2001). Some thoughts on the history of rural special education: A first hand account. *Rural Special Education Quarterly, 20*(1/2), 22–29.

Collins, B. C., & Schuster, J. W., & Grisham-Brown, J. (2002). *Success story: Ned.* Unpublished manuscript.

Collins, B. C., Schuster, J. W., & Nelson, C. M. (1992). Teaching a generalized response to the lures of strangers to adults with severe handicaps. *Exceptionality, 3,* 67–80.

Collins, B. C., Stinson, D. M., & Land, L. (1993). A comparison of in vivo and simulation prior to in vivo instruction in teaching generalized safety skills. *Education and Training in Mental Retardation, 28,* 128–142.

Cook, B. G. (2002). Special educators' views of community-based job training and inclusion as indicators of job competencies for students with mild to moderate disabilities. *Career Development for Exceptional Individuals, 25,* 7–24.

Cooper, K. J., & Browder, D. M. (1998). Enhancing choice and participation for adults with severe disabilities in community-based instruction. *Journal of the Association for Persons with Severe Handicaps, 23,* 252–260.

Cuvo, A. J., & Klatt, K. P. (1992). Effects of community-based, videotape, and flash card instruction of community-referenced sight words on students with mental retardation. *Journal of Applied Behavior Analysis, 25,* 499–512.

Donnellan, A. M. (1984). The criterion of the least dangerous assumption. *Behavior Disorders, 9,* 141–150.

Everington, C., & Stevenson, T. (1994). A giving experience: Using community service to promote community living skills and integration for individuals with severe disabilities. *Teaching Exceptional Children, 26*(3), 56–59.

Frederick-Dugan, A., Test, D.W., & Varn, L. (1991). Acquisition and generalization of purchasing skills using a calculator by students who are mentally retarded. *Education and Training in Mental Retardation, 26,* 381–387.

Gast, D. L., Collins, B. C., Wolery, M., & Jones, R. (1993). Teaching preschool children with disabilities to respond to the lures of strangers. *Exceptional Children, 59,* 301–311.

Gumpel, T. P., & Nativ-Ari-Am, H. (2001). Evaluation of a technology for teaching complex social skills to young adults with visual and cognitive impairments. *Journal of Visual Impairment and Blindness, 95,* 95–107.

Hall, M. G., Kleinert, H. L., & Kearns, J. F. (2000). Going to college! Postsecondary programs for students with moderate to severe disabilities. *Teaching Exceptional Children, 32*(3), 58–65.

Hamre-Nietupski, S., McDonald, J., & Nietupski, J. (1992). Integrating elementary students with multiple disabilities into supported regular classes: Challenges and solutions. *Teaching Exceptional Children, 24*(3), 6–9.

McDonnell, J., Hardman, M. L., Hightower, J., Keifer-O'Donnell, R., & Drew, C. (1993). Impact of community-based instruction on the development of adaptive behavior of secondary-level students with mental retardation. *American Journal on Mental Retardation, 97,* 575–584.

Mechling, L. C., Gast, D. L., & Langone, J. (2002). Computer-based video instruction to teach persons with moderate intellectual disabilities to read grocery aisle signs and locate items. *Journal of Special Education, 35,* 224–240.

Miracle, S., McNabb-Kuebler, E., Hardy, W., Pinto, J., & Davis, G. (n.d.). *Woodford County Schools community-based instruction manual.* Versailles, KY: Woodford County Schools.

Morse, T. E., & Schuster, J. W. (2000). Teaching elementary students with moderate intellectual disabilities how to shop for groceries. *Exceptional Children, 66,* 273–288.

Neef, N. A., Lensbower, J., Hockersmith, I., DePalma, V., & Gray, K. (1990). In vivo versus simulation training: An interactional analysis of range and type of training exemplars. *Journal of Applied Behavior Analysis, 23,* 447–458.

Nietupski, J., Hamre-Nietupski, S., Clancy, P., & Veerhusen, K. (1986). Guidelines for making simulation an effective adjunct to in vivo community instruction. *Journal of the Association for Persons with Severe Handicaps, 11,* 12–18.

Rainforth, B., & York, J. (1987). Integrating related services in community instruction. *Journal of the Association for Persons with Severe Handicaps, 12,* 190–198.

Sailor, W., Halvorsen, A., Anderson, J., Goetz, L., Gee, K. Doering, K., & Hunt, P. (1986). Community intensive instruction. In R. Horner, L. Meyer, & H. Fredericks (Eds.), *Education of learners with severe handicaps: Exemplary learning strategies.* Baltimore: Brookes.

Smith, R. L., Collins, B. C., Schuster, J. W., & Kleinert, H. L. (1999). Teaching table cleaning skills to secondary students with moderate/severe disabilities: Facilitating observational learning during instructional downtime. *Education and Training in Mental Retardation and Developmental Disabilities, 34,* 342–353.

Snell, M. E., & Browder, D. M. (1986). Community-referenced instruction: Research and issues. *Journal of the Association for Persons with Severe Handicaps, 11,* 1–11.

Sprague, J. R., & Horner, R. H. (1984). The effects of single instance, multiple instance, and general case training on generalized vending machine use by moderately and severely handicapped students. *Journal of Applied Behavior Analysis, 17,* 273–278.

Stokes, T. F., & Baer, D. M. (1977). An implicit technology of generalization. *Journal of Applied Behavior Analysis, 10,* 349–367.

Taylor, P., Collins, B. C., Schuster, J. W., & Kleinert, H. L. (2002). Teaching laundry skills to high school students with disabilities: Generalization of targeted skills and nontargeted information. *Education and Training in Mental Retardation and Developmental Disabilities, 37,* 172–183.

Wolfe, P. S. (1994). Judgment of the social validity of instructional strategies used in community-based instructional sites. *Journal of the Association for Persons with Severe Handicaps, 19,* 43–51.

CHAPTER NINE

WORKING WITH STUDENTS WITH MEDICAL NEEDS:
Health and Vitality

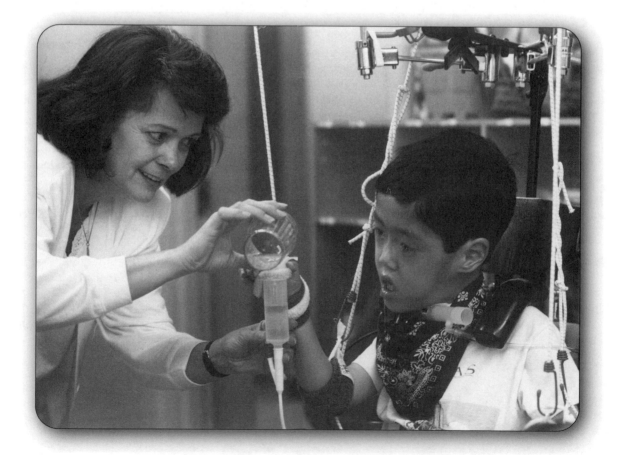

On completion of this chapter, the reader will meet the following objectives:

- Define terminology related to the health care of students with moderate and severe disabilities.

- Write health care information and appropriate health care–related objectives for an Individual Education Plan (IEP) or Individual Transition Plan (ITP).

- Discuss legal decisions regarding the responsibilities of school districts to provide health-related procedures.

- Describe the type of information and training teachers should obtain from school districts and health care professionals regarding policies and procedures for working with children with medical needs in the school setting.

- Describe the type of information teachers should obtain from parents and health care professionals regarding precautions and emergencies for working with students with various types of medical needs in the school setting.

- Discuss various health care skills that should be taught and issues that should be addressed in working with students with moderate and severe disabilities.

The preceding chapters discussed what, how, and where students with moderate and severe disabilities should be taught in order to receive an appropriate education. Chapters 9 and 10 will expand on this topic by discussing services that persons with moderate and severe disabilities should receive in regard to health care and behavioral needs, with a special focus on what should take place in the educational system.

In the past few decades, there has been an increase in the number of children and students with physical and health disabilities. In 1990 Lehr listed the reasons for an increase in children with complex health care needs as being advances in technology, changes in attitude (e.g., adoption of the principle of normalization), more programs for young children, and group care for children with communicable diseases, such as acquired immunodeficiency disorder (AIDS). According to Heller, Fredrick, Dykes, Best, and Cohen (1999), numbers reported by the U.S. Department of Education in 1996 included 60,604 students identified as having orthopedic impairments, 106, 509 identified as having other health impairments, and 89,646 identified as having multiple disabilities. They attributed an increase in these over time to a higher survival rate of smaller babies, surgical interventions, and improved treatments due to better medical technology.

FIGURE 9.1

Overlap of Persons with and Without Mental Disabilities and Medical Needs

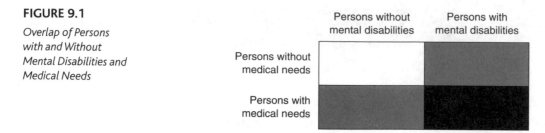

With the advent of the principle of normalization, deinstitutionalization also is a contributing factor due to an increase of persons with disabilities and health care needs living with their families and receiving services within community settings (Lehr & McDaid, 1993), although lack of medical personnel trained in developmental disabilities, Medicaid disincentives, and geographic inaccessibility can be community barriers to receiving adequate services (Hayden & DePaepe, 1991). Morningstar et al. (2001) reported that 10,000 to 68,000 children required some kind of medical technology in 1992 (e.g., ventilator assistance: 680–2,000, parental nutrition: 350–700, device-based respiratory or nutritional support: 1,000–6,000, ventilator assistance or parental nutrition: 2,300–8,700) and noted that 80% to 90% of children with chronic conditions now survive to adulthood; the shift from institutional to community care has put the responsibility for such health care–related services on the educational system.

The focus of this chapter will be on the health and vitality of persons with moderate and severe disabilities who reside in community settings, with particular attention to school settings. As noted in Chapters 1 and 2, persons with moderate and severe disabilities often have medical needs in addition to a mental disability. In some cases the medical condition is linked to the mental disability, causing the medical condition to be categorized as either (a) a factor causing the mental disability (e.g., traumatic brain injury), (b) a factor related to the mental disability (e.g., Down syndrome), or (c) an outcome resulting from the mental disability (e.g., malnutrition).

In some cases a medical condition, a physical impairment, or a sensory impairment (or a combination) may be so severe that persons may function as if they have a mental disability when they do not (e.g., deafblindness). In others a medical condition may be unrelated to the mental disability and just happen to occur in persons with mental disabilities as it would if they did not have mental disabilities. (Figure 9.1 illustrates this concept.) For example, asthma is the leading cause of school absenteeism across all children (Getch & Neuharth-Pritchett, 1999). In addition, 100,000 children under the age of 19 have diabetes, a condition that can occur as early as 6 months of age (Rosentahal-Malek & Greenspan, 1999).

While some medical conditions are unrelated to the mental disability, there is evidence that persons with moderate and severe disabilities may have a greater risk for particular medical conditions found in persons without disabilities, such as cardiovascular disease (Draheim, McCubbin, & Williams, 2002) and osteoporosis (Center, Beange, & McElduff, 1988). Quality of health care for persons with moderate and severe disabilities may be a contributing factor to their state of health and vitality (Walsh & Kastner, 1999); for example, thyroid and cardiac functions must be monitored in persons with Down syndrome, and pressure sores may need to be monitored in persons with significant cognitive or severe multiple disabilities who are nonambulatory.

There are numerous examples of ways in which persons with moderate and severe disabilities may be at risk for serious medical conditions. Problems with the respiratory tract are the leading cause of death among persons with significant cognitive disabilities or severe cerebral palsy, and there is evidence that those who receive tube feedings via a gastrostomy tube experience an increase in pneumonia over those who receive tube feedings via a jejunostomy tube (Taylor, 2002). Children with feeding problems also may be at risk for malnourishment (Brotherson, Oakland, Secrist-Mertz, Litchfield, & Larson, 1995).

Down syndrome and the overall smaller size (i.e., height and weight) of persons with mental disabilities are factors that cause an increased prevalence of osteoporosis, creating a risk factor for fractures and prolonged hospitalization in a group that is already at risk for having a greater number of falls than persons without disabilities (Center et al., 1988). Low bone mineral density associated with cerebral palsy and Down syndrome may lead to an increase in fractures; likewise, persons with seizure disorders or who take seizure medication also may exhibit an increase in fractures (Ryder et al., 2003).

Persons with moderate and severe disabilities may be at risk for communicable diseases. In 1990 Lehr stated that human immunodeficiency virus (HIV) was a leading cause of both mental retardation and death. Of 8,294 adults identified with HIV or AIDS in New Jersey from 1993 to 1996, Walkup, Sambamoorthi, and Crystal (1999) found that 119 also had a diagnosis of mental retardation. Factors associated with mental retardation, such as unhealthful sexual behavior, vulnerability to sexual abuse, dependence on others, and denial or reluctance from staff to deal with sexual issues, make persons with moderate and severe disabilities at risk for contracting HIV or AIDS (Jacobs, Samowitz, Levy, & Levy, 1989). Persons with moderate and severe disabilities (especially those with Down syndrome) also may be at elevated risk for contracting hepatitis (especially hepatitis A or B) through group living conditions (e.g., institutionalization), medical care, sexual contact, or wounds resulting from aggressive or self-injurious behavior (Woodruff & Vazquez, 2002).

Brain disorders also can be associated with moderate and severe disabilities. Traumatic brain injury is the most common cause of death and disability in children in the United States; of more than one million children having traumatic brain injury, between 9% and 38% are referred to special education for services (Keyser-Marcus et al., 2002). Traumatic brain injury has become so prevalent that the condition was identified as a specific special education category under the Individuals with Disabilities Education Act (IDEA) of 1990 (Witte, 1998). Seizure disorders, a condition that may be associated with brain trauma, can be found in 14% to 44% of persons with mental disabilities with an increase in the likelihood of seizures linked to the severity of the disability (Morgan, Baxter, & Kerr, 2003); although it is rare for seizures to be fatal, they can result in injuries or sudden death with the overall mortality rate for those with seizure disorders being two to three times greater than for those without seizure disorders (McKee & Bodfish, 2000).

In addition to medical needs, persons with moderate and severe disabilities may have dental needs that can affect their state of health and vitality. For example, prescription medications, altered salivary flow, and edible reinforcers, such as candy, can induce dental decay; behaviors associated with stereotypy, such as thumbsucking, or genetic syndromes, such as tongue thrusting, can result in malocclusions; medical conditions can contribute to soft tissue complications (e.g., side effect of seizure medication) or bruxism (i.e., grinding associated with cerebral palsy); and behavioral patterns, such as physical aggression or self-injury, can result in fractured teeth (Waldman, Perlman, & Swerdloff, 2001).

The severity of the health care needs of students can affect their ability to receive educational services. When Borgioli and Kennedy (2003) interviewed the parents of students with multiple disabilities who experienced absences from school due to hospitalizations across 48 Tennessee school districts, they found that 61% of the hospitalizations were for emergency reasons and were unplanned. Most of the unplanned hospitalizations were due to infections, while most of the planned hospitalizations were due to orthopedic surgeries. Absences lasted an average of 28.9 days (6.7 spent in the hospital and 22.2 spent recovering). The students averaged 2.4 hospitalizations over a five-year period. The authors noted that this is equivalent to one summer vacation every five years. Only one family stated that they had a transition plan during their child's hospitalization so that educational programming could continue.

The health care needs of children with moderate and severe disabilities can also affect their families. For example, Brotherson et al. (1995) examined the quality of life in eight families whose children used feeding tubes and found that feeding tubes can be a mixed blessing. On the positive side, the tubes promoted weight gain, increased alertness, and decreased irritability. On the negative side, the tubes increased financial stress (e.g., cost of formula and medical supplies), created difficulty in finding respite (e.g., babysitters who could perform the tube feeding), decreased social support from family and friends, and increased social stigma by making the child's disability more visible. In addition, parents struggled with conflicting information or lack of information from professionals.

In summary, dealing with health and vitality issues is one of the challenges in providing services to persons with moderate and severe disabilities. The remainder of this chapter will define terminology associated with health care needs, describe components that should be included in the IEPs and ITPs of students with moderate and severe disabilities who have health care needs, discuss the issues involved in providing appropriate health care services, and suggest strategies for working with students with moderate and severe disabilities who have health care needs.

DEFINING THE TERMS

Before considering educational needs of students with health care needs, it is useful to define associated vocabulary. According to Heller et al. (1999), physical and health impairments include orthopedic impairments, other health impairments, and multiple disabilities. **Physical** or **orthopedic impairments** may be congenital in origin, caused by disease, or due to other causes. The term **other health impairment** refers to "limited strength, vitality, or alertness, due to chronic or acute health problems such as heart conditions, tuberculosis, rheumatic fever, nephritis, asthma, lead poisoning, leukemia, or diabetes, that adversely affects a child's educational performance" (Department of Education, 1992, p. 44802). Heller et al. (1999) noted that this category can "include students who have technology-assisted or complex health care needs" (p. 220). Heller et al. also noted that **multiple impairments** is a term that refers to persons who have both orthopedic and other health impairments.

The term **complex health care needs** describes a heterogeneous population that includes students labeled as "(a) having chronic illnesses, (b) being technology-dependent, or (c) being medically fragile" (Lehr, 1990, p. 3). **Chronic illnesses** include conditions (e.g., burns), injury traumas (e.g., spinal cord injury), or illnesses (e.g., diabetes) that may last months or a lifetime (Lehr, 1990, p. 3). A student who is **technology dependent** is "one who needs both a medical device to compensate for the loss of a vital body function and substantial and ongoing nursing care to avert death or further disability" (U.S. Congress, 1987). Examples include dependence on ventilators, intravenous drugs, respiratory or nutritional support, apnea monitors, dialysis, catheters, or colostomy bags. Students who are considered **medically fragile** are those "who are in constant need of medical supervision to prevent life-threatening situations" (Katsiyannis & Yell, 2000, p. 317).

Students with health care needs may require **school health services** that are "provided by a qualified school nurse or other qualified person" (IDEA Regulations, 34 C.F.R. § 300.16) or **medical services** that are "provided by a licensed physician for diagnostic or evaluation purposes" (Katsiyannis & Yell, 2000, p. 319). School health services may be required under the law if the service "is necessary to assist a child with disabilities in benefiting from special education, (b) must be performed during school hours, and (c) can be provided by a person other than a licensed physician" (Katsiyannis & Yell, 2000, p. 319). Lehr (1990) listed the needs of students with complex health care needs as (a) entitlement to a free and appropriate public school education, (b) education in a least restrictive environment, (c) a health care plan as part of the IEP, (d) treatment as a child and student over treatment as a patient, and (e) interaction with peers without health care issues. To meet these needs, Lehr further stated that schools must agree to perform health care procedures in the school setting, determine who will be responsible for administering the procedures, provide adequate preparation in performance of the procedures, and determine ways to meet student transportation needs. The following section addresses the IEP and ITP of students with moderate and severe disabilities who have health care needs.

Addressing Health Care Needs Through the IEP and ITP

Health care needs should be addressed when the educational team is writing the IEP or ITP for a student. The following sections contain ways in which this can be approached.

Planning for the Educational Program

There are two ways to approach writing the IEP for a student with a moderate or severe disability who has health care needs. The first is to address how the health care needs of the student will be met. The second is to view the implementation of a health care procedure as an educational opportunity to teach skills to the student.

Supplying Information on Health Care Procedures   When writing the IEP, Lehr and McDaid (1993) suggested that a health care plan also should be written if a student has health care needs. This would contain (a) the health history of the student, (b) special health care needs, (c) baseline health status, (d) medication and dietary needs, (e) transportation requirements, (f) intervention and emergency plans, and (g) procedures to document contact with emergency services.

When students are medically fragile, Prendergast (1995) suggested including additional information. First, the level of care the child will receive should be specified.

This can be (a) **direct care,** in which a nurse delivers the service, (b) **indirect care,** in which a nurse is available to the team but not to the child, or (c) **consultation,** in which a nurse is available to the school for consultative services. Second, two staff members who will be responsible for delivering the health care service (primary and backup) should be identified for each health care goal. Third, a checklist may be useful in assuring that the following items are covered during the meeting: (a) assessment data, (b) medical summary, (c) medical orders, (d) nursing interventions, (e) equipment, (f) schedule, (g) safety issues, (h) emergency protocol, (i) authorization for treatment, and (j) health-related services. Health-related services may include but are not limited to seizure monitoring, teeth and gum care, medicine administration, skin care, bowel care, nutrition monitoring, therapeutic management, cardiopulmonary resuscitation, shunt monitoring, cast care, glucose monitoring, colostomy/ileostomy care, nasogastric or gastrostomy tube feeding, clean intermittent catheterization, and tracheostomy care (p. 40).

The health care plan for a student with asthma developed by Getch and Neuharth-Pritchett (1999) is a good example of a health care plan that can accompany an IEP. The plan included the student's name, date of birth, parents' telephone numbers, emergency telephone numbers, emergency procedures, allergy triggers, asthmatic symptoms, medicine dosage, and medicine side effects.

Regardless of the health care need, the IEP team will want to address specific information within the context of the IEP or the health care plan. This is illustrated in Example 9.1.

EXAMPLE 9.1   **WRITING HEALTH CARE INFORMATION IN THE IEP**

The administration of medication related to a child's health care need is often an issue in providing educational services for students with moderate and severe disabilities. The following example (Smith & Leathervy, 1993, p. 83) illustrates how this may be written in the child's IEP or accompanying health care plan. Note that the team will want to check with local school district policies (e.g., who can give medication) before specifying such information.

Required Procedure: Date:	Person(s) Responsible:	Date Begin:	End:
The student will receive medication three times per day each day he is at school.	Teacher (Primary) Instructional Assistant (Backup)	August, 2005	June, 2006

Viewing Health Care Procedures as Instructional Opportunities   The Division for Physical and Health Disabilities of the Council for Exceptional Children has issued a position statement that specialized health care procedures are self-help or independent living skills that should be included as educational objectives on the IEP (Heller, Frederick, Best, Dykes, & Cohen, 2000). The objective may be for the student to learn to perform the procedure independently, to partially participate in the procedure, or to direct someone else to perform the procedure. In addition to addressing the health care procedure as a skill to be taught to a student, the delivery of health care procedures can be viewed also as opportunities to embed the instruction of unrelated skills, such as language, motor, or functional academic skills (e.g., math, reading). Example 9.2 illustrates both types of objectives.

EXAMPLE 9.2 ADDRESSING HEALTH CARE PROCEDURES IN IEP OBJECTIVES

IEP objectives can be written to address the instruction of health care skills, as shown in the following example of an objective for performing catheterization (Smith & Leatherby, 1993):

> When given the materials needed for catheterization and given the verbal command to do so, the student will catheterize himself by independently performing 100% of the steps of catheterization two out of two times each day of the school year (p. 83).

IEP objectives can also be written to embed the instruction of other skills within the performance of the health care procedures, as shown in the following example of an objective for the motor skill to extend the arm (Smith & Leatherby, 1993):

> When involved in an activity (described below) and given a verbal cue to "reach for _____" when the item is placed two to four inches in front of the student, he will extend his right forearm from the elbow to make contact with the item within 15 seconds, four out of five opportunities for three consecutive days.
>
> Examples of activities in which the student will practice reaching for items by extending the arm are as follows:
>
> 1. reaching for switch to operate appliance during snack time
> 2. reaching for switch to operate video game during leisure time
> 3. reaching for coat hook to hang up coat during arrival time
> 4. reaching for switch to operate electric can opener to open can of formula for G-tube feeding
> 5. reaching for the supplies during G-tube feeding to assist with feeding during lunch (p. 83)

Planning for Transition

There are two types of transitions that should be addressed in working with students with moderate and severe disabilities who have health care needs. First, students should have educational needs addressed during illnesses and hospitalizations. Second, students should have health care needs addressed during the transition from school to adulthood.

As noted previously, educational services often discontinue for extended periods when a student with a moderate or severe disability is hospitalized or is recovering from an illness or surgery. Borgioli and Kennedy (2003) suggested that ITPs be written for students who miss extended periods of school due to medical needs and that a transdisciplinary, family-centered approach be used in determining who will be responsible for (a) delivering educational services, (b) training others who deliver educational services, and (c) monitoring educational services outside of the school setting (e.g., hospital, home).

Second, the health care needs of students with moderate and severe disabilities should be addressed when they transition from the educational system to adulthood. Based on longitudinal in-depth interviews with 12 participants over a two-year period, Morningstar et al. (2001) found that the majority of students who were supported by medical technology received minimal planning during transition to adulthood and that the level of planning was dependent on the cognitive ability of the student. The parents who were interviewed had concerns for the future of their children and the lack of adult services available to their children.

Morningstar et al. recommended several strategies that can be used in developing the ITP. These included (a) determining if the student can manage health care needs independently and focusing on helping the student be more independent, (b) including knowledgeable persons (e.g., nurse, physician) and future health care providers on the transition team as goals are written, and (c) identifying health care advocates for students who may need assistance in communicating. In addition, Umbarger, Turnbull, Morningstar, Reichard, and Moberly (2001) suggested that transition teams investigate future funding for medical needs through (a) public sources (e.g., Medicaid, supplemental social security income [SSI], the Rehabilitation Act, IDEA) and (b) private sources (i.e., insurance policies, civic organizations, private foundations, national associations, institutions of higher education) since family income may not be sufficient to cover necessary costs during adulthood.

LEGAL ISSUES IN PROVIDING SCHOOL HEALTH CARE SERVICES

In determining educational placements and programming and in implementing the IEPs and ITPs of students with moderate and severe disabilities who have health care needs, the educational team may experience confusion over policies and funding. Under IDEA, all students are entitled to a free and appropriate public education that may include special and related services. Related services include school health services (those provided by the school nurse or other qualified personnel) and medical services (those determined by but not provided by a physician). Those students who do not qualify for health care services under IDEA may qualify for health care services under section 504 of the Rehabilitation Act of 1973.

Thomas and Hawke (1999) noted that related services addressed through the courts have included climate control, special diets, medication administration (e.g., parent right to refuse to medicate, school obligation to medicate even if parents are unwilling to sign waiver of liability), emergency care (e.g., lack of school liability in some states if parents have "do not resuscitate" orders), medical evaluation (e.g., school obligation to pay only for medical evaluation for identification and evaluation regardless of parent request for other evaluations), and school health services. Table 9.1 provides an overview of selected court cases that have addressed the interpretation of the law and the ability of school districts to provide school health care.

It is clear that the courts have wrestled with the responsibility of schools to provide complex and costly services, such as tracheostomy monitoring. Several authors (Bartlett, 2000; Katsiyannis & Yell, 2000; Rapport, 1996, Thomas & Hawke, 1999) have noted that, in most cases, the courts have held school districts to the **bright line test,** in which a medical service must be covered by schools as a related service if it can be performed by someone other than a physician. Bartlett (2000) recommended that special education funding be increased to cover expenses in areas where districts are held to the bright line test and inferred that money could be better spent in advocating for the change of laws rather than challenging laws through

TABLE 9.1   *Overview of Selected Legal Cases Regarding Provision of Health Care Services in School Settings Based on Bartlett (2000), Katsiyannis and Yell (2000), Rapport (1996), and Thomas and Hawke (1999).*

Case	Year	Issue	Outcome
Board of Education v. Rowley	1982	Provision of language interpreter for student with hearing impairment	Appropriate program has access to special services with programming left to educators and parents (not courts)
Department of Education v. Katherine D.	1984	School refusal to provide education for child with cystic fibrosis and tracheostomy tube	School must provide medical service because it can be performed by school nurse or other qualified person
Irving Independent School District v. Tatro	1984	School refusal to provide clean intermittent catheterization	School must provide medical service because it can be performed by school nurse or other qualified person
Detsel v. Board of Education	1986, 1987	Provision of services for student needing constant supervision with respirator	Cost and complexity of providing constant nursing assistance more than district could bear
Detsel v. Sullivan	1990	Provision of services for student needing constant supervision with respirator	Service could be funded in school setting through Medicaid
Bevin H. v. Wright	1986, 1987	Cost of constant nursing care for student with tracheostomy and gastrostomy tubes	Cost and complexity of providing constant nursing assistance more than district could bear
Granite School District v. Shannon M.	1992	Cost of constant nursing care for student with tracheostomy tube	Homebound educational program more appropriate
Neely v. Rutherford County Schools	1994, 1995	Provision of constant services for child with tracheostomy tube	School must provide specialized medical supervision; decision later reversed because medical services excluded under IDEA
Fulginiti v. Roxbury Township Public Schools	1996	Provision of constant services for child with severe multiple disabilities including need for tracheostomy tube	Cost and complexity of medical services undue burden to school system and not required under IDEA
McComb County Intermediate School District v. Joshua S.	1989	Provision of tracheostomy supervision by nurse during transportation to and from school	School district must provide medical service during transportation as well as in school setting

(Continued)

(continued)			
Cedar Rapids Community School District v. Garret F.	1996,1997, 1999	School refusal to provide services for child needing tracheostomy care, catheterization, and positioning	School must provide service since it can be performed by nurse; decision upheld by Supreme Court
Skelly v. Brookfield LaGrange Park School District 95	1996, 1997	Provision of tracheostomy supervision by nurse during transportation to and from school	Child moved to homebound services because school not responsible for medical service during transportation
Morton Community School District 709 v. J. M.	1997, 1998	Refusal of school district to provide constant ventilator monitoring	Ventilator monitoring was related service that could be provided in school setting by nurse

the court system. Even when it is determined that school districts are responsible for providing medical services, Heller et al. (2000) noted the lack of national legislation regarding the performance of school health care procedures and the variance in Nurse Practice Acts across states as to who can perform specific procedures.

Katsiyannis and Yell (2000) suggested that state educational agencies develop a uniform set of policies and procedures to assist school districts, investigate various sources to secure funding for medical services, provide technical assistance for schools, and ensure proper coverage for liability. In addition, Katsiyannis and Yell suggested that local educational agencies develop guidelines in compliance with those from the state, examine the level of liability coverage, explore additional funding sources, contract with health care providers for complex health care services, and collaborate with other agencies.

ISSUES IN TRAINING PERSONNEL

As stated in the previous section, there is a legal basis for health care procedures being performed in public schools if the procedures can be performed by persons other than physicians.

Some health care procedures may be performed by nurses or other licensed health care professionals, but many will need to be performed by school personnel, such as teachers or instructional assistants. The Council for Exceptional Children's Division of Physical and Health Disabilities has issued a position statement that teachers should "maintain a safe, healthy environment for their students," including "learning about their students' specialized healthcare procedures, planning for emergencies related to the procedures, and being educated to recognize problems and implement the plan" as well as being skilled in universal precautions, first aid, and CPR (Heller et al., 2000, p. 175). Thus, adequate training to perform health care procedures can be an issue.

Heller et al. (2000) reported that the Division of Physical and Health Disabilities surveyed its members to determine the skills needed in educational settings and who was performing those skills. The results revealed that the most frequently performed procedures were tube feedings (67.3%), clean intermittent catheterizations (55.6%), and suctioning (48.2%). In addition, more than 20% of the respondents reported ventilator management, an intrusive and complex procedure. A nurse performed the procedures most often followed by the teacher or instructional assistant. More than one third of teachers or instructional assistants took responsibility for performing tube feedings, colostomy care, clean intermittent catheterizations, suctioning, and tracheostomy care. Nurses were followed by teachers, instructional assistants, and clerical staff in administering medication and in performing first aid. Most training of health care procedures consisted of one-to-one training with the student for both medical and nonmedical personnel. Most school personnel had received training in infection control, universal precautions, cardiopulmonary resuscitation, and first aid, although much of the training was not current. The majority of schools had written procedures for emergency management, first aid, medication administration, and special health care procedures.

It is clear that there are training issues for both health care and educational professionals. These issues are addressed in the following sections. Before proceeding, however, take time to check your own competencies for performing health care and physical management procedures by working through Activity 9.1.

ACTIVITY 9.1   Rating Your Degree of Competency in Health Care and Physical Management Procedures

In a nationwide survey of special education teachers and related service professionals (e.g., occupational, physical, speech/language therapists) who work in school settings, Cross, Collins, & Boam-Wood (1996) gathered information on the health management, physical management, communication, and educational practices that special education teachers perform in their classrooms as well as their perceived degree of competency in those practices. Take time to work through a list of the health and physical management practices listed below that were included in the survey. First note which procedures you are expected to perform. Then rate each skill from "not well trained" (1) to "well trained" (4). When you are finished, check your responses with those who responded to the survey.

CHECKLIST

Procedure	Not Well Trained		Well Trained	

Health Management Procedures

Procedure				
Cardiopulmonary resuscitation	1	2	3	4
Catheterization	1	2	3	4
Colostomy/ileostomy procedures	1	2	3	4
Diet/glucose monitoring	1	2	3	4
Medication administration	1	2	3	4
Seizure management	1	2	3	4
Shunt care	1	2	3	4
Teeth and gum care	1	2	3	4
Tracheostomy care/suctioning	1	2	3	4
Tube feeding (e.g., GI, NGI)	1	2	3	4

Physical Management Procedures

Procedure				
Cast care	1	2	3	4
Feeding/eating procedures	1	2	3	4
Handling and positioning	1	2	3	4

Prosthetic/ orthotic care	1	2	3	4
Skin care (e.g., breakdown)	1	2	3	4
Use of basic terminology (e.g., prone, supine)	1	2	3	4
Use of simple adaptive devices (e.g., pointers, grips)	1	2	3	4
Use of specific equipment (e.g., standers, wheelchairs)	1	2	3	4
Use of splints	1	2	3	4
Use of technical assistive/adaptive devices (e.g., electronic switches)	1	2	3	4
Working with bone/joint deformities	1	2	3	4

RESULTS (CROSS ET AL., 1996)

When the respondents were broken into groups, the special education teachers reported that they most often worked as direct service providers in classroom settings, with most embedding services within classroom activities in addition to sending students for pull-out services. Many reported that they had little training in working within a team although most worked as part of an interdisciplinary team as part of their job.

In health management procedures, 30% or more of the special education teachers reported performing seizure management, CPR, and medication administration. When compared to therapists, the special education teachers viewed themselves as less trained in CPR and better trained in seizure management. None of the special education teachers reported performing tracheostomy care and suctioning, and only a few reported performing colostomy/ileostomy procedures, diet/glucose monitoring, shunt care, and tube feeding; none of the respondents reported being well trained in these procedures.

In regard to physical management procedures that they performed, more than 30% of the special education teachers selected the use of simple adaptive devices followed by use of technical assistive/adaptive devices, basic terminology, and special equipment; a minimal number selected the use of splints, orthotic/prosthetic care, and cast care. Across physical management skills, the special education teachers did not perceive themselves as well trained.

Issues in the Ability of Health Care Professionals to Work with Persons with Mental Disabilities

Availability and training are both issues that affect the ability of health care professionals to work with persons with mental disabilities. Heller et al. (2000) reported both a shortage of school nurses and high caseloads (1,200 to 5,000) for nurses serving school districts and suggested that the expertise of special education teachers can be valuable in assisting nurses in task analyzing health care procedures and providing instructional strategies as well as in assisting therapists in making adaptations.

The problem with the training of nurses in the area of disabilities extends beyond the school to the community since more adults with mental retardation are now residing in community settings. When Walsh, Hammerman, Josephson, & Krupka (2000) surveyed nurses in New Jersey, they found that 87% reported encountering persons with developmental disabilities in their work, but a quarter had no experience with developmental disabilities. Only 10% of the nurses had received educational content on developmental disabilities (e.g., case management, Americans with Disabilities Act) in their training programs; yet the majority stated that this content should be included.

Walsh and Kastner (1999) asserted that there is a need to restructure the entire health care system to include a network of specialized developmental disability providers and practitioners with experience in working with persons with developmental disabilities. They based this assertion on such obstacles to health care for persons with disabilities as inadequate medical information, the cognitive and verbal limitations of patients, and difficulty in communicating with multiple caregivers. They also reported that solutions ranked as useful by physicians have included (a) distributing a list of physicians with experience in developmental disabilities, (b) expanding referral opportunities, (c) providing specific information on informed consent with persons with developmental disabilities, (d) training individuals to provide patient support, and (e) making clinical information available.

Issues in the Ability of Educational Personnel to Work with Persons with Health Care Needs

The second issue revolves around the training of educational personnel. In some cases teachers need information on working with students with medical needs that are found in the general population (e.g., asthma). In other cases teachers need information on working with specific medical conditions that result in the need for special education services (e.g., traumatic brain injury). Finally, teachers who serve students with complex health care needs have a need for specific training based on the individual needs of each student (e.g., tube feeding). In other words, teachers need specialized training for specific students as well as a broad base of generalized training for conditions that may occur across students. Training may include first aid and CPR, physical care, general health and nutrition, infection control, skin care, elimination and oral hygiene, childhood diseases, community resources, using a transdisciplinary team approach, and IEP writing (Lehr, 1990). The Council for Exceptional Children has generated a comprehensive list of knowledge and skills for all beginning special education teachers who serve students with physical and health disabilities (Heller et al., 1999). These include competencies in foundations, characteristics, instruction, planning, and environmental management.

Based on a survey of teachers serving students with severe and multiple disabilities in Kansas, Mulligan-Ault, Guess, Struth, and Thompson (1988) found that the top procedures performed in their classrooms were seizure monitoring (88%), teeth and gum care (87%), medication administration (85%), and emergency seizures (79%). The authors separated health care procedures into categories that should be the responsibility of (a) teachers—seizure monitoring, skin breakdown prevention, bowel habits, postural drainage, handling and positioning, percussion, gastrostomy feeding, prosthesis care, and oxygen supplementation; (b) nurses—medication administration, diet monitoring, shunt care, glucose monitoring, colostomy/ileostomy care, catheterization, machine suctioning, tracheostomy tube and tie changing, and enema administration; (c) teachers and nurses—emergency seizure procedures, skin breakdown treatment, and oxygen supplementation with mask; (d) teachers and instructional assistants—teeth and gum care; and (e) teachers, nurses, and instructional assistants—CPR.

Based on a more recent survey of teachers, institutions of higher education, school system directors, and state departments of education, Heller et al. (1999) generated a list of health care procedures and skills in which teachers perceived themselves as not being well trained. The list included (a) teaching self-management skills, (b) working with students who are chronically or terminally ill, (c) participating in a transdisciplinary team for transitioning (e.g., home to hospital, rehabilitation to school), (d) modifying reading for nonverbal students with physical disabilities, and (e) teaching students to use augmentative communication devices and systems or assistive technology devices. Of those surveyed, special education teachers with a degree that focused on physical and health disabilities reported being the best trained across these skills. Most of the special education teachers surveyed, however, received degrees with a concentration that was generic or focused on another area of special education.

Results from institutions of higher education in the Heller et al. (1999) survey revealed that 42.3% offered a special education degree with a concentration in physical and health disabilities and 61.5% employed a professor with expertise in that area. In addition, results from state departments of education revealed that 30 states did not have certifications in physical and health disabilities. The overall outcome of the Heller et al. survey was that a large number of special education teachers serving students with physical disabilities lacked knowledge and skills in half of the necessary competencies. This is one of the reasons the Council for Exceptional Children has advocated for special education certification in the area of physical and health disabilities.

Strategies for Working with Health Care Needs and Persons with Moderate and Severe Disabilities

The professional literature in special education contains numerous suggestions for working with students across a variety of medical conditions. While these are summarized in the following sections, it is imperative that teachers consult state and local school district policies regarding responsibility and liability. For example, the Kentucky Systems Change Project developed a policy manual for local school districts regarding services for students with special health care needs (Smith & Leatherby, 1993).

Across medical conditions, the recommendations in the Kentucky manual for working with students with special health care needs included (a) consultations with physicians on procedures, schedule, equipment, and side effects; (b) training in procedures by a licensed health care professional; (c) consultations with parents on emergency procedures; (d) documentation of procedures, outcomes, and problems; and (e) sanitary procedures and disposal. The manual also listed additional recommendations for working with students with other health concerns that included (a) acquiring specific information on the medical condition or device or knowing the signs of complications. While teachers were allowed to perform most procedures following training by a licensed health care professional, nurses were responsible for administering medication via injections or tubes and for feeding via nasogastric tubes.

In addition, the manual listed precautions for classroom teachers that were specific to working with students with special health care needs and other health concerns. The precautions for working with students with special health care needs are overviewed in Table 9.2, and the precautions for working with students with other health concerns are overviewed in Table 9.3.

TABLE 9.2 *Example of State Policies for Providing Medical Services in School Settings Based on Smith, Leatherby, and Deters (1993a).*

Procedure	Precautions
Cast care	Cast protected from indentations, soiling, and entry of foreign objects; pressure sores reduced through frequent repositioning; skin observed for proper circulation; discomfort reported to parents or LHCP[1]
Catheterization	Gloves worn during procedure with attention to latex allergies, possible testing for nitrates in urine, appropriate fluid disposal
Gastrostomy tube (G-tube) feeding	Gloves worn during contact with G-tube or stoma, G-tube reinserted by LHCP, consultation with physician on positioning, close observation for problems (e.g., vomiting, skin irritation around stoma), caution in combining formula with medications
Glucose monitoring (diabetes)	Reporting of inadequate insulin coverage to physician, awareness of behavioral symptoms of problems in nonverbal students
Ileostomy and colostomy	Caution in positioning student when bag is closed with clamp, adequate supply of materials (e.g., pouches), insurance of privacy, gloves worn during procedure with attention to latex allergies, use of sanitary procedures, special diet considerations
Medication administration	Single designated person responsible for entire process, new medication first given outside of school setting, medicine spoon used for proper dosage, students with oral motor and feeding problems monitored for choking, immediate reporting of improper administration, consultation with LHCP for side effects
Nasogastric tube (NG-tube) feeding	Caution in combining formula with medications, monitoring of formula intolerance (e.g., vomiting), procedures for unclogging NG-tube, awareness of skin irritation where tube is taped to skin, discontinuance of feeding if tube slips into esophagus, gloves worn during contact with NG-tube
Seizure intervention and monitoring	Emergency procedures for seizure lasting longer than 10 minutes
Tracheostomy care and suctioning	Symptoms of respiratory distress (e.g., bluish coloring of fingernails), positioning for suctioning, avoidance of gag reflex during suctioning, gloves worn during contact with mucus secretions
Ventilator monitoring	Ventilator plugged in, emergency generator available, emergency calling system in classroom, emergency numbers readily available, distress signal for student or awareness of symptoms of distress, avoidance of clothing that obstructs or sheds, avoidance of getting anything in tracheostomy, appropriate educational placements

[1]LHCP = licensed health care professional

TABLE 9.3 *Example of State Policies for Other Health Concerns in School Settings Based on Smith, Leatherby, and Deters (1993b).*

Concern	Precautions
Bowel and joint deformities	Training from physical therapist in lifting, handling, and carrying; physical management techniques embedded across educational activities; signs of fractures or joint dislocations during exercise; signs of joint contractures reported to physical or occupational therapist
Bowel care	Gloves worn during toileting, medical intervention for impacted bowels
Congenital heart disease	Sign and symptoms of heart distress (e.g., shortness of breath), especially during early childhood; physical activity restrictions
Feeding disorders	Avoidance of problematic foods, training in choking and CPR procedures, handwashing prior to and following feeding, disposable napkins or one washcloth per student, one student fed at a time, one set of gloves per student worn when feeding students with contagious conditions or when feeder has open wounds or sores on hands
Orthotics care (braces and splints)	Proper placement and fit of orthotic devices, signs of discomfort, reporting of pressure points that remain longer than 20 minutes, reduced time wearing new device or after extended periods without device, training in ambulation and movement with device
Prosthetics care (artificial limbs)	Skin irritations caused by poor hygiene, emotional needs of child wearing device, participation in physical education, frequent changing of underclothing due to excessive perspiration and elevated temperature
Shunt monitoring	Immediate reporting of symptoms of shunt malfunction, emergency procedures for shunt malfunction
Skin care	Gloves worn during application of topical treatments, changing of dressings, or dealing with open sores or injuries

Strategies for Working with Students with Medical Needs

Based on the information presented thus far in this chapter, it is clear teachers need to be versed in strategies for working with students with health care needs. While specific training should be conducted to meet the unique needs of students in each classroom, the following sections provide an overview of strategies from the professional literature. These include implementing general health care and specific medical procedures in classroom settings and increasing the ability of persons with mental disabilities to perform or partially participate in health care procedures and to make informed decisions about their health care needs as they transition to adulthood.

Implementing General Health Care Procedures in the Classroom Edens, Murdick, and Gartin (2003) asserted that teachers should be versed in numerous universal precautions to prevent infections, such as tuberculosis, hepatitis B, HIV, herpes, or cytomegalovirus, in the classroom. These included correct procedures for

(a) handwashing, such as using one paper towel to dry hands and another to clean faucet, using warm or hot water, and washing each area of the hand for 10 to 30 seconds; (b) putting on gloves, such as removing jewelry that might puncture gloves; (c) removing gloves, such as pinching palm and pulling one glove inside out over the other before balling for disposal; (d) cleaning and disinfecting contaminated areas, such as wearing protective clothing, soaking up fluids with paper towels, cleaning contaminated areas with soap and water, and disinfecting area and sink after washing; and (e) using protective barriers, such as gloves, masks, aprons, and eye wear. Edens et al. noted that precautions should include being aware of latex allergies (common in children who have had multiple surgeries) and always carrying two pairs of gloves.

Working with Specific Medical Conditions   The first step in working with students with medical conditions is to gather information. For children who are medically fragile, this may include information on the medical diagnosis and treatments, anticipated frequency of absences and hospitalizations, ongoing medications, necessary adjustments to the classroom schedule and environments, and safety considerations (Prendergrast, 1995). While the information on working with other students with less critical medical conditions may not be as complex, it still may be as crucial, as illustrated in the following two examples.

First, Getch and Neuharth-Pritchett (1999) stated that teachers who work with students with asthma need to (a) understand the condition, (b) know policies for medication and emergency treatment, (c) be aware of the side effects of medications, (d) recognize early warning signs, (e) know and eliminate triggers, (f) communicate with family and medical personnel, and (g) be familiar with resources to educate other children. In a second example, Rosenthal-Malek and Greenspan (1999) suggested strategies for teachers who work with students with diabetes. These included (a) allowing the student to leave the room when needed and follow a routine without being conspicuous, (b) encouraging students with diabetes to talk about their feelings and describe their symptoms, (c) communicating with parents, (d) educating other class members about the condition, (e) knowing what to do in an emergency and how to make accommodations to meet the requirements of the law, and (f) keeping current on advice from diabetes experts.

In addition to the need for information and strategies on dealing with medical needs, teachers need to know how to make adaptations in educational procedures to accommodate students with medical needs. For example, Keyser-Marcus et al. (2002) stated that teachers who work with students with traumatic brain injury need to know the characteristics and that traumatic brain injury requires a mulitidisciplinary team approach as students transition from the hospital to the school setting. Further suggestions for classroom teachers included the following strategies. For problems with concentration, teachers should allow mini breaks, supply earplugs, place students in the front of the classroom, and break assignments into small segments. For problems with memory, teachers should help students use a memory notebook and checklist, provide daily repetitions, and record lectures. For problems with executive functioning, teachers should provide organizers, assess discrimination skills, color code, and structure choices. For communication problems, teachers should provide assistive technology, reduce distractions, encourage word substitutions, and provide opportunities to practice language. Finally, teachers should teach compensatory strategies, including the use of external aids, such as planners, and internal aids, such as mnemonics.

Suggestions by Witte (1998) can be added to this list. In addition to recommending a low teacher/student ratio, instructional repetition, highly structured lessons, behavioral programming, and task analyses, Witte recommended "SOS"—an educational focus on (a) **S**tructure—home-school collaboration, teacher inservice, environmental stimulation, and monitoring; (b) **O**rganization—consistent classroom routine, clear identification of work, assignment book, tape-recording of material, and life skills; and (c) **S**trategies—compensatory instruction, peer role models, direct instruction, and modeling.

Increasing the Ability of Students with Moderate and Severe Disabilities to Address Their Own Health Issues

In addition to being responsible for the immediate health care concerns of their students, teachers should also use strategies to increase the independence of students with health care needs as they grow older. This may include teaching them how to perform or participate in health care procedures, how to use procedures to decrease health care risks, and how to advocate for their health care needs.

Basic instructional strategies are useful in teaching students how to independently perform or partially participate in medical procedures. For example, Bosner and Belfiore (2001) used a system-of-least-prompts strategy to teach an adolescent female with Down syndrome, moderate mental retardation, and insulin-dependent diabetes to self-administer insulin injections. (See Chapter 6 for a description of the system of least prompts.) They taught the task-analyzed medical procedure in two chunks with 11 steps per chunk. On three of the steps (inserting syringe, pushing plunger, removing syringe), the student partially participated under the guidance of an adult. The instructional procedure consisted of a hierarchy of prompts that included general verbal prompts, specific verbal prompts, partial physical guidance, and full physical guidance, as well as initial simulation with an orange. Once the student acquired the procedure, she generalized the skill from her home to the home of a friend and from performing the procedure with her mother to performing it with her father.

Another strategy is to teach persons with moderate and severe disabilities to be compliant when others perform health care procedures for them. For example, Altabet (2002) noted that dentists may be reluctant to treat patients with mental disabilities because patients may resist treatment or fail to cooperative during the treatment process. Thus, Altabet recommended the use of a desensitizing procedure that used modeling, shaping, paired relaxation, and reinforcement. In a research investigation, patients worked through simulations in which they could enter the dentist's office and sit in the dental chair then continue to sit as sounds and odors were added and they were touched by the dentist. When this procedure was used with 35 patients with severe and profound mental disabilities, 19 showed an increase in number of steps they could complete without the need for sedation or restraint, including traveling to and entering the office, sitting in the dental chair, opening mouth, and tolerating touch on teeth.

It also is important for teachers to educate persons with moderate and severe disabilities on ways to decrease health risks. For example, persons with moderate and severe disabilities may have a difficult time understanding preventative measures for sexually transmitted diseases. Jacobs et al.(1989) noted that person with mental disabilities are vulnerable to contracting HIV or AIDS due to unhealthful sexual behaviors, sexual abuse, and dependency on others. Once contracted, LeRoy, Powell, and Kelker (1994) stated that communicable diseases, such as AIDS, may result in social isolation, long-term hospitalization, parental illness and death, family problems, and associated learning difficulties. In addition, students with mental disabilities may have a lack of understanding about spreading diseases and fall prey to peer pressure for unsafe sexual activity or drug activity. Jacobs et al. (1989) stated that the problem is compounded by staff denial that persons with mental disabilities are sexually active, staff who are uncomfortable in discussing sexuality and AIDS, and the inability of persons with mental disabilities to understand concepts such as disease and death.

Jacobs et al. (1989) recommended that staff who conduct AIDS prevention programs group persons by their functioning level, ensure confidentiality, build trust, and be nonjudgmental. Once a student contracts the disease, LeRoy et al. (1994) stated that teachers are responsible for a number of variables that include (a) inclusion of the student in school, (b) interdisciplinary team management, (c) early and frequent assessment (e.g., medical status, psychological and educational development, behavior, and family support), (d) sensitive and nonjudgmental services with a family focus, (e) confidentiality and safety, (f) currency on medical research, (g) attention to quality of life, and (h) advocacy. (More information regarding sex education programs for persons with moderate and severe disabilities can be found in Chapter 13.)

As students transition to adulthood, the ability to make decisions about their own health care increases. According to Cea and Fisher (2003), this includes the ability to understand information about a medical disorder, weigh the risks and benefits of various treatments, and communicate a choice of treatments. Cea and Fisher interviewed adults with mild and moderate mental retardation regarding three vignettes: (a) a psychiatrist's recommendation for psychopharmacological treatment, (b) a dentist's recommendation for orthodonture work to correct misalignment of teeth, and (c) a physician's recommendation for a series of injections to prevent allergic reaction to pollen and dust. They found that the ability to provide responses decreased as the complexity of the situation increased. At least one half of the respondents with moderate mental disabilities indicated at least partial understanding of the vignettes but had difficulty weighing the risks and benefits of the treatments. They concluded that some adults with moderate mental disabilities are capable of giving consent for treatment and suggested that their ability to do so could be enhanced with educational techniques.

Friedman (1998) suggested that advance directives should be used when persons with mental disabilities make decisions regarding health care treatments. These are written instructions that specify treatments in advance (i.e., instruction directives) or designate another person to make those decisions if the person is incapacitated (i.e., proxy directives). Although a number of states have legislation authorizing living wills and appointment of health care proxies, Friedman stated that the assessment of decision-making capacity, standards for surrogate decision making, and family involvement in advance directives should be considerations with persons with mental disabilities.

Best Practices
Health and Vitality

1. Using a team approach, seek out information from licensed health care professionals and parents in developing health care plans for students with health care needs.

2. If you must perform a health care procedure, obtain direct training from a licensed health care professional and schedule periodic monitoring.

3. Document all health care procedures performed for students, as well as any related concerns.

4. Obtain written policies from school districts or agencies before implementing health care procedures.

5. In writing the IEP, address (a) the performance of or partial participation in health care procedures and (b) the embedding of related skills within health care procedures.

6. In writing the ITP, address (a) the future medical needs of students and (b) the ability to be self-advocates in future health care.

Conclusion

The purpose of this chapter has been to create an awareness that providing an appropriate education for students with moderate and severe disabilities includes addressing their health and vitality. Because persons with moderate and severe disabilities tend to have a greater number of medical needs than what is found in the general population, most of the teachers and staff who work with them will find that they must address a myriad of health care needs over time and it is not uncommon for many to be life threatening. Thus, teachers and staff need to be versed in terminology, the writing of health care plans and objectives, legal policies and requirements, and educational strategies in addition to receiving specific training to address individual needs. Best practices in health and vitality in regard to working with persons with moderate and severe disabilities are listed above, and a performance-based assessment activity follows at the end of this chapter.

Questions for Review

1. Write an IEP objective that (a) focuses on teaching a health care objective to a student, (b) focuses on embedding a skill within a health care procedure, and (c) focuses on meeting health care needs within a transition plan.

2. What type of procedures can be performed by a classroom teacher within an educational setting?

3. What type of health care information should the instructional team gather at the time a child with complex health care needs is placed in an educational setting?

4. Contrast a direct service model to a consultative service model. In each model, who is responsible for delivering services? For training the person who delivers services? For monitoring the health care of the student?

5. List basic health care skills that teachers should have regardless of whether or not a student has an identified disability.

Performance-Based Assessment

You have received notice that you will be receiving a student in your classroom who has complex health care needs. Generate a list of questions that you will want to discuss with the team prior to working with the student. What information will you want for the student's health care plan?

Select one of the following health care procedures and practice writing (a) an objective that increases the student's independence in performing the procedure and (b) an objective that embeds related skills in the procedure.

Procedures

Glucose monitoring	Catheterization
Medication administration	Tube feeding

References

Altabet, S. C. (2002). Decreasing dental resistance among individuals with severe and profound mental retardation. *Journal of Developmental and Physical Disabilities, 14,* 297–305.

Bartlett, L. (2000). Medical services: The disputed related service. *The Journal of Special Education, 33,* 215–223, 247.

Borgioli, J. A., & Kennedy, C. H. (2003). Transitions between school and hospital for students with multiple disabilities: A survey of causes, educational continuity, and parental perceptions. *Research and Practice with Severe Disabilities, 28,* 1–6.

Bosner, S. M., & Belfiore, P. J. (2001). Strategies and considerations for teaching an adolescent with Down syndrome and type I diabetes to self-administer insulin. *Education and Training in Mental Retardation and Developmental Disabilities, 36,* 94–102.

Brotherson, M. J., Oakland, M. J., Secrist-Mertz, C., Litchfield, R., & Larson, K. (1995). Quality of life issues for families who make the decision to use a feeding tube for their child with disabilities. *Journal of the Association for Persons with Severe Handicaps, 20,* 202–212.

Cea, C. D., & Fisher, C. B. (2003). Health care decision-making by adults with mental retardation. *Mental Retardation, 41,* 78–87.

Center, J., Beange, H., & McElduff, A. (1998). People with mental retardation have an increased prevalence of osteoporosis: A population study. *American Journal on Mental Retardation, 103,* 19–28.

Cross, D. P., Collins, B. C., & Boam-Wood, S. (1996). A survey of interdisciplinary personnel preparation. *Physical Disabilities: Education and Related Services, 2,* 13–32.

Department of Education. (Sept. 29, 1992). *Federal register. 34 CFR Parts 300–301. Assistance to states for the education of children with disabilities program and preschool grants for children with disabilities, Final Rule, 57 (189),* (pp. 44801–44802) Washington, DC: Author.

Draheim, C. C., McCubbin, J. A., & Williams, D. P. (2002). Differences in cardio-vascular disease risk between non-diabetic adults with mental retardation with and without Down syndrome. *American Journal of Mental Retardation, 107,* 201–211.

Edens, R. M., Murdick, N. L., & Gartin, B. C. (2003). Preventing infection in the classroom: The use of universal precautions. *Teaching Exceptional Children, 35*(4), 62–66.

Friedman, R. I. (1998). Use of advance directives: Facilitating health care decisions by adults with mental retardation and their families. *Mental Retardation, 36,* 444–456.

Getch, Y. Q., & Neuharth-Pritchett, S. (1999). Children with asthma: Strategies for educators. *Teaching Exceptional Children, 31*(3), 30–36.

Hayden, M. F., & DePaepe, P. A. (1991). Medical conditions, level of care needs, and health-related outcomes of persons with mental retardation: A review. *Journal of the Association for Persons with Severe Handicaps, 16,* 188–206.

Heller, K. W., Fredrick, L. D., Best, S., Dykes, M. K., & Cohen, E. T. (2000). Specialized health care procedures in the schools: Training and service delivery. *Exceptional Children, 66,* 173–186.

Heller, K. W., Fredrick, L. D., Dykes, M. K., Best, S., & Cohen, E. T. (1999). A national perspective of competencies for teachers of individuals with physical and health disabilities. *Exceptional Children, 65,* 219–234.

Individuals with Disabilities Education Act of 1997 Regulations, 34 C.F.R. § 300 et seq.

Jacobs, R., Samowitz, P., Levy, J. M., & Levy, P. H. (1989). Developing an AIDS prevention education program for persons with developmental disabilities. *Mental Retardation, 27,* 233–237.

Katsiyannis, A., & Yell, M. L. (2000). The Supreme Court and school health services: *Cedar Rapids v. Garret F. Exceptional Children, 66,* 317–326.

Keyser-Marcus, L., Briel, L., Sherron-Targett, P., Yasuda, S., Johnson, S., & Wehman, P. (2002). Enhancing the schooling of students with traumatic brain injury. *Teaching Exceptional Children, 34*(4), 62–76.

Lehr, D. H. (1990). Providing education to students with complex health care needs. *Focus on Exceptional Children, 22*(7), 1–12.

Lehr, D. H., & McDaid, P. (1993). Opening the door further: Integrating students with complex health care needs. *Focus on Exceptional Children, 25*(6), 1–7.

LeRoy, C. H., Powell, T. H., & Kelker, P. H. (1994). Meeting our responsibilities in special education. *Teaching Exceptional Children, 26*(4), 37–44.

McKee, J. R., & Bodfish, J. W. (2000). Sudden unexpected death in epilepsy in adults with mental retardation. *American Journal on Mental Retardation, 105,* 229–235.

Morgan, C. L., Baxter, H., & Kerr, M. P. (2003). Prevalence of epilepsy and associated health service utilization and mortality among patients with intellectual disability. *American Journal on Mental Retardation, 108,* 293–300.

Morningstar, M. E., Turnbull, H. R., Lattin, D. L., Umbarger, G. T., Reichard, A., & Moberly, R. L. (2001). Students supported by medical technology: Making the transition from school to adult life. *Journal of Developmental and Physical Disabilities, 13,* 229–259.

Mulligan-Ault, M., Guess, D., Struth, L., & Thompson, B. (1988). The implementation of health-related procedures in classrooms for students with severe multiple impairments. *Journal of the Association for Persons with Severe Handicaps, 13,* 100–109.

Prendergast, D. E. (1995). Preparing for children who are medically fragile in educational programs. *Teaching Exceptional Children, 27*(2), 37–41.

Rapport, M. J. (1996). Legal guidelines for the delivery of special health care services in schools. *Exceptional Children, 62,* 537–549.

Rosenthal-Malek, A., & Greenspan, J. (1999). A student with diabetes is in my class. *Teaching Exceptional Children, 31*(3), 38–43.

Ryder, K. M., Williams, J., Womack, C., Nayak, N. G., Nasef, S., Bush, A., Tylavsky, F. A., & Carbone, L. (2003). Appendicular fractures: A significant problem among institutionalized adults with developmental disabilities. *American Journal on Mental Retardation, 108,* 340–346.

Smith, P. D., & Leathervy, J. L. (1993). *Services for students with special health care needs: Guidelines for local school districts.* University of Kentucky Interdisciplinary Human Development Institute Kentucky Systems Change Project: Lexington, KY.

Smith, P. D., Leatherby, J. L., & Deters, J. (1993a). Specific health care procedures (pp. 30–57). In P. D. Smith & J. L. Leatherby *Services for students with special health care needs: Guidelines for local school districts.* Lexington, KY: University of Kentucky Interdisciplinary Human Development Institute Kentucky Systems Change Project.

Smith, P. D., Leatherby, J. L., & Deters, J. (1993b). Other health care concerns (pp. 58–79). In P. D. Smith & J. L. Leatherby *Services for students with special health care needs: Guidelines for local school districts.* Lexington, KY: University of Kentucky Interdisciplinary Human Development Institute Kentucky Systems Change Project.

Taylor, H. M. (2002). Pneumonia frequencies with different enteral tube feeding access sites. *American Journal on Mental Retardation, 107,* 175–180.

Thomas, S. B., & Hawke, C. (1999). Health-care services for children with disabilities: Emerging standards and implications. *The Journal of Special Education, 32,* 226–237.

Umbarger, G. T., Turnbull, H. R., Morningstar, M. E., Reichard, A., & Moberly, R. L. (2001). Funding challenges during transition to adulthood for young adults who use medical technology. *Journal of Developmental and Physical Disabilities, 13,* 141–167.

U.S. Congress, Office of Technology Assessment. (1987). *Technology-dependent children: Hospital vs. home care—A technical memorandum.* (OTA-TM-H-38). Washington, DC: U.S. Government Printing Office.

Waldman, H. B., Perlman, S. P., & Swerdloff, M. (2001). Children with mental retardation/developmental disabilities: Do physicians ever consider needed dental care? *Mental Retardation, 39,* 53–56.

Walkup, J., Sambamoorthi, U., & Crystal, S. (1999). Characteristics of persons with mental retardation and HIV/AIDS infection in a statewide Medicaid population. *American Journal on Mental Retardation, 104,* 356–363.

Walsh, K. K., Hammerman, S., Josephson, F., & Krupka, P. (2000). Caring for people with developmental disabilities: Survey of nurses about their education and experience. *Mental Retardation, 38,* 33–41.

Walsh, K. K., & Kastner, T. A. (1999). Quality of health care for people with developmental disabilities: The challenge of managed care. *Mental Retardation, 37,* 1–15

Witte, R. (1998). Meet Bob: A student with traumatic brain injury. *Teaching Exceptional Children, 30* (3), 56–60.

Woodruff, B. A., & Vazquez, E. (2002). Prevalence of hepatitis virus infections in an institution for persons with developmental disabilities. *American Journal on Mental Retardation, 107,* 278–292.

CHAPTER TEN

SUPPORTING STUDENTS WITH THE MOST CHALLENGING BEHAVIORS:

Functional Behavioral Assessment and Intervention

On completion of this chapter, the reader will meet the following objectives:

- Identify five different classes of challenging behaviors that may be exhibited by persons with moderate and severe disabilities.
- Explain the process for conducting a functional behavioral assessment.
- Rank behavioral interventions from least to most intrusive and provide a rationale for selecting an intervention based on using the least intrusive alternative.
- Discuss issues involved in using aversive procedures.
- Explain the components that lead to the success of a behavioral support plan.

As noted in Chapter 2, students with moderate and severe disabilities may have challenging behaviors in addition to cognitive, physical, and sensory impairments. While teachers may become skilled in classroom behavior management techniques to decrease disruptive behaviors (e.g., off task, out of seat) and increase desirable behaviors (e.g., work completion, raising hand before talking), additional skills are needed in dealing with more challenging behaviors.

This chapter will provide an overview of behavioral assessment and intervention techniques that have been and are being used with success to identify causes of challenging behaviors and to develop appropriate intervention techniques. In addition, the chapter will present the issues involved in selecting appropriate intervention techniques.

TYPES OF CHALLENGING BEHAVIORS

Challenging behaviors can be separated into five categories: (a) aggression and disruption, (b) noncompliance, (c) self-injury, (d) stereotypy, and (e) social withdrawal. These categories of behavior, however, must be further defined in specific behavioral terms before assessment and intervention can occur. Defining behavior provides a means to focus on the behavior that is occurring and to measure the behavior to determine if an intervention is effective. For example, stating that a child has aggressive behavior is too broad to provide helpful information. The term *aggressive* could refer to either physical or verbal aggression. Each of these subcategories can be further defined. Physical aggression may refer to aggression toward people (e.g., hitting) or toward objects (e.g., breaking), and verbal aggression can refer to threats toward others or cursing.

Most behaviors can be identified as excesses or deficits or as occurring within the presence of an inappropriate stimulus (Wolery, Bailey, & Sugai, 1988). For example, the stereoptyic behavior of hand flapping is a problem due to an excess in occurrence, the disruptive behavior of being out of seat is a problem due to a deficit in the duration of sitting, and the disruptive behavior of shouting is appropriate at a ballgame but not in a classroom.

Once the behavior is identified and defined, it is important to question why the behavior should be changed. An acceptable rationale for changing a behavior may be that the behavior can cause injury to the person exhibiting the behavior or to others in the environment. Another acceptable rationale is that the behavior, while not harmful, is intense enough to be disruptive to the learning process of the person exhibiting the behavior or to others in the environment. An additional acceptable rationale is that the continuance of the behavior may result in the person being confined to more restrictive environments at present or in the future. Before reading further, assess your ability to categorize behaviors by working through Activity 10.1.

ACTIVITY 10.1   Categorizing Challenging Behaviors

Test your ability to categorize challenging behaviors by matching the following behaviors and categories. Are there any behaviors where the context would be important? Are there any behaviors that are a problem only when there is an excess or a deficit in the behavior? Are there any behaviors where more information is needed? Are there any behaviors that could fit into more than one category? How might you further define some of these behaviors before categorizing them?

CATEGORIES

Noncompliance:
Aggression/disruption:
Social withdrawal:
Self-injury:
Stereotypy:

BEHAVIORS

Banging walls	Hand mouthing	Refusing to talk
Biting	Head banging	Rocking
Chewing fingers	Hitting	Scratching
Covering face	Kicking	Screaming
Cursing	Nail biting	Scribbling
Eating inedibles	Off-task talking	Slapping
Eye poking	Obscene gesturing	Spitting
Face scratching	Pinching	Stomping
Grabbing	Pulling hair	Touching others
Hair pulling	Pushing	Throwing items
Hand biting	Refusing requests	Whining
Hand flapping	Refusing to look	Yelling

Aggressive and Disruptive Behavior

Aggressive and **disruptive behaviors** often go hand in hand. In examining the behavior of an adult male with profound mental disabilities, Smith and Churchill (2002), for example, found that the disruptive behaviors of crying, reaching, and foot stomping were often precursors to the aggressive behaviors of hitting and kicking.

As previously stated, aggression can be physical or verbal and can be directed toward others or toward objects. Physical aggression can result in injury to others within the environment and or to personal property. Verbal aggression can escalate into physical aggression by the perpetrator or by the targets of the aggression. Whether physical or verbal in nature, aggression is disruptive to the learning environment and decreases access to less restrictive environments. In defining the aggression of two children with moderate and severe disabilities, Fisher, Adelinis, Thompson, Worsdell, and Zarcone (1998) identified specific behaviors that were both physical and verbal and that were directed toward others or toward property.

These included hitting, kicking, pushing, pulling hair, throwing objects (both toward others and in general), biting, cursing, breaking and tearing objects, and banging on objects.

While aggression is disruptive to the learning environment, other more general disruptive behaviors can occur that are not as volatile. Some of these behaviors are not a problem until they increase enough in intensity, frequency, or duration to affect the learning process in a negative way. For example, Romaniuk et al. (2002) defined the disruptive behaviors of seven elementary school students (four with moderate disabilities or autism) as including whining; crying; being out of seat; making off-task comments; touching or hugging therapist; using materials in an inappropriate manner; making inappropriate gestures, noises, or faces; covering face with hands; scribbling; yelling; and saying "shut up." Some behaviors with the potential for being dangerous to the person who performs them may be categorized as disruptive because the instructor must disrupt the learning process in order to deal with them. For example, Fisher et al. (1998) defined the dangerous disruptive behaviors of two children with moderate and severe disabilities as standing on furniture, touching light sockets, and striking the ceiling. Like aggression, disruptive behaviors can decrease access to less restrictive environments.

Noncompliant Behavior

Although it may not be as disruptive as the behaviors defined in the previous section, **noncompliant behavior** can have a detrimental effect on learning. When a person refuses to participate in a task, to follow a direction, or to make a verbal response, the instructor has no way of determining the ability of the person or whether learning has taken place. In defining disruptive behaviors of seven elementary school students, Romaniuk et al. (2002) included noncompliant behaviors as putting head on table and making refusal statements. In truth, any behavior can be identified as being noncompliant if it is in direct opposition to directions that were delivered (e.g., person talks aloud when told to be quiet, child runs when told to walk). Repeated acts of defiance can decrease access to less restrictive environments.

Self-Injurious Behavior

Self-injurious behaviors are those that are of sufficient intensity, frequency, or duration to result in physical injury or tissue damage to the person who performs them. In addition to being disruptive to the learning process of the person who performs them, these behaviors can be disruptive to the learning environment in general in that action is required on behalf of the instructor.

The professional literature contains an abundance of investigations that have focused on the reduction of self-injurious behaviors, especially head banging or head hitting (Kahng, Iwata, & Lewin, 2002). For example, Moore, Mueller, Dubard, Roberts, and Sterling-Turner (2002) focused on the self-injurious behaviors of a 6-year-old girl with profound disabilities that included hitting herself (i.e., making forceful contact between the head and hand), banging her head (i.e., striking objects with the head), and biting herself (i.e., closing teeth on hand or wrist). In another example, Piazza et al. (1998) focused on pica, a subcategory of self-injurious behavior in which inedible objects are consumed that can result in physical injury. The authors identified the pica of three children with moderate and severe disabilities as including eating furniture, clothing, oxygen tube, string, hair, keys, rocks, plastic game pieces, crayons, coins, cloth, paper, toy pieces, twigs, rocks, and a dead animal.

Self-injurious behaviors can be life threatening or result in permanent physical damage. Because they may be automatically or intrinsically reinforced, protective equipment may be worn by the person, such as a helmet for head hitting and head banging or a baseball cap with gauze for extreme hair pulling (i.e., trichotillomania) (Borrero, Vollmer, Wright, Lerman, & Kelley, 2002).

Stereotypic Behavior

While **stereotypic behavior** (also called self-stimulatory behavior) may not result in physical injury to the person or others in the environment, it can be disruptive to the learning process due to its intensity, frequency, or duration. In addition, stereotypic behavior can be stigmatizing, thus decreasing access to less restrictive environments. Like self-injurious behavior, decreasing stereotypic behavior can be challenging because it may be automatically or intrinsically reinforced. In analyzing the behavior of 41 students with fragile X syndrome (the majority of whom had mental retardation, developmental delays, autism, or multiple disabilities), Symons, Clark, Roberts, and Bailey (2001) defined stereotypic behaviors exhibited by the students as rocking back and forth or side to side, flapping hands, or jumping up and down three times or more in succession.

Social Withdrawal

Social withdrawal can be ignored since it is not disruptive to the learning environment and does not result in physical damage to the person or others. Still, social withdrawal can be a challenging behavior because the instructor cannot determine if learning has taken place if the person refuses to speak or interact in any other way. In addition, social withdrawal decreases access to less restrictive environments where the person must interact with others (e.g., working, socializing, shopping).

FUNCTIONAL BEHAVIORAL ASSESSMENT

In recent years the process of **functional behavioral assessment** has gained popularity in determining the conditions that cause a behavior to occur or result in a behavior being maintained over time. The outcome of a functional behavioral assessment is that an appropriate intervention can be identified based on the antecedents, function, and consequences of a behavior. For example, the function of a behavior may be to communicate displeasure or needs, to gain attention, or to escape the performance of difficult tasks. Identifying the function of a behavior allows the interventionist to alter setting events and antecedents that precede a behavior, to teach or increase alternate behaviors that are more acceptable, or to alter the consequences (e.g., reinforcers) that maintain a behavior.

Functional behavioral assessment is such a useful tool that it was included in the IDEA Amendments in 1997 (Murdick & Gartin, 1999). According to the law, the local educational agency is to convene an IEP meeting to develop a functional behavioral assessment plan and to implement an appropriate behavioral intervention based on its results no later than 10 days following a disciplinary action.

Horner and Carr (1997) listed the steps in a functional behavioral assessment as conducting (a) interviews, (b) descriptive observations, and (c) functional analyses.

Murdick and Gartin (1999) added a preliminary step of gathering demographic information, such as name, age, sex, grade, school, residence, date, and disability. The steps of a functional assessment are described in the following sections.

Interviews The interview process should involve talking with those who have contact with the person with challenging behaviors across settings. This may include the parents or caregivers, family members, school or agency staff, job coaches or employers, and peers. These persons will be able to identify the specific challenging behaviors that are being exhibited and the conditions under which those behaviors seem to occur. It also is helpful to identify settings in which the challenging behavior does not occur. Thorough interview notes will provide clues to conditions, times of day, activities, and settings where the behavior can be verified and analyzed.

Descriptive Direct Observation Once the interviews are completed, challenging behaviors should be observed in each setting where they were reported. An initial running narrative is useful in further defining the behavior as it occurs and the conditions that appear to be in place at that time. For example, helpful information recorded on a student who was described as being aggressive during physical education class might include (a) the size, temperature, and acoustics of the setting; (b) the number, age, and behavior of other students in the setting; (c) the student-to-instructor ratio; (d) the availability and appropriateness of materials; (e) the type of activity taking place when the behavior occurs; and (f) the appropriateness of the activity to the person's physical ability and age. In addition, the behaviors should be defined in observable and measurable terms (e.g., physical aggression equals the intentional directing and throwing of a basketball at other students involved in the class in such a manner or with such an intensity that it could result in personal injury or pain; verbal aggression equals cursing the instructor when told to put down the ball).

It also is useful to conduct a descriptive observation in settings where the behavior does not occur. For example, the same student who exhibited aggressive behavior during a structured physical education class may have appropriate behavior in a community leisure activity, such as bowling or playing softball. This type of information is helpful in identifying the specific variables that differ across the two settings, such as the type of activity, noise level, social composition of the participants, coaching or teaching techniques, skill level of the participant, and student preference for the activity.

As part of the descriptive observation, an **A-B-C analysis** can be performed to determine the antecedents that precede a behavior and the consequences that follow it. This is done by structuring the observation notes across three columns with the labels of antecedent (*A*), behavior (*B*), and consequence (*C*). As the observation progresses, the column is filled in by focusing the observation on the target person's behavior (*B* column), the actions or words that precede that person's behavior (*A* column), and the actions or words that follow that person's behavior (*C* column). After observing for a duration of 10 to 20 minutes, patterns may begin to emerge, such as a child receiving attention only in response to inappropriate behavior or inappropriate behavior occurring only in response to directions to work on tasks that may be difficult. Repeating the A-B-C analysis across other conditions, such as settings, activities, and times of day, will strengthen hypotheses about the causes of inappropriate behavior. The A-B-C analysis can be a useful instrument for the classroom teacher who needs a sample of what is occurring under typical conditions in the classroom setting without having to control all of the potential variables. Activity 10.2 contains the notes from a behavioral observation using an A-B-C analysis format and gives the reader the opportunity to analyze the notes to formulate a hypothesis about the function of the behavior.

ACTIVITY 10.2   Analyzing an A-B-C Analysis

Name: Wendy; 14-year-old female with multiple disabilities, including severe mental retardation, severe hearing impairment, and attention deficit disorder

Behavior: Referred for unspecified aggressive behavior at school

Time of observation: 9:30 to 9:45 a.m.

Setting events: Segregated high school classroom for students with moderate and severe disabilities; classroom filled with preschool- and elementary-school-age toys (e.g., Play-Doh, Lite-Brite); four other students in classroom playing with toys; Wendy has just entered classroom and is pointing to her hair

Antecedent	Behavior	Consequence
Teacher: "Get your hairbrush."	Wendy gets her hairbrush.	Teacher: "Good job."
Teacher: "Do you want your hair done?"	Wendy: "Yes."	Teacher: "Sit."
Teacher brushes Wendy's hair.	Wendy keeps saying "Mommy" and pointing to her backpack.	
Teacher: "What do you want?"	Wendy: "Mommy."	
Teacher: "Sit still so I can fix your hair."	Wendy sits still.	Teacher: "Do you want a hair band?"
Teacher fixes hair: "Do you want to look?"	Wendy: "Yeah." She looks in mirror.	Teacher: "Is that OK?"
	Wendy: "Mommy."	Teacher puts away backpack.
Teacher points to drink: "Do you want to finish this?"	Wendy takes sip of drink.	
Teacher gets out nail polish.		
Teacher: "Let's do your nails."	Wendy extends her hand.	Teacher: "Wendy's going to be pretty."
Teacher polishes Wendy's nails.	Wendy: "Mommy, Papa." She points to empty drink.	Teacher: "At lunch, you can have more."
	Wendy knocks over drink.	Teacher cleans up spilled drink.
Teacher: "Go to the table."	Wendy sits at table and puts out foot. "High heels."	Teacher: "Wendy has boots."
Teacher shows picture to Wendy: "What's this?"	Wendy pushes picture away: "Papa."	Teacher: "Look; this is a living room."
	Wendy does not attend; looks around room and tries to get out of seat.	Teacher holds Wendy down: "Couch is in living room."
Teacher: "Look at the refrigerator; put it in the kitchen."	Wendy puts a refrigerator picture on the kitchen picture and gets up and runs across room.	Teacher picks up pictures she dropped.
	Wendy gets out beads and starts stringing them.	Teacher: "Put those down. We're doing pictures right now."
Teacher goes to answer phone.	Wendy continues stringing beads.	Teacher talks on phone, ignoring Wendy.

Do you have suggestions for curricular and environmental modifications that might improve Wendy's behavior? Does the teacher need to change any personal behaviors?

Functional Analysis or Systematic Manipulation of Variables   In addition to an A-B-C analysis, a large body of literature supports a systematic functional analysis as a way to determine the function of a behavior. This can be of particular help in determining the function of challenging behaviors that are severe in nature. Most functional analyses follow the prototype developed by Iwata, Dorsey, Slifer, Bauman, and Richman (1994) in which the researchers compared problem behaviors during carefully manipulated conditions that included (a) escape, in which demands are withdrawn when behavior occurs; (b) attention, in which attention is given when behavior occurs; (c) alone, in which behavior occurs in the absence of materials or people; and (d) play, in which materials and attention are present without demands. In addition, researchers have varied the procedures by comparing conditions such as those that follow: (a) with and without protective equipment (e.g., Borrero et al., 2002), (b) with interspersal of easy and difficult demands (e.g., Ebanks & Fisher, 2003), (c) with high interaction and low frequencies of interaction (Hall, Neuharth-Pritchett, & Belfiore, 1997), (d) with various types of aversive noises (McCord, Iwata, Galensky, Ellingson, & Thomson, 2001), (e) with alternative edible items (Piazza, Roane, Keeney, Boney, & Abt, 2002), (f) with choices of tasks (Romaniuk et al., 2002), (g) with instruction and transition (Symons et al., 2001), (h) with fixed and variable schedules for delivering reinforcement (Van Camp, Lerman, Kelley, Contrucci, & Vorndran, 2000), and (i) with vibrating and nonvibrating toys (Van Camp, Lerman, Kelley, Roane et al., 2000).

Based on the outcomes of functional analyses, hypotheses regarding the function of a behavior can be generated and tested to determine effective interventions. This can be done using an A-B-A-B research design in which *A* shows the behavior during a baseline condition and *B* shows the behavior during an intervention condition. The intervention would be considered effective if behavior improved only during the *B* (i.e., intervention) condition. Examples of effective interventions based on functional analyses include (a) using antecedent prompting with the interspersal of easy tasks to decrease self-injurious behavior and aggression (Ebanks & Fisher, 2003); (b) using extinction with functional communication training to decrease aggression and disruption (Fisher et al., 1998); (c) slowly increasing the volume level of noises over time to decrease self-injurious behavior, aggression, and disruption (McCord et al., 2001); (d) providing alternate edibles that require low effort to decrease pica (Piazza et al., 2002); (e) placing contingencies on precursor behaviors to decrease self-injurious behavior and aggression (Smith & Churchill, 2002); and (f) eliminating vibrating toys to decrease self-injurious behavior (Van Camp, Lerman, Kelley, Roane et al., 2000).

Examples of Functional Assessments

Because behavior may be specific to a setting, it is important to focus on the settings where inappropriate behavior occurs as well as on the persons in whose presence it occurs. The following examples demonstrate how functional assessments have been conducted in both the home and classroom settings.

Behavioral Assessment in the Home   A behavioral assessment conducted by Girolami and Scotti (2001) is an example of a functional behavioral assessment that was conducted in the home setting. The purpose of the assessment was to determine the function of the challenging behaviors exhibited at mealtime by three young children (i.e., 28 to 32 months of age) with developmental disabilities.

During parent interviews, the researchers used a functional analysis intervention form to identify challenging behaviors (e.g., throwing food, slapping caregiver's hand, spitting food, turning head to side, showing aggression toward caregiver, making negative vocalizations), the time they occurred (e.g., mealtimes), and the person present during the behaviors (e.g., parent). In addition, they interviewed parents regarding potential alternate behaviors to replace the challenging behaviors exhibited by the children using a motivation assessment scale. These included saying or gestering "no more" or replacing the food in the serving dish.

In conducting an A-B-C analysis, a researcher observed each parent feeding his or her child across three separate meals. The researcher recorded antecedents and consequences as well as setting events and circumstances.

The researchers then conducted a systematic functional analysis in each of the homes of the children since this was the natural setting where the behaviors were occurring. Prior to the functional analyses, the researchers determined the foods the children preferred and did not prefer by placing two spoonfuls of two different foods at a time side by side on a tray and waiting to see which food the child consumed, refused, or expelled within 20 seconds. This was repeated until the researchers identified a preferred and nonpreferred food for each child. Finally, the researchers decided to use a system-of-least-prompts procedure (verbal, gesture, and physical prompts) to assist the child in consuming a nonpreferred food during the functional analyses.

The functional analyses consisted of six 10-minute conditions conducted during mealtime in the home. During each condition, the researcher presented a food every 20 seconds. Depending on the condition, the following procedures took place: (a) attention—researcher voiced statements of concern and disapproval in response to refusal of a nonpreferred food, (b) demand—researcher turned away from the child and withdrew the food for 20 seconds in response to refusal of a nonpreferred food, (c) tangible toy—researcher placed a toy in front of the child in response to refusal of a nonpreferred food, (d) tangible food—researcher placed a preferred food in front of the child in response to refusal of the nonpreferred food, (e) alone—researcher placed a nonpreferred food in front of the child and left the room, and (f) control—researcher presented a preferred food with attention while toys were available for play.

For the most part, the results of the behavioral assessment were consistent across the various components (interview, observation, functional analysis) of the assessment. The challenging behavior of two of the children seemed to be maintained by being allowed to escape eating. For the third child, the interview with the functional analysis intervention form and the A-B-C analysis observation indicated that the child's behavior was maintained by the parent's attention (negative reinforcement) when he refused to eat, while the functional analog assessment (i.e., functional analysis across conditions) and the motivation scale indicated that the child's behavior was maintained by access to a tangible toy (positive reinforcement) when he refused to eat. Based on the results of the functional assessment, the researchers were able to make recommendations for home interventions to each child's parents.

Behavioral Assessment in the Classroom   A behavioral assessment conducted by Hall et al. (1997) is an example of a functional behavioral assessment that was conducted in the classroom setting. The purpose of the assessment was to determine the function of the disruptive and aggressive behaviors (e.g., hitting, kicking, running from the teachers, throwing or destroying objects) exhibited during instruction in an inclusive third-grade setting by a 9-year-old male with Down syndrome and moderate disabilities.

During the descriptive analysis phase of the assessment, the researchers gathered information from teacher reports and interviews. They then conducted an informal observation to identify antecedents and consequences to the target behaviors in the classroom setting. The antecedents consisted of (a) instruction—teacher-directed activity, (b) high interaction—one-to-one play with teacher or student, and (c) low interaction—unstructured group play. The consequences consisted of (a) attention from the teacher, (b) removal of the task, (c) ignoring by teacher, and (d) receipt of tangible. The results of the observation showed that the behavior appeared to be maintained by **negative reinforcement** (i.e., escape from demands).

The researchers then conducted a systematic functional analysis by alternating three conditions. In the first condition, the student received constant instruction in which inappropriate behavior was followed by removal of materials, removal of attention, and return of the materials when behavior was again appropriate. In the second condition, the student received varied instruction that differed from the first condition only in that the work activity was changed every two minutes. In the third condition, the student received interaction in the form of teacher reprimand for inappropriate behavior during activities with peers. The functional analysis revealed that inappropriate behavior occurred most often during constant instruction.

Based on the functional assessment, the resulting behavioral intervention consisted of teaching the student to request an alternate activity for a brief period while he was waiting during a group activity. Thus, he used more appropriate behavior to gain attention from staff and remained busy in an appropriate manner while waiting his turn during an instructional activity.

COMPREHENSIVE BEHAVIORAL INTERVENTION

Once the behavioral assessment is complete, the next step is to develop an appropriate intervention plan. According to Murdick and Gartin (1999), the steps of developing a behavioral intervention plan include (a) developing a long-term goal and short-term objectives, (b) listing the persons who will implement the plan as well as the time and place the plan will be implemented, and (c) identifying the responses to appropriate and inappropriate behaviors. These steps are followed by evaluating the plan and making revisions as needed.

The field of applied behavioral analysis contains a wealth of research-based behavioral procedures that have been effective in increasing desirable behaviors and in decreasing undesirable behaviors. In selecting an appropriate intervention, it is preferable to select the least intrusive alternative. In other words, if two procedures are equally effective, the one that is less restrictive and more positive is the best choice.

Hierarchy of Behavioral Interventions

The following sections describe various behavioral interventions to decrease challenging behaviors in a hierarchy from least to most intrusive. Later sections will discuss issues to consider in selecting behavioral interventions.

Medical Intervention   One of the first considerations in changing behavior is to ensure that there are no medical reasons for the behavior by consulting a physician.

For example, a physician can determine if head banging is due to a chronic ear infection, if rumination (i.e., regurgitation of foods) is due to food allergies, or if stereotypic behavior is associated with seizures. In some cases surgery (e.g., tubes inserted in ears), changes in diet, or medication (e.g., antiepileptic) may be warranted. Since such behaviors have a medical basis, behavioral intervention would not be expected to have an effect on the behavior.

Kennedy and Meyer (1998) noted that psychotropic medications often are prescribed for persons with challenging behaviors. Based on a review of the use of those that are commonly prescribed for behavior, they suggested (a) that a number of variables (e.g., medical and behavioral intervention history, least restrictive placement options, quality of life, support needs) should be considered in determining whether to use pharmaceuticals to decrease challenging behaviors, (b) that a team of individuals should be involved in the decision-making process (e.g., family, health care professionals, educators, psychologists, case workers), (c) that the use of a psychotropic medication should be part of a comprehensive behavioral intervention package, and (d) that periodic reviews of the treatment should take place.

Bosch (2001) demonstrated how medical treatments can be part of effective behavioral intervention plans in describing four case studies of persons with challenging behaviors. In the first case, medications (Tegretol, Depakote, Tenex, and Risperdal) were part of a behavior intervention plan to decrease the destructive and aggressive behavior of a 6-year-old male with atypical development. In the second case, a change in diet, dental work, and bowel management were part of an intervention plan to decrease disruptive and self-injurious behavior of an 18-year-old female with a severe to profound disability. In the third case, a change in medication (Clonidine) dosage and schedule and a change in feeding formula and schedule were part of a behavior intervention plan to decrease aggressive and self-injurious behaviors in a 10-year-old male with a severe to profound disability. In the fourth case, dental treatment for caries and medical treatment for constipation were part of a behavior intervention plan to decrease disruptive and self-injurious behaviors in a 27-year-old female with a severe to profound disability. (Further details on these case studies are presented later in this chapter.)

Environmental Modification   Once medical reasons have been considered, the next least intrusive alternative for decreasing challenging behaviors is to analyze setting events and environmental factors to determine their effect on behavior. It is easier to manipulate the environment of a person to change behavior than it is to implement a behavior intervention program. In analyzing the environment, a number of variables should be considered, such as the social and physical environment; scheduling; instructional materials, activities, and methods; functional communication skills; and protective equipment. If feasible, each variable can be altered one at a time to determine its effect on the behavior.

Changing the social environment can be as simple as reassigning seating so a person is not next to someone who provokes inappropriate behavior or serves as a poor role model. In some cases behavior may change when the setting changes. For example, a person in a segregated environment may imitate inappropriate behaviors, such as stereotypy, that are performed by persons in the environment. When moved to an inclusive environment where there are better role models and more stimulating social interactions, the behavior may change in a positive way.

Changes in the physical environment of a setting also can influence a person's behavior. For example, temperatures that are too warm or too cold, inadequate lighting, a noisy and distracting background, and uncomfortable furniture can result in challenging behaviors. In the case of someone who is nonverbal, aggressive or disruptive behavior can be a way of communicating discomfort in the physical environment. Changing the temperature, installing better lighting, or installing carpet to reduce noise can have a positive effect on behavior without implementing a behavioral intervention procedure.

In some cases challenging behavior results when a clear schedule is lacking. Having a clear and structured schedule can enable persons to know what is expected of them. Once a schedule is set, activities can be scheduled so easy tasks follow difficult tasks, thus reinforcing the performance of the difficult task using the **Premack Principle** (i.e., make a high-frequency behavior contingent on the performance of a low-frequency behavior [Alberto & Troutman, 1995]). For example, a person can be told that snack time will follow participation in math class or a coffee break will follow cleaning an office. Also, choice can be built into a schedule. Instead of telling a person what to do, good options can be presented (e.g., "It is time for math. Would you like to use a number line or a calculator to complete your problems?" "It is time clean house. Would you like to do the dishes or make the bed first?").

Some challenging behaviors are the result of boredom with instructional materials or activities. This can be countered by introducing novel materials that are interesting to the person, such as writing with a colored gel pen versus a pencil, and by attempting to ensure that tasks are meaningful to the person who is asked to perform them, such as cutting out coupons to go shopping versus cutting straight lines drawn on paper. Providing variation in materials and activities can keep interest high while decreasing avoidance behaviors.

The manner in which instruction is conducted can decrease challenging behaviors. For example, whole group instruction may lead to excessive waiting, during which inappropriate behaviors occur (see Hall et al., 1997). In addition, error correction may result in negative statements (e.g., reprimands, such as "You did that wrong.") that punish participation rather than positive statements (e.g., praise, such as "You did a great job!") that reinforce participation. Errorless response-prompting procedures (such as those presented in Chapter 6) decrease frustration because they are fast-paced to prevent boredom and frustration. In addition, they provide prompting when the student does not know how to respond, thus reducing frustration and increasing the likelihood that instruction will end with positive reinforcement (e.g., praise). Whenever a student is exhibiting challenging behavior during instructional trials or sessions, the instructor should consider trying a different procedure. For example, students who need a physical prompt may have better behavior with a time delay procedure that employs a physical prompt when the student needs assistance rather than a system of least prompts, in which the students must wait through the delivery of a series of prompts before physical guidance is provided.

The ability to communicate in an appropriate manner is a major variable that should be considered in analyzing challenging behaviors. As may be deduced from a functional analysis, some challenging behaviors occur as a way of communicating such emotions as anger or boredom or as a way of communicating such needs as assistance, food, or comfort. **Functional communication training** (i.e., teaching a person to communicate in an appropriate way) can be an effective way to reduce inappropriate behavior. When the person does not have the means to communicate verbally, an **augmentative communication system** can be an acceptable alternative. The augmentative communication system, however, should be assessed for appropriateness. For example, a system that is based on minimal effort, such as one in which entire phrases are stated with the push of a single key, may result in a greater improvement in behavior than a system that requires more effort, such as a one that requires the user to push multiple keys to spell out words, letter by letter.

Durand (1999) found that functional communication training resulted in a decrease in inappropriate behavior (e.g., self-injury—hand biting, face slapping, head banging; aggression—hitting; disruption—screaming, crying, throwing objects) across five children (ages 5 to 15 years) with moderate and severe disabilities. Based on the results of a functional behavioral assessment, Durand selected individualized communicative responses (e.g., "I need help," "I want more") for each student that were programmed into an Introtalker (an electronic augmentative communication device). Following functional communication training, the students generalized their ability to use the augmentative device from the classroom to the community.

Hetzroni and Roth (2003) also reported the effectiveness of an augmentative communication system in reducing the challenging behaviors (e.g., biting, screaming) of children ages 12 to 19 years with moderate and severe disabilities. After using a functional behavioral assessment to determine the communicative function of the challenging behaviors of the children (e.g., seek attention, request assistance, escape work), the school staff (e.g., teacher, assistant, counselor, speech language pathologist, physical therapist, occupational therapist) individualized an electronic augmentative communication system with appropriate messages for each of the children. For example, one student could hit a single switch to activate the message, "Teacher, come please," while another student could select from 16 picture symbols linked to messages, such as "Teacher, I need help" or "Good morning," that were programmed on a vocal output augmentative device. The use of the augmentative communication devices was effective in reducing the challenging behaviors.

With some behaviors, the addition of protective equipment can decrease the behavior since the person is no longer receiving automatic reinforcement from performing the challenging behavior or because the person is unable to perform the challenging behavior while the equipment is in place. As long as the equipment does not restrict the movement of the person, it can be considered a precautionary intervention rather than a punishment. For example, Borrero et al. (2002) found that wearing a baseball cap with gauze decreased the head hitting and head banging of an 8-year-old male with a profound disability, and a helmet decreased the hair pulling (i.e., trichotillomania) of a 35-year-old male with a moderate disability. A related problem was that the presence of the equipment also prevented the function of the inappropriate behavior from becoming apparent during a functional behavioral assessment. Le and Smith (2002) also found that, while protective equipment, such as an oven mitt, medical gloves, or a helmet, suppressed the self-injurious behaviors of face slapping, fingernail biting, and head banging when worn by three adults with profound disabilities, the protective equipment also interfered with the researchers' ability to determine the function of the behaviors. Thus, protective equipment should be viewed as a measure that prevents a behavior from occurring while it is worn with the understanding that the behavior may recur in the absence of the equipment.

Manipulation of Reinforcement Contingencies   Once curricular and environmental modifications have been exhausted, the next least intrusive alternative for decreasing challenging behavior is to use **differential reinforcement** strategies to increase appropriate or desirable behaviors. Once acceptable reinforcer preferences (e.g., attention, praise, edibles, access to desired materials, time alone) are identified on an individual basis for the person whose behavior is to be changed, systematic and contingent delivery and withholding can increase desirable behavior while decreasing undesirable behavior.

There are several variations of differential reinforcement (see Alberto & Troutman, 1995). With differential reinforcement of other behavior (DRO), the person receives reinforcement in the absence of a target behavior, such as being praised in the absence of tantruming. With differential reinforcement of incompatible behavior (DRI), the person is reinforced for performing a behavior that cannot be performed at the same time that an opposite behavior is performed, such as being praised for being on task instead of off task. With differential reinforcement of alternate behavior (DRA), the person is reinforced for performing an appropriate replacement behavior that is preferred over an inappropriate behavior, such as being praised for raising hand before speaking instead of shouting out comments at will. With differential reinforcement of low rates of behavior (DRL), the person is reinforced for performing a target behavior at a lower frequency that is more acceptable than when it is performed at a higher frequency, such as being praised for being out of seat no more than five minutes during a 60-minute session.

The professional literature has numerous examples of differential reinforcement being delivered to decrease challenging behaviors of persons with moderate and severe disabilities. Based on the conclusion that his inappropriate behavior was maintained by attention, Anderson and Long (2002), for example, used differential reinforcement of other behavior to decrease the aggressive (e.g., hitting, kicking, pinching, pulling hair) and disruptive (e.g., throwing objects, knocking over furniture) behaviors of a 13-year-old boy with a moderate to severe disability by having the instructor deliver praise on the average of every two minutes throughout the day if the boy was not displaying the target behaviors. In a more systematic application, Kahng, Abt, and Schonbachler (2001) delivered differential reinforcement of other behavior in the form of physical contact and praise for one minute at the end of a specified interval (average length of 15 minutes) if a 15-year-old girl with a profound disability was not engaging in aggressive behavior (e.g., hitting, kicking, punching, grabbing, pulling hair) at the moment that a timer sounded.

Both contingency contracts and token economies (see Alberto & Troutman, 1995) can be used in combination with differential reinforcement. **Contingency contracts** are an excellent way to make persons aware of the consequences of their actions. Whether written or drawn in pictures, contingency contracts are binding documents that make clear the target behavior to be increased or decreased and the length of time the behavior must occur for the reinforcers to be delivered. The contract also may specify consequences for inappropriate behavior. The contract goes into effect once all involved parties sign the document. Written and picture contingency contracts can be found in Example 10.1.

EXAMPLE 10.1 SAMPLE CLASSROOM CONTRACT

EFFECTIVE DATES: Fall semester

REVIEW DATES: Weekly

We agree to the following conditions:

1. Each time Sandra completes activities from her schedule, she can earn an individual item from her reinforcer menu.

2. When Sandra has a great day following directions and requests, she can earn an item from her reinforcer menu for the class.

Signed:_____ Date:_____
      (special education teacher)

Signed:_____ Date:_____
      (general education teacher)

Signed:_____ Date:_____
      (parent)

Signed:_____ Date:_____
      (student)

Reinforcer Menu

INDIVIDUAL REINFORCERS	REINFORCERS FOR CLASS
Playing on computer for 5 min	Class free time for 5 min
Reading a book	Videotape for class to watch
Getting free time for 5 min	Game for class to play
Listening to tape for 5 min	Extra 5 min of recess
Being line leader	Special snack
Sitting by teacher at lunch	
Doing an art activity	
Eating a small snack	

Token economies are a way to simulate conditions often found in the real world by delaying reinforcement. Instead of receiving a desired reinforcer at the moment that an appropriate behavior occurs, the person receives a **secondary reinforcer,** such as a token, point, or coin, that can be traded in for a **primary reinforcer,** such as an edible, drink, activity, or toy, at a specified time. Token economies work well with differential reinforcement formats. For example, a person may receive praise and a token at the end of each interval (e.g., two minutes) that an inappropriate behavior is absent. At the end of the session (e.g., two hours), the tokens could be traded for free time or a snack in the same way that money can be accumulated and spent in the natural environment.

Mildly Intrusive Punishment Procedures

The science of applied behavior analysis contains a number of effective procedures that can be used to decrease inappropriate behaviors that are mildly intrusive. Two common mildly intrusive procedures are extinction and response cost (see Alberto & Troutman, 1995). Using the "fair pair rule," it is wise to reinforce desirable behaviors when undesirable behaviors are punished. That way, the person whose behavior is being changed learns how to act as well as how not to act.

Extinction is a mildly punishing procedure in which a reinforcer that is maintaining a behavior is withheld. This is effective when the reinforcer can be controlled. An example is withholding attention for inappropriate behavior that is being used to gain attention, such as not attending to crying. To be effective, extinction must be used on a consistent basis. Failure to do so can result in **spontaneous recovery** in which the behavior recurs due to being inadvertently reinforced over time. There are other drawbacks to the use of extinction as well. The use of extinction is accompanied by the likelihood of an **extinction burst** in which the behavior occurs at a higher intensity or for a longer duration before it decreases because the person is trying harder to access the previously available reinforcer. In addition, there is a possibility of increased aggression in response to losing a previously available reinforcer. Lerman, Iwata, and Wallace (1999) analyzed 41 sets of data from persons who were treated with extinction and found that extinction bursts and aggression occurred in half of the cases. Based on this finding, the authors suggested that extinction be used as part of a treatment package, such as in conjunction with differential reinforcement.

Response cost, another mildly punishing procedure, is the removal of a reinforcer in response to the occurrence of an inappropriate behavior. For example, a desired activity, such as playtime, may be shortened or cancelled or an earned reinforcer, such as a token, may be deducted when an inappropriate behavior occurs. While effective, the procedure should be used with caution so a person will not lose more reinforcers than have been earned. If this is possible, there should be a way to earn back what has been lost. Another problem in implementing response cost is that inappropriate behavior can increase in intensity (e.g., shouting) when the reinforcer is removed.

Again, the professional literature is full of investigations in which mildly intrusive punishing procedures have been effective in decreasing inappropriate behavior. In most cases these procedures have been paired with reinforcement for appropriate behavior. For example, Fisher et al. (1998) paired functional communication training with extinction in decreasing the aggression (e.g., hitting, kicking, biting, pulling hair) of a 14-year-old girl with a severe disability whose behavior appeared to be attention getting as well as a response to the disruption of preferred activities with a demand that required a gross motor response (e.g., being told to move when looking out a window). Functional communication training consisted of learning to present a card that read "stop" in response to an undesirable request, and extinction consisted of ignoring inappropriate behavior.

Intrusive Punishment Procedures   The professional literature also contains a number of intrusive punishment procedures that have been effective in decreasing challenging behaviors. These include time-out, overcorrection, and the application of aversives (Alberto & Troutman, 1995). Consideration should be given to the use of these procedures because they can result in unwanted side effects. If used, it is crucial that punishment procedures be paired with reinforcement procedures.

The time-out procedure can be categorized in two ways. In **nonseclusionary time-out,** reinforcement is removed from the student within the environment where the behavior is occurring. For example, a teacher may remove materials and attention from a student who is disrupting a group lesson. When the student demonstrates appropriate behavior, the materials and attention are returned. In **seclusionary time-out,** the student is removed from the environment where the reinforcement is available when inappropriate behavior occurs. For example, a student who is disrupting the class with inappropriate behavior is taken to a secluded area of the same room or to a different room. When the student demonstrates appropriate behavior, the student is allowed to return to the original setting. In both cases time-out will be effective if the student values the attention received and the activity being conducted within the original setting and wants to return. The procedure would not be effective if the performance of the behavior is maintained by intrinsic or automatic reinforcement. For example, self-injurious or stereotypic behaviors may continue in a timeout setting. Also, removal from a setting may be reinforcing to the student who wants to escape the completion of nonpreferred tasks.

Overcorrection also can be categorized in two ways. With **restitutional overcorrection,** the person must make amends by performing a behavior that restores the environment to a state that goes beyond correcting the damage done by the student. For example, a student who spits on the floor would have to wash the target area as well as the floor of the entire room. With **positive practice overcorrection,** the person must repeatedly demonstrate the appropriate way to perform a behavior. For example, a student who ran down a hallway would be required to return and practice walking down the hall five times or for five minutes. With either type of overcorrection, it is desirable to have the punishment be related to the behavior. Also, a problem may arise if the person refuses to perform a behavior and must be forced to comply.

The direct application of aversives is the most intrusive punishment procedure. Because of potential undesirable side effects, the procedure should be used only as a temporary measure in cases that are life threatening and have the potential for causing danger. TASH (TASH, 2000) identified aversive procedures as including the application of substances that are aversive to the senses: (a) auditory, such as loud noises; (b) olfactory, such as ammonia; (c) tactile, such as electric shock; (d) taste, such as shaving cream or vinegar; and (e) visual, such as blindfolding. TASH also identified aversive procedures as including those that put restrictions on a person's movement, such as physical restraint, or restriction on a person's rights, such as the withholding of nutrition.

Issues in Selecting Behavioral Interventions

While it is clear that a number of behavioral procedures are available for increasing appropriate behaviors and decreasing inappropriate behaviors, the current trend is to provide positive behavioral support within a comprehensive intervention. The arguments and issues that support this trend are described in the following sections.

Aversiveness and Intrusiveness   Numerous persons and groups in the field of disabilities have been vocal in advocating against the use of aversives in decreasing challenging behaviors. In 1986 TASH passed a resolution on the use of aversives as follows:

> Therefore be it resolved, that TASH, an international advocacy association of people with disabilities, their family members, other advocates and people who work in the disability field, affirms the right of persons with disabilities to freedom from aversive procedure of any kind. TASH is unequivocally opposed to the use of aversive procedures under any circumstance and calls for the cessation of the use of all such procedures (TASH, 2000).*

TASH based the resolution against aversives on the logic that aversives (a) cause pain, (b) have potential side effects (e.g., tissue damage, stress), (c) dehumanize the person, (d) cause discomfort of those involved in delivering the intervention, and (e) can result in rebellion.

In 1988 Iwata asserted that aversive procedures are "default technologies" because they are used when reinforcement procedures fail. As such, he argued that the field of applied behavior analysis should refrain from advocating for such aversive procedures but should, instead, continue to ensure that such technologies are used in an appropriate manner until they can be replaced. Since that time, the research base to support the use of more positive procedures has increased.

---

*Printed with permission from TASH. For more information about TASH, visit www.tash.org.

Helmstetter and Durand (1991) identified a number of issues in the use of aversive procedures that include (a) mixed results in generalization, (b) potential for misuse, (c) side effects (e.g., fear, withdrawal, crying, aggression), (d) disregard for other factors that influence behaviors (e.g., communication deficits, setting events), and (e) violation of a person's constitutional rights to speech and privacy. These issues are apparent in a research investigation conducted by Magee and Ellis (2001) that evaluated the use of physical restraint (10-second basket-hold timeout) to decrease the physical aggression (e.g., hitting, kicking) and physical touching (e.g., touching the genital areas of others) of a 13-year-old male with Down syndrome. When high levels of problem behaviors occurred during physical restraint, the researchers concluded that the restraint was either causing or maintaining the inappropriate behavior. When physical restraint was discontinued, the target behaviors were eliminated with the less intrusive procedures of differential reinforcement and extinction.

Court cases also have addressed the use of aversives in behavioral interventions and have left some latitude for their use under specific conditions. In examining the case law on the use of aversive interventions, including electric shock, noxious substances, corporal punishment, restraints, and time-out, with persons with disabilities since 1990, Lohrmann-O'Rourke and Zirkel (1998) found the following:

1. The use of electric shock may be permissible under limited circumstances.
2. The use of noxious substances is limited to cases where it is justified by data and is used with safeguards.
3. The use of corporal punishment is subject to state standards, and consideration in its use may or may not be based on the presence of a disability.
4. There is some latitude in the use of physical restraint, depending on the boundaries set in the IEP, the relationship to the disability, the nature and extent of the restraint, and the circumstances under which it is applied.
5. Time-out is to be used in accordance with state and local standards regarding justification, relationship to the disability, degree of intrusiveness or isolation, failure of less restrictive procedures, IEP boundaries, and parental consent.

Positive Behavioral Support and Teamwork   In 2005 TASH reprinted a classic article by Horner et al. (1990) advocating a "nonaversive" approach to providing behavioral support. In this position paper, the authors asserted that an emerging technology for dealing with challenging behaviors was causing the use of aversive interventions to be justified only as a temporary measure during crisis management. The authors listed the following practices as themes in providing positive behavioral support: (a) lifestyle changes providing access to activities in inclusive settings, (b) functional analysis, (c) multicomponent interventions, (d) manipulation of ecological and setting events, (e) antecedent manipulations, (f) instruction on adaptive behavior, (g) environments with effective consequences, (h) minimal use of mild punishers, and (i) social validation of procedures with consideration for human dignity. Fifteen years later Snell (2005) reflected that several of these themes had been the basis of significant changes in the practices used to deal with challenging behaviors during subsequent years.

While the research literature is full of examples of the effectiveness of punishment in decreasing challenging behaviors, the current research base builds a case for positive behavioral support as an alternative to punishment. For example, Kahng et al. (2002) reviewed 396 investigations on the treatment of self-injurious behaviors that were published in 63 professional journals between 1964 and 2000; since 1980 the authors found a decrease in the use of punishment procedures, such as time-out and overcorrection, and an increase in interventions involving reinforcement, such as differential reinforcement of other behaviors or alternate behaviors.

Positive behavioral support can be implemented at different levels. For example, Turnbull et al. (2002) described three components to be considered in implementing schoolwide behavioral support: (a) universal support—a schoolwide positive reinforcement system, (b) group support—group contingencies for students with chronic behavior problems, and (c) individual support—individualized specific behavior intervention programs for students with the most challenging behaviors. They noted that a large number of students will need less intense support, while a small number of students will need intensive support.

Horner and Carr (1997) pointed out that behavioral intervention should be comprehensive in nature and can include (a) functional communication training, (b) curricular revision, (c) setting event changes, and (d) involvement of students in making choices. The premise is that several positive behavioral strategies can be used together to optimize the chances for successful intervention. For example, Wheeler, Carter, Mayton, and Thomas (2002) increased task engagement and decreased the self-injurious behavior of head hitting in a 7-year-old girl with blindness and a moderate disability by implementing a comprehensive intervention with the following components: (a) presenting a choice of nonpreferred tasks, (b) presenting a preferred activity on completion of a nonpreferred task, (c) giving specific task directions with hand-over-hand assistance, and (d) providing praise for any attempt to engage in appropriate behavior (differential reinforcement of alternate behavior).

Team involvement is crucial in implementing a positive behavioral support plan so the intervention can be developed with viewpoints from various perspectives (e.g., communication, reinforcer identification) across settings, such as home, school, and work. Bambara, Gomez, Koger, Lohrmann-O'Rourke, and Xin (2001) described four case studies in which teams implemented positive behavioral supports for adults with mental retardation who had challenging behaviors, such as sexually inappropriate behavior, aggression, destruction, and self-injury. Team members consisted of agency directors, behavioral specialists, program supervisors, direct support staff, consultants, and family members. Through their efforts around the clock, the teams were able to reduce behaviors for extended periods of time (e.g., two years) so the persons they supported could participate with success in less restrictive environments, such as a general education classroom or a competitive work setting. Bambara et al. found that these teams operated in an atmosphere where everyone was heard, the members were there to support each other, and the teams were person centered.

Bosch (2001) built a case for the inclusion of persons from a wide variety of backgrounds in decreasing self-injurious and aggressive behaviors in persons with mental disabilities that may include (a) community members, (b) dentists, (c) family members, (d) nutritionists, (e) occupational therapists, (f) physical therapists, (g) physicians or nurse practitioners, (h) psychiatrists or psychologists, (i) recreation therapists, (j) speech/language pathologists, (k) social workers, and (l) teachers. As discussed earlier in this chapter and as shown in the Table 10.1, Bosch found teaming to be successful in four case studies.

Self-Management of Behavior   Although teamwork can be effective in decreasing inappropriate behaviors, teaching students to regulate or manage their own behavior

TABLE 10.1   *Examples of Interdisciplinary Teaming to Decrease Challenging Behaviors Based on Bosch (2001).*

Descriptive Information	Team Members	Behavioral Support Plan
Aggression (e.g., hitting, biting) in 6-year-old male with communication disorder, attention-hyperactivity disorder, seizure disorder, atypical development	Neurologist, psychiatrist, educator, speech/language pathologist	Medication, interspersal requests, escape extinction, functional communication training
Self-injurious behavior (e.g., hand chewing) in 18-year-old female with severe to profound mental disability, neuromuscular disorder, seizure disorder, impaired oral skills, mild malnutrition, esophagitis, constipation	Orthopedist, physician, speech/language pathologist, dentist, nurse, physical therapist, occupational therapist, psychologist	Diet changes, dental work, positioning, interspersed requests, nonexclusionary time-out, functional communication training, choice making, active involvement, consistency, structure
Self-injury (e.g., head banging, destruction, and aggression) in 10-year-old male with scoliosis, seizure disorder, gastrostomy, severe to profound mental disability, hearing loss, microcephaly, reflux, sinus infections, communication deficits	Audiologist, nutritionist, psychologist, speech/language pathologist	Medication, feeding schedule, interspersal requests, escape extinction, functional communication training
Tantruming and self-injury (e.g., finger chewing) in 27-year-old female with severe to profound mental disability, encephalopathy, quadriplegia, low weight, scoliosis, dysphagia	Physician, dentist, nutritionist, speech/language pathologist, psychologist	Dental treatment, internal medical intervention, diet changes, functional communication training, escape extinction, differential reinforcement of appropriate behavior

is a worthwhile strategy in that it may lead to less restrictive environments and increased inclusion in the future. For example, Mithaug (2002) taught six students with pervasive developmental disorders, autism, or developmental delays to use choice cards in selecting classroom tasks and to reward themselves for task completion during independent work time. Wehmeyer, Yeager, Bolding, Agran, and Hughes (2003) found that such self-regulation and student-directed strategies also decreased problem behaviors that included inappropriate touching or verbalizations and the failure to attend of three adolescents with developmental disabilities (e.g., mild to moderate mental disabilities, autism) in inclusive general education settings. The self-regulation strategies included (a) antecedent cues—pictures, (b) self-monitoring—recording performance of target behavior, (c) self-evaluation—measuring progress, and (d) self-reinforcement—earning preferred reinforcer. Inappropriate behaviors decreased while appropriate behaviors increased.

Validity Regardless of the intervention procedure that is selected, it is important to consider the validity of the procedure (Helmstetter & Durand, 1991). This can be done by asking (a) whether the change in behavior occurred as a result of the intervention (e.g., Did head banging decrease because a behavioral intervention was implemented or because a child's earache ended?), (b) whether the intervention was implemented as specified in the behavior plan (e.g., Did the teacher remember to deliver reinforcers at the end of each interval specified in the behavior plan?), and (c) whether the resulting change in behavior was meaningful (e.g., Did decreasing disruptive classroom episodes of tantruming from five per hour to two per hour improve the classroom learning environment enough to justify the time and effort put into implementing an intervention?) (Voeltz & Evans, 1983). It is possible that the responses to such questions may affect the conclusions that can be drawn regarding a behavioral intervention or may show one procedure to be preferable to another.

Best Practices
Challenging Behaviors

1. Use a functional behavioral assessment to determine the function of challenging behavior and an appropriate behavioral intervention.
2. In selecting a behavioral intervention, consider the least intrusive alternative, and attempt to make environmental and curricular changes before using behavioral strategies.
3. Use an interdisciplinary team approach in both behavioral assessment and intervention.
4. Use a positive behavioral support plan to avoid the side effects that are associated with the use of aversive procedures.
5. Apply the fair pair rule by increasing appropriate behaviors while decreasing inappropriate behaviors.
6. Recognize that positive behavioral support plans should be comprehensive in nature.

Conclusion

It is clear that a variety of strategies exist for decreasing challenging behaviors exhibited by students with moderate and severe disabilities. The implementation of a functional behavioral assessment can help identify the functions of challenging behaviors and lead to appropriate intervention. The involvement of a team of persons working together across settings can result in a comprehensive intervention across settings.

Daniels (1998) posed a number of questions that can be useful for those involved in selecting appropriate behavioral interventions in inclusive settings. These included assessing the following:

1. Whether behavior is a result of inappropriate curriculum or teaching strategies (e.g., group size and composition)

2. Whether behavior is a result of the student's inability to grasp concepts being taught

3. Whether behavior is a result of the student's disability

4. Whether behavior is a result of other factors (e.g., inappropriate curriculum)

5. Whether the teacher can control causal factors (e.g., amount and type of feedback)

6. Whether behavior is setting specific

7. Whether behavior can be self-regulated or self-managed

8. Whether behavioral strategies are appropriate without violating a student's rights

9. Whether reinforcement strategies can be effective

10. Whether punishment (e.g., response cost, timeout, overcorrection) is appropriate and, if it is, what precautions should be in place

A team containing persons who think through each of these questions is on the right path to finding an appropriate intervention.

Questions for Review

1. List five categories of challenging behavior, and provide two examples of each.
2. Explain each of the steps for conducting a functional assessment.
3. What is an A-B-C analysis, and what does it reveal?
4. How can hypotheses be tested to determine the function of a behavior?
5. Using a hierarchy of interventions, which are least intrusive?
6. Why are intrusive and aversive behavioral interventions undesirable? Can they ever be justified?
7. What have the courts ruled in regard to the use of aversives?
8. What components might a comprehensive behavior support plan include?

Performance-Based Assessment

You have conducted a functional behavior assessment on Charlotte, a middle school student with moderate mental retardation who is in a self-contained classroom for students with disabilities, and have come up with the following information:

1. The class contains nine students with one teacher and three instructional assistants.
2. The teacher seldom acknowledges the student but tends to let one instructional assistant work with the student.
3. The student has a limited vocabulary of two- to three-word utterances.
4. The assistant seldom follows through on making Charlotte comply with directions.
5. Charlotte's behaviors appear to be hitting, throwing, kicking, cursing, and self-mutilating.

6. Past behavioral interventions have included physical restraint, timeout in the corner, and response cost (staying in room during lunch, art, or field trips).

7. The teacher often sends Charlotte home early when her behavior escalates at school.

8. Potential reinforcer preferences include sustained adult interaction and escape from work by going home or to the office.

9. IEP objectives include matching objects, reading survival signs, giving personal information, and tying shoes.

10. During instruction, Charlotte is easily distracted and is successful in maintaining adult interaction by refusing to do work and changing the subject.

11. When the assistant persists in instructional requests, Charlotte's behavior escalates (e.g., saying "no" and throwing objects).

12. Instruction consists of error correction with little opportunity for praise.

Describe components that you might include in a positive behavioral support plan for this student.

References

Alberto, P. A., & Troutman, A. C. (1995). *Applied behavior analysis for teachers* (4th ed.). Upper Saddle River, NJ: Merrill/Prentice Hall.

Anderson, C. M., & Long, E. S., (2002). Use of a structured descriptive assessment methodology to identify variables affecting problem behavior. *Journal of Applied Behavior Analysis 35,* 137–154.

Bambara, L. M., Gomez, O., Koger, F., Lohrmann-O'Rourke, S., & Xin, Y. P. (2001). More than techniques: Team members' perspectives on implementing positive supports for adults with severe challenging behaviors. *Journal of the Association for Persons with Severe Handicaps, 26,* 213–228.

Borrero, J. C., Vollmer, T. R., Wright, C. S., Lerman, D. C., & Kelley, M. E. (2002). Further evaluation of the role of protective equipment in the functional analysis of self-injurious behavior. *Journal of Applied Behavior Analysis, 35,* 69–72.

Bosch, J. J. (2001). An interdisciplinary approach to self-injurious and aggressive behavior. *Journal of Developmental and Physical Disabilities, 13,* 169–178.

Daniels, V. I. (1998). How to manage disruptive behavior in inclusive classrooms. *Teaching Exceptional Children, 30*(4), 26–31.

Durand, V. M. (1999). Functional communication training using assistive devices: Recruiting natural communities of reinforcement. *Journal of Applied Behavior Analysis, 32,* 247–267.

Ebanks, M. E., & Fisher, W. W. (2003). Altering the timing of academic prompts to treat destructive behavior maintained by escape. *Journal of Applied Behavior Analysis, 36,* 355–359.

Fisher, W. W., Adelinis, J. D., Thompson, R. H., Worsdell, A. S., & Zarcone, J. R. (1998). Functional analysis and treatment of destructive behavior maintained by termination of "don't" (and symmetrical "do") requests. *Journal of Applied Behavior Analysis, 31,* 339–356.

Girolami, P. A., & Scotti, J. R. (2001). Use of analog functional analysis in assessing the function of mealtime behavior problems. *Education and Training in Mental Retardation and Developmental Disabilities, 36,* 207–223.

Hall, A. M., Neuharth-Pritchett, S., & Belfiore, P. J. (1997). Reduction of aggressive behaviors with changes in activity: Linking descriptive and experimental analyses. *Education and Training in Mental Retardation and Developmental Disabilities, 32,* 331–339.

Helmstetter, E., & Durand, V. M. (1991). Nonaversive interventions for severe behavior problems. In L. H. Meyer, C. A. Peck, & L. Brown (Eds.), *Critical Issues in the Lives of People with Severe Disabilities* (pp. 559–600). Baltimore: Brookes.

Hetzroni, O. E., & Roth, T. (2003). Effects of a positive support approach to enhance communicative behaviors of children with mental retardation who have challenging behaviors. *Education and Training in Mental Retardation and Developmental Disabilities, 38,* 95–105.

Horner, R. H., & Carr, E. G. (1997). Behavioral support for students with severe disabilities: Functional assessment and comprehensive intervention. *Journal of Special Education, 31,* 84–104.

Horner, R. H., Dunlap, G., Koegel, R. L., Carr, E. G., Sailor, W., Anderson, J., Albin, R. W., & O'Neill, R. E. (1990). Toward a technology of "nonaversive" behavioral support. *Journal of the Association for Persons with Severe Handicaps, 15,* 125–132.

Iwata, B. A. (1988). The development and adoption of controversial default technologies. *The Behavior Analyst, 11,* 149–157.

Iwata, B. A., Dorsey, M. F., Slifer, K. J., Bauman, K. E., & Richman, G. S. (1994). Toward a functional analysis of self-injury. *Journal of Applied Behavior Analysis, 27,* 197–209.

Kahng, S., Abt, K. A., & Schonbachler, H. E. (2001). Assessment and treatment of low-rate high-intensity problem behavior. *Journal of Applied Behavior Analysis, 34,* 225–228.

Kahng, S., Iwata, B. A., & Lewin, A. B. (2002). Behavioral treatment of self-injury 1964 to 2000. *American Journal on Mental Retardation, 107,* 212–221.

Kennedy, C. H., & Meyer, K. A. (1998). The use of psychotropic medication for people with severe disabilities and challenging behavior: Current status and future directions. *Journal of the Association for Persons with Severe Handicaps, 23,* 83–97.

Le, D. D., & Smith, R. G. (2002). Functional analysis of self-injury with and without protective equipment. *Journal of Developmental and Physical Disabilities, 14,* 277–290.

Lerman, D. C., Iwata, B. A., & Wallace, M. D. (1999). Side effects of extinction: Prevalence of bursting and aggression during the treatment of self-injurious behavior. *Journal of Applied Behavior Analysis, 32,* 1–8.

Lohrmann-O'Rourke, S., & Zirkel, P. A. (1998). The case law on aversive interventions for students with disabilities. *Exceptional Children, 65,* 101–123.

Magee, S. K., & Ellis, J. (2001). The detrimental effects of physical restraint as a consequence for inappropriate classroom behavior. *Journal of Applied Behavior Analysis, 34,* 501–504.

McCord, B. E., Iwata, B. A., Galensky, T. L., Ellingson, S. A., & Thomson, R. J. (2001). Functional analysis and treatment of problem behavior evoked by noise. *Journal of Applied Behavior Analysis, 34,* 447–462.

Mithaug, D. K. (2002). "Yes" means success: Teaching children with multiple disabilities to self-regulate during independent work. *Teaching Exceptional Children, 35*(1), 22–27.

Moore, J. W., Mueller, M. M., Dubard, M., Roberts, D. S., & Sterling-Turner, H. E. (2002). The influence of therapist attention on self-injury during a tangible condition. *Journal of Applied Behavior Analysis, 35,* 283–286.

Murdick, N. L., & Gartin, B. C. (1999). Complying with IDEA: Using functional assessment of behavior to plan programs for students with mental retardation. *Education and Training in Mental Retardation and Developmental Disabilities, 34,* 464–472.

Piazza, C. C., Fisher, W. W., Hanley, G. P., LeBlanc, L. A., Worsdell, A. S., Lindauer, S. E., & Keeney, K. M. (1998). Treatment of pica through multiple analyses of its reinforcing functions. *Journal of Applied Behavior Analysis, 31,* 165–189.

Piazza, C. C., Roane, H. S., Keeney, K. M., Boney, B. R., & Abt, K. A. (2002). Varying response effort in the treatment of pica maintained by automatic reinforcement. *Journal of Applied Behavior Analysis, 35,* 233–246.

Romaniuk, C., Miltenberger, R., Conyers, C., Jenner, N., Jurgens, M., & Ringenberg, C. (2002). The influence of activity choice on problem behaviors maintained by escape versus attention. *Journal of Applied Behavior Analysis, 35,* 349–362.

Smith, R. G., & Churchill, R. M. (2002). Identification of environmental determinants of behavior disorders through functional analysis of precursor behaviors. *Journal of Applied Behavior Analysis, 35,* 125–136.

Snell, M. E. (2005). Fifteen years later: Has positive programming become the expected technology for addressing problem behavior? A commentary on Horner et al. (1990). *Research and Practice for Persons with Severe Disabilities, 30,* 11–14.

Symons, F. J., Clark, R. D., Roberts, J. P., & Bailey, D. B. (2001). Classroom behavior of elementary school-age boys with fragile X syndrome. *The Journal of Special Education, 34,* 194–202.

TASH resolution on the use of aversive procedures (2000). *TASH Newsletter, 26*(11), 6.

Turnbull, A., Edmondson, H., Griggs, P., Wickham, D., Sailor, W., Freeman, R., Guess, D., Lassen, S., McCart, A., Park, J., Riffel, L., Turnbull, R., & Warren, J. (2002). A blueprint for schoolwide positive behavior support: Implementation of three components. *Exceptional Children, 68,* 377–402.

Van Camp, C. M., Lerman, D. C., Kelley, M. E., Contrucci, S. A., & Vorndran, C. M. (2000). Variable-time reinforcement schedules in the treatment of socially maintained problem behavior. *Journal of Applied Behavior Analysis, 33,* 545–557.

Van Camp, C. M., Lerman, D. C., Kelley, M. E., Roane, H. S., Contrucci, S. A., & Vorndran, C. M. (2000). Further analysis of idiosyncratic antecedent influences during the assessment and treatment of problem behavior. *Journal of Applied Behavior Analysis, 33,* 207–221.

Voeltz, L. M., & Evans, I. M. (1983). Educational validity: Procedures to evaluate outcomes in programs for severely handicapped learners. *Journal of the Association of Severe Handicaps, 8,* 3–15.

Wehmeyer, M. L., Yeager, D., Bolding, N., Agran, M., & Hughes, C. (2003). The effects of self-regulation strategies on goal attainment for students with developmental disabilities in general education classrooms. *Journal of Developmental and Physical Disabilities, 15,* 79–91.

Wheeler, J. J., Carter, S. L., Mayton, M. R., & Thomas, R. A. (2002). Structural analysis of instructional variables and their effects on task-engagement and self-aggression. *Education and Training in Mental Retardation and Developmental Disabilities, 37,* 391–398.

Wolery, M., Bailey, D. B., & Sugai, G. M. (1988). *Effective teaching: Principles and procedures of applied behavior analysis with exceptional students.* Boston: Allyn & Bacon.

CHAPTER ELEVEN

PLANNING FOR THE LIFE SPAN:
Longitudinal Transition

On completion of this chapter, the reader will meet the following objectives:

- Define transition within the context of the life span.
- Identify the ages at which an ITP is required by law and the components for each type.
- Identify factors that may exacerbate the transition process for families of children with moderate and severe disabilities.
- List factors that may be perceived as challenges or barriers in the transition process.
- Discuss the process of longitudinal programming and strategies that may be helpful at various points in the life span.

As discussed in Chapter 4, longitudinal programming assists students with moderate and severe disabilities in achieving the criterion of ultimate functioning (Brown, Nietupski, & Hamre-Nietupski, 1976). Using an ecological inventory approach, the focus of longitudinal instruction is on teaching functional skills that will be needed in future environments (Brown et al., 1979). This chapter will revisit the concept of longitudinal programming by describing the lifelong process of transitioning from early childhood to adulthood. Later, Chapter 12 will provide vocational, residential, and recreational options for adulthood following a seamless transition from school to the adult community.

Transitions are changes from one state of being to another that occur in a progressive fashion over the life span of a person. Thus, transitions can be from one domain (e.g., educational, residential, community) to the next or from one stage of life (e.g., childhood, adolescence, adulthood) to the next. **Longitudinal transitions** consist of changes over time that are planned and involve preparation for future environments or stages prior to transitioning so transitions are smooth instead of abrupt. This is accomplished through longitudinal programming, the process of selecting target skills for instruction that will lead to independent functioning in the next environment. To begin to clarify your understanding of the concept of transitioning, complete Activity 11.1.

LEGAL AND HISTORICAL FOUNDATIONS OF TRANSITION

In 1981 Brown et al. set the historical foundation for using longitudinal programming for persons with moderate and severe disabilities as a means of facilitating a seamless transition to adulthood. Brown et al. argued that unacceptable services for students with severe disabilities include (a) untrained service providers, (b) segregated educational services, (c) educational services limited to school settings, (d) a nonfunctional and chronological-age-inappropriate curriculum, (e) uninvolved parents

---

ACTIVITY 11.1   Lifelong Transitions

To understand the impact of transitions in the life cycle, create a time line like the one shown below and list the major transitions you have had in your own life. Think about the births, deaths, illnesses, moves, relationships, unexpected events, and career changes that have occurred. Have any been more challenging than others? Why? What type of support enabled you to make each transition? Did any of the transitions result in failure? Later in this chapter, we will revisit this time line.

- Birth
- Begin elementary school
- Move to another state
- Enroll in new school

- Enter secondary school
- Graduate and begin college
- Graduate with undergraduate degree and begin employment
- Marry and move to new state
- Have children
- Return to graduate school
- Begin new employment

Before continuing, consider what your life would be like if you had a moderate or severe disability. Would all of these transitions have occurred? If so, which would have required the most support? What type of support?

---

and guardians, and (f) lack of preparation for future community environments. Brown et al. then proposed the following. First, educational and related services should be delivered around the clock and throughout the year across a variety of natural school and nonschool environments to students placed in natural proportions in neighborhood, chronological-age-appropriate schools. Second, the curriculum should consist of individualized, chronological-age-appropriate, functional skills needed across both current and future environments. Third, a longitudinal, comprehensive, and individualized transition plan that provides for direct instruction in future environments should be developed with involvement from parents or guardians, sending and receiving personnel, and related service personnel.

Although the term *transition* is often used to refer to launching to adulthood, Activity 11.1 demonstrated that the process of transitioning begins with birth and is a continuing process, as argued by Brown et al. (1981). Federal special education and disability legislation has mandated that special attention be paid to transitioning at the points when students enter and exit school services. Through IDEA and its amendments, legislation has ensured funding for transition services as well as formal ITPs (Johnson, Stodden, Emanuel, Luecking, & Mack, 2002; Kohler & Field, 2003).

As contrasted by Repetto and Correa (1996), early childhood and secondary transition plans differ in several ways. First, early intervention transition plans are required as part of the Individualized Family Service Plan (IFSP), while secondary transition plans are required as part of the IEP. Second, early intervention transition plans are required at least 90 days before a child enters preschool (preschool services can begin on the third birthday), while secondary transition plans can begin at age 14 and are required by age 16. Third, those who participate in writing the early childhood transition plan include the family, professionals from the birth-to-two lead agency, and the local education agency, as advised by the state education agency, while those who participate in the writing of the secondary transition plan include the student's teacher; the local education agency; and if desired, the parents or guardian, the student, and representatives from adult agencies. Fourth, the content of the early childhood transition plan includes the required components of the IFSP;

determination of eligibility for preschool services; transition goals, objectives, and services; placement options, visits, and determination; staff training of receiving program; child orientation for transition to the program; sharing of records; and arrangement of nonschool services. On the other hand, the content of the secondary transition plan includes the components of the required IEP; transition outcomes; transition services for instruction, employment, community experience, adult living, and if appropriate, daily living or vocational evaluation; a statement if services are not needed in a specific area; and responsibilities of participating agencies. Finally, the early childhood transition plan requires evaluation of parent satisfaction with the implementation of the plan, while the secondary transition plan requires evaluation that the plan was implemented and reviewed on an annual basis. Example 11.1 shows the typical information that would be found on a transition plan for a secondary school student with moderate to severe disabilities.

EXAMPLE 11.1 A SAMPLE TRANSITION PLAN

Date: Review Date:
Name: Age: Grade:
Student ID#:   Disability:

Transition Service Needs	
Employment	Competitive
	Supported
Living Arrangements	Independent
	Group Home
	Family
Community Participation	Supported
	Unsupported

Required Transition Services	
Agency Responsibilities	Agency Responsible

In 1985 Wehman, Kregel, and Barcus (1985) focused on vocational transition in particular and defined this as a "carefully planned process, which may be initiated either by school personnel or adult service providers, to establish and implement a plan for either employment or additional vocational training" of a student with disabilities "who will graduate or leave school in three to five years" and noted that "such a process must involve special educators, vocational educators, parents and/or the student, an adult service system representative, and possibly an employer" (p. 26). Furthermore, Wehman et al. asserted that there are three stages to vocational transition: (a) school instruction, (b) planning for the transition process, and (c) placement into meaningful employment.

In 1988 Hasazi and Clark followed through on Wehman's focus on vocational transition in noting that practices in the 1980s included the development of an ITP with interagency collaboration, paid work experiences, vocational training at employment sites, participation in vocational programs, and instruction in job-seeking skills. At the time, they predicted that future trends would include the hiring of school-based employment specialists, an increase in employment opportunities during the secondary school years, the development of specific outcomes to evaluate program effectiveness, state legislation and policies, an emphasis in self-advocacy, and changes in demographics and occupational structures by the year 2000 that would include an increase in racial and ethnic diversity and a decrease in lower-skilled job opportunities. These predictions have been validated as the years have passed.

Based on the concept that transitioning is a longitudinal process and not limited to the early childhood (birth to 3 years) and secondary (16 to 21 years) periods mandated by law, Repetto and Correa (1996) asserted that transition planning should include the years of age 4 to 15 as well across the following components. First, the curriculum would proceed from a developmental approach to a functional skill approach, ending with vocational, residential, and community inclusion. Second, the location of services would proceed from home and preschool to elementary, middle, and secondary school, ending with inclusive vocational, residential, and community settings. Third, futures planning would begin with the IFSP and progress through the IEP and the secondary ITP. Fourth, multiagency collaboration would progress from early childhood agencies to school-associated agencies, ending with adult service providers. Finally, the focus of transition would progress from being family centered to being student centered, ending with self-advocacy.

FAMILY ISSUES ASSOCIATED WITH TRANSITION

As described in Chapter 4, specific times of transition, such as accessing school services and adult services for the first time, can be predicted as stressors for families. While having their children launch into the adult world can be stressful for all families, it can be even more so when the children have disabilities. For example, Whitney-Thomas and Hanley-Maxwell (1996) surveyed parents of children in their junior and senior years of secondary school and found that the parents of children with disabilities had more concerns with the transition process to adulthood than did the parents of children who did not have disabilities.

When children have moderate and severe disabilities, the concerns about launching can be expanded to include the failure to launch as well as the lack of adult options. As noted by several researchers, the transition to adulthood is often the time when parents first discover the lack of adult options that are available for their children. For example, Kraemer and Blacher (2001) noted the lack of adult options when they focused on the transition of children with severe disabilities between the ages of 20 and 24. In interviewing 52 families in California, they found that most of the families were aware of the mandate for transition and that most of their children were engaged in experiences to facilitate a successful transition, including working on a functional curriculum that included daily living and social skills in conjunction with community-based instruction and paid or volunteer work experiences. In terms of employment, the parents wanted their children to participate in competitive or supported employment but tended to see sheltered workshops or day activity centers as more realistic options. In terms of residential placement, more expected their children to live in group homes rather than a more independent and less restrictive setting. Although the parents were pessimistic about the future options for their children, they were satisfied with their level of involvement in the transition process.

In 1992 Thorin and Irvin reported the results of a survey of 42 members of 19 families with children with severe disabilities, ages 15 to 25 years, in Oregon. When presented with a list of concerns related to school, work life, residential services, professionals, daily life, family life, and the future, the respondents rated residential concerns (e.g., interactions with providers, attainment of services, quality of services) as being the most stressful.

Ten years later, Cooney (2002) reported similar results from a two-year qualitative investigation (i.e., document reviews, interviews, observations) that centered on the transitioning to adulthood of nine students with significant disabilities. Cooney found that the students desired jobs, relationships, pay, a place of their own, and independence, while the parents wanted their children to find fulfillment based on their strengths and capabilities. On transition, parents discovered a lack of program options and alienation of their children within the adult service system. The professionals who assisted with the transition process tended to be skeptics characterized as "realistic" and to base outcomes on eligibility for existing options rather than on attempting to find a match for the desires and preferences of the persons with disabilities and their families. Cooney concluded that this type of perspective in professionals involved in the transition process destines persons with disabilities for a life of "clienthood" and dependency. Also, it results in confusion as to the roles of parents and professionals during the transition process. Thus, Cooney suggested that more balanced partnerships between parents and professionals are needed in regard to transition.

Family concerns for the future of their children with disabilities are not limited by nationality or ethnicity. Heiman (2002) reported concerns of 32 parents of children with disabilities (i.e., mental, physical, learning) in Israel. Their concerns included the ability of their children to complete an education, find employment, and achieve financial and physical independence. They also worried about how their children would be able to manage without parents, find a place to live, and have adequate adult support (e.g., financial, emotional). Although the parents tended to be both optimistic and realistic in expressing their concerns, none were involved in taking steps to secure their children's future welfare and security.

Although some concerns for the future are shared, differences across cultures also exist. Geenen, Powers, and Lopez-Vasquez (2001) surveyed 308 urban parents of children with disabilities, ages 13 to 22 years, who were African American, Hispanic American, Native American, and European American to determine their perspectives on transition. The authors found that (a) African American parents placed emphasis on talking to their children about transition and teaching them to use public transportation, (b) Hispanic and Native American parents placed emphasis on teaching cultural values and beliefs, and (c) European American parents were more involved in school transition meetings. Based on the results of their investigation, the authors concluded that racism, discrimination, insensitivity, and cultural responsiveness can be barriers to transition in culturally and linguistically diverse families and suggested that schools should be more sensitive to diversity when transitioning students with disabilities.

In addition to parents, siblings also share concerns for the future of a child with disabilities. Chambers, Hughes, and Carter (2004) interviewed the families of 11 students with significant cognitive disabilities and found that both parents and siblings lacked information about adult options and assumed the child would be in a restrictive environment, such as living at home and working in a segregated setting, on exiting school.

These investigations point out the need to value the role of families in the transition process. Transition should be a collaborative effort, not a process left to professionals alone. This is exemplified in Example 11.2.

| EXAMPLE 11.2 | AN EXAMPLE OF MISCOMMUNICATION BETWEEN FAMILIES AND PROFESSIONALS IN PREPARING STUDENTS FOR TRANSITION |

In looking to the future, Meers (1992) predicted that that the future opportunities for employment would be as janitors; nurse's aides, orderlies, and nurses; sales clerks, general clerks, and cashiers; waiters and food service workers; secretaries; and truck drivers. In planning transition activities, professionals may make assumptions based on such lists, rather than in collaboration with the student and family.

A secondary school in Washington erred in this manner when school officials assumed that most special education students would transition to janitorial work in adulthood (Cook, 2003). Thus, they had 25 out of 100 students with disabilities in the Work Experience Program pick up trash, search for recyclables, and haul away the trash without pay.

Although the district said that parents had given permission for the work activity, several objected, saying they never were notified. One enraged parent protested that his son would not be going through trash cans when he completed school, while another reported that his daughter was teased and called "Stinky" as a result of the activity.

As a result of the practice, a lawsuit was filed and later dropped. Although the school district claimed that the practice of having students assist custodians was due to the fact that there were not enough available job sites in the community, they halted the practice and found less stigmatizing jobs for the students, such as working in retail businesses.

CHALLENGES AND SOLUTIONS FOR SUCCESSFUL TRANSITIONING

In a seamless transition, the last day of a student's school career should be identical to the first day of adult life. The idea is to shape the skills needed for transition over time while moving the student in a stepwise fashion out of the school system and into the world of adult services. The professional literature has identified a number of challenges in achieving a seamless transition and proposed guidelines and models based on the experiences and projects of the authors.

Challenges to Successful Transition

Given the continuing discrepancies in the adult outcomes of transitioning between persons with and without disabilities, it is clear that there are challenges that must be addressed. Wehman (1992) assessed past progress in meeting challenges while looking to the future. In particular, Wehman noted past progress includes an (a) increased awareness of the poor postschool outcomes for students with disabilities, (b) positive legislative advances (e.g., Individuals with Disabilities Education Act, Rehabilitation Act Amendments, Americans with Disabilities Act), (c) advances in technology (e.g., robotics, computers), (d) high expectations for vocational preparation from families and students, and (e) grant support for model transition programs. This progress is tempered with an awareness that there still is a need for rigorous legislation in medical rehabilitation, vocational rehabilitation, and behavior intervention;

for a labor force trained across areas of need (e.g., hotel, retail, fast food, factory, office, hospital services); and for transition to remain a part of educational reform.

The professional literature is full of references to the challenges faced in creating a seamless transition throughout the life cycle and between secondary school and adulthood, in particular. For example, Repetto and Correa (1996) identified barriers to transition as including an (a) episodic curriculum that consists of nonintegrated academics; (b) lack of respect for the IEP as a working document; (c) intervention limited to the student rather than the family, community, and school; and (d) family reluctance to make long-term plans for the future.

Research investigations have provided data to support the challenges to transition. Based on interviews with 44 secondary school special education teachers, Zhang and Stecker (2001) found that teachers often have needs identified prior to the transition meeting and expect the family and student to sign the transition document, downplaying the role of self-determination in selecting options. Thoma, Rogan, and Baker (2001) also noted a lack of self-determination in reporting the results of a qualitative study of the transition meetings of eight students with moderate and severe disabilities. In addition to the transition meetings being run by the professionals on the transition team instead of in a collaborative fashion, the professionals discouraged student and family involvement by scheduling meetings at school at the convenience of the professionals, focusing the meetings on student deficits, and using an excess of professional jargon.

Even when communication is open, transitions face other challenges. The results of a qualitative investigation of 11 secondary school students with moderate and severe disabilities during their last year of school (Gallivan-Fenlon, 1994) revealed a number of discrepancies among the students, their families, and professionals. First, there were differences in expectations and aspirations for adult life, with the students voicing the desire to work and parents and service providers advocating for more restrictive placements along a continuum, such as sheltered workshops and day treatment centers. Second, transition activities and experiences sometimes included instruction in the community skills needed for transition, but specific transition planning often was done at the last minute with a lack of information regarding agencies and services and a reliance on professionals to tell the family what to do. Finally, the outcomes of transition were mixed, with some of the young adults experiencing work and friendships while others sat at home alone watching television; those who transitioned to supported employment earned higher wages than those who worked in sheltered workshops.

Part of the problem with teachers who are involved in transitioning students with disabilities is that their knowledge may have gaps in the area of adult services. When Knott and Asselin (1999) surveyed 214 teachers who were responsible for the transition of students with mental disabilities, they found that the teachers rated themselves as best at involving students and their families in the process, individualizing transition plans, and providing vocational instruction; they rated themselves worst at having knowledge of adult services and family support agencies and noted that they did not have a high degree of involvement in the evaluation of the process.

According to Johnson et al. (2002), a number of challenges must be met for successful transitioning to adulthood to occur. The first challenge is to ensure that students with disabilities have access to a full range of general education curricular options and learning experiences, such as vocational education, service learning, community work experiences, and adult living skills. The second challenge is to base high school graduation on meaningful indicators of a student's learning and skills as would be done through alternate assessment, taking into account the implications that arise from different diploma options. The third challenge is to provide students with access to an array of postsecondary educational, vocational, and residential opportunities by providing information on options and support. The fourth challenge is to facilitate student and family participation in the transition process through placing value on open communication and self-advocacy during meetings. The fifth and final challenge is to improve collaboration and linkages with adult service agencies. Repetto and Correa (1996) asserted that if the challenges of transition are met, the benefits of a longitudinal seamless transition throughout life are lower dropout rates, continued family involvement, less fragmentation of the curriculum and supporting services, lifelong learning for the student, and generalization to adulthood of the skills that have been taught.

Factors That Facilitate Successful Transition

There are a number of factors that help overcome barriers and challenges, leading to successful transitioning. The professional literature contains numerous guidelines for successful transitioning and a number of descriptions of model transition programs that have been successful. A sampling of these are described in the following sections.

Guidelines   Repetto and Correa (1996) provided guidelines for successful transitioning across five components. First, a coordinated functional curriculum should be taught across settings (e.g., classroom, home, community) with flexible scheduling, appropriate teaching strategies, and embedded academic skills. Second, the educational program should be implemented across settings within the context of school and community partnerships, should include orientation visits to the receiving program, and should have related services embedded in natural environments. Third, futures planning should be based on student portfolios and include individualized objectives. Fourth, multiagency collaboration should be a lifelong process under the guidance of a transition coordinator during regularly scheduled accessible meetings and with the family taking the lead role.

Kohler and Field (2003) proposed a framework for effective transition practices with the following components. First, student-focused planning should be based on the student's goals, visions, and interests. Second, the emphasis of student development should be on life, employment, and occupational skills identified through the practice of self-determination. Third, interagency and interdisciplinary collaboration should occur among community businesses, organizations, and agencies. Fourth, family involvement should be composed of participation, empowerment, and training. Last, program structure and attributes should be based on philosophy, planning, policy, evaluation, and resource development. Based on this framework, Kohler and Field concluded that a general education framework alone may not be sufficient to support successful transitioning, but all students, with and without disabilities, could benefit from the identified components.

Team Planning   The use of the McGill Action Planning System (MAPS) is one way to facilitate longitudinal programming for adulthood throughout the school years (Vandercook, York, & Forest, 1989). This process requires that the individual, family members, friends, and both regular and special educators work together to design an educational program that will address the future of the student with moderate to severe disabilities. Across one to three sessions, the team work together to identify the student's history; dreams for the future; nightmares (e.g., being alone); personal characteristics; strengths, gifts, and abilities; needs; and ideal day.

Model Descriptions   The professional literature has reported numerous secondary transition models that have led to successful outcomes. For example, Certo et al. (2003) described the Transition Service Integration Model that was implemented across 234 students with significant support needs in 14 school districts in California and Maryland. In the model, three agencies representing special education, rehabilitation, and developmental disabilities worked with the school system during the final year of school to ensure a seamless transition. Working together, the agencies shared responsibilities and redirected resources into the transition year of each student. During the transition year, representatives from the three agencies shared an office and oversaw instruction on functional, chronological-age skills in natural community settings.

In another example, Lombard (1994) focused on the challenges of rural transitioning in describing the Collaborative Transition Model implemented in Wisconsin. The model was guided by a small internal steering committee that gathered transition support and cooperation from various sources including school, adult agencies, and family. Once this group came together, a transition core team (e.g., family members, agency personnel, educators, employers) was identified. The team conducted a community needs assessment to evaluate available community options (e.g., employment). They then developed a community action plan to fill in the voids identified through the assessment. Once this was completed, students with disabilities were identified for transition planning from middle through secondary school. In-school transition planning then took place through a process of assessment and development of the IEPs and ITPs followed by enrollment in vocational classes with support. Continued follow-up occurred in postschool settings with a plan for annual evaluation.

In a final example, White and Bond (1992) described the Special Transitional Education Project in Montana, a five-year program that included vocational evaluation, inclusion in general education and adapted vocational classes, community living instruction, career exploration, long-range transition planning, and community agency support. In addition to learning vocational skills, students spent time learning life skills in an apartment complex. The program emphasized being punctual, remaining on task, using etiquette, following instructions, having appropriate social interactions, working independently, taking appropriate breaks, and observing safety rules. Based on their experiences, White and Bond recommended making transition a priority, hiring a full-time specialist for guiding work and residential experiences, and using paraprofessionals to maximize program effectiveness.

Summary

In summary, the challenges to transition include episodic instruction on a fragmented curriculum, the tendency of professionals to make decisions for students and their families using unfamiliar jargon, the lack of coordination between sending and receiving agencies involved in the transition, family reluctance to plan for the future, and failure to follow through on transition activities. Likewise, factors that may facilitate successful transitioning include multiagency collaboration, instruction on skills needed for future environments, instruction across school and nonschool settings (including future settings), delivery of related services in natural contexts and environments where they will be needed, and the use of self-determination by the person making the transition in regard to transition outcomes.

LONGITUDINAL PROGRAMMING AND TRANSITIONING

As previously stated, it is important to bear in mind that transitioning is a lifelong process that is not restricted to the four or five years prior to adulthood. Thus, it is important to begin planning for the future as soon as a child is born. It is not uncommon for the family of typical children to begin a college fund when a child is young; to teach children activities, such as sports and the arts, that will give them lifelong pleasure or become a vocation; or to enroll children in special courses that will increase the likelihood that they will be accepted to the schools of their choice (e.g., colleges, specialized programs) that will expand their vocational options. In the same manner, it is crucial that family members of children with moderate and severe disabilities begin to plan early for the future. Even as early as the time a child enters the school system, activities may include exploring future vocational and residential options, teaching functional skills that will be needed in future environments, planning future guardianship and financial security, and becoming familiar with agencies that provide support beyond the school system. The least dangerous assumption in regard to transition is to increase options by gathering information and planning early rather than decreasing options by adopting an attitude that there will be time for planning later then being faced with the harsh reality that it is too late. The following sections provide suggestions for longitudinal programming throughout the life cycle. Before continuing, however, take time to complete Activity 11.2.

ACTIVITY 11.2   Planning for Transition Throughout the Life Cycle

In Activity 11.1 you identified transitions in your own life. Look again at your time line. What kinds of activities or types of support were beneficial to you in making each transition that was successful? Did your parents take you on a tour of your new school before you enrolled? Did you attend a college orientation prior to the first day of class? Did you correspond with roommates before you met them? Did you have an older sibling who gave you advice before you began dating or a parent who accompanied you as you learned to drive while you had a learner's permit? Was there a new-employee orientation or an assigned mentor in your workplace? Did you receive solace from a friend or family member if you lost someone due to death? How did you deal with illness? What agencies assisted you if an unexpected disaster occurred?

Again, imagine that you have a moderate or severe disability. What kinds of activities or sources of support would be helpful in making transitions?

Early Transition

As soon as it is determined that a child can benefit from preschool services, the transition from home to school is planned, and by the age of 3 years, an IFSP is written. The preschool setting, however, may differ from the school setting in a number of ways, such as whether a specific disability is labeled to obtain appropriate services, whether the program has an academic focus, or whether there are expectations for independent performance in a larger setting. Thus, attention needs to be paid to activities that can facilitate the transition process into the elementary school program. Several activities can help families with transitioning from the preschool setting to elementary school.

Providing Information and Orientation   The transition from preschool to kindergarten can be a time of stress for family members. Just when they have come to feel comfortable with staff and have secured the support services needed for their child within a small environment, it is time to enter the arena of school services. The changes are numerous and may include larger classes, longer days, more staff, and a greater age span across students in the school. Instead of eating meals family style in the classroom, children may need to learn to negotiate long food lines in noisy cafeterias. Instead of activity-based instruction based on the child's interests across learning centers, children may be required to sit at desks or tables for extended periods of time and engage in more academic tasks. Instead of keeping personal items in labeled cubbyholes in the classroom, children may be assigned lockers in the hall. The variation in such procedures across schools and even classrooms may be great, making it difficult to predict the skills that will be needed upon transition. In addition, the time of transition to the school system may be the first time that a special education label, such as mental retardation or learning disability, is placed on a child in order to secure appropriate services.

The transition process from early childhood to school consists of preparing the family, the child, and the receiving party. In analyzing the survey responses of 3,595 kindergarten teachers who had at least one child with special needs in their classrooms, La Paro, Pianta, and Cox (2000) found that there may be differences in how teachers transition students with and without disabilities. The practices for kindergarten transition most often reported for the students with special needs were information seeking, such as reading their records and contacting their preschool teachers, while the practices most often reported for the entire class were information sharing, such as sending a letter or talking to the family, holding an open house, or sending a flyer to the child after school ended or before school began in addition to conducting kindergarten registration. The practice for first-grade transition most often reported for the students with special needs was engaging in individualized planning and activities, while the practice most often reported for the entire class was visiting the first-grade classroom.

Fowler, Schwartz, and Atwater (1991) stated that the role of professionals in the transition process should be to (a) agree on the exit criteria from preschool, (b) discuss this with the family, (c) notify receiving agencies, (d) evaluate the child's current level of development, (e) determine eligibility for future services through a staff meeting, (f) develop the initial IEP if the child is to receive special education services, (g) identify various placement options, (h) visit the placement options with the child, and (i) engage in follow-up to ensure that the transition was successful. Fowler et al. also suggested that the family stress associated with transitioning can be reduced by providing families with information about the next environment and ensuring their active participation in the transition process, bearing in mind that the skills the family acquires in negotiating initial transitions may serve them well in negotiating future transitions.

Longitudinal Programming   Young children can be prepared for transition through longitudinal programming that teaches the skills that will be needed in the next environment. The first step of longitudinal programming is to conduct an environmental survey of the next environment (Fowler et al., 1991) to determine the skills that will be needed following transition. For example, a school setting may require a child to perform a specific arrival sequence (e.g., exit bus, locate classroom, hang coat in locker, greet teacher, take seat), say the Pledge of Allegiance, take part in circle time, complete independent and large-group activities, and transition to the lunchroom or playground when bells ring. These experiences can be provided in the preschool classroom or experienced during visits in the next setting prior to final transition.

When Troup and Malone (2002) made site visits to 11 inclusive elementary classrooms, they found that the expectations for student behavior varied across settings. In the majority of the classrooms, however, students were expected to sit at small tables, to participate in group activities in which sitting time was interspersed with opportunities for movement, to perform seatwork based on visual and verbal directions, to complete a district-wide curriculum, to raise hands to signal the need for assistance, to perform toileting needs independently, and to receive related services through a pull-out model. Based on their observations, Troup and Malone concluded that, although some of the kindergarten procedures they observed may not be appropriate for all children, preschool teachers can prepare students for transition to kindergarten by teaching them to practice following multistep directions during large-group activities and teaching them the underlying concepts (e.g., counting, letter recognition) that they will be expected to perform on worksheets in the school setting. Troup and Malone also suggested that needed supports should be in place for children with special needs before school begins, that placement in smaller inclusive classes may result in better teacher-child interactions and individualized instruction, and that classes that do not employ developmentally appropriate practices should be approached with caution.

Early Planning for Adult Outcomes   Even when their children are young, the family members of children with moderate and severe disabilities should be encouraged to begin planning for the future of their children in the event that their children outlive them. Most families will not be aware of the waiting lists for adult services that their children will encounter in attempting to gain access to adult programs. For example, the national data reported 218,186 individuals with developmental disabilities who were on waiting lists for adult community support services in 1998, with the highest numbers reported in New York (50,225), Pennsylvania (28,000), Louisiana (13,958), North Carolina (12,654), and Texas (11,084); one family in Utah was reported to have been on a waiting list for 18 years before being classified as "critically in need of services" for an additional 10 years ("The List," 1998). In talking with family members, professionals can suggest making plans for the future that include guardianship, finances (e.g., insurance, trusts), and school arrangements, as well as making considerations for housing needs, people who can provide a circle of support, transportation needs, and medical needs (Future planning, 1998).

School Transitions

Once a child enters the school system, the process of transitioning does not end. Several activities are useful as a student progresses through elementary, middle, and secondary school settings. These include using transition portfolios to transmit information, continuing the practice of longitudinal programming, and as the student ages, increasing the focus on adult outcomes.

Transition Portfolios   Perhaps the greatest challenge to successful transitioning throughout the school years is getting sufficient information from one teacher to the next so the flow of educational programming and services will not be disrupted. Demchak and Greenfield (2000) described the usefulness of a transition portfolio in working with Jeff, a 14-year-old middle school student with severe and multiple disabilities (e.g., cognitive and motor disabilities, communication disorder, hearing and visual impairments). The portfolio contained information pertinent to creating an appropriate educational program in the next environment, such as personal information, medical information, positioning strategies, suggestions for educational programming, effective methods for communication, reinforcement strategies, and positive behavior supports. A more detailed description of a transition portfolio can be found in Example 11.3.

EXAMPLE 11.3 A TRANSITION PORTFOLIO

Demchak and Elquist (2001) created a sample portfolio with guidelines for students with disabilities to facilitate longitudinal transitioning throughout the school years. The intent was to transmit information from one grade level to the next to assist team members in creating appropriate educational programming. The portfolio was laid out in sections with an attractive and inviting design. There were places to insert specific information as well as pictures when they might be useful, such as those used to demonstrate positioning or show adaptive equipment. The sections of the transition portfolio designed by Demchak and Elquist are described below and can be used as a framework for creating a similar instrument.

Section	Sample of Information to Be Inserted	Sample of Pictures to Be Inserted
Cover sheet	Basic information, such as name, date of birth, and address	Photograph of student
Important People	Names of friends in activities	Photographs of student with friends
Parent/Caregiver Information	Names and phone numbers; student strengths, need for support, plans for future	
Current Teacher Information	Name and phone number; student strengths, successes, adaptations, instructional strategies, plans for future	

Medical Information	Names of doctors; allergies and reactions; medications, directions, and side effects; vision and hearing needs; seizure information; other health care needs	
Adaptive Equipment, Positioning and Handling	Names and phone numbers of physical and occupational therapists; equipment and activities with guidelines	Student use adaptive equipment and strategies with examples of proper/improper use
Educational Programming Strategies and Adaptations	Instructional matrix of schedule and IEP objectives; types and use of adaptations	
Communication Methods	List of verbal responses, manual signs, objects, and gestures used by student to communicate; communicative intent of various forms of expression; communication devices with symbols and activities	Pictures used to communicate
Reinforcement Strategies	Descriptions of reinforcers	
Positive Behavioral Support	Positive behavioral support plan components	
Problem Solving and Team Notes	Dates, foci, and summaries of meetings; list of team members	

Longitudinal Programming Longitudinal programming should continue with the same practices suggested for the initial transition to kindergarten. That is, an ecological survey of each new school setting should be performed as a student progresses from grade to grade, and skills should be taught that will be needed in that environment prior to transition. In addition, time can be devoted to progressively exposing a child to a new school building prior to an actual transition. At each grade level, the skills needed for the next environment can be taught in the months or years preceding the transition, with an eye on the skills that will be needed for ultimate criterion to be reached in adulthood. This concept is illustrated in Example 11.4.

EXAMPLE 11.4 LONGITUDINAL PROGRAMMING OF A FUNCTIONAL SKILL

As mentioned in this chapter, most children begin taking care of personal belongings when they are away from home by placing them in a cubbyhole that bears their name in the preschool classroom. This skill can be practiced across settings by placing belongings in a cubbyhole in a church school class or in the dressing room of a public recreational facility. In the elementary school, the cubbyhole may be replaced by a locker within the classroom. In the middle or secondary school settings, the lockers may be outside of the classroom, identified by numbers rather than names, and secured with locks. Again, students may have the opportunity to practice using lockers across settings, such as in athletic locker rooms or in facilities for the arts (e.g., art, music, or dance classes).

When asked which skills would be most useful for a student preparing to transition to middle school, a middle school teacher once replied that teaching the students to use a combination lock would be most valuable because she found that she was spending hours of instructional time across several weeks at the beginning of the school year teaching this skill when the time could have been devoted to the middle school curriculum. Fetko, Schuster, Harley, and Collins (1999) validated opening and closing locks on lockers as a skill needed in adulthood when they surveyed 20 local businesses to determine if (a) employees used lockers to store personal items at the business site and (b) the business sites employed persons with disabilities. Half of the businesses (e.g., fast-food restaurant, retail store, hotel, recreational facility, grocery store) responded "yes" to both questions. Based on the results of the survey, Fetko et al. taught four secondary school students with severe disabilities to use a keyed lock to secure their personal belongings in school hallway lockers. Although adaptations, such as painting the keyhole red, were needed, the students generalized the skill to open smaller locks on other lockers.

Transition Outcomes, Goals, and Objectives   The closer students come to the end of their school program, the more crucial it becomes to teach the skills that will be needed for adulthood. In 1985 Wehman et al. asserted that the least effective school program for transition consisted of segregated services with classroom-based instruction focusing on a developmental curriculum, and the most effective school program for transition consisted of inclusive services with community-based instruction on a functional curriculum. Wehman et al. also stated that transition meetings should orient family members to receiving community agencies and familiarize them with the responsibilities of special education, vocational education, and vocational rehabilitation.

Since Wehman et al. made these recommendations, transition initiatives have become law and have resulted in improved outcomes for students with disabilities, although further improvements are needed. As evidence of this, Frank and Sitlington (2000) compared students with mental disabilities from Iowa one year following graduation in 1985 and one year following graduation in 1993. Although they found that those who graduated in 1993 were better off than the earlier comparison group, they stated that those who graduated in 1993 still were behind their peers without mental disabilities. Frank and Sitlington recommended an increase in the enrollment of students with mental disabilities in vocational programs, supported community-based employment, school to work efforts, and postsecondary education.

Self-determination should be evident in the goals and objectives of the transition plan as well as in the outcomes. A model created by Steere and Cavaiuolo (2002) shows how postschool outcomes can be identified as the first step in creating goals and objectives on the IEP. To illustrate their model, Steere and Cavaiuolo provided the following examples. To attain a postschool outcome of employment in a supermarket, an annual IEP goal might be to learn to manage time and follow a schedule with corresponding short-term IEP objectives of (a) completing vocational activities by checking off each activity from a list without assistance and (b) identifying the clock face time by which activities on a list must be completed. To attain a postschool outcome of independent living in an apartment, an annual IEP goal might be to prepare meals with corresponding short-term IEP objectives of (a) preparing a meal by following a pictorial recipe without assistance and (b) using the stove and oven without assistance. To practice using this model, complete Activity 11.3.

ACTIVITY 11.3   Connecting Transition Outcome to IEP Goals and Objectives

Select a transition outcome in the area of community living (e.g., shopping, using transportation) or recreational activities (e.g., participating in a sport, being an active member of a club). Write an IEP goal that addresses the skills needed to perform the activity. Then brainstorm two short-term objectives that could be included on the IEP to increase the probability that the student's educational program will someday result in the desired transition outcome.

Postsecondary Transitions

Although community-based instruction is an important component of longitudinal programming for students with moderate and severe disabilities throughout their school years, the focus of their entire education should move from the secondary school setting to the community setting when a student reaches the age of eighteen. As described in the following sections, a community-based program should be implemented using a model of self-determination as the transition to adulthood takes place.

Community-Based Programs   Although students with disabilities can receive school services to the age of 21, it is impossible to put an inclusive philosophy into practice in a school-based program when their same-age peers exit the school system around the age of 18 years to enter postsecondary programs or participate in competitive employment and begin to practice independent living. In recognition of the need to prepare students for adulthood in inclusive environments with same-age peers, a number of schools are adopting community-based programs for students with moderate and severe disabilities. At this point, an intense focus on the functional skills needed for adulthood can facilitate a seamless transition to less restrictive residential and employment settings and a more normalized pattern of life.

According to Grigal, Neubert, and Moon (2002), appropriate goals of postsecondary programs for students with significant disabilities may include (a) obtaining employment, (b) participating in college classes, (c) increasing community mobility, (d) accessing adult agency support, (e) improving social and communication skills, (f) learning self-determination skills, (g) developing friendships, and (h) acquiring age-appropriate leisure and recreational skills. A program to meet these goals can be implemented in an age-appropriate educational setting, such as a university or community college, or in a community setting, such as a retail business. For example, Grigal, Neubert, and Moon (2001) described 13 school-funded postsecondary programs in Maryland for students from age 18 to 21 years with a range of disabilities. The programs were housed on college campuses or in community settings (e.g., sheriff's office), most with an assigned space, and served a small number of students (e.g., four to eight students per program). Options across programs included (a) participation in college courses, such as art, music, or physical education; (b) supervision by adult agency staff in overnight settings, such as apartments, to practice independent living skills, such as cooking; (c) job training; (d) community-based instruction of functional skills, such as banking, dining in restaurants, or shopping; and (e) recreational activities, such as participation in community service clubs, religious organizations, or volunteer programs. Program components that appeared to contribute to the success of the programs included interagency collaboration, the waiving of tuition for college classes, and parent involvement. Grigal et al. noted, however, that inclusion, staffing, scheduling, and transportation were challenges in program implementation.

As an example, Hall, Kleinert, and Kearns (2000) described a successful community-based postsecondary program for students with moderate and severe disabilities located on the campus of a four-year college. In addition to practicing functional skills in the community, participating in leisure activities with same-age peers, and learning vocational skills in employment settings, the students attended college classes that included social work, family studies, ecology, radio production, and physical education. According to Hall et al., there were benefits (a) for the students with disabilities that included learning with same-age peers, acquiring recreational skills, and developing vocational skills; (b) for the college students that included friendships, hands-on experiences related to college majors, and knowledge of diversity; (c) for the special education teachers that included awareness of community resources, understanding of age-appropriate behavior, and experience with making modifications in natural settings; (d) for the parents that included an understanding of their child's needs, a community network, and a circle of friends for their child; and (e) for the college that included learning opportunities for faculty, experiences for future teachers, and collaboration with the school district and community.

To set up a similar community-based postsecondary program, the authors suggested the following time line and corresponding activities: (a) six to nine months in advance—meet with involved parties, conduct personal future-centered planning meetings, meet with community leaders, and obtain approval from school and college; (b) one to two months in advance—present program to faculty, identify potential classes and activities; (c) start of semester—transition students to campus, allow students to select classes, finalize details (e.g., schedule, transportation, and support); and (d) ongoing—provide faculty support, evaluate student participation in jobs and activities, maintain contact between school and college, celebrate success with reception.

Focus on Vocational Skill Instruction   Regardless of whether postsecondary programs are housed on or away from the school campus, a major goal should be vocational preparation, with the goal of finding paid employment that will continue when the students exit the school system. Moon, Diambra, and Hill (1990) recommended such an outcome-oriented transition process for students with severe disabilities that consisted of hiring a transition or supported-employment expert to design the vocational transition program, accessing the assistance of adult-services providers, obtaining administrative support, and assigning staff (paraprofessionals) to the role of employment specialist. To monitor individual vocational progress, Moon et al. also suggested using a transition skills checklist to record the prompt level needed to complete the target skill and to rate associated job performance skills, such as promptness in getting to work, and community skills, such as using public transportation in getting to work.

Self-Determination and Person-Centered Planning   **Self-determination** is an integral component of transition. Defined as a combination of skills, knowledge, and attitudes, self-determination is evident in the ability to make choices, solve problems, set and attain goals, take risks and use safety precautions, self-regulate, self-advocate, and demonstrate self-awareness and self-knowledge (Steere & Cavaiuolo, 2002). Although self-determination is linked to positive outcomes (Agran, Blanchard, & Wehmeyer, 2000), successful implementation of a self-determination model is challenged when transition outcomes are too vague, are perceived as unrealistic, or are not revised over time, as well as when the connection between postschool outcomes and IEP objectives and goals are unclear, when expectations for the future are too low, and when there is a lack of action on transition plans (Steere & Cavaiuolo, 2002). Based on an analysis of the transition meetings of 237 students with mental retardation between the ages of 14 and 21 years in Colorado, student participation in transition meetings is higher when special education services are delivered in general education settings, teachers have perceptions of student job-related competencies, there is a noncontrolling family environment, and students have the ability to self-regulate and self-monitor their performance (Spencer & Sands, 1999).

When Agran et al. (2000) implemented a self-determination model of instruction with 19 students with disabilities (including moderate and severe disabilities), they found that 17 of the students made progress on goals that included increasing academic skills, following directions, using transportation, completing vocational tasks, improving conversation, and learning computer skills. The model consisted of teaching self-regulated problem-solving skills to the students so they could set their own goals based on self-analysis of their needs, wants, and preferences; developing action plans to achieve the goals; and teaching students to self-evaluate their progress, making goal revisions when needed.

As the student with a moderate or severe disability nears the time to exit school services, person-centered planning becomes crucial in facilitating a transition to a least restrictive environment based on the dreams and preferences of the student. Miner and Bates (1997) described five steps to be completed during person-centered transition planning. These included (a) developing a personal profile, (b) determining a future lifestyle, (c) identifying action steps and the parties responsible, (d) identifying needed service system changes, and (e) following up on the recommendations. These steps are illustrated in Activity 11.4.

ACTIVITY 11.4   Person-Centered Transition Planning

To better understand the process of person-centered transition planning, imagine that you are the person who will be transitioning (e.g., to the workplace, to retirement) as you complete the steps suggested by Miner and Bates (1997) that are listed below. (Permission to print an overview of the these steps with corresponding figures has been granted by the Council for Exceptional Children.)

STEP ONE: CREATE A PERSONAL PROFILE

Circle of Support Map

On a blank sheet of paper, draw five circles. The smallest will be in the middle of the page, and each circle will be progressively larger as it is drawn around the previous circle. Inside Circle 1, write your name. Inside Circle 2, list those who are closest to you (those people with whom you have interactions or communication on a regular basis and with whom you share your life). Inside Circle 3, list those you consider to be friends, even though you are not as close to them. Inside Circle 4, list groups of people to which you belong and with whom you interact on a regular basis. Inside Circle 5, list people you see only when you pay them to be with you. Compare your Circle of Support Map to the one in Figure 11.1. Analyze the people you have listed. Which ones do you think would be willing to provide support for you on a frequent or an occasional basis? Which would do this for free, and which would need to be reimbursed?

Community Presence Map

Take another sheet of blank paper. In the center draw a house and write your name in the middle. On the left side of the house, list the settings where you go on a daily basis. On the right side of the house, list the settings where you go on a weekly basis. Underneath the house, list the settings where you go on an occasional basis. When you have finished, compare your Community Presence Map to

FIGURE 11.1

Circle of Support Map based on Miner and Bates (1997).

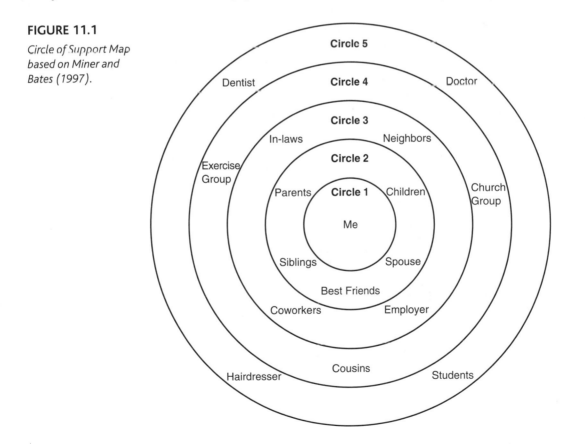

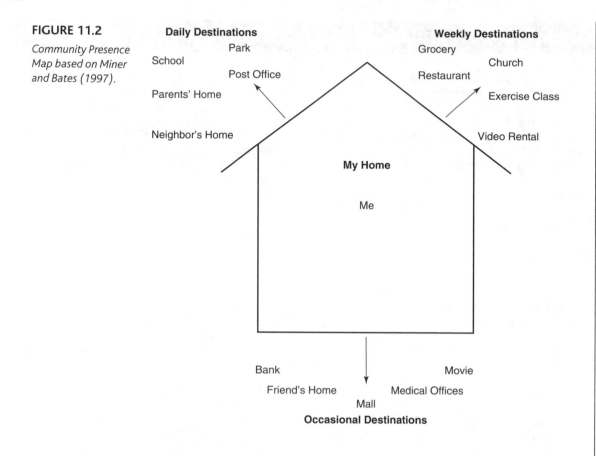

FIGURE 11.2

Community Presence Map based on Miner and Bates (1997).

Daily Destinations
Park
School
Post Office
Parents' Home
Neighbor's Home

Weekly Destinations
Grocery
Church
Restaurant
Exercise Class
Video Rental

My Home

Me

Bank
Friend's Home
Mall
Movie
Medical Offices

Occasional Destinations

the one in Figure 11.2. Next, compare the settings where you go to the people you listed on the Circle of Support Map. Which of the people you listed could provide support in each of the settings that you listed?

List of what works and what does not work

Make a list of what works and does not work in your life. For example, are you a "day person" or a "night person"? Do you enjoy individual or group activities? Do you prefer activities that are sedentary or active? Do you prefer to cook at home or eat in a restaurant? Do you prefer to live alone or with a roommate or family member? Do you like living in a rural or urban setting? Try to sort out your choices and preferences without being confined by the reality of your life. How many of your preferences could be possible, given the support identified in the previous activities?

List of gifts and capacities

Compile another list—this one of the areas in which you excel. What are your natural talents? In what area do you

show promise, given the support that you need? Could any of these gifts and capacities be used to your advantage in seeking employment or recreational activities? In joining groups? In earning an income?

STEP TWO: PLAN FOR A FUTURE LIFESTYLE

Based on the information you compiled in Step 1, list feasible options for where you might live, work, and spend leisure time and who might be able support you in your choices.

STEP THREE: CREATE AN ACTION PLAN

Identify three to four activities that could help you attain the goals you set for the future in Step 2. Then, specify people or agencies that could be responsible for assisting you in the process.

STEP FOUR: IDENTIFY CHANGES THAT ARE NEEDED

How does the present service system need to be changed to help you attain your goals? Is there an agency that can offer support, or would working with a specific individual be more helpful? What lists of services might require applications (e.g., scholarships, insurance, employment agency, realty office)? Which have a waiting list?

STEP FIVE: FOLLOW-UP

Set a schedule for periodic reviews as your transition progresses. As indicated, you should feel free to alter the plan based on personal preferences and as previous options are eliminated or new options are added.

Best Practices
Longitudinal Transition

1. Recognize that families of children with moderate and severe disabilities may need added support during times of transition.
2. To increase the options they will have, encourage families to begin planning for long-range outcomes for their children at an early age.
3. Use longitudinal programming through the school years to create a smooth flow to a seamless transition to adulthood.
4. Use strategies that facilitate longitudinal programming, such as ecological surveys of future environments, transition portfolios, community-based programming, self-determination, personal futures planning, and adult outcome-based goals and objectives.

Conclusion

This chapter has described the transition process with an emphasis on longitudinal programming to achieve desired transition outcomes. Chapter 12 focuses on residential, vocational, and recreational options available to students with moderate and severe disabilities as they transition to adulthood. Although current adult services are often bleak, outcomes could be improved if families begin to plan for adult transitions when a child is still young and if students, families, and professionals can work together to advocate for better alternatives (e.g., community-based programs, long-range outcomes, ITPs that focus on self-determination, functional skill instruction for future environments, more funding for support programs) as they transition through the school system. Before proceeding to Chapter 12, however, stop to assess your knowledge of the transition process by completing the Performance-Based Assessment at the end of this chapter.

Questions for Review

1. Define transition as it relates to the life span.
2. When are ITPs required by law?
3. Who must be included in transition planning meetings?
4. How might a family of a child with a moderate or severe disability be affected during times of transition?
5. Describe one activity that can facilitate longitudinal programming (a) in the early years, (b) during the school years, and (c) during postsecondary years.

6. What are the steps of personal futures planning?
7. Why is self-determination crucial in transitioning to adulthood?
8. What components might be included in a postsecondary community-based program?

Performance-Based Assessment

Imagine that you are writing an ITP for a child or student with moderate to severe disabilities at either entrance or exit to the school system as you answer the following questions:

1. What guidelines for professional behavior should be followed at the transition meeting?
2. What considerations should be given to student or family preferences?
3. Who should be included in the transition meeting?
4. How can self-determination be encouraged?
5. What transition activities might be implemented to transition to the next environment? When should they be implemented and by whom? What typical community agencies might be contacted?
6. What skills might be targeted to facilitate attainment of desired adult outcomes?

References

Agran, M., Blanchard, C., & Wehmeyer, M. L. (2000). Promoting transition goals and self-determination through student self-directed learning: The self-determined learning model of instruction. *Education and Training in Mental Retardation and Developmental Disabilities, 35,* 351–364.

Brown, L. Branson, M. B., Hamre-Nietupski, S., Pumpian, I., Certo, N., & Gruenewald, L. (1979). A strategy for developing chronological age-appropriate and functional curricular content for severely handicapped adolescents and young adults. *The Journal of Special Education, 13,* 81–90.

Brown, L., Nietupski, J., & Hamre-Nietupski, S. (1976). Criterion of ultimate functioning. In M. A. Thomas, Ed. *Hey! Don't forget about me!* Reston, VA: The Council for Exceptional Children.

Brown, L., Pumpian, I., Baumgart, D., Vandeventer, P., Ford, A., Nisbet, J., Schroeder, J., & Gruenewald, L. (1981). Longitudinal transition plans in programs for severely handicapped students. *Exceptional Children, 47,* 624–630.

Certo, N. J., Mautz, D., Pumpian, I., Sax, C., Smalley, K., Wade, H. A., Noyes, D., Luecking, R., Wechsler, J., & Batterman, N. (2003). Review and discussion of a model for seamless transition to adulthood. *Education Training in Mental Retardation and Developmental Disabilities, 38,* 3–17.

Chambers, C. R., Hughes, C., & Carter, E. W. (2004). Parent and sibling perspectives on the transition to adulthood. *Education and Training in Developmental Disabilities, 39,* 79–94.

Cook, R. (2003). Work of special ed students irks parents. *Yahoo! News.* Retrieved October 10, 2003, from http://www.mccranky.com/movies/killbill/43.html.

Cooney, B. F. (2002). Exploring perspectives on transition of youth with disabilities: Voices of young adults, parents, and professionals. *Mental Retardation, 40,* 425–435.

Demchak, M., & Elquist, M. (2001). *"Could you please tell my new teacher?" A parent/teacher guide to successful transitions.* Reno, NV: Nevada Dual Sensory Impairment Project.

Demchak, M., & Greenfield, R. G. (2000). A transition portfolio for Jeff, a student with multiple disabilities. *Teaching Exceptional Children, 32* (6), 44–49.

Fetko, K. S., Schuster, J. W., Harley, D. A., & Collins, B. C. (1999). Using simultaneous prompting to teach a chained vocational task to young adults with severe intellectual disabilities. *Education and Training in Mental Retardation and Developmental Disabilities, 34,* 318–329.

Fowler, S. A., Schwartz, I., & Atwater, J. (1991). Perspectives on the transition from preschool to kindergarten for children with disabilities and their families. *Exceptional Children, 58,* 136–145.

Frank, A. R., & Sitlington, P. L. (2000). Young adults with mental disabilities—Does transition planning make a difference? *Education and Training in Mental Retardation and Developmental Disabilities, 35,* 119–134.

Future planning for your child takes more than a will (1998). *TASH Newsletter, 24* (5), 13–14.

Gallivan-Fenlon, A. (1994). Their senior year: Family and service provider perspectives on the transition from school to adult life for young adults with disabilities. *Journal of the Association for Persons with Severe Handicaps, 19,* 11–23.

Geenen, S., Powers, L. E., Lopez-Vasquez, A. (2001). Multicultural aspects of parent involvement in transition planning. *Exceptional Children, 67,* 265–282.

Grigal, M., Neubert, D. A., & Moon, M. S. (2002). Postsecondary options for students with significant disabilities. *Teaching Exceptional Children, 35,* 68–73.

Grigal, M., Neubert, D. A., & Moon, M. S. (2001). Public school programs for students with significant disabilities in post-secondary settings. *Education and Training in Mental Retardation and Developmental Disabilities, 36,* 244–254.

Hall, M., Kleinert, H. L., & Kearns, F. J. (2000). Going to college! Postsecondary programs for students with moderate and severe disabilities. *Teaching Exceptional Children, 32,* 58–65.

Hasazi, S. B., & Clark, G. M. (1988). Vocational preparation for high school students labeled mentally retarded: Employment as a graduation goal. *Mental Retardation, 26,* 343–349.

Heiman, T. (2002). Parents of children with disabilities: Resilience, coping, and future expectations. *Journal of Developmental and Physical Disabilities, 14,* 159–172.

Johnson, D. R., Stodden, R. A., Emanuel, E. J., Luecking, R., & Mack, M. (2002). Current challenges facing secondary education and transition services: What research tells us. *Exceptional Children, 68,* 519–531.

Knott, L., & Asselin, S. B. (1999). Transition competencies: Perception of secondary special education teachers. *Teacher Education and Special Education, 22,* 55–65.

Kohler, P. D., & Field, S. (2003). Transition-focused education: Foundation for the future. *The Journal of Special Education, 37,* 174–183.

Kraemer, B. R., & Blacher, J. (2001). Transition for young adults with severe metal retardation: School preparation, parent expectations, and family involvement. *Mental Retardation, 39,* 423–435.

La Paro, K. M., Pianta, R. C., & Cox, M. J. (2000). Teachers' reported transition practices for children transitioning into kindergarten and first grade. *Exceptional Children, 67,* 7–20.

Lombard, R. C. (1994). The collaborative transition model: An interdisciplinary approach to meeting the transition needs of rural communities. *Rural Special Education Quarterly, 13*(1), 24–28.

Meers, G. D. (1992). Getting ready for the next century: Vocational preparation of students with disabilities. *Teaching Exceptional Children, 24,* 36–39.

Miner, C. A., & Bates, P. E. (1997). Person-centered transition planning. *Teaching Exceptional Children, 30*(1), 66–69.

Moon, M. S., Diambra, T., & Hill, M. (1990). An outcome-oriented vocational process. *Teaching Exceptional Children, 23*(1), 47–50.

Repetto, J. B., & Correa, V. I. (1996). Expanding views on transition. *Exceptional Children, 62,* 551–563.

Spencer, K. C., & Sands, D. J. (1999). Prediction of student participation in transition-related actions. *Education and Training in Mental Retardation and Developmental Disabilities, 34,* 473–484.

Steere, D. E., & Cavaiuolo, D. (2002). Connecting outcomes, goals, and objectives in transition planning. *Teaching Exceptional Children, 34*(6), 54–59.

The list goes on and on (1998). *TASH Newsletter, 24*(5), 17–19.

Thoma, C. A., Rogan, P., & Baker, S. R. (2001). Student involvement in transition planning: Unheard voices. *Education and Training in Mental Retardation and Developmental Disabilities, 36,* 16–29.

Troup, K. S., & Malone, D. M. (2002). Transitioning preschool children with developmental concerns into kindergarten: Ecological characteristics of inclusive kindergarten programs. *Journal of Developmental and Physical Disabilities, 14,* 339–352.

Vandercook, T., York, J., & Forest, M. (1989). The McGill Action Planning System: A strategy for building the vision. *Journal of the Association for Persons with Severe Handicaps, 14,* 205–215.

Wehman, P. (1992). Transition for young people with disabilities: Challenges for the 1990's. *Education and Training in Mental Retardation, 27,* 112–118.

Wehman, P., Kregel, J., & Barcus, J. M. (1985). From school to work: A vocational transition model for handicapped students. *Exceptional Children, 52,* 25–37.

White, S., & Bond, M. R. (1992). Transition services in large school districts: Practical solutions to complex problems. *Teaching Exceptional Children, 24*(4), 44–47.

Whitney-Thomas, J., & Hanley-Maxwell, C. (1996). Packing the parachute: Parents' experiences as their children prepare to leave high school. *Exceptional Children, 63,* 75–87.

Zhang, D., & Stecker, P. M. (2001). Student involvement in transition planning: Are we there yet? *Education and Training in Mental Retardation and Developmental Disabilities, 36,* 293–303.

CHAPTER TWELVE

ENTERING ADULTHOOD:
Options for Work and Community Living

On completion of this chapter, the reader will meet the following objectives:

- Contrast traditional and community-based continua of settings for employment and residential living.
- Describe advantages and disadvantages to the various work and residential options currently available to persons with moderate and severe disabilities.
- Elaborate on why families may choose one option for adult living over another.
- Define *supported employment* and *supported living*.
- Discuss strategies for supporting community inclusion for adults with moderate and severe disabilities.

To this point, this text has focused on the principles involved in educating students with moderate and severe disabilities and the issues that must be considered in implementing best practices. As has been noted, the purpose of an education is to prepare a student for adulthood. Yet as described in Chapters 4 and 11, transition to adulthood is often a stressful process for a number of reasons. Hanley-Maxwell, Whitney-Thomas, and Pogoloff (1995) termed the transition to adulthood as "the second shock" for parents, with entry into the school system being the first. In a qualitative study, Hanley-Maxwell et al. found that parents of children with mild to severe disabilities had visions for the future of their children that included living in a safe, happy residence with a strong social network and meaningful activities to fill their free time. Instead, the parents found long waiting lists for adult services and minimal social networks. In addition, Campbell and Essex (1994) found that many parents of children with mild to severe disabilities failed to plan for the adulthood of their children due to a lack of information on available services and a lack of understanding by professionals in how to guide them.

The problems associated with transitioning to adulthood do not appear to be limited by geography. When compared, persons with disabilities in both rural and suburban areas have access to the almost the same amount of paid support, such as job coaches or case managers, but informal support, such as family members, friends, and coworkers, may be higher in suburban areas (Kellow & Parker, 2002). Turnbull and Turnbull (1999) addressed the challenges in providing adult support when they described their experiences in arranging comprehensive lifestyle support for their son. In presenting JT's weekly schedule, they demonstrated that ensuring that their son engaged in normalized age-appropriate activities (e.g., meals at home and in restaurants, work, exercise, recreation, shopping) and lived in a home of his own required the involvement of the extended family, friends, a housemate, a therapist, and a job coach.

Even when parents are involved in supporting the adulthood of their children, the lack of options for adults with disabilities is disturbing, given that some options tend to be associated with a higher quality of life. For example, Kraemer, McIntyre, and Blacher (2003) assessed 188 families of children with moderate and severe disabilities, ages 18 to 26 years, and found that those who worked in the community after transitioning from school experienced a higher quality of life than those who transitioned to sheltered workshops or day activity centers. Specifically, higher adaptive functioning, larger social networks, paid work experiences during school, and less parental stress had a positive impact on quality of life while limited parental knowledge of adult services and a smaller social network had a negative impact.

According to data gathered in the National Longitudinal Transition Study from 1987 to 1990, quality of life for adults with disabilities is determined by five components: (a) social relationships, (b) employment, (c) independence, (d) esteem, and (e) support from others (Heal, Khoju, Rusch, & Harnisch, 1999). In addition to physical growth, Jordan and Dunlap (2001) stated that adulthood also entails privileges, such as the right to vote, marry, have consensual sex, and live apart from one's family, that may be withheld from adults with more severe cognitive disabilities. The ability to exercise such rights often is contingent on the type of guardianship that has been awarded. In a review of 121 court cases in Michigan, Millar and Renzaglia (2002) found that guardianship is a complex issue, with a range of variations of partial or plenary guardianship of the person and of the estate. Being placed under guardianship can interfere with self-determination since the individual may lose the power to make medical, residential, program, financial, travel, and personal (e.g., type of dress or activity) decisions. Typically, persons with mild and moderate disabilities had partial guardians appointed, while persons with severe and profound disabilities were more likely to have plenary guardians appointed. In a study of students following their exit from school, those who were able to exercise more self-determination fared better in terms of both employment and residential independence (Wehmeyer & Palmer, 2003).

This chapter will examine the employment and residential options available to persons with moderate and severe disabilities in adulthood as well as the issues associated with those options. Later, Chapter 14 will address the issues involved in self-determination that affect the adult lives of persons with moderate and severe disabilities.

Employment Options for Adults with Moderate and Severe Disabilities

In 1996 Blackorby and Wagner reported the findings of the National Longitudinal Transition Study of Special Education Students. Based on a study of 8,000 youth, ages 13 to 21 years, who received special education services, they found that students with disabilities were less likely to be employed than were their peers without disabilities five years following their exit from secondary school. Also, females, African Americans or Hispanic Americans, and persons with mental retardation were less likely to be employed. In addition, the discrepancy in competitive wages for persons with disabilities tended to increase over time, possibly because persons with disabilities were less likely to be promoted to higher-paying positions.

More recent statistics reported by Certo et al. in 2003 do not show significant improvement. A new millennium has begun with adults with disabilities still less likely to be employed than their peers without disabilities and more likely to live in households with an annual income of less than $15,000. For example, McDermott, Martin, and Butkus (1999) analyzed employment data for persons with cognitive disabilities in South Carolina and found that those who were most likely to be employed had higher IQ (i.e., mild range of mental retardation) and adaptive behavior scores, had fewer emotional or health problems, were younger (18 to 49 years), were male, and lived in subsidized housing. In analyzing national data, Yamaki and Fujiura (2002) found that the majority of adults with developmental disabilities living in community settings were unemployed, and those who were employed had low incomes (less than $1,000 per month), even when government support and employment wages were combined.

In employing persons with moderate and severe disabilities, there are a number of activities that must take place. These include determining appropriate individualized employment options, identifying individual preferences and skills for types of employment, providing specific instruction in job skills, and providing adequate support to maintain employment. These activities are described in the following sections.

Employment Options

Just as there is a continuum of employment options for persons without disabilities (e.g., self-employment, full- or part-time competitive employment, contractual, salaried, or hourly wages), there should be a continuum of appropriate options for persons with moderate and severe disabilities. In 1988, Taylor urged the replacement of a traditional continuum of more restrictive options in favor of a continuum of less restrictive, community-based options, as shown in Table 12.1.

Although the placement team may determine that some restrictive options may be determined to be appropriate for some persons with multiple severe and significant cognitive disabilities (including those with complex health care needs or the most challenging behavior), consideration of less restrictive options should be

---

TABLE 12.1   *Comparison of Traditional and Community-Based Vocational Continua (based with permission on Taylor, 1988).*

Vocational Continua

Traditional		Community-Based
Work Activity Center	Most Restrictive	Specialized Industrial Training
Day Treatment Center	↑	Mobile Crews
Sheltered Workshop		Enclaves
Work Station		Individual Supported Jobs
Transitional Employment Services	↓	Independent Competitive
Competitive Employment	Least Restrictive	Employment

encouraged for the majority of persons with moderate and severe disabilities for several reasons. First, the programming in more restrictive placements may be inappropriate. In an examination of one hundred day activity centers for adults with severe disabilities, Reid, Parsons, and Green (2001) found that the adults spent only half of their time engaged in purposeful behaviors and not all of these activities were age appropriate (i.e., the same activity using the same materials in which same-age peers without disabilities would participate).

Second, more restrictive settings may be inappropriate for adults with moderate and severe disabilities because, even if they are paid, wages may be minimal. For example, McDermott et al. (1999) compared the employment of persons with cognitive disabilities in South Carolina and found that those who were engaged in competitive employment earned higher wages than those working in sheltered workshops. Specifically, those working in the manufacturing or lumber industries earned the highest wages (average of $199 per week), while those working in sheltered workshops earned the lowest wages (average of $65 per week). Other higher-paying jobs in competitive employment were found to be in hotel/motel, retail, small-business, or service (e.g., daycare center) settings.

Third, less restrictive options, such as supported employment, are less costly to operate than more restrictive options, such as day activity centers and sheltered workshops (Rusch, Chadsey-Rush, & Johnson, 1991). Instead of the costs associated with maintaining a separate facility and a large staff, competitive employment uses existing work sites and natural supports, such as coworkers and managers, that allow a single job coach to serve several employees within or across sites and to fade services when they no longer are needed.

Finally, there is evidence that persons with disabilities who are engaged in supported employment are happy. Specifically, supported employees who participated in interviews conducted by Test, Carver, Ewers, Haddad, and Person (2000) indicated that they liked the work, the friends they made at work, and the money they earned. In addition, they were satisfied with the support they received from their job coaches.

If the goal for persons with moderate and severe disabilities is to spend time engaged in purposeful, age-appropriate activities in community settings and to earn higher wages, then competitive employment should be considered as the first option before moving to more restrictive options on the continuum. In competitive employment, wages are paid at the prevailing rate in an integrated setting within the community (Powell & Moore, 1992). If necessary, support can be provided to ensure that the person with a disability receives the assistance necessary to gain and maintain employment (Wehman, 1988). Thus, **supported employment** consists of work in an integrated, community setting with wages paid at the prevailing rate.

When the practice of supported employment was in its infancy, Wehman (1988) listed a number of components necessary for its implementation. These included (a) funding, (b) technical assistance and staff development, and (c) coordinated agency services. A decade later, Wehman, West, and Kregal (1999) examined the implementation of supported employment practices over time and found that a number of needs to enhance this option continued to exist. These included (a) ensuring that choice and self-determination are part of the process, (b) increasing wages and benefits, (c) ensuring equal access to employment opportunities, (d) individualizing levels of support, (e) providing opportunities for career advancement, and (f) ensuring integration within the workplace. When asked for the factors that influenced their ability to provide supported employment, agencies responding to a survey listed

(a) philosophy and mission, (b) state and federal funding, (c) family preferences, and (d) positive agency experiences (McGaughey, Kiernan, McNally, Gilmore, & Keith, 1995).

Mank, Cioffi, and Yovanoff (2003) collected survey data from 13 vocational programs across eight states that confirmed the continuing need to improve the practice of supported employment for persons with disabilities by showing that, over a decade, wages and hours worked failed to increase and the types of jobs in which employment was obtained failed to change. The survey data showed that most supported employees continued to work half time (i.e., 22 hours per week) for an hourly wage of approximately $6 and were most often employed in food service or custodial/janitorial jobs.

Rusch et al. (1991) identified three placement options for implementing a supported employment model: (a) individual placement, (b) clustered placement, and (c) mobile work crew. In an individual placement, a job coach provides temporary support for a single person hired by an employer, such as a cook in a restaurant. In a clustered placement, a job coach provides continual support for a small group of persons at a specific integrated work site, such as a hotel cleaning crew. Finally, in a mobile work crew, a job coach provides continuous support for a small group of persons across community locations, such as a lawn service.

Powell and Moore (1992) stated that funding issues may be of concern in providing supported employment and noted that supported employment can be funded from a variety of sources, including state agencies, such as the Departments of Mental Retardation or Developmental Disabilities, Mental Health, or Vocational Rehabilitation and the Department of Labor. In addition, Powell and Moore, noted that parents might have concerns that their children will lose benefits. Thus, it is advantageous to involve persons on the placement team who are familiar with social security programs that protect the benefits of persons who are employed. They should also know about programs that provide incentives to employers through the Department of Labor.

Other concerns of the family also should be considered in implementing supported employment. Specifically, Lustig and Thomas (1997) identified a number of stressors that may affect families of supported employees in addition to the normative stressors associated with launching to adulthood. These included concerns about the employee getting along with coworkers, being taken advantage of, being physically but not socially included, finding transportation, and having adequate supervision during nonworking hours, as well as the stressor of interacting with coordinating agencies. Thus, Lustig and Thomas recommended that support should be provided for the family as well as for the employee. Based on interviews with school transition programs and vocational agencies, Hagner, Butterworth, and Keith (1995) stated that families of persons with severe disabilities can be involved in person-centered career planning through meetings or "open houses" and through frequent personal contacts. They also observed that the family network could be an outlet for making contact with potential employers.

Employment Preferences

Person-centered planning is associated with higher job satisfaction and longer terms of employment, and an emphasis on self-determination requires consideration of the preferences of the candidate for employment. For example, Menchetti and Garcia (2003) examined the level of job match to their work preferences for 83 supported employees and found that that those with moderate to high job matches made higher wages ($6.11 to $6.49 per hour versus $6.00 per hour), worked more hours (105 to 118 hours per month versus 103 hours per month), and remained longer in job sites (44 to 52 months versus 37 months) than those with low job matches. Thus, Menchetti and Garcia recommended that career planning needs to match the vision statements (i.e., "I want. . . .") of persons with disabilities to both the occupation and the location where they are placed.

If candidates for employment have difficulty with verbal expression, preferences can be determined by giving them the opportunity to select pictures (Becker, 1981) or video segments of persons performing jobs that appeal to them (Ellerd, Morgan, & Salzberg, 2002). However, Ellerd et al. (2002) found that it is preferable to have candidates select from paired choices rather than to respond positively or negatively to single choices.

A second means of assessing the job preferences of persons with limited communication skills is to present a variety of tasks then collect duration data to determine the tasks that maintain a person's attention. For example, Worsdell, Iwata, and Wallace (2002) presented a choice of seven tasks per person (e.g., boxing disks, stamping cards, filing paper, stuffing envelopes, assembling pens, packaging supplies) to four persons with mental disabilities and found that each person selected and worked on one task to the exclusion of the others.

Finally, preferences for jobs can be assessed by observing reactions of the individuals performing them. Parsons, Reid, and Green (2001) determined whether or not three adults with multiple severe behaviors "liked" the jobs they were asked to perform by recording facial expressions, such as smiling or frowning; verbalizations, such as laughing, yelling, or crying; and other behaviors, such as clapping hands, pushing away objects, and stomping feet. For each of the adults, the investigators were able to determine "likes" that included mulching and bagging leaves and "dislikes" that included cleaning the porch and wiping the counter.

In 1991 Rusch et al. suggested implementing a supported employment model by surveying the community for potential jobs, analyzing those jobs, and matching persons to specific jobs and providing training. A decade later Nietupski and Hamre-Nietupski (2000, 2002) proposed using a job carving approach instead. In the job carving process, the skills and support needs of candidates are first identified and "ideal job match hypotheses" are generated. The job coach then targets businesses that match the hypotheses, determines jobs in which hiring the candidate might prove to be beneficial (e.g., provide savings in cost and time), and develops a hiring proposal. For example, a candidate may enjoy clerical tasks, such as copying and filing. Instead of waiting for a job opening for clerical work to be posted before applying, a job coach would approach an agency where clerical work consumed employee time that could be devoted to more specialized tasks, such as making sales, analyzing data, and writing reports, and would propose that the productivity of current employees could be increased if a person with disabilities who had the necessary clerical skills was hired to perform specific time-consuming clerical tasks for employees.

Employment Skills and Instruction

To maintain employment and receive promotions, an employee must have a number of skills in addition to those that are specific to the task. Rusch and Hughes (1988) and Brady and Rosenberg (2002) divided these skills into three categories:

(a) performance or work-required skills—independence, attendance, punctuality, personal appearance, hygiene, and communication; (b) adaptability or work-required duties—rate of performance, quality and quantity of work, safety procedures, time management, problem-solving, and motivation; and (c) social skills or work-required behavior—appropriate social interaction, acceptance of criticism, stress tolerance, honesty, initiative, and endurance.

Facilitation of Adaptability   Rusch and Hughes (1988) suggested that there are several strategies to promote employee adaptability. First, employee independence can be observed and evaluated on the job, with expectations determined by the performance of their peers. Second, adaptability can be promoted by teaching self-instruction, self-monitoring, and self-reinforcement strategies to employees. Third, coworkers can be enlisted to assist in facilitating adaptability, such as prompting the employee to look at a watch. Fourth, employee independence can be transferred over time to work-related stimuli, such as clocks, whistles, or coworker behavior.

It may be necessary to implement a variety of approaches to identify the best way to promote adaptability in an individual. For example, Mautz, Storey, and Certo (2001) found that the addition of a communication device increased the workplace social interactions of an employee with severe cognitive disabilities after they had tried changing his job duties (receiving shipments to returning items on the floor) and providing natural support during work and breaks (coworker without disabilities).

Instruction of Tasks   As described in Chapter 6, systematic instruction can be effective in teaching specific tasks to persons with moderate and severe disabilities. These procedures have been effective in teaching adults to perform tasks across a continuum of adult settings.

In work activity centers, Lancioni, Dijkstra, O'Reilly, Groeneweg, and Van den Hof (2000) taught two adults with severe disabilities to access picture and auditory prompts from a palmtop computer in preparing food, cleaning a living area, and setting a table, while Jones and Collins (1997) taught three women with moderate disabilities to perform microwave cooking tasks using a system of least prompts that included the addition of safety and nutritional information. In a sheltered workshop setting, Maciag, Schuster, Collins, and Cooper (2000) taught adults with moderate and severe disabilities to construct shipping boxes using a simultaneous-prompting procedure. Although these skills were taught in more restrictive settings, Browder and Minarovic (2000) demonstrated how systematic instruction also can be used in competitive work settings (e.g., grocery store, cafeteria, clothing factory) when they used a progressive time delay procedure to teach three adults with moderate disabilities to read job-specific sight words that included sweep, bag, bread, dishwasher, fold, and tally.

Employment Support

Some employees with disabilities need more support than others. For example, those with mild disabilities are more likely to be able to work at a job independently than those with more severe and profound disabilities because they are more likely to have better adaptive behavior skills (e.g., social skills), academic skills (e.g., reading), and communication skills (e.g., verbal language) as well as fewer medical and behavioral problems. When Kregel and Wehman (1989) examined the background of 1,411 persons receiving supported employment across eight states, they found that the majority had mild disabilities and only a small percentage (less than 8%) had severe and profound disabilities. Thus, it cannot be assumed that all persons with disabilities working in competitive employment settings will require the same amount of support. Instead the level of support should be evaluated and individualized through informal or formal observation. This can be done using instruments such as the Job Observation and Behavior Scale described by Brady and Rosenberg (2002).

The level of support provided for an employee can be determined from a hierarchy of least to most intrusive options. The least intrusive options would consist of supports that can be used independently, such as picture, audiotape, or computer prompts. Steed and Lutzker (1997) provided a book of picture prompts (i.e., photographs) for a man with profound disabilities to enable him to set a table, vacuum, and dust in a community center and an office. Post, Storey, and Karabin (2002) provided an audiotape (i.e., taped reminders with music) and a sheet to self-record behavior for a man with mild disabilities to remind him to stay focused on bagging and labeling coffee beans in a store. Davies, Stock, and Wehmeyer (2002) provided a palmtop computer with picture and audio prompts for 10 employees with mild and moderate disabilities to enable them to assemble boxes and package software. In each of these investigations, the support from the adaptive devices was sufficient for the employee to complete the targeted tasks.

A more intrusive means of providing support in employment sites is to provide personal assistance. This can come from families, employers, coworkers, or job coaches (Hagner et al., 1995). In terms of providing training and support, Nisbet and Hagner (1988) described five models, as follows:

1. Job coach—Job coach responsible to agency provides initial training and support then fades
2. Mentor—Job coach responsible to agency provides initial training then transfers responsibility for support to coworker responsible to company
3. Training consultant—Job coach responsible to agency teaches coworker(s) responsible to company to provide training and support
4. Job sharing—Job coach responsible to agency trains coworker responsible to both agency and company to be job sharer
5. Attendant—Attendant responsible to supported employee provides support

Each of the above models can be used effectively. For example, Hood, Test, Spooner, and Steele (1996) paid a coworker to support two men with severe, multiple disabilities in completing laundry tasks for a hotel. After being trained by a job coach, the coworker was able to provide support that resulted in the employees maintaining their productivity with a high degree of accuracy and high employer satisfaction ratings. In another example, Lee, Storey, Anderson, Goetz, and Zivolich (1997) compared the effect of training by a (a) job coach and (b) mentor (e.g., restaurant manager trained by job coach) on the social integration of 30 employees with severe disabilities who worked in a chain of pizza restaurants; they found that the mentor model resulted in more reciprocal social interactions with coworkers who did not have disabilities.

Self-determination can enter into the decision of whether to provide support from a device or an assistant by giving employees a choice. When Reid, Parsons, Green, and Browning (2001) gave three adults with multiple disabilities the choice of working with or without adaptive devices to complete a collation task at a publishing company, the employees chose working with an adaptive device over having support from a job coach; productivity was at least 96% whether assistance came from the device or the job coach.

Summary

In looking to the future, Meers (1992) predicted that needed occupations would include janitors, nurse's aides, salesclerks, cashiers, waiters, general clerks, professional nurses, food preparation and service personnel, secretaries, and truck drivers and suggested that agencies be involved in preparing persons with disabilities for employment at an early age. Since it has been against the law since 1994 for employers to discriminate against persons with disabilities who can perform jobs, spending the day in a productive manner should be a goal for all adults, regardless of ability, and providing sufficient support can enable most adults with moderate and severe disabilities to meet that goal. Before continuing, work through Activity 12.1, which details the work experiences of a woman with a moderate mental disability.

ACTIVITY 12.1   Solving Employment Issues

Jane is a 40-year-old woman with Down syndrome and a moderate mental disability. She has excellent communication and social skills, enjoys working with other people, completes assigned tasks, and takes pride in her grooming. She also has a keen interest in local and national politics and exercises her right to vote in each election. When her mother died, she moved into a local group home but has retained close contact with a brother who lives in the same city. Staff at the group home assist Jane with budgeting her money and offer physical protection since her outgoing nature makes her vulnerable. From the group home, Jane can take walks in her neighborhood and has access to local businesses. She also has access to a nearby bus stop and can take the bus to a restaurant or the mall.

Jane's case manager assisted her in finding employment in a local fast-food restaurant located on a direct bus route. Jane liked dressing in a uniform for the job, enjoyed conversation with the diners, and was consistent and thorough in completing the job tasks to which she was assigned. During her lunch hour each day, she went to the employee lounge and ate her lunch while watching the local news to keep current with the political scene, such as campaigns for mayor, governor, president, etc. She then discussed this with the diners and the residents of her group home and delighted in debating the pros and cons of being a democrat or a republican. Other employees knew that Jane watched the noon newscast and often asked her to share what she had learned.

One day Jane took her lunch to the employee lounge and found a new employee watching a soap opera instead of the news. When Jane attempted to change the station, the employee stopped her and told her that she always watched her soap opera at that time each day. Jane became angry and began throwing items at the employee and the television set. The manager heard the noise, saw the damage to the property, and fired Jane from the job she had held with minimal support for almost 20 years.

Although Jane's case manager intervened and sought legal recourse for Jane, the restaurant management refused to reinstate her in her job. With the incident on her employment record, she was unable to find work in a similar competitive setting. The case manager finally placed her in a sheltered workshop where she assembles boxes each day with other adults with disabilities. Instead of riding the bus independently, Jane now rides a van with other adults with disabilities. Although her wages have been cut, Jane appears happy because she is able to watch the noon news and discuss politics with the workshop staff.

How do you react to this case study? Discuss each facet. Could the initial incident have been handled differently by the restaurant management? Could the case worker have explored other options? Is the fact that Jane appears to be satisfied in a more restrictive setting problematic?

RESIDENTIAL OPTIONS FOR ADULTS WITH MODERATE AND SEVERE DISABILITIES

In addition to determining the best option for adults with moderate and severe disabilities to spend their days in a productive manner, the transition team needs to work with persons with disabilities and their families in determining the best residential options when they transition, by choice or necessity, from their homes. This is a decision that many parents postpone until age or illness forces them to make decisions.

In addition to proposing a community-based continuum for employment as shown in Table 12.1, Taylor (1988) also proposed a community-based continuum for residential options to replace a traditional continuum with more restrictive options, as shown in Table 12.2. For example, the most restrictive option in a traditional continuum would be a public institution, while the most restrictive option in a community-based continuum would be a small community-based facility, such as an intensive-care facility for persons with mental retardation. More than a decade later, the traditional continuum still exists for a variety of reasons.

In analyzing residential data collected on 461 families across two states since 1988, Seltzer, Krauss, Hong, and Orsmond (2001) found that their children with mental disabilities moved to a variety of residential options that included (a) group homes and foster homes—64.1%, (b) partially staffed or unstaffed apartments—17.5%, (c) nursing homes or institutions—14.5%, and (d) the homes of relatives—3.9%. The mothers of these adults reported that most were on waiting lists prior to moving and that they continued to maintain close contact (e.g., visit, telephone) with their children after they moved. In addition, contact with siblings tended to increase following the move. When Pruchno and Patrick (1999) analyzed the placement decisions of older mothers of adult children with mental disabilities, they found that they were more likely to place their children within a formal residential system than

---

TABLE 12.2   *Comparison of Traditional and Community-Based Residential Continua (based with permission on Taylor, 1988).*

Residential Continua

Traditional		Community-Based
Public Institution	Most Restrictive	Small Community ICFs/MR[1]
Private Nursing Homes		Group Homes
Private Institutions	↑	Small Group Homes
Community ICFs/MR[1]		Foster Care
Group Homes		Supervised Apartments
Foster Care	↓	Semi-Independent Living
Semi-Independent Living		Independent Living
Independent Living	Least Restrictive	

[1]ICFs/MR = Intensive Care Facilities for Persons with Mental Retardation

with family members, and the degree of caregiving required by their children was a determining factor in their decisions for placement.

Current data (Lakin, Prouty, Polister, & Coucouvanis, 2003) show a trend toward community-based residential places of persons with mental disabilities. From 1977 to 2002, the number of persons living in larger institutional facilities decreased from 207, 356 to 74, 194, while the number of persons living in smaller community-based settings increased from 40, 444 to 323, 028. The following sections will discuss the issues associated with three residential models from most to least restrictive: (a) institutions, (b) group homes, and (c) supported independent living.

Institutions

Timberlake (1999) reported the formation of an advocacy group to protest cuts in a state budget that would result in the closing of a state hospital for persons with mental retardation and the transfer of its residents to community-based homes. The group planned to ask the state to increase funding to keep the facility open for adults with intense needs. This example is representative of those families with children with severe and profound disabilities who believe their needs are best served in residential facilities. In following 100 families of children with severe and profound disabilities for 10 years, Hanneman and Blacher (1998) found that the families that chose residential placements for their children made their decisions based on (a) the child's appearance (e.g., less normative), (b) the mother's occupation (e.g., educated and working outside of the home), (c) a large number of siblings, (d) caregiving burdens, and (e) the age of the parents (e.g., younger mother, older father). The ability of the family to cope and the amount of social support they had did not appear to make a difference. In analyzing the adaptation of 106 families after placing family members with mental disabilities in large residential facilities, Baker and Blacher (2002) found that the majority (86%) reported an increase in peace of mind and a decrease in negative feelings, such as stress and guilt. Adaptation was found to be highest in families of adults than in families of younger children, possibly because it is normal for adults to leave the family home. Example 12.1 further illustrates the reasons families may select institutional settings for their children with disabilities, and Activity 12.2 centers around a state institution that is making an attempt to improve its services.

ACTIVITY 12.2   Evaluating an Institutional Setting

Ward (2004a) described how a state institution has been making efforts to improve the quality of life for its residents. While describing the institution as a series of cottages on 200 acres of a parklike setting, Ward noted that the facility had been plagued by a lack of supervision for its residents that allowed them to engage in life-threatening behaviors (e.g., pica) and the extended delivery of medications that resulted in detrimental side effects for the residents. After the state intervened, 60 residents moved to less restrictive settings, the state increased funding from $28 million to $45 million, and the facility increased the staff from 800 to 1,300 to support the 300 remaining residents (142 persons with significant cognitive disabilities). Still dissatisfied with the level of progress, the state took over management from the private company that ran the facility and contracted with a consultant to make changes.

Since that time, the consultants have worked to improve medical treatment and to address the "wishes, aspirations, and dreams" of the residents, who range in age from teenagers to senior citizens. Changes have included the following: (a) private or semiprivate rooms decorated to the residents' tastes (e.g., jungle theme, ice cream shop theme); (b) darkened room with flashing lights, bubble machine, and projection of pictures on the wall to calm behaviors of the residents; (c) decrease in the use of physical restraints and drugs for challenging behaviors; (d) incentives, such as snacks, to reward compliance; (e) small classes with activities that included working with wooden blocks, playing with plastic animal toys, coloring pictures, and identifying numbers; and (f)

field trips to participate in activities, such as washing laundry or making crafts.

Think back to what you have read in the previous chapters of this text, especially those that focused on functional and age-appropriate skills, community inclusion, and challenging behaviors. What improvements have been made in this setting? What improvements still need to be implemented?

EXAMPLE 12.1 Why a Family Chose an Institutional Setting

In 1999 Owen wrote a poignant and thoughtful article about her sister, Donna, a 41-year-old woman with autism and a profound mental disability. Owen described Donna as a person with a variety of positive attributes that included physical attractiveness, a friendly personality, and the ability to show personal preferences but also with enough challenging behaviors (e.g., limited communication skills, awkward physical motor skills, short attention span, stereotypical running, obsessive compulsive tendencies, crying and tantruming) to require constant attention. After attempting to meet Donna's needs in their home for 18 years, her family placed her in a minimally restrictive facility where she was physically abused before being asked to leave. With no other options open to them at the time, Donna's parents admitted her to the state institution where she had been residing for almost 20 years. The family found that the setting proved to be a positive placement. The facility's staff implemented a positive behavior program in a consistent and caring manner, and the family could bring Donna home for a visit on a weekly basis.

Owen continued to describe the family's stress when they learned that the state planned to close the institution in lieu of community-based homes. While she acknowledged that institutions were costly options, she maintained that there were not enough community homes to accommodate people with Donna's needs, argued that the institutional setting provided Donna with a life with human dignity, and expressed resentment that advocates of community-based living would deny her family their freedom of choice, as follows:

> The extremists, however, want all such institutions closed, and closed now. They will not accept that there are good institutional homes; in fact, to them, the very phrase is an oxymoron. . . . Freedom means different things to different people. At Central State, Donna is as free as she can ever be. She is free from fear and from the terror of trying to fit into a world she can't understand, and which can't understand her. She is free from being an outcast, having at last become a part of her own little community. In this home, she has the freedom to experience the basic human right of dignity (p. F4).

Group Homes

A newspaper article pointed out the support that some families have for group homes as a residential placement for their children with disabilities ("Covington home," 2002). According to the article, cuts in funding and difficulty in recruiting adequate staff caused the closing of a number of group homes in the northern region of a state. A dozen residents had one month to find new housing in a state where almost 2,000 adults with disabilities were on a waiting list for housing. Although a program offered to move the residents to other regions of the state, families were displeased because this would cause them to have to live a great distance from people they loved, including their family and friends. A guardian was quoted as saying that an adult for whom he was responsible "has relatives here. He has a job here. . . . I don't want him moving to someplace that would be like the dark side of the moon for him. He needs to be here" (p. C4).

Duvdevany, Ben-Zur, and Ambar (2002) compared the lifestyle of persons with mild and moderate disabilities living at home and living in group homes; they found that those living in group homes reported more satisfaction with their lifestyle (e.g., residence, community, services, employment), while those living at home reported more self-determination, such as choices in domestic, financial, health, social, and work domains. The level of satisfaction can be attributed to factors that may vary across group homes, such as the physical condition, staff, and coresidents. Stancliffe and Lakin (1998) examined costs as well as lifestyle when they compared residential settings for 116 adults with severe and profound mental disabilities. Their data revealed that community-based residences, such as community group homes, were less costly, had higher staffing per resident, and resulted in higher outcomes (e.g., social activities, community integration, contact with family, personal choice) for residents than institutional settings, such as large intensive-care facilities. A sampling of research studies that have investigated similar factors follows.

Egli, Rober, Feurer, and Thompson (1999) had 63 college students rate 18 group homes for their "homelikeness" and found that this was associated with the visual appearance as well as the sound (i.e., reverberation). The residences that were not built as group homes received the highest ratings. Baker, Freeman, and High (2000) observed 16 staff members across three group homes (four to six residents with mild and moderate mental disabilities across facilities with two to three staff per shift) during the following activities: (a) instruction, (b) personal care, (c) leisure, and (d) household management. While the frequency of communication differed across activities and residents, some required more attention than others but not across staff members or homes. In other words, some activities were more conducive to communication than others, and some residents required more attention than others. Wiltz and Reiss (2003) compared 93 dyads of housemates with mild to severe disabilities who lived in group homes and were identified as being compatible or incompatible, based on frequency of conflict and complaint. They found that incompatible housemates had a higher motivation for vengeance and acceptance and had a lower tolerance for anxiety, pain, and frustration. Thus, they recommended that residents should use self-determination in selecting housemates based on compatible characteristics, such as whether they enjoy socializing or prefer being left alone. With the results of these investigations in mind, the reader can evaluate the homelikeness of a group setting for persons with disabilities found in Activity 12.3.

ACTIVITY 12.3   Evaluating a Group Setting

Hoye (2003) described a communal rural farm as an example of a group home setting with a familylike atmosphere. Founded 20 years ago to provide a community option to institutional living for adults with moderate and severe disabilities, the farm was the home of 18 adults who lived in small groups in cottages that were supervised by "house parents." Chores on the 26-acre farm consumed most the residents' day. This included growing crops of flowers and vegetables that they sold in their greenhouse and at large events. Other activities were domestic, such as canning homemade tomato juice, or recreational, such as softball games with community members without disabilities. The farm was supported by the farming efforts of the residents and volunteers from the community.

Based on the limited description you have been given, can you evaluate this setting for homelikeness? What are the positive attributes of the setting? Are there ways in which it could be improved?

Supported Living

In 1991 Nisbet, Clark, and Covert defined **supported living** as "small living arrangements where support is provided as necessary" (p. 128) and noted that this was replacing group homes as the model of choice for persons with severe disabilities. In writing the story of his life, Chris Dixon (2003) built a case for supported community living.

A man with severe disabilities (e.g., physical, communication, medical), Chris related how he lived at home in a typical family until his mother had a stroke and his father died. At the age of 43, he was placed in a group home where, even though he knew the staff cared about him, he felt as if his life were confined and regimented (e.g., based on meeting objectives) within a group of strangers: "I was afraid. Everything was different. They watched me like I was in jail. . . . I was frustrated and unhappy" (p. 31).

After a serious illness, Chris moved to a nursing home. Again, Chris stated that the staff were nice, but he felt out of place with residents who were so much older: "Again, there was another whole set of rules, and again, this was not by my choice. I was afraid when I got there. . . . It was [a] very old place, with lots of old people and it made me pretty sad" (p. 31).

Finally, Chris received support for community living in an apartment with a roommate he chose. For the first time, he could eat what he liked, manage his own finances, go shopping, and watch television whenever he wanted: "I ate what I wanted, and when I wanted. . . . I have help with my banking and shopping and I have my privacy when I need it" (pp. 31–32).

As time passed, Chris lived with and without a roommate but received continual personal assistance to meet his needs (e.g., dressing, preparing meals, going to and getting up from bed). In time, he enrolled in college classes, volunteered in a hospital, and worked as a teacher's assistant. At the time that he wrote his story, Chris had a new communication device and was involved in self-advocacy.

Several investigations have compared community-based supported living to other options. Emerson et al. (2001) compared cost and quality of life across several models implemented in the United Kingdom: (a) residential campuses—large buildings with 94 to 144 residents each, (b) village communities—campus of several units with 7 to 8 residents each, (c) group homes or staffed houses—dispersed community houses with 1 to 8 residents each. The investigators found that the cost of dispersed community group homes and staffed housing was 15% higher than residential campuses and 20% higher than village communities. The higher costs, however, seemed to result in better outcomes. For example, campuses were associated with the lowest quality of living, and community housing options were associated with the highest quality of living based on the homelikeness of the settings, staffing ratios, planning and management procedures, prescription of antipsychotic medications, and reliance on psychiatric support. In addition, persons living in dispersed community housing had more opportunities to make choices, had larger social networks, and engaged in more recreational or community activities, although they also had more exposure to crime and verbal abuse. Those with mild and moderate mental disabilities tended to live in community settings, while those with more severe disabilities tended to live in more restrictive settings.

Investigators have made similar comparisons in the United States. Spreat and Conroy (2001) compared residential factors for persons with profound disabilities who lived in state institutions and who later moved from state institutions to small community-based homes. Although they found integration to be higher in the community, they noted that those in the community had more difficulty having some of their medical and nonmedical needs (e.g., technology) met.

In another investigation, Stancliffe, Abery, and Smith (2000) compared the personal control exercised by 74 residents with mild to profound disabilities across (a) semi-independent living arrangements—1 to 2 residents, (b) supported living sites—1 to 4 residents, and (c) community-based intensive-care facilities for persons with mental retardation—6 to 12 residents in a group home or up to 44 residents in an apartment complex. They found that residents living in arrangements with fewer people (e.g., one to five) exercised more self-control over their lives and that personal control was influenced by the personal characteristics of the residents (e.g., adaptive or challenging behaviors), their competency in self-determination (e.g., skills, attitude, knowledge), and environmental variables (e.g., staff, lifestyle, social network). Finally, when Stancliffe, Hayden, and Lakin (2000) compared the individual habilitation plans of 155 adults with mental retardation residing in either an institution or the community, they found that, in addition to having more objectives, the objectives for the community residents were more age appropriate and covered more domains and content areas, including meal planning, self-care, community participation, money management, and household chores.

Supported living appears to be an optimal model for persons with moderate and severe disabilities in the least restrictive environment. Yet supported living services can be difficult to obtain, as depicted in Example 12.2.

EXAMPLE 12.2 OBTAINING SUPPORTED LIVING SERVICES

Richardson (2000) described the difficulty Carolyn and her family encountered in trying to obtain supported living services. Carolyn was a 33-year old woman with Down syndrome, a cognitive disability, diagnosed depression, erratic behavior, and limited self-help and functional academic skills. Her parents were retired and both suffered from age-related physical problems (e.g., arthritis) that made it difficult for them to continue to care for their daughter themselves. When they placed Carolyn in an institutional setting, they noticed that drug intervention was inducing undesirable side effects, such as the loss of the ability to communicate, and brought her home. At that point, they put Carolyn on a waiting list for community-based services from the state and built a home for her next door to their own. After eight years passed, Carolyn was number 190 on the waiting list to get the state funding necessary to enable her to move in to the new home with support (i.e., professional caregiver).

Summary

As illustrated in Example 12.3, it is clear that a number of residential options continue to be available to persons with moderate and severe disabilities. Data trends, however, show that there has been a shift in favor of less restrictive placements for students with disabilities. For example, more students who are deaf or blind are receiving services in their home communities rather than in state-run facilities ("Board to require," 2004). In reviewing the professional literature on the costs of residential options over a quarter of a century, Walsh, Kastner, and Green (2003) reported conflicting data and pointed out that the tendency to serve more capable persons in the community and to serve those with more intense needs in larger facilities makes cost comparisons difficult. Thus, they suggested that instead of asking which option is less expensive, determination of residential placements should be based on questions that revolve around the needs of the individual: "'What does this person need? Where is the best place to provide for these needs?' and 'at what cost?'" (p. 117). By examining the needs of the individual, the transition team can consider such variables as staffing needs, functional skill needs, and quality of life.

EXAMPLE 12.3 AN EXAMPLE OF OPTIONS WITHIN A STATE

A recent newspaper article (Ward, 2004b) illustrated the issues encountered by a state in moving toward less restrictive options. In contrast to states that have discontinued institutional placements as alternatives, such as Virginia, New Hampshire, and New Mexico, Kentucky ranks 49th in the nation in placing persons with moderate and severe disabilities in smaller residential settings (i.e., 15 or fewer residents) and 50th in the nation in financing community support services. In examining options in Kentucky, the author of the article provided figures relating to residential options and the opinions of persons who support various options on the continuum of residential services. These statistics and opinions illustrate the problems that may be encountered across a number of other states.

Facts

At the time the article was written, 3,613 persons with mental retardation in Kentucky resided in smaller settings that received public funding. Of these, 45% lived in settings with 16 or more residents, compared to 23% nationally. It cost the state an average of $53,000 per person per year to serve persons in smaller settings (e.g., group homes) and an average of $139,604 per person per year to serve persons in larger settings (e.g., institutions), with $100 million going to support institutions on an annual basis. More than 2,000 persons were on the waiting list for the Supports for Community Living program. Persons with more severe disabilities tended to live in institutional settings; for example, 142 out of 303 residents at a state-run institution had profound mental retardation and multiple disabilities. In addition, the state had 10,643 persons with mental retardation living with elderly caregivers who eventually would need alternate residential options.

Opinions

Persons who supported various residential options in Kentucky were vocal. Advocates for supported living tended to be professionals in the field of disabilities who voiced opinions that institutions had outlived their usefulness as the only option available to families of persons with disabilities and did not provide the quality of life that residents should have. Advocates for institutional living tended to be family members who voiced opinions that the state could not afford to provide the necessary intensive one-on-one care for persons with complex medical needs and challenging behaviors and that people should have a choice to select more restrictive settings. The arguments were best summarized by Dr. Harold Kleinert of the University of Kentucky Interdisciplinary Human Development Institute when he stated, "We've got a long way to go" (p. B2).

In changing the mind-set to a focus on the individual, Racino (1995) pointed out that there is a difference in community integration and independent living across a number of dimensions. For example, integration is an activity with dependence on agencies and requires the viewpoint that some type of compensation must be made for a person's disabilities. In contrast, independent living can be viewed as a right to freedom and self-control based on the preferences of the individual with the disability being accepted as the person connects with others in the community.

As proponents of the supported living model, Shepard and Mayfield (2003) dispelled a number of myths by asserting that services are not setting specific and (as in the previously mentioned case of Chris Dixon) can be provided in natural settings around the clock, if necessary. In addition, Shepard and Mayfield stated that the quality of supported living can be enhanced when a person with disabilities has his or her own room, makes his or her own rules, has a schedule based on personal needs, is supported by a variety of staff, has control over the hiring of services, and is connected to people and activities within the community.

COMMUNITY INVOLVEMENT

The previous sections contained material regarding community work and residential options for persons with moderate and severe disabilities with a focus on supported employment and supported residential settings within the community. Being a part of a community, however, goes beyond having a job and a home. Community living requires involvement in activities with persons without disabilities. Persons with disabilities need to have the same opportunities to participate in recreational, religious, volunteer, and continuing-education activities that their peers without disabilities enjoy. Just as educational inclusion must be precipitated by physical inclusion in school settings, community inclusion is precipitated by physical inclusion in work and residential settings. As in educational inclusion, however, strategies may be necessary to ensure that community inclusion occurs. This is illustrated by the following two examples.

First, Jones et al. (2001) found an increase in activities both within residences (e.g., entertaining guests or being entertained by others) and within the community (e.g., visiting cafes, churches, sports events, and concerts) after they implemented Active Support training for staff across 38 residences where adults with severe disabilities resided. A two-day staff workshop consisted of (a) considering residents' preferences, (b) drawing up corresponding activity and support plans, (c) learning to provide individualized support, (d) learning how to reinforce engagement during activities, (e) writing task analyses, and (f) preparing opportunity plans for the following week. In the second example, Harlan-Simmons, Holtz, Todd, and Mooney (2001) described the effect of the Community Membership Project of the Center on Aging and Community on the lives of three older adults with developmental disabilities. In each of the cases, an adult "community-builder" worked through the following stages to support the adults with disabilities within the community: (a) getting to know you—spending time with the person in a community setting and interviewing those who know them well; (b) developing a vision—identifying personal characteristics, such as strengths, interests, and habits; (c) getting connected—matching the person to community activities, settings, and members and identifying supports; and (d) cultivating relationships—assisting community interactions through techniques, such as teaching communication strategies before decreasing involvement. The resulting community involvement of the residents included taking drum lessons, volunteering for Meals on Wheels, and working with children at a YMCA summer day camp. Activity 12.4 contains other examples of attempts at community inclusion for your consideration.

ACTIVITY 12.4   Evaluating Community Inclusion

This chapter has drawn from a number of newspaper articles to provide real-life examples of the options available to adults with moderate and severe disabilities. In this activity three additional recent news articles are reviewed. These illustrate efforts at including persons with moderate and severe disabilities in community settings. As you read through these examples, can you find ways that persons with disabilities benefit from the activities that are described? Can you find ways in which the activities could be improved? In particular, consider factors that may or may not be stigmatizing to the participants.

The first two articles described community-based art classes conducted for adults with disabilities in separate regions of a state. In the first setting (Stinnett, 2004), the classes were taught by an artist at a training center through state funding for the arts and resulted in a special exhibit in the gallery of a public library as well as note cards and art prints designed by the students that were for sale at the training center. In the second setting (Gabriel, 2003), the classes focused on both visual and performing arts taught by artists at a community studio funded by a service agency for adults with disabilities and resulted in an artist with disabilities being featured in a juried exhibit of 350 artists without disabilities, as well as the students helping to teach classes to children at a local children's museum.

The third article (McClure, 2002) focused on an annual event rather than on a continuing activity. The event was a prom for persons over the age of 16 with physical and mental disabilities that was organized by a local church. During the year the article was written, 800 persons with disabilities and 700 volunteers attended the event. Family members were quoted as saying that the event was the highlight of the year for their family members with disabilities as they described their excitement in shopping for formal clothing, having hair and makeup done, and dancing and socializing with other people. The organizing pastor said that the prom was designed to give those "who might not have had the opportunity to go to a regular prom a really memorable experience" (p. E3).

Best Practices
Adult Options

1. Consider a variety of factors in determining employment and residential setting for adults with disabilities, making sure that individual preferences of the person being placed are documented and family preferences are noted.

2. Do not assume that persons with greater cognitive disabilities, medical needs, and challenging behaviors must be in the most restrictive setting (recall the least dangerous assumption).

3. Instead of focusing on "Where?" and "What does it cost?" focus placement decisions on "Why?" and "How?" as well as "Who is responsible?"

4. Do not assume that physical placement in community settings will ensure community inclusion.

5. Work to change the mind-set of providers from helping to providing support and from "doing activities for" to "doing activities with."

Conclusion

This chapter has presented a continuum of adult work and residential options for person with moderate and severe disabilities with an emphasis on selecting less restrictive options. While this chapter does not assert that all persons with moderate and severe disabilities can or should be served in independent settings, it does assert that those who are involved in placement decisions should consider a variety of factors, such as medical needs, challenging behaviors, and individual and family preferences, in attempting to provide support in the least restrictive setting possible for all persons. In other words, asking "Why?" and "Why not?" is as important as asking "Where?" This chapter also touched on community inclusion activities aside from work and residential settings and pointed out, through examples, that sometimes there is room for improvement even when the best of intentions are involved. At this point, stop to assess your understanding of adult options by completing the Performance-Based Assessment at the end of this chapter.

Questions for Review

1. Define *supported employment* and *supported living*.

2. How can work preferences be determined for an individual with minimal communication skills?

3. How can job carving be used to identify potential employment settings?

4. Describe various means of providing support for persons with mental disabilities. Are some preferable to others? Why or why not?

5. Why might parents be opposed to less restrictive employment and residential settings?

6. Discuss the discrepancies in cost across residential options for adults with mental disabilities.

7. Why is self-determination a critical component in determining adult options for work and living?

8. How can community inclusion be facilitated?

Performance-Based Assessment

The following scenario represents a difficult placement decision confronting the family of a child with a severe disability. Based on what you learned in this chapter, identify the options that might be available to the family and how you might work with them to ensure that they make the best decision possible for the future well-being of their adult child. Consider both work and residential options, as well as strategies for community inclusion.

Greta is a 21-year-old woman with significant cognitive and multiple severe disabilities who resides in a rural community with her elderly parents and is the youngest of several siblings. Greta requires assistance to manipulate her wheelchair within the home and communicates through eye gaze. She can indicate simple choices (e.g., what she wants to eat or wear when given a choice of two items) by smiling. She appears happy when receiving attention from people in her community, and most know her by name. Her most consistent motor skill is her palmar grasp. Until this point, all of her needs (e.g., dressing, eating, bathing) have been met by her parents. Greta has not been taught vocational or domestic skills because her parents always have argued that she would live with them and would not need these skills. Now her parents realize that they no longer can provide for caregiving needs as they age. For example, they can no longer get her in and out of their van to go out into the community and have difficulty bathing her and getting her in and out of her bed. They do not, however, want her siblings to accept responsibility for her because they are raising families of their own.

References

Baker, B. L., & Blacher, J. (2002). For better or worse? Impact of residential placement on families. *Mental Retardation, 40,* 1–13.

Baker, D. J., Freeman, R., & High, R. (2000). Resident-directed communication patterns in community homes for persons with disabilities. *Mental Retardation, 38,* 489–497.

Becker, R. L. (1981). *Reading-free interest inventory: M F.*

Blackorby, J., & Wagner, M. (1996). Longitudinal post school outcomes of youth with disabilities: Findings from the National Longitudinal Transition Study. *Exceptional Children, 62,* 399–413.

Board to require higher scores, more services: Plan spreads more of $16 million to outside students (2004, August 12). *Lexington Herald-Leader,* p. C1.

Brady, M. P., & Rosenberg, H. (2002). Job Observation and Behavior Scale: A supported employment assessment instrument. *Education and Training in Mental Retardation and Developmental Disabilities, 37,* 427–433.

Browder, D. M., & Minarovic, T. J. (2000). Utilizing sight words in self-instruction training for employees with moderate mental retardation in competitive jobs. *Education and Training in Mental Retardation and Developmental Disabilities, 35,* 78–89.

Campbell, J. A., & Essex, E. L. (1994). Factors affecting parents in their future planning for a son or daughter with developmental disabilities. *Education and Training in Mental Retardation and Developmental Disabilities, 29,* 222–228.

Certo, N. J., Mautz, D., Pumpian, I., Sax, C., Smalley, K., Wade, H. A., Noyes, D., Luecking, R., Wechsler, J., & Batterman, N. (2003). A review and discussion of a model for seamless transition to adulthood. *Education Training in Developmental Disabilities, 38,* 3–17.

Covington home for disabled closes. (2002, November 23). *Lexington Herald-Leader,* C4.

Davies, D. K., Stock, S. E., & Wehmeyer, M. L. (2002). Enhancing independent task performance for individuals with mental retardation through use of a handheld self-directed visual and audio prompting system. *Education and Training in Mental Retardation and Developmental Disabilities, 37,* 209–218.

Dixon, C. (2003). My story. *TASH Connections, 29,* 31–32.

Duvdevany, I., Ben-Zur, H., & Ambar, A. (2002). Self-determination and mental retardation: Is there an association with living arrangement and lifestyle satisfaction? *Mental Retardation, 40,* 379–389.

Egli, M., Rober, T., Feurer, I., & Thompson, T. (1999). Architectural acoustics in residences for adults with mental retardation and its relation to perceived homelikeness. *American Journal on Mental Retardation, 104,* 53–66.

Ellerd, D. A., Morgan, R. L., & Salzberg, C. L. (2002). Comparison of two approaches for identifying job preferences among persons with disabilities using video CD-ROM. *Education and Training in Mental Retardation and Developmental Disabilities, 37,* 300–309.

Emerson, E., Robertson, J., Gregory, N, Hatton, C., Kessissoglou, S., Hallam, A., Knapp, M., Järbrink, K., Walsh, P. N., & Netten, A. (2001). Quality and costs of community-based residential supports, village communities, and residential campuses in the United Kingdom. *American Journal on Mental Retardation, 105,* 81–102.

Gabriel, M. (2003, June 25). Arc of Bluegrass seeks to open doors and mind: Disabled artists contribute to public projects. Lexington, KY: *Lexington Herald-Leader,* p. E2.

Hagner, D., Butterworth, J., & Keith, G. (1995). Strategies and barriers in facilitating natural supports for employment of adults with severe disabilities. *Journal of the Association for Persons with Severe Handicaps, 20,* 110–120.

Hanley-Maxwell, C., Whitney-Thomas, J., & Pogoloff, S. M. (1995). The second shock: A qualitative study of parents' perspectives and needs during their child's transition from school to adult life. *Journal of the Association for Persons with Severe Handicaps, 20,* 3–15.

Hanneman, R., & Blacher, J. (1998). Predicting placement in families who have children with severe handicaps: A longitudinal analysis. *American Journal on Mental Retardation, 102,* 392–408.

Harlan-Simmons, J. E., Holtz, P., Todd, J., & Mooney, M. F. (2001). Building social relationships through valued roles: Three older adults and the community membership project. *Mental Retardation, 39,* 171–180.

Heal, L. W., Khoju, M., Rusch, F. R., & Harnisch, D. L. (1999). Predicting quality of life of students who have left special education high school programs. *American Journal on Mental Retardation, 104,* 305–319.

Hood, E., Test, D. W., Spooner, F., & Steele, R. (1996). Paid co-worker support for individuals with severe and multiple disabilities. *Education and Training in Mental Retardation and Developmental Disabilities, 31,* 251–265.

Hoye, S. (2003, October 23). Planting a future: Quest Farm teachers the disabled how to be farmers. *Lexington Herald-Leader,* p. E1.

Jones, E., Felce, D., Lowe, K., Bowley, C., Pagler, J., Gallagher, B., & Roper, A. (2001). Evaluation of the dissemination of activity support training staffed community residences. *American Journal of Metal Retardation, 106,* 344–358.

Jones, G. Y., & Collins, B. C. (1997). Teaching microwave skills to adults with disabilities: Acquisition of nutrition and safety facts presented as non-targeted information. *Journal of Physical and Developmental Disabilities, 9,* 59–78.

Jordan, B., & Dunlap, G. (2001). Construction of adulthood and disability. *Mental Retardation, 39,* 286–296.

Kellow, T., & Parker, R. I. (2002). Self-perceptions of adequacy of support among persons with mental retardation living in suburban versus rural communities. *Education and Training in Mental Retardation and Developmental Disabilities, 37,* 328–338.

Kraemer, B. R., McIntyre, L. L., & Blacher, J. (2003). Quality of life for young adults with mental retardation during transition. *Mental Retardation, 41,* 250–262.

Kregel, J., & Wehman, P. (1989). Supported employment: Promises deferred for persons with severe disabilities. *Journal of the Association for Persons with Severe Handicaps, 14,* 293–303.

Lakin, K. C., Prouty, R., Polister, B., & Coucouvanis, K. (2003). Selected changes in residential service systems over a quarter century, 1977–2002. *Mental Retardation, 41,* 303–306.

Lancioni, G. E., Dijkstra, A. W., O'Reilly, M. F., Groeneweg, J., & Van den Hof, E. (2000). Frequent versus nonfrequent verbal prompts delivered unobtrusively: Their impact on the task performance of adults with intellectual disability. *Education and Training in Mental Retardation and Developmental Disabilities, 35,* 428–433.

Lee, M., Storey, K., Anderson, J. L., Goetz, L., & Zivolich, S. (1997). The effect of mentoring versus job coach instruction on integration in supported employment settings. *Journal of the Association for Persons with severe Handicaps, 22,* 151–158.

Lustig, D., & Thomas, K. (1997). Adaptation of families to the entry of young adults with mental retardation into supported employment. *Education and Training in Mental Retardation and Developmental Disabilities, 32,* 21–31.

Maciag, K. G., Schuster, J. W., Collins, B. C., & Cooper, J. T. (2000). Training adults with moderate and severe mental retardation in a vocational skill using a simultaneous prompting procedure. *Education and Training in Mental Retardation and Developmental Disabilities, 35,* 306–316.

Mank, D., Cioffi, A., & Yovanoff, P. (2003). Supported employment outcomes across a decade: Is there evidence of improvement in the quality of implementation? *Mental Retardation, 41,* 188–197.

Mautz, D., Storey, K., & Certo, N. (2001). Increasing integrated workplace social interactions: The effects of job modification, natural supports, adaptive communication instruction, and job coach training. *Journal of the Association for Persons with Severe Handicaps, 26,* 257–269.

McClure, M. (2002, November 27). Boogie night: Jesus Prom organizers find blessing in serving. *Lexington Herald-Leader,* p. E3.

McDermott, S., Martin, M., & Butkus, S. (1999). What individual, provider, and community characteristics predict employment of individuals with mental retardation? *American Journal on Mental Retardation, 104,* 346–355.

McGaughey, M. J., Kiernan, W. E., McNally, L. C., Gilmore, D. S., & Keith, G. R. (1995). Beyond the workshop: National trends in integrated and segregated day and employment services. *Journal of the Association for Persons with Severe Handicaps, 20,* 270–285.

Meers, G. D. (1992). Getting ready for the next century: Vocational preparation of students with disabilities. *Teaching Exceptional Children, 24*(4), 36–39.

Menchetti, B. M., & Garcia, L. A. (2003). Personal and employment outcomes of person-centered career planning. *Education and Training in Mental Retardation and Developmental Disabilities, 38,* 145–156.

Millar, D. S., & Renzaglia, A. (2002). Factors affecting guardianship practices for young adults with disabilities. *Exceptional Children, 68,* 465–484.

Nietupski, J. A., & Hamre-Nietupski, S. (2000). A systematic process for carving supported employment positions for people with severe disabilities. *Journal of Developmental and Physical Disabilities, 12,* 103–119.

Nietupski, J. A., & Hamre-Nietupski, S. (2002). A business approach to finding and restructuring supported employment opportunities. In P. Wehman (Ed.).

Supported employment in business: Expanding the capacity of workers with disabilities. St. Augustine, FL: Training Resource Network.

Nisbet, J., Clark, M., & Covert, S. (1991). Living it up! An analysis of research on community living. In L. H. Meyer, C. A. Peck, & L. Brown (Eds.), *Critical Issues in the Lives of People with Severe Disabilities* (pp. 115–144). Baltimore: Brookes.

Nisbet, J., & Hagner, D. (1988). Natural supports in the workplace: A reexamination of supported employment. *Journal of the Association for Persons with Severe Handicaps, 13,* 260–267.

Owen, C. (1999, March 14). Yes, it's an institution, but it's home. Lexington, KY: *Lexington Herald-Leader,* pp. F1, F4.

Parsons, M. B., Reid, D. H., & Green, C. W. (2001). Situational assessment of task preferences among adults with multiple severe disabilities in supported work. *Journal of the Association for Persons with Severe Handicaps, 26,* 50–55.

Post, M., Storey, K., & Karabin, M. (2002). Cool headphones for effective prompts: Supporting students and adults in work and community environments. *Teaching Exceptional Children, 34,* 60–65.

Powell, T. H., & Moore, S. C. (1992). Benefits and incentives for students entering supported employment. *Teaching Exceptional Children, 24*(3), 16–19.

Pruchno, R. A., & Patrick, J. H. (1999). Effects of formal and familial residential plans for adults with mental retardation on their aging mothers. *American Journal on Mental Retardation, 104,* 38–52.

Racino, J. A. (1995). Community living for adults with developmental disabilities: A housing and support approach. *Journal of the Association for Persons with Severe Handicaps, 20,* 300–310.

Reid, D. H., Parsons, M. B., & Green, C. W. (2001). Evaluating the functional utility of congregate day treatment activities for adults with severe disabilities. *American Journal on Mental Retardation, 106,* 460–469.

Reid, D. H., Parsons, M. B., Green, C. W., & Browning, L. B. (2001). Increasing one aspect of self-determination among adults with severe multiple disabilities in supported work. *Journal of Applied Behavior Analysis, 34,* 341–344.

Richardson, M. (2000, August 2). Mental health money will help foster independence. *Lexignton Herald-Leader,* p. A1, A12.

Rusch, F. R., Chadsey-Rusch, J., & Johnson, J. R. (1991). Supported employment: Emerging opportunities for employment integration. In L. H. Meyer, C. A. Peck, & L. Brown (Eds.), *Critical Issues in the Lives of People with Severe Disabilities* (pp. 145–169). Baltimore: Brookes.

Rusch, F. R., & Hughes, C. (1988). Supported employment: Promoting employee independence. *Mental Retardation, 26,* 351–355.

Seltzer, M. M., Krauss, M. W., Hong, J., & Orsmond, G. I. (2001). Continuity or discontinuity of family involvement following residential transitions of adults who have mental retardation. *Mental Retardation, 39,* 181–194.

Shepard, S., & Mayfield, C. (2003). Learning to listen: The key to supported living. *TASH Connections, 29,* 8–9.

Spreat, S., & Conroy, J. W. (2001). Community placement for persons with significant cognitive challenges: An outcome analysis. *Journal of the Association for Persons with Severe Handicaps, 26,* 106–113.

Stancliffe, R. J., Abery, B. H., & Smith, J. (2000). Personal control and the ecology of community living settings: Beyond living unit size and type. *American Journal on Mental Retardation, 105,* 431–454.

Stancliffe, R. J., Hayden, M. F., & Lakin, K. C. (2000). Quality and content of individualized habilitation plan objectives in residential settings. *Education and Training in Mental Retardation and Developmental Disabilities, 35,* 191–207.

Stancliffe, R. J., & Lakin, K. C. (1998). Analysis of expenditures and outcomes of residential alternatives for persons with developmental disabilities. *American Journal on Mental Retardation, 102,* 552–568.

Steed, S. E., & Lutzker, J. R. (1997). Using picture prompts to teach an adult with developmental disabilities to independently complete vocational tasks. *Journal of Developmental and Physical Disabilities, 9,* 117–133.

Stinnett, D. B. (2004, March 14). Creativity within: Program gives disabled a mode of artistic expression. Henderson, KY: *The Gleaner,* p. C1.

Taylor, S. J. (1988). Caught in the continuum: A critical analysis of the principle of the least restrictive environment. *Journal of the Association for Persons with Severe Handicaps, 13,* 41–53.

Test, D. W., Carver, T., Ewers, L., Haddad, J., & Person, J. (2000). Longitudinal job satisfaction of persons in supported employment. *Education and Training in Mental Retardation and Developmental Disabilities, 35,* 365–373.

Timberlake, J. (1999, June 15). Groups unite to help retarded adults: New coalition wants Kentucky to spend $30 million for care. *Lexington Herald-Leader,* p. B3.

Turnbull, A., & Turnbull, R. (1999). Comprehensive lifestyle support for adults with challenging behavior: From rhetoric to reality. *Education and Training in Mental Retardation and Developmental Disabilities, 34,* 373–394.

Walsh, K. K., Kastner, T. A., & Green, R. G. (2003). Cost comparison of community and institutional residential settings: historical review of selected research. *Mental Retardation, 41,* 103–122.

Ward, K. (2004a, August 3). State facility for retarded sees progress. *Lexington Herald-Leader,* pp. A1, A5.

Ward, K. (2004b, August 4). Institutions vs. group homes: State ranks low in treating disabled in community settings. *Lexington Herald-Leader,* pp. B1–2.

Wehman, P. (1988). Supported employment: Toward equal employment opportunity for persons with severe disabilities. *Mental Retardation, 26,* 357–361.

Wehman, P., West, M., & Kregel, J. (1999). Supported employment program development and research needs: Looking ahead to the year 2000. *Education and Training in Mental Retardation and Developmental Disabilities, 34,* 3–19.

Wehmeyer, M. L., & Palmer, S. B. (2003). Adult outcomes for students with cognitive disabilities three-years after high school: The impact of self-determination. *Education and Training in Mental Retardation and Developmental Disabilities, 38,* 131–144.

Wiltz, J., & Reiss, S. (2003). Compatibility of housemates with mental retardation. *American Journal on Mental Retardation, 108,* 173–180.

Worsdell, A. S., Iwata, B. A., & Wallace, M. D. (2002). Duration-based measures of preference for vocational tasks. *Journal of Applied Behavior Analysis, 35,* 287–290.

Yamaki, K., & Fujiura, G. T. (2002). Employment and income status of adults with developmental disabilities living in the community. *Mental Retardation, 40,* 132–141.

PART THREE

Identifying Issues That Affect the Lives of Persons with Moderate and Severe Disabilities

CHAPTER THIRTEEN

DEALING WITH DIFFICULT ISSUES:
A Sampling of Basic Human Rights

On completion of this chapter, the reader will meet the following objectives:

- Describe historical events in which the human rights of persons with disabilities have been violated.
- Provide a rationale for sex education for persons with moderate and severe disabilities.
- Describe the difference between providing sex education and sexual support.
- State why persons with moderate and severe disabilities may be vulnerable as both victims of abuse and as alleged criminal offenders.
- Discuss the ethical issues involved in making life-and-death decisions for persons with disabilities who cannot advocate for themselves.

The previous sections of this text have addressed the principles and foundations of providing appropriate programs and services for persons with moderate and severe disabilities, with particular emphasis on education. There are other issues, however, that affect a person's quality of life that may become confusing when the person also has a disability. In particular, history has shown that persons with moderate and severe disabilities may be denied a number of basic rights due to societal perceptions that devalue their lives and the difficulty they may have in communicating choices that affect their lives based on age, cognitive ability, or limited communication skills. The intent of the final chapters of this text is to provide information for those who serve as advocates for persons with moderate and severe disabilities and to highlight the process of self-determination.

In a number of cases, it is possible for basic rights to become entangled in ethical questions, and sometimes it is difficult to find clear-cut answers to those questions. This chapter will focus on three areas, in particular, in which basic human rights may be an issue in the lives of persons with moderate and severe disabilities. In each case much is revealed about how society has valued human life and worth in the past and how society continues to value human life and worth in a changing world. The following sections have been condensed to focus on (a) the right to sexual fulfillment, (b) the right to personal safety, and (c) the right to life. It is not the intent of this chapter to provide all of the answers to the questions that surround these basic rights; instead, these sections raise issues so advocates can be armed with information when involved in making decisions that affect the lives of persons with moderate and severe disabilities. The final chapter of this text will then focus on self-determination.

The Right to Sexual Fulfillment

Discussions of sexuality and persons with moderate and severe disabilities often evoke strong opinions and emotions. Conflicts may occur over permission for persons with mental disabilities to participate in sex education classes, to initiate and continue intimate relationships, and to exercise various forms of sexual expression (Hingsburger, 2004). One reason for this response is that society often views persons with moderate and severe disabilities as "eternal children" based on their cognitive ability and ignores that, as their bodies mature, they experience the same emotional attachments, physical responses, and sexual drives as persons without disabilities. Lesseliers and Van Hove (2002) stated that society holds two conflicting attitudes in regard to sexuality and disabilities. The first is that people with disabilities need to be protected from the sexual world, and the second is that the world needs to be protected from the sexuality of persons with disabilities. Irwin (1997) supported this viewpoint in acknowledging similar myths in which persons with disabilities may be viewed as not interested in or incapable of having sexual relationships or they may be viewed as overly interested in sexual acts to the point of being out of control.

Research has examined societal attitudes toward the sexuality of persons with mental disabilities. For example, Oliver, Anthony, Leimkuhl, and Skillman (2002) asked adults without disabilities to rate pictures of persons with and without mental disabilities engaged in various heterosexual or homosexual intimate behaviors in public and in private that included holding hands, kissing, having sexual relations, masturbating, getting married, having children, and using birth control. Across groups, the greatest difference between what was considered acceptable for persons without disabilities over those with disabilities was in getting married and having children. In addition, older adults tended to be more conservative in their ratings of the pictures in general than younger adults were.

The repression of sexuality in persons with disabilities has a long historical foundation, and it is not uncommon to continue to find supporters of involuntary sterilization. Stories of healthy sexual relationships between persons with moderate and severe disabilities are still novel enough to elicit coverage in the news or to be the subject of movies. For example, Adler (1998) reported on an emotion-filled wedding between two adults with Down syndrome in Missouri (see Example 13.1), and a made-for-television movie that aired in 2003 centered on the true story of the marriage of a couple who had been institutionalized for having cognitive disabilities ("'Normal' circumstances," 2003).

EXAMPLE 13.1 A Celebration of Marriage

The fact that the marriage of two persons with Down syndrome became a syndicated news story (Adler, 1998) is evidence that marriage between persons with moderate and severe disabilities is a novelty. The author of the story, however, noted that the marriage of Jim and Jodi was an example of an increasing trend in which persons with developmental disabilities establish lasting intimate relationships.

The romance between Jim and Jodi progressed in the way that most romances progress. Over a period of four years, they talked on the telephone, went bowling and dancing, and became known as a couple in the workshop where they were employed. Still, their families had to adjust to the idea when they decided that they wanted to marry. They had questions as to where they would live, if they were capable of independent living, if they would be able to resolve marital spats, and if they would be able to achieve sexual intimacy. Perhaps the most pressing concern was if they would be emotionally and physically capable of caring for a baby should a pregnancy occur.

To assuage these fears, the families helped when the couple moved into their own apartment more than a year before the wedding. Jodi's brother moved into an apartment in the same complex so he could act as a natural support. In addition, the families secured other supports that included social services, a driver, a shopping assistant, and an occasional cook. The anticipated problems arose, such as arguments over housework and turnover in support personnel, but nothing was insurmountable. In addition, after the families counseled the couple on birth control, Jim and Jodi chose to practice contraception rather than have children. This example is evidence that, with adequate planning and support, persons with developmental disabilities can participate in sustained intimate relationships that enrich their lives.

Historical Foundation

In recounting the history of sterilization, Brantlinger (1992) reported that, during much of the 20th century, half of the United States had laws allowing involuntary sterilization. For example, Indiana legalized involuntary sterilization in 1907 and did not repeal the law until 1975. Although involuntary sterilization was declared unconstitutional in the 1970s, many states continue to have laws that restrict sexual relations, marriage, and child-rearing by persons with developmental disabilities. Such laws have resulted from fears associated with **eugenics,** a theory that perpetuates the idea that persons with mental retardation will give birth to persons with mental retardation (Elkins & Andersen, 1992) and that mental retardation is associated with a number of societal woes, such as criminal behavior. Brantlinger (1992) noted that the problem of involuntary sterilization is exacerbated for those with developmental disabilities because persons with mental retardation, especially those with moderate and severe disabilities, are often in positions where decisions regarding their lives are made by others.

The 1927 case of Carrie Buck highlights the mind-set behind involuntary sterilization (Elkins & Andersen, 1992). Although she had not been deemed mentally incompetent, Carrie Buck was institutionalized after having given birth to a child out of wedlock and underwent involuntary sterilization based on an opinion issued by the U.S. Supreme Court that "three generations of imbeciles" (in the words of Chief Justice Holmes) was enough. (Later studies of Ms. Buck's life questioned whether she, in fact, had a disability.)

Data do not support the theory of eugenics. Ninety percent of persons with mental retardation do not give birth to children with mental retardation; in addition, 89% of persons with mental retardation are born to parents without mental retardation (Elkins & Anderson, 1992). In spite of these data, attitudes and values are difficult to change. Brantlinger (1992) made this point when she interviewed 50 persons (e.g., legal, medical, and social services personnel) involved with making decisions regarding sterilization for persons with mental disabilities and found that their attitudes were based on the values they held regarding sterilization, sexuality, and disabilities.

Even though sterilization of men is a simple, less costly, and possibly reversible procedure with few risks, sterilization tends to be a female issue because women most often bear the responsibility for birth control (Ferguson & Ferguson, 1992).

Although Elkins and Andersen (1992) acknowledged that there may be concerns over the parenting skills of persons with mental retardation, they suggested that sterilization should be considered as a last resort when other types of contraception are not feasible, giving consideration to a person's ability to make decisions, to engage in sexual activity and procreate, and to parent. They also noted that some procedures that are performed for other reasons, such as excessive menstrual bleeding and pain, may result in sterilization and that some medical conditions, such as epilepsy, increase risks involved in pregnancy and the use of contraceptives. In these cases the benefits of sterilization should be weighed against risks that include infection, hemorrhage, and fatal reaction to anesthesia, and, if used, sterilization should occur using the least invasive procedure possible; for example, tubal ligation should be considered before hysterectomy. Elkins and Andersen reported that most of today's judges are unwilling to make decisions favoring sterilization and noted that the *Relf v. Weinberger* case in 1974 resulted in a 30-day waiting period between the time of consent given by a person with mental retardation and the performance of the actual procedure.

Even if today's legal system is reluctant to allow involuntary sterilizations, families may view sterilization as a desirable when children have cognitive disabilities. For example, Fredericks (1992), the father of a son with Down syndrome, acknowledged that his son could not pass the test to drive a car but was capable of fathering a child. In addressing sterilization from the viewpoint of a parent, Fredericks stated the decision should be based on several considerations that include (a) how a parent with mental retardation would be perceived by the child, (b) how the child would perceive the parent's limitations when the child surpassed the parent's abilities, (c) whether the child would resent the parent, and (d) how the parent would deal with the child's resentment. It was Fredericks's contention that, even though persons with disabilities have the right to parent, it is often their parents or family members who must bear the responsibilities associated with unwanted pregnancies and inadequate care provided for grandchildren. (Later in this chapter, Example 13.2 will illustrate some of the problems that can be associated with inadequate parenting when a mother has mental retardation.)

Taking state laws into account, it seems appropriate that the decision regarding sterilization should be made by the individual with disabilities with input from family and medical personnel. Professionals in the field of disabilities, however, should be prepared to share information on services that may impact the final decision. Once that information is shared, as is the case with persons without disabilities, the ultimate decision should be respected.

Sex Education

While sterilization may appear to be a drastic form of birth control, it is viewed as a fail-proof way to prevent unwanted pregnancies, especially for women with disabilities who may be sexually victimized and for persons who, due to cognitive limitations or medical reasons, cannot practice other methods of birth control. The practice of relying on sterilization falls short, however, in addressing the problem of sexually transmitted diseases.

Sex education can provide an alternative to involuntary sterilization by addressing the core of the problem—the need to teach persons with disabilities how to diminish the chance of being victimized, how to use alternate birth control methods to prevent conception, and how to decrease exposure to sexually transmitted diseases. According to Blanchett and Wolfe (2002), providing sex education for persons with disabilities is a way to (a) prevent sexual abuse; (b) decrease the spread of sexually transmitted diseases, such as HIV and AIDS; (c) decrease unwanted pregnancy; and (d) increase appropriate sexual and social behavior. Abramson, Parker, and Weisberg (1988) noted that persons with mental disabilities who have been segregated, in particular, may demonstrate atypical means of sexual expression, such as public masturbation, and may need to be shown alternate or more appropriate means. In addition, sex education should focus on practices that facilitate emotional and physical well-being, such as maintaining good sexual hygiene and giving informed consent.

The practice of masturbation in appropriate places by appropriate means also should be given consideration in developing a sex education program in that this practice may alleviate sexual tension without the risk of unwanted pregnancy ("Developmental disabilities," 2005). Video materials are available for teaching appropriate masturbation to both females with disabilities (e.g., Hingsburger & Haar, 2000) and males with disabilities (e.g., Hingsburger, 1995).

One of the challenges in providing sex education for persons with mental disabilities is combating the idea that it is OK to have sex with anyone, a belief that puts persons at risk for sexual abuse and sexually transmitted diseases (Garwood & McCabe, 2000). Thus, sex education needs to include a focus on appropriate and inappropriate behavior within the context of different relationships (e.g., boyfriend, parent, stranger) and how to say "no" and report abuse. For example, the Circle Concept (Walker-Hirsch & Champagne, 1991) focuses on appropriate behavior with various circles of people (hug, handshake, wave, private, far away, and stranger circles).

The concept of sexual consent, in particular, may be difficult to teach since it involves both affirmative and negative responses and requires that the person giving consent understands the request, makes the response free of coercion, and is aware of the outcome (McAfee & Wolfe, 2000). In a survey, Kennedy and Niederbuhl (2001) found that 1,000 members of the American Psychological Association believed that the most important prerequisites to giving sexual consent included the ability to perform actions, such as saying "no"; making choices; selecting an appropriate place or time for sex; recognizing persons who pose sexual threats; and having the ability to understand outcomes, such as the possibility of pregnancy, over the ability to understand specific sexual information, such as terminology, preference, diseases, and the mechanics of performance and reproduction.

Because sex education covers skills that are critical for safety and are related to basic human rights, comprehensive sex education should be included on the IEPs of students with moderate and severe disabilities and should be taught by knowledgeable personnel using the best methodologies available (Wolfe & Blanchett, 2000). Furthermore, society cannot demand appropriate sexual behavior in persons with cognitive disabilities unless it has been taught (Whitehouse & McCabe, 1997).

In 2002 Blanchett and Wolfe noted an increase in published sex education curricula for persons with mental disabilities and conducted an evaluation of 12 specific curricula that included five curricula developed for persons with disabilities, five general sex education curricula, and two curricula specifically focused on prevention of sexually transmitted diseases and pregnancy published from 1988 to 1997 across the following variables:

1. Demographics—age, disability, and reading level of the target audience, as well as the recency of publication and cost
2. Goals and objectives—cognitive or affective, as well as measurable

3. Scope and sequence—prerequisite concepts, misconceptions about sex, and terminology addressed in a logical and sequential manner

4. Concepts—information included on biology and reproduction, health and hygiene, relationships, self-protection, and self-advocacy

5. Instructional methods—medium, format, strategies, and opportunity for evaluation included

6. Curriculum development and evaluation—testing and revision based on feedback, staff development and suggestions for collaboration, diversity of ability and ethnicity, and references included

7. Adaptations—applications for daily life included

Blanchett and Wolfe (2002) concluded that all of the curricula they evaluated would be appropriate for students with disabilities and suggested that teachers first determine the type of curriculum needed by students then match student needs to the content, that they pick and choose from various curricula or combine curricula when necessary, and that they use published curricula as a starting point in instruction and review and modify lesson goals, objectives, and activities, as needed. (Readers are referred to Blanchett and Wolfe for a list of the reviewed curricula that contains titles, publishers, and costs as well as specific evaluation results. Readers also are referred to Irwin [1997] for a list of additional resources on sexuality and disabilities.)

In addition to evaluating the content and format of curricula for appropriateness, it also is critical to evaluate its effectiveness with the participants who use it. Caspar and Glidden (2001) used a pencil/paper pre- and post-test with "yes" or "no" responses to measure changes in sexual values, opinions, attitudes, perceptions, and empowerment of 12 adults with mild and moderate mental disabilities who resided in a residential facility and participated in a sex education program. Specifically, the curriculum consisted of overhead slides, handouts, videotapes, and tests that covered sexually transmitted diseases, birth control, reproduction, and hygiene. The participants attended six sessions, each lasting two to three hours (a total of 16 hours). The evaluation results showed that the sexual knowledge and attitudes of the participants improved, and the authors noted that the participants voiced their appreciation for the program and were willing to rearrange their schedules to attend sessions. Although the curriculum appeared to be effective, their evaluation had the

---

ACTIVITY 13.1   Misunderstanding the Content of Sexual Curricula

A mother reported how her daughter with cognitive disabilities misinterpreted information she had received regarding unwanted sexual advances. The young woman had been taught several different bits of information. She knew that there were "good touches" and "bad touches," that touches could be sexual, that it was her right to say "no" to bad touches, that *rape* was a term to be used to describe the act of a person touching her body without her permission, that predators could be strangers, and that, if being raped, she could get help by yelling. The woman put all of this information together and overgeneralized it. Thus, when anyone touched her anywhere on her body,

even in an innocent way such as tapping her on the shoulder to get her attention, she screamed, "Rape!" and retreated in fear.

In considering this example, think about ways in which self-protection skills can be taught. How might "good" and "bad" touches be differentiated in a way that is clearer? How could the act of rape be made clearer? What other misconceptions did the woman have that could be taught in a different way? Would pictures or video be helpful? What about role-playing? How can self-protection be taught without making someone overly fearful and still ensure his or her safety?

limitation of being based on what the participants said instead of their actions. As illustrated in Activity 13.1, this can be a problem.

Garwood and McCabe (2000) used a more detailed process to evaluate the effectiveness of two sex education curricula with six men with mental retardation who lived at home. The evaluation instrument *(Sexuality, Knowledge, Experience, and Needs for People with Intellectual Disability)* consisted of 248 items presented across three comprehensive interviews per participant. The first curriculum, *Co-Care,* was taught during ten weekly two-hour sessions and covered feelings, body language, social skills, human life cycle, puberty, body awareness, private and public behavior, sexual relationships, conception, pregnancy and childbirth, contraception, menstruation, and protective behaviors. The second curriculum, *Family Planning Victoria,* was taught during six weekly one-hour sessions and covered self-awareness, feelings, body awareness, public and private body parts and behavior, relationships and friendships, protective behaviors, sexual relationships, contraception, and AIDS.

Evaluation results revealed that the men had minimal increases in sexual knowledge following participation in both curricula. Thus, Garwood and McCabe (2000) recommended that sex education curricula need to be simplified and time needs to be devoted to supplementing group instruction with one-to-one sessions. The results of this evaluation show that comprehensive interviews may be more revealing than yes/no, paper/pencil evaluations. Even interviews, however, rely on self-report and may not reveal whether participants will apply what they have learned.

When persons have more severe disabilities, formative evaluation measures based on observation may be preferable to summative evaluation measures based on self-report. Epps, Stern, and Horner (1990) reported an example of one-to-one instruction in which formative data demonstrated that three middle school students and one adult with severe and profound mental disabilities acquired and generalized the ability to perform menstrual self-care behaviors. Instruction consisted of the use of multiple exemplars of materials, such as thin and thick pads in various colors with and without stains, taught in a forward-chaining format. Through experimental analyses, they found that training using simulations on self was more effective than training using simulations on a doll. Although the procedure generalized to in vivo probes, maintenance was mixed. While this type of one-to-one instruction may be effective, it is limited by ethics to teaching specific types of skills, such as performing hygienic skills or putting on a condom, instead of acts of sexual expression.

The *LoveTalks* sex education program for adults with disabilities (Plaute, Westling, & Cizek, 2002) has taken a different approach by incorporating self-determination. The program consists of five sessions, each two to three hours in length, in which the participants discuss topics that they generate themselves, such as personal hygiene, sexual language, relationships, intimacy, birth control, and sexually transmitted diseases. The participants then follow through with special projects to put their discussions into practice, such as visiting a hospital to observe babies or meet with a gynecologist and taking steps toward establishing a relationship by hosting a singles party or placing a personals ad. The unique aspect of this program is that it can move from describing the mechanics of sex and reproduction to discussions of intimacy.

Sexual Support

There is a difference between offering sex education and offering the sexual support that is needed for intimacy. Sexual support involves facilitating social interactions that build friendships and intimate relationships and requires moral reasoning and sensitivity (Dukes, 2004). The drive for intimacy may be greater than the drive for sex and meeting a person's intimacy needs may be more important than meeting a person's sexual needs (Hingsburger, VanNoort, & Tough, 2000).

Lesseliers and Van Hove (2002) pointed out the need for sexual support when they interviewed 34 adults with mental retardation who lived in staffed residences and attended sheltered workshops. They found that these adults experienced a variety of conflicting emotions connected to their sexuality. For example, they experienced intimacy and desire without encouragement from staff or parents, they experienced guilt and disapproval in their relationships, they had painful confrontations that included sexual abuse, and they were denied the choice to marry or have children. Based on the interviews, the authors concluded the need for a higher degree of self-determination, space for privacy and intimacy in residential settings, changes in program practices to support human rights, sex education and counseling, and more respectful attitudes by parents and staff toward the sexual fulfillment of persons with disabilities.

The New York Behavior Management Services Sexuality Clinic is an example of services that have been expanded to serve persons with disabilities who have sexually problematic behaviors, such as sexual touching, public exposure and masturbation, and rape. Based on their experiences at the clinic, Hingsburger and his colleagues (Hingsburger et al., 2000; Hingsburger & Tough, 2002) have made a number of observations on the way programs for persons with disabilities fail to facilitate sexual expression and intimacy. For example, caregivers for persons with disabilities may contribute to sexual problems when they fail to promote healthy sexuality and intimacy or fail to correct misinformation. Acts of repression, such as making people feel that sex is "dirty" and limiting opportunities for privacy, may have undesirable results, such as persons with disabilities concluding that sexual acts should be performed in a public place (e.g., park) because they have been told not to perform them in a private place (e.g., bedroom).

Based on their work with adolescents with disabilities, Hingsburger et al. (2000) have a number of recommendations for parents of preteen children with disabilities, as follows:

1. Recognize that children are sexual beings.
2. Ensure that a child's circle of friends is age appropriate.
3. Increase supervision when sexual development begins.
4. Provide guidance (instead of medication or punishment) for budding relationships.
5. Be open to discussions on sexuality.
6. Respect dreams for the future (e.g., marriage and children, heterosexual or homosexual relationship).
7. Be sensitive to needs to conform to fashions and trends.
8. Be open to and support relationships between persons with disabilities (even in an age of inclusion).
9. Provide access to sex education classes and materials.
10. Remain calm when sexual activity occurs.

In working with adults, recommendations from Hingsburger and Tough (2002) include ensuring that (a) healthful sexual environments are facilitated by clear policies on sexual expression where persons can feel "whole," (b) trained staff view persons with disabilities as sexual beings, (c) persons with disabilities are encouraged to be self-advocates for sexual rights, and (d) relationship training focuses on intimacy as well as sexual acts.

Because gay sexuality has yet to be fully embraced by society, persons with mental disabilities who are lesbian, gay, or bisexual may experience discrimination based on both their disability and their sexual preference, causing sexual intimacy to be unattainable. This issue is illustrated in Example 13.2.

EXAMPLE 13.2 A STORY OF A FAILED RELATIONSHIP

Willard (2004) illustrated the impact that the repression of a sexual relationship can have on a person with disabilities when he recounted the story of two boys who grew up as friends in an institutional setting in the 1980s. As time passed, the boys began to experience love and sexual desire for each other. As young men, they acted on those feelings. When they were discovered by the staff, they were forbidden to have future contact with each other and were subsequently sent to separate facilities as a result of their behavior. While sexuality was forbidden in the institution, it appears that homosexuality carried even more of a taboo.

Based on this story, Willard, who lives in a residential facility and works in the disability community, recommended three "golden rules" for fostering intimacy for persons with disabilities. First, relationships between persons should not be patronized. Second, interactions should be facilitated when couples are attracted to each other. Third, privacy should be respected, and the relationships of persons with disabilities should be treated with dignity.

A TASH forum on gay sexuality and severe disabilities (Blanchett, 2002) reported that statistics on the general population most likely hold true for persons with disabilities. For example, 10% of the population is gay, and there is a greater incidence of suicide for students who are gay. Expressing sexual preference, especially same-sex preferences, is an issue with persons with disabilities because they may have limited communication skills and caregivers who have sexual biases. In addition, sex education curricula may focus on heterosexual sexuality, thus limiting options for sexual expression. To address these issues, Blanchett (2002) recommended (a) adopting sex education curricula that respect diversity; (b) being accepting of sexual expressions by persons, regardless of sexual preference; (c) including persons with disabilities in gay support groups; (d) providing diversity trainings for parents, teachers, and caregivers; (e) assuring that advocacy organizations have a gay voice; (f) conducting research on ways to support persons who are gay and have disability support needs; and (g) including persons with disabilities in research focusing on gay issues. (The reader is referred to Harley, Hall, and Savage [2000] who have prepared a basic foundation in gay issues and appropriate terminology to be used in discussing sexual orientation for service providers who need preparation in working with persons with disabilities who are gay, lesbian, or bisexual.)

Summary

The issues surrounding the right to sexual fulfillment by persons with disabilities are difficult and often accompanied by strong emotions. Families and other members of society sometimes have trouble recognizing that the need for sexual expression and intimacy occurs with physical maturation, regardless of cognitive limitations. Due to personal biases or fear, sexual expression may be repressed, often resulting in behaviors that are inappropriate and undesirable. Sometimes the good intentions of caregivers lead to less fulfilling lives for persons with disabilities. Overcoming historical biases and personal opinions is difficult, but sex education needs to be revised to include self-determination and support in the areas of sexuality and intimacy. In addition, the effectiveness of programs that focus on sexuality needs to be evaluated in ways that demonstrate changes in life style rather than self-reports of understanding sexual acts and should be individualized to meet personal needs rather than the general needs of the group.

Recognizing the right to sexual fulfillment raises a number of issues in working with persons with moderate and severe disabilities, and it may be difficult for families and professionals to provide appropriate support that is not limited by their own fears and values. Although the communication skills of persons with moderate and severe disabilities may not be adequate to voice sexual desires, the age when the performance of sexual behaviors begins is an indication that it is time for some type of intervention and that support is needed. This may be as simple as teaching a person to discriminate between appropriate and inappropriate settings for specific behaviors, such as masturbation, and as complex as enhancing the opportunity for lasting intimate relationships. This section has touched on just a few of the issues involved in ensuring that the right to sexual fulfillment is respected. However, it is clear that this is an area that needs to be addressed in greater detail for both children and adults with moderate and severe disabilities to enhance quality of life as well as to increase personal safety (as will be further addressed in the next section).

THE RIGHT TO PERSONAL SAFETY

All of us have the right to personal safety. That is, we have a right to be free from abuse and harm. As is true in the general population, persons with moderate and severe disabilities can be either victims or offenders or both. As illustrated by the case study of Ronai (1997) in Example 13.3, there are unique issues that arise with the presence of a cognitive disability. This section will address a number of those issues as they relate to both victims and offenders.

EXAMPLE 13.3 WHEN THE VICTIM AND THE OFFENDER ARE THE SAME PERSON

In sharing the experiences of growing up as the child of a woman with mental retardation, Carol Rambo Ronai (1997) illustrated the pain that can be caused when abuse is associated with a cognitive disability. Now a college professor, Ronai shared the graphic and disturbing story of a childhood in which she experienced both love and hatred toward her mother, Suzanne.

Carol's mother was a woman who delighted in playing with Barbie dolls with her daughter, who defended her daughter in childhood disputes by mooning other children, and who got the wrong answers when she tried to help her child with her homework. Suzanne was married to a man who was a rapist and a pedophile, who abused both Carol and her mother, and who was in and out of the penal system. Suzanne contributed to the abuse of her child by passively watching her husband perform sexual acts on Carol and failing to report this behavior to family or authorities. Her love for her child was evident in the small ways she tried to protect her, such as hiding the sheets when Carol wet the bed so she would not be punished by her father, but Suzanne's love for her child was not strong enough to cause her to leave her husband.

When Carol became courageous enough to report the sexual abuse herself, she found that her grandmother was angry because the embarrassing situation reflected negatively on her social status, and her mother was angry because she could no longer see her husband. In time, it was Carol who, although still a child, took on the responsibility of securing social services and benefits that she and her mother needed for survival. As the years passed, Carol grew up, obtained an education, married, became a mother, and pursued a career while refusing to maintain contact with Suzanne, who had become a stereotypical "bag lady." Although Carol was justified in her resentment toward her "mentally retarded" mother, it is important to remember that Suzanne also was a victim of emotional, physical, and sexual abuse.

Persons with Disabilities as Victims

The statistics on the abuse of persons with moderate and severe disabilities are difficult to measure since many cases may go unreported due to inadequate communication skills to describe what has occurred, inadequate cognitive skills to recognize abuse when it occurs, inadequate physical skills for self-protection, and the inability to come across as a credible accuser. A number of cases of abuse against persons with disabilities go unreported because caregivers are afraid of administrative reprisal and negative publicity or do not believe that authorities will act on their allegations (Sorenson, 2003). Those cases that are reported in the news tend to be heartbreaking. For example, Kocher (2004) and Matthews (2004) reported the case of a woman who was successful in arguing for denial of parole for her husband, who was incarcerated for abusing their child. The man had repeatedly beat his child about the head to stop her crying when she was an infant, leaving her with severe multiple disabilities (i.e., profound mental retardation, poor eyesight, limited motor skills).

In spite of the problems in gathering data, several authors have reported current statistics on the victimization of persons with disabilities:

1. Approximately 5 million crimes are committed against persons with disabilities in the United States each year (Sorenson, 2003).
2. Persons with developmental disabilities are four to ten times more likely to be a victim of financial, physical, or sexual abuse (Davis, 2000).
3. Fifteen thousand to 19,000 persons with disabilities are raped in the United States each year (Davis, 2000).
4. A survey in Oregon found that 70% of women with developmental disabilities had been victims of sexual assault by family, caregivers, or strangers, with 50% of the women experiencing repeated assaults (Dubin, 2003).
5. Only 3% of the sexual assaults against persons with disabilities are reported to authorities (Sorenson, 2003).
6. Fifty percent of persons with disabilities who are sexually abused report incest (Strickler, 2001).

7. Seventy-two percent of adolescents and adults with Fetal Alcohol Syndrome or Fetal Alcohol Effects have been victimized because they failed to recognize situations that put them at risk (Kelly, 2003).

8. Seventy to 90% of persons with disabilities who are abused report that it occurred prior to their 18th birthdays (Strickler, 2001).

9. Thirty-three out of 1,000 children in the United States are abused each year, and children with disabilities are four to ten times more likely to be victims of abuse (Strickler, 2001).

10. Children with disabilities experience 1.7 times more maltreatment (2.8 times more emotional neglect, 2.1 times more physical abuse, 1.8 times more sexual abuse, and 1.6 times more physical neglect) than children without disabilities (Vig & Kaminer, 2002).

11. Boys are 35% more likely to experience physical abuse than girls (Strickler, 2001).

12. Girls are 2.5% more likely to experience sexual abuse than boys (Strickler, 2001).

13. Ninety-nine percent of the offenders of women and children are known by the victims (16.8% family, 15.2% acquaintances, 9.2% service providers, 8.2% strangers, and 2.2% step-family; Strickler, 2001).

In addition to these statistics, there is evidence that persons with disabilities may become victims of abuse in settings, such as group homes or institutions, where they are dependent on others and lack the ability or opportunity to report mistreatment (Focht-New, 1996). As recently as 2005, The Arc of Illinois called for the closing of an institution housing 200 persons with disabilities following reports of deaths due to inadequate health care, abuse, and neglect; excessive use of restraints; failure to address life-threatening behaviors, such as pica; failure to provide protection from sexual assault; the absence of active treatment and programming; the lack of effective communication; missing documentation; and multiple uninvestigated injuries ("More deaths," 2005).

Strickler (2001) asserted that inadequate adaptive skills increase the likelihood of abuse and listed nine factors that put persons with mental retardation, in particular, at risk for being abused: (a) increased physical dependency on others, (b) denial of human rights, (c) low perception that abuse will be discovered, (d) lack of credibility, (e) lack of education about appropriate or inappropriate sexual behavior, (f) social isolation and tendency to be easily manipulated, (g) physical helplessness and vulnerability, (h) inclusion without self-protection skills, and (i) economic dependency on others. Strickler also noted that persons with mild and moderate mental disabilities may be more at risk than those with severe and profound disabilities because their reactive behaviors to the abuser may accelerate the cycle of abuse and because they may try harder to "fit in," making them vulnerable to sexual abuse. Other problems associated with mental retardation include the tendency to obey caregivers instead of challenging them and the fear of being left homeless or without a support network due to retribution from caregivers.

Strickler (2001) reported that persons with disabilities, and women in particular, are especially vulnerable to sexual abuse. Part of the problem can be attributed to the myth that persons with disabilities are asexual, to the repression of sexuality in persons with disabilities, and to inadequate or inaccurate sexual information that has been disseminated by peers.

Reporting crimes against persons with disabilities may be problematic for a number of reasons. According to Sorenson (2003), crimes against persons with disabilities result in low rates of police follow-up, prosecution, and conviction because the cognitive and communication skills of the victims make cases difficult to investigate and bring to trial. In addition, police may display unhelpful characteristics, such as disbelief, anger, and sarcasm.

Although persons with mental retardation may have trouble communicating the occurrence of abuse, symptoms of abuse may be manifested as a result of post-traumatic stress disorder (Pease, 2003). Symptoms of abuse may include aggressive, disruptive, or defiant behavior; self-injurious behaviors; agitation, jumpiness, or distractibility; insomnia; or depression. It is possible that some symptomatic behaviors may be mistaken for behavior problems. For example, a person experiencing flashbacks of an episode of abuse may be assumed to be having a hallucination. Women with disabilities who have been sexually abused may respond through social withdrawal or self-destructive behaviors and may be committed to a hospital setting with an inappropriate diagnosis (Strickler, 2001).

Vig and Kaminer (2002) have noted a number of considerations associated with children who have disabilities and abuse. In particular, children with disabilities may be especially vulnerable to maltreatment due to added stress on their caregivers. Family stress may result in physical, sexual, or emotional abuse. Factors that put families at risk for abusing their children include (a) family or parent characteristics, such as social isolation, attachment problems, substance abuse, mental illness, cognitive disabilities, or a previous experience of being abused; (b) child characteristics, such as temperament, personality, or physical traits; and (c) environmental factors, such as poverty, low level of educational attainment, low socioeconomic status, under-employment, or unemployment. As noted in Chapter 3, abuse can result from an interaction among various factors or as a result of a pile-up effect. The presence of a child with disabilities in a family may be accompanied by a need for physical care, increased medical appointments, financial problems, an inadequate support network, and a lack of information, resources, and respite.

Vig and Kaminer (2002) also noted that the consequences of childhood abuse follow children with disabilities into adulthood in ways such as a decrease in IQ scores or an increase in school problems (e.g., grade retention, dropout rates, suspension, expulsion). In particular, physical abuse may result in an increase in problem behaviors, such as physical aggression, and neglect may result in an increase in social problems, such as inadequate food, clothing, shelter, or medical treatment. Even if the child is not the direct target of abuse, exposure to domestic violence in families can be manifested in the child through anxiety, oppositional behavior, or depression.

While there is a clear potential for persons with developmental disabilities to become victims of abuse, there also are a number of practices that professionals can employ to address the problem. Strickler (2001) recommended intervention programs for those who are at risk for abuse or who have experienced abuse, including education on sexuality, abuse, and neglect. In addition, Strickler recommended requirements for service agencies to provide staff training in violence, sexuality, and mental retardation and to make sure that services are accessible, available, and appropriate for persons with mental disabilities.

Vig and Kaminer (2002) had a number of recommendations for working with children with disabilities, in particular. First, they suggested that professionals need to recognize various forms of maltreatment. For example, a lack of supervision can be neglect, and inappropriate disciplinary practices can be physical abuse. Second, professionals need to screen for developmental problems on a routine basis and refer children for comprehensive multidisciplinary evaluation when indicated. Third, professionals need to recognize the competencies of caregivers and provide guidance in implementing treatments as needed. Finally, professionals should be familiar with a number of resources (e.g., mental health, education, pharmacology) and monitor progress as interventions are implemented over time. (The National Association of Counsel for Children (2005) has recommended guidelines by Nathanson [2004] in interviewing children with disabilities who are involved in domestic violence.)

In dealing with post-traumatic stress disorder with persons with disabilities, Pease (2003) had several recommendations that included the following. Professionals should (a) work to strengthen coping strategies (i.e., actions that will make the person feel better), (b) provide information (e.g., explanation of symptoms and therapy), (c) use a soothing vocabulary (e.g., "I know you are scared, but I will make you feel safe."), (d) understand that correct words may be missing or misunderstood by the victims (See Activity 13.1 about "rape."), and (e) act as a "cognitive prosthesis" in role-playing both sides of an event to help a person think through responses.

One of the challenges in reporting abuse is in increasing the credibility and believability of the victim and in providing ways to improve communication. The use of detailed anatomical dolls and drawings can be dismissed as leading. Valenti-Hein (2002) investigated this topic by comparing the use of dolls and pictures to the use of a live model. She selected 30 adults with mild or moderate mental disabilities who attended sheltered workshops to participate in the investigation. She then showed each participant anatomical dolls and drawings as well as a live model on which blue stickers had been placed on specific body parts and asked the participants to place blue stickers on the same parts on their own bodies. There was little difference between verbal responses and responses using tools (e.g., dolls, stickers) for participants with mild disabilities, but those with moderate disabilities performed best with a live model. Thus Valenti-Hein recommended that live models may facilitate communication for persons with moderate disabilities who are involved in crime investigations.

In addressing violent crimes against women with developmental disabilities, Dubin (2003) recommended several steps to be followed in working with police that also can be applied to any victim. Immediately following the crime, the police should be notified, pictures should be taken of injuries, the mode of communication should be made clear, and a 24-hour contact number should be provided. During the police interview, compound questions (e.g., "Who were you with and what happened?") should be avoided and leading yes/no questions should not be asked. Finally, the appointment of an advocate is desirable because some women with developmental disabilities may attempt to hide an episode of abuse, especially if the offender is a person of authority, such as a family or staff member. Ward and Bosek (2002) reported that interventions that work for men may be ineffective with women and suggested that services implemented to promote safety for women with disabilities take place in an environment with a welcoming atmosphere, that discussions take into account that the women may have difficulty expressing feelings, and that activities be used in place of lectures. Ward and Bosek also described a program implemented with a women's group in Alaska that included teaching ways to say "no," responsible dating behavior, the difference between public and private talk, and safety rules in public places. They noted that, once information was taught, there was a need for community practice of the concepts that had been taught.

Lee and Tang (1998) described the Behavioral Skills Training Program, a sexual abuse prevention program for adolescent females with developmental disabilities. Topics included body ownership, private body parts, private touching and looking, appropriate reasons for touching and looking, forced touching, and responsibility. The program presents multiple exemplars of stories of appropriate and inappropriate touching as well as role-playing responses (say "no," walk away, tell someone). Lee and Tang evaluated the effectives of the program as it was taught in two sessions to 72 female adolescents in China and found that the participants acquired knowledge through the program and showed some maintenance in a two-month follow-up. Example 13.4 describes another safety program for adults with moderate and severe disabilities that illustrates some of the problems that may occur in regard to generalization.

EXAMPLE 13.4 TEACHING SELF-PROTECTION SKILLS TO ADULTS WITH MODERATE AND SEVERE DISABILITIES

One way to teach self-protection skills to persons with moderate to severe disabilities is through role-playing. As illustrated in the following example, however, teaching a skill to criterion does not ensure that generalization will occur.

Collins, Schuster, and Nelson (1992) taught three adults with severe mental retardation to resist the lures of strangers. To facilitate generalization across persons, they used an array of confederate "strangers" varying in age, gender, ethnicity, and physical characteristics. To facilitate generalization across lures, they varied the type of lure the strangers delivered to include general lures (e.g., offer a ride in a car), incentive lures (e.g., offer a snack), and authority lures (e.g., directive from supervisor). Finally, to facilitate generalization across settings, they conducted daily probe and instructional trials across a variety of community settings.

Each day a stranger delivered a predetermined lure in a predetermined setting. If the participant agreed to go with the stranger, the instructor interrupted the event and conducted three instructional trials in which the participant practiced saying "no" to the stranger and walking away. Although all of the participants reached criterion after several weeks of instruction, maintenance results were mixed and two of the three participants agreed to accompany a novel stranger during a novel probe in a novel setting.

In reflecting on this investigation (Collins, 1992; Collins, Nelson, & Ryall, 1992), the investigators noted that teaching self-protection skills to adults with moderate or severe disabilities that generalize is a difficult undertaking because they are likely to have history of being reinforced for going with strangers, such as medical personnel, related service personnel, instructors, and adult services staff. In addition, ethics prevent the instructional use of "scare tactics" in which the participants may experience emotional trauma.

It is crucial that caregivers never assume that the simple delivery of information or the simple teaching of a safe response will ensure that a person with a disability will generalize the information or response when it is needed. Safety programs must address and assess generalization if the safety of the participants is to be ensured.

Persons with Disabilities as Offenders

Just as persons with mental disabilities can be victims of abuse, they can act as offenders also. Current statistics include the following:

1. Nine percent of the general population commit sexual crimes while 10 to 15% of persons with mental retardation commit sexual crimes (Davis, 2000).

2. One percent of the general population engage in sexual misconduct while 12.5% of persons with mental retardation engage in sexual misconduct (Davis, 2000).

3. As of 2002, 44 persons with mental retardation had been executed for criminal acts (Keyes, Edwards, & Perske, 2002).

4. As of 1997, 11 of 40 states that have the death penalty had enacted laws against executing persons with mental retardation (Keyes, Edwards, & Perske, 1997).

Since these statistics reflect persons with all degrees of mental retardation as a group (i.e., anyone with an IQ below 70), it is difficult to determine the number of criminal offenders who have moderate and severe disabilities. Although there is no link between mental retardation and criminal behavior, certain characteristics of persons with moderate and severe disabilities may cause them to be vulnerable to participating in crime (Davis, 2000).

Persons with mental disabilities may participate in crimes because they can be easily persuaded, manipulated, or frightened into performing behaviors; because they want to please those in authority by complying with their requests; because they may not realize that some behaviors are unacceptable (e.g., being charged with indecent exposure for public urination); or because they are modeling behaviors they learned through being a victim of abuse (Davis, 2000; Keyes et al., 1997). The most frequent offenses performed by persons with mental disabilities are sexual in nature, such as indecent exposure or sexual assault; although this may be attributed to behavioral or cognitive reasons, sexual crimes also may be due to a lack of sex education and knowledge regarding appropriate means of sexual expression (Ward, Trigler, & Pfeiffer, 2001).

In a national survey of community service providers (Ward et al., 2001), 240 respondents identified the most common categories of inappropriate sexual behavior exhibited by persons with mental disabilities as (a) inappropriate sexual behavior in public, such as exposing genitals, masturbating, stripping, and engaging in consensual sex (92% of respondents); (b) inappropriate sexual behavior involving others, such as touching, grabbing genitals, rubbing against others, making unsolicited sexual requests and comments, engaging in voyeurism, fondling without permission, and stalking (63% of respondents); (c) sexual activity involving minors, such as engaging children to watch sexual behavior, soliciting children, masturbating to a child's picture, inappropriately touching a child, and molesting a child (63% of respondents); and (d) assaultive or nonconsensual sexual behaviors, such as nonconsensual intercourse or rape (51% of respondents). The respondents also reported the occurrence of additional categories, such as obsessive sexual behaviors (e.g., fetishes), high-risk sexual behaviors (e.g., prostitution), and inappropriate sexual stimulation (e.g., self-mutilation).

The survey conducted by Ward et al. (2001) also examined the issues in providing services to ensure community safety, with 74% of community service workers identifying close supervision (e.g., 24-hour supervision, low client/staff ratio) as the most frequent intervention, followed by behavioral interventions, such as contracts; mental health services, such as individual or group therapy; environmental interventions, such as alarms on doors; sex education; and legal sanctions, such as an offender registry. Staff issues (e.g., turnover) and gaps in service delivery (e.g., sex education) were only two of the reasons listed as problematic in addressing areas of community safety. Eighty-one percent of the respondents believed the services they provided were inadequate to deal with persons with disabilities who are identified as offenders; this was due to lack of expertise, as well as issues within the service system, lack of funding, and access to resources.

Once accused of or indicted in a crime, persons with mental disabilities do not fare well in the criminal justice system for a number of reasons. They are more likely to be arrested, to confess to crimes they did not commit, and to give incriminating evidence (Linhorst, Bennett, & McCutchen, 2002). In addition, they are more likely to be unjustly convicted and incarcerated for crimes they did not commit (Keyes et al., 1997). Once in prisons, they have trouble adjusting and tend to serve longer sentences due to breaking rules (Linhorst et al. 2002).

In analyzing the problem of persons with disabilities as offenders, several themes raise concern. First, a number of characteristics related to cognitive disabilities may play a part in the commission of an offense, such as failure to discriminate between appropriate and inappropriate behaviors. Second, some persons may be innocent and still confess to or be convicted of a crime because they want to please the accuser. Third, those who commit crimes may not understand what they did was wrong and may not fare well when incarcerated. Finally, service agencies may have a difficult time addressing the issues when persons with disabilities are identified as offenders. These concerns can be addressed in a number of ways.

First, persons with disabilities need education on safety issues, how to talk with police, and their rights as citizens (Davis, 2000). Second, services need to be established and funded to work with persons with mental disabilities who become involved with the criminal justice system (Linhorst et al., 2002). Third, police need to be aware of fair practices in interrogating persons with disabilities who are accused of crimes (Perske, 1991).

Behavior Risk Management is a model program that has addressed the needs of adolescent and adult males with disabilities who have a history of inappropriate sexual behavior (Ward & Bosek, 2002). The program has the following components: (a) weekly group meeting for identifying risk factors and developing coping skills, (b) sex education, (c) identification of high-risk situations, (d) weekly watching of tapes that focus on coping, (e) staff living in close proximity, and (f) environmental precautions, such as alarms on doors and windows, television viewing under staff supervision, screening of printed materials, random searches, and staff accompaniment in the community. Due to their behavior, the participants are forced to relinquish some of their personal rights; however, the strict components enable the participants to live within a community setting while protecting the rights of others. An example of a high school program initiated to prevent juvenile offenses by students with moderate to severe disabilities can be found in Example 13.5.

EXAMPLE 13.5 A PROGRAM TO PREVENT SECONDARY SCHOOL STUDENTS WITH MODERATE AND SEVERE DISABILITIES FROM COMMITTING JUVENILE OFFENSES

Two teachers who worked with students with moderate and severe disabilities in a secondary school setting found themselves with a dilemma when their students were involved in the commission of two offenses due to peer pressure from students without disabilities who attended their school. In the first incident, a student pulled a fire alarm at the request of peers, and in the second incident, a student dialed 9-1-1 in a nonemergency situation at the insistence of peers. In both cases the peers found the situations humorous and the students with disabilities were trusting and eager to please.

Instead of approaching the problem by punishing the peers without disabilities, the teachers involved peers without disabilities and a general education teacher in formulating a solution (Collins, Hall, Rankin, & Branson, 1999). The teachers first collaborated in identifying common peer pressures experienced by secondary school students without disabilities. They then used a procedure similar to the one described in Example 13.4 to teach the students with disabilities to resist peer pressure. Each day general education students acted as confederates in applying peer pressure to the students with disabilities in natural school settings. These were peers that the students knew through their inclusive speech class. If the students with disabilities succumbed to the peer pressure, one of the special education teachers intervened and, using a constant time delay procedure, assisted the student in role-playing an appropriate response of saying "no" and walking away. Over time, the students with disabilities demonstrated the ability to resist multiple exemplars of peer pressure that were harmful to their health (e.g., smoking), harmful to their achievement (e.g., skipping class), or harmful to others (e.g., stealing).

Summary

Everyone has a right to personal safety. Persons with moderate and severe disabilities, however, may be more vulnerable to harm than persons without disabilities. They may suffer abuse at the hands of family, friends, acquaintances, or strangers and not be able to communicate what has happened due to poor communication skills. If they are able to communicate, they may not be believed. In some cases, they may not comprehend that they are being abused or that the behaviors directed toward them are out of the ordinary. Thus, self-protection skills are crucial.

The same variables that contribute to victimization also play a role in persons with disabilities becoming offenders. Again, vulnerability may cause persons to perform criminal acts to please others. A lack of comprehension skills can result in a person innocently performing inappropriate behaviors without realizing that the behaviors are wrong or out of context. Educational programs are warranted to teach persons with moderate and severe disabilities to discriminate between appropriate and inappropriate behaviors. In cases where a person cannot discriminate, support is needed to ensure safety for those who might be victims and to ensure justice for those who may be offenders.

This section has touched on a few of the issues related to personal safety, with a special focus on abuse. Because this topic is so critical in the lives of persons with disabilities, the reader is referred to authors who have written full chapters or texts on this subject (e.g., Conley, Sgroi, Sobsey).

THE RIGHT TO LIFE

It is not uncommon to find examples in society where less value is placed on the lives of persons who deviate from the norm. This includes persons with cognitive or physical disabilities. The problem can be exemplified through the idea that changing the physical characteristics associated with Down syndrome will change how a person is perceived by society. Although a case can be built that reducing the size of the tongue can improve speech and breathing, it is more difficult to build a case that other cosmetic procedures, such as inserting chin implants and decreasing epicanthal folds in the eyelid, will improve quality of life by making children more accepted and less vulnerable to teasing. Two questions arise: (a) Do the possible outcomes justify the exposure to possible complications (e.g., severe sutures, infection, pain, potential aspiration) when the cognitive ability remains the same? and (b) Does the problem of acceptance rest with society or with the child?

Surveys indicate that the problem appears to rest more with the inability of parents to accept physical differences associated with Down syndrome than with the health-related or psychological experiences of their children (Goeke, 2003; May, 1988). The recent emergence of promising practices, such as the use of models with Down syndrome in children's catalogs and the marketing of dolls with the features associated with Down syndrome (Knight Ridder News Service, 2003; "The faces," 1998), reflect an effort toward accepting and embracing differences rather than trying to change them.

The example of the acceptance (or lack of acceptance) of physical appearances is illustrative of how society places less value on persons who are different. This applies to both physical and cognitive differences. In many cases the more severe the disability, the less valued the life. The following sections will examine various points at which decisions are made that affect the right to life for persons with disabilities. The first section will examine the historical practice of euthanasia following the birth of children with disabilities, and the second section will examine current issues regarding the right to life, including issues that arise prior to and following the birth of children with moderate and severe disabilities.

Historical Issues Affecting the Right to Life

Euthanasia is the practice of mercy killing and is based on the premise that the quality of life is so dismal for some people that death is preferable to life. Euthanasia can be **active,** in which an act of commission is performed to end a life, or euthanasia can be **passive,** in which an act of omission fails to sustain a life (Lusthaus, 1985). In the case of persons with disabilities, euthanasia may occur because lives are so devalued that cognitive factors, such as IQ or self-awareness, and physical differences, such as malformed limbs or cranial deformities, are considered justification for the termination of life.

A philosophy that the worth of lives could be measured was in place in Nazi Germany in the 1930s and 1940s when mass extermination practices began with those who had cognitive and physical disabilities and, in time, developed into a **slippery slope** that extended to include other groups of people whose lives also were determined to be of lesser value (Lusthaus, 1985; Powell, Aiken, & Smylie, 1982). Mostert (2002) identified the societal factors in Europe that led to the practice of genocide as (a) a scarcity of basic resources (e.g., food, heating) stemming from World War I that caused those with more severe disabilities to be considered "useless eaters" and (b) the rise of Darwinism and the eugenics movement in the 1920s that led to the concept that certain races were superior and should not be diluted by the reproduction of those with cognitive or physical disabilities.

The acceptability of euthanasia as a practice for terminating lives based on the presence of disabilities continued into the 1970s and 1980s in the United States, as exemplified by the case of Phillip B., whose parents requested that he not receive heart surgery to sustain his life because he had mental retardation as a result of Down syndrome (Powell et al., 1982); the case of Baby Doe, whose parents refused surgery to correct an esophageal feeding problem needed to sustain life because the child had Down syndrome (Schaffer & Sobsey, 1990); and the case of conjoined twins who were denied medical treatment and nourishment (Smith, 1989). Based on a series of legal cases involving euthanasia and cognitive disabilities, the Council for Exceptional Children adopted a position in 1988 that all children with mental retardation have the right to medical care and treatment needed to sustain their lives (Smith, 1989).

Coulter (1988) argued that euthanasia may be justified when there is no doubt that a disability will result in death, as in the case of infants born with anencephaly (i.e., absence of cranium and brain tissue), and advocated harvesting of organs as soon as death is certain as a way to save lives of other infants with life-threatening conditions (e.g., heart or kidney defects). Instead of harvesting organs prior to death (an act of active euthanasia), the infant would be allowed to live on a ventilator without other medical interventions until brainstem function ceased (an act of passive euthanasia). For parents who did not choose to terminate pregnancy due to the presence of anencephaly, this was a way to allow the death of their newborn child to result in life for others.

Perhaps the most compelling reasons for opposing euthanasia for children born with disabilities have come from cases built by persons with disabilities and their families. An analysis of 204 letters sent to Congress following the Baby Doe case (Turnbull, Guess, & Turnbull, 1988) revealed reasons that fell into the following categories: (a) the positive attributes of persons with disabilities, (b) the positive effects persons with disabilities have had on their families, (c) the guarantee of equal treatment under the 14th Amendment to the Constitution, (d) the sanctity of life, (e) the possibility of mistakes in diagnoses from the medical profession, (f) the inaccuracy of medical predictions, (g) the difficulty in drawing lines (i.e., slippery slope), and (h) the danger of repeating historical abuses.

Other professionals writing in the field of special education also have identified a number of factors that appear to play a role in the decision-making processes of families and physicians in making life-and-death decisions for children with mental and physical disabilities (Powell et al., 1982; Smith 1989). These include values systems regarding the sanctity of life, definitions of the quality of life, economics, parental rights, legal precedents, the emotional state of the family, and the intent to prevent suffering. With this in mind, Smith (1989) recommended that special educators be a voice of advocacy for children with disabilities, and Powell et al. (1982) urged adoption as an alternative for families who find themselves incapable of caring for a child with disabilities.

Current Issues Affecting the Right to Life

Since the 1980s ethical issues that relate to the right to life of persons with disabilities have continued to evolve. Advances in prenatal testing have resulted in life-and-death decisions being made prior to birth while the survival of children with complex health care needs have resulted in difficult decisions being made regarding the continuance of life. These issues are discussed in the following sections.

Genetic Testing   According to Mahowald, Verp, and Anderson (1998), 1 in 30 newborn infants has a major birth defect and 5% to 12% of pediatric hospitalizations are due to genetic conditions. New strides in prenatal testing and genetic counseling have allowed women to identify the likelihood or presence of disabilities and medical disorders in their unborn children.

It is a fact of life that all people do not place equal values on human life. Issues related to the right to life (and the right to reproduce) can be linked to eugenics, the belief that human characteristics are linked to single genes (Smith, 1994). For example, the Eugenics Special Interest Group, a small organization within the Mensa Society, whose members have IQs in the upper 2% of the population, recommended in 1991 that amniocentesis be routine for all pregnancies and that all pregnancies be terminated when Down syndrome is identified in the fetus. Since that time the Human Genome Project has been an international effort to construct a detailed map of human chromosomes ("Prenatal genetic screening," 1992–1994). In recent decades the Human Genome Project has mapped up to 100,000 human genes, an important endeavor in the field of mental disabilities since approximately 750 genetic disorders are associated with mental retardation (around one third of those with mental retardation), and lower IQs are more likely to be associated with genetic causes (Hodapp & Fidler, 1999).

The ability to link traits and disorders to genes raises a number of ethical issues. No one can dispute that the ability to identify and cure diseases at a genetic level could prevent a great deal of suffering and pain. Even if genetic diseases and disorders cannot be changed, genetic counseling may cause persons with increased reproductive risks to select adoption over natural pregnancy or to arm themselves with information prior to conception. The American Medical Association ("Prenatal genetic screening," 1992–1994) has identified a number of issues, however, that raise difficult questions. These include the following:

1. Will the ability to select and manipulate disorders and traits increase selective abortions of affected fetuses?
2. How much latitude should parents have in making choices about their offspring?
3. Should human genomes be altered? If so, for what reason (e.g., prevent diseases or genetic disorders, change cosmetic appearance, increase cognitive ability, change gender)?
4. Does the expense of altering human genomes justify the outcome? Will manipulative or preventative procedures be accessible to all or only to those who can afford them?
5. Will early-detection procedures lead to discriminatory practices, such as insurance denial, for those who refuse to have testing or refuse to abort affected fetuses?
6. Will parents who select to give birth to a child with a diagnosed disease or disorder suffer ostracism from society?
7. How can a slippery slope be avoided? Where will the line be drawn as to which traits or disorders should be changed or which diseases will be covered by insurance?
8. Will the role of the physician change from providing treatment to providing counseling and preventing outcomes?

In cases where women choose to abort a fetus based on prenatal testing, the type of disability appears to play a role in the decision-making process (Roberts, Stough, & Parrish, 2002), with abortion high for diagnoses that are linked to cognitive disabilities, such as Down syndrome and anencephaly, and low for diagnoses of physical conditions, such as gastro disorders and cleft palates or lips. While some disabilities seem to be more acceptable to society than others, there is a danger that decisions may be based on misinformation. For example, the perception may be that persons with Down syndrome always have severe cognitive disabilities when, in reality, most persons with Down syndrome have cognitive disabilities that fall in the mild or moderate range of mental retardation. This perception is illustrated in Example 13.6.

EXAMPLE 13.6 PRENATAL RIGHT-TO-LIFE DECISIONS BASED ON THE PRESENCE OF DOWN SYNDROME

Down syndrome occurs in about 1 in 1,000 births, with 4,000 to 5,000 babies with Down syndrome born each year (Poirot, 1998). Learning during pregnancy that the expected child will have Down syndrome is an adjustment and forces decisions on the right to life. Some parents choose to terminate the pregnancy, while others choose to give birth and either keep the child and put the child up for adoption. In a bestselling book, Beck (1999) wrote of her experiences when she was told that she would give birth to a child with Down syndrome while a doctoral student at Harvard in the late 1980s. At the time she could find few positive resources regarding the prognosis of children with Down syndrome and was pressured by professors, medical staff, and family to terminate the pregnancy. Beck, however, made the decision to give birth to her son and to work to dispel the myths surrounding Down syndrome. As illustrated in the following quotes from news articles, a variety of attitudes continue to exist regarding Down syndrome.

1. Mother who chose to abort a child with Down syndrome with the support of her husband, family, and priest:

   I've done things in my life that I have questioned, but, I truly believe that I made the right decision. I really have a very strong belief in fate and things working out for the best. Because if we had had that little boy, we would have never gone on for a third child and I would never have known my daughter. And that's the good I feel that has come out of that incident in my life (Breeze, 1997, p. 2).

2. Parents who chose to give birth to and keep children with Down syndrome:

   We have never ever regretted that he was born with an extra chromosome, that he's exactly the way he is.. . . . If I could wave a wand and make Conner different, I would not even consider it (Moore, as cited by Poirot, 1998, p. 3).

   We had a lot of support from our families and good health insurance and Grady is a sweet, quiet, precious baby, who hasn't had any of the major health problems associated with Down's. . . . We were prepared for a lot more difficulties (McGrew, as cited by Poirot, 1998, p. 3).

3. Doctor from Harvard Medical School, noting recent trends:

   There are a lot of people who want babies who need them, and babies with Down syndrome are in such demand there's a waiting list in most major cities. . . . I could find you a family in 15 minutes that want to adopt a baby with Down syndrome. That's a startling departure from 20 years ago" (Crocker, as cited by Poirot, 1998, p. 3).

Research has addressed the connection between attitudes, prenatal testing, and the continuance or termination of pregnancies when the fetus is diagnosed with a disability or medical condition. Bell and Stoneman (2000) focused their research on young adults who had not yet experienced pregnancy. Based on data collected from 166 undergraduate students across 19 disciplines, they found that the respondents were more likely to consider abortion when the fetus was diagnosed with Down syndrome than when the diagnosis was spina bifida or hemophilia. Those with more positive attitudes toward disabilities were the least likely to abort based on prenatal testing, but having a family member with a disability was not a determining factor. In addition, those who attended church were more accepting toward chronic illnesses than toward physical or cognitive disabilities. Pro-abortion reasons cited by 105 of the students included the negative effect a child with a disability or disease would have on the quality of life for the family.

Roberts, Stough, and Parrish (2002) focused their research on 69 women who were pregnant and at risk for giving birth to a child with a disability in determining the role of genetic counseling on the decision to continue their pregnancies. The results showed that the majority of the women sought counseling on the recommendation of their physicians or due to their age. Sixty-five percent of the women said they would terminate their pregnancies if the fetus had a diagnosed disorder (equal response for Down syndrome or spina bifida) and cited social reasons over medical reasons for making this decision; those who had access to resources, such as books and articles or genetic counseling, were more likely to continue their pregnancies.

The demand for genetic counseling is on the rise, with Mahowald, Verp, and Anderson reporting in 1998 that 3,000 health care professionals in the United States were certified in genetic counseling by the American Board of Medical Genetics or the American Board of Genetic Counseling. With the need for genetic counselors continuing to grow, a number of issues arise in relation to insurance policies, when and for whom genetic tests should be offered, the liability incurred when genetic counseling is not provided and children are born with disabilities, and the ability of genetic counselors to remain neutral while providing information.

Bowe (1995) suggested that the issues of prenatal testing and genetic counseling fall into three major ethical categories: (a) prenatal testing, (b) genetic engineering or manipulation, and (c) medical intervention. First, prenatal testing is not authorized under IDEA, raises issues about confidentiality and invasion of privacy, makes parents vulnerable to directive counseling (e.g., recommendation for an abortion) that may conflict with their personal and religious values, and may be confusing (e.g., What is meant by a 10% chance of Down syndrome?). Second, genetic engineering or manipulation has implications for whether funding will be directed toward preventing disabilities instead of offering special education services and raises issues as to whether a person has a right to a life without a disability. Third, medical intervention may be considered futile in certain genetic disorders (e.g., anencephaly), raising issues of discrimination if treatment is not offered based on quality of life.

The field of genetic counseling is a new frontier as the human genomes linked to disabilities are identified and new technologies for prenatal testing and genetic manipulation emerge. The Committee on Assessing Genetic Risks of the Institute of Medicine has recommended that (a) screening for genetic defects be contingent on evidence that screening is needed for detection and treatment, (b) testing be limited to disorders that can be cured or prevented, (c) confidentiality be breached in communicating with relatives only when there is a high probability of irreversible effects or fatality, (d) genetic carrier status be revealed only to a person's spouse with that person's permission, (e) legislation prevent insurance companies from taking genetic risks into account in providing coverage, and (f) legislation prevent companies from collecting genetic information that is unrelated to their employees' jobs (Mahowald et al., 1998). In addition, the American Medical Association has recommended that the criteria for conducting genetic screening include a clear benefit for the child and be equally available to everyone regardless of socioeconomic status; furthermore, the focus of genetic manipulation should be on curing diseases rather than changing cognitive ability or physical traits ("Prenatal genetic screening," 1992–1994). Finally, Bowe (1995) has recommended that multidisciplinary teams be assembled to give different perspectives when families are making right-to-life decisions during pregnancy. Although all of these recommendations are based on sound reasoning, it is unlikely that they will be accepted and put into practice without continued debate.

The ethics of genetic research becomes more positive in tone when the focus moves from debating the right to life prior to birth to enhancing the quality of life following birth. Sandon (2004) suggested that lack of health care has been an important factor in a recent increase in abortions in the United States and cited the case of a family that chose to continue with a pregnancy after the mother was exposed to rubella. The child was born with severe, multiple disabilities and a critical need for medical and educational services, placing a burden on the parents even though they viewed the child as a blessing. Sandon concluded that "The pro-life advocates must always keep in mind that life does not end at birth; the pro-choice people should be attentive to eliminating conditions that encourage abortion" (p. H4).

Hodapp and Fidler (1999) noted that the role of genetics in special education is growing as the Human Genome Project identifies specific genes that are linked to intelligence, language, personality, and behavior. Although it would be impossible to develop separate educational certifications or classes for the numerous etiologies related to moderate and severe disabilities, identification of traits that are linked to specific genetic syndromes may provide special education teachers with knowledge regarding characteristics that can and cannot be changed due to genetic factors and knowledge regarding characteristics linked to genetic factors that may be strengths that can be utilized in the educational process. Although this information may be useful, caution in placing too much emphasis on genetics is warranted due to (a) the role that the environment plays in the performance of children with mental disabilities that are genetic, (b) individual differences within classes of genetic disabilities, (c) causes of behaviors aside from genetics, and (d) changes in ability and behavior as children with genetic disabilities grow older.

Do Not Resuscitate Orders While professionals in the field of special education may serve as a resource for parents who are making decisions about the right to life while the fetus is in utero, their role becomes more involved once a child is born.

As explained in Chapter 9, special educators who work with children with moderate and severe disabilities may be confronted with a number of life-threatening medical conditions, some of which are linked to specific genetic disorders. When a child is considered to be medically fragile, one of the right-to-life issues teachers may face is whether or not to follow Do Not Resuscitate (DNR) orders.

DNR orders are written by a physician at the request of a child's guardian and specify that the teacher cannot perform CPR if the child goes into cardiac or respiratory arrest, an act of passive euthanasia. This poses several problems for the classroom teacher (Brown & Valluzzi, 1995). First, the teacher is forced to treat the child in a way that is different from how other students without disabilities are treated.

Second, the teacher may be found negligent of tending to the child's best interests if intervention is withheld and found guilty of practicing medicine without a license if treatment is provided. Third, any death of a child within a classroom setting is traumatic for those in the classroom environment, but even more so if students observe the teacher doing nothing to save the child's life. Fourth, deliberate refusal to honor DNR orders may be viewed as violating freedom of choice for the parents (and possibly the child, if the child has had input into the decision). Fifth, honoring DNR orders may cause the teacher to violate personal religious and ethical beliefs in regard to the right to life.

It is crucial that school districts establish policies concerning DNR orders and make this clear to parents and guardians. The American Academy of Pediatrics (Committee on School Health and Committee on Bioethics, 2000) has recommended the following protocol for pediatricians who have received a request from a family to write DNR orders. First, pediatricians, families, and school officials (e.g., nurse, teacher, administrators) should meet to discuss and come to an agreement on in-school medical intervention. This process should be conducted in an atmosphere of negotiation and compromise, and the final outcome should be reviewed by the board of education and legal counsel, with continued reviews and revisions every six months. The pediatrician and school district should then work with local emergency medical services regarding how intervention should be implemented. In addition, the pediatrician should assist the school in developing age-appropriate materials for students regarding death and dying and should be available to assist the teacher if the DNR orders are accepted.

According to Brown and Valluzzi (1995), one option for teachers is to notify a health care professional when the decision to fulfill a DNR order must be made and to allow that person to make the ultimate decision. If DNR orders are accepted, documentation from the physician and the parents or guardians needs to be included on the IFSP or IEP. If the DNR orders are denied, the district needs to inform the parents or guardians of this decision in writing and an emergency plan needs to be in place for dealing with the medical care of the student. Regardless of the decision, the staff need training on appropriate procedures.

It goes without saying that the death of a child in the school setting is a traumatic experience for both staff and students and can occur even in cases where it was not anticipated. In the case of accepting DNR orders, however, advance preparation is crucial in lessening the trauma associated with death and should include (a) the designation of a site away from the classroom where the body can be placed until appropriate personnel arrive (e.g., medical examiner, coroner), (b) arrangements with local emergency medical services for transporting the body, (c) verification that DNR orders will be executed in compliance with the law (e.g., child will wear a bracelet with DNR orders), (d) designation of a mortuary by the family if they cannot be reached, and (e) use of a vehicle on school grounds that does not resemble a hearse ("Do-Not-Resuscitate orders," 2000).

Summary

The ethics of right-to-life decisions continues in the 21st century. Although mass genocide of persons with disabilities is no longer practiced, cases of euthanasia based on disabilities still make the news. For example, Lannen (2003) reported a murder-suicide in which a mother chose to take her own life and the life of her

22-year-old daughter with cognitive disabilities when caregiving responsibilities became too difficult for her to manage.

More recently, the case of Terri Schiavo attracted a great deal of attention from the community of persons with disabilities, many of whom argue that Ms. Schiavo was put to death because she had a disability (brain injury) in direct violation of the rights ensured under the Americans with Disabilities Act (Stothers, 2005). The Web site of the U.S. disability rights group Not Dead Yet contains multiple similar stories of people with disabilities and their families who continue to worry about the practice of involuntary euthanasia and its effect on their right to life. Based on the assumption that having the right to make decisions regarding one's own mortality is in opposition to having that decision made by others, Not Dead Yet has recommended the adoption of a series of safeguards for persons with disabilities ("Eight things," 2005).

While science has been responsible for a wide range of improvements in the lives of persons with disabilities, science has also opened the doors on a number of ethical issues in regard to the right to life of persons with disabilities. According to Mostert (2002), there are a number of implications for professionals. First, professionals need to remain informed on current advances in science and technology and should recognize that the media may be either a positive or a negative influence on practices. Once armed with reliable information, professionals then should serve as advocates in maintaining the value of persons with disabilities that may be diminished by research and in working with medical professionals and families who are making decisions regarding the right to life.

Best Practices
Difficult Issues Regarding Human Rights

1. Recognize that persons with moderate and severe disabilities may need someone who is prepared to advocate for their human rights when they are incapable of doing this in an effective manner.

2. In advocating for the right to sexual fulfillment, consider the need for both sex education and sexual support, remembering that need for intimacy is often overlooked.

3. Recognize that personal characteristics, such as vulnerability, that are associated with moderate and severe disabilities can increase the likelihood of victimization as well as being identified as an offender.

4. Remain informed of current research in the field of genetics, and be aware of ensuing policies that may jeopardize the basic right to life of persons with disabilities.

5. Once you have shared information in a nonjudgmental manner, be respectful of the decisions made by persons with disabilities or their caregivers that may differ from your personal value system.

Conclusion

This chapter has examined historical foundations and ethical issues related to persons with moderate and severe disabilities across three basic human rights: (a) the right to sexual fulfillment, (b) the right to personal safety, and (c) the right to life.

The intent of this chapter was not to provide answers to difficult questions, but to raise awareness of the need for information in those who advocate for persons with disabilities. Advocacy by professionals is important enough that the Council for Exceptional Children has included advocacy in the standards for special educators (Gartin, Murdick, Thompson, & Dyches, 2002). In particular, the Council for Exceptional Children has stated that special educators should advocate for their students through speaking, writing, and actions, yet Gartin et al. found that special education teachers are in need of advocacy training and fear personal and professional risks if they participate in advocacy activities. In recognition of the need for advocacy for basic human rights in a changing world, the previous best practices were offered.

Questions for Review

1. How have the terms *slippery slope* and *eugenics* been applied in the history of persons with disabilities?
2. Why is it difficult to evaluate the effectiveness of sex education and self-protection programs that are taught to persons with disabilities?
3. In what ways may persons with moderate and severe disabilities be more vulnerable to victimization than persons without disabilities?
4. What characteristics might cause a person with moderate or severe disabilities to be falsely identified as an offender?
5. What is the difference between sex education and sexual support? How can opportunities for intimacy be enhanced?
6. What ethical issues regarding disabilities are raised with the advent of the Human Genome Project?
7. What are DNR orders and how should school districts respond to them?
8. What are signs that a person with a disability may have been a victim of abuse?

Performance-Based Assessment

Professionals often find themselves in situations where they are asked to intervene in the lives of persons with disabilities in a supportive and nonjudgmental manner. Select one of the following scenarios and tell what interventions might be appropriate.

1. Robbie is an 8-year-old child with a moderate mental disability who has asked his teacher about explicit sexual acts. When the teacher asked him how he was aware of these acts, he confided that he saw them when he was watching television with his parents.
2. Steve is a 10-year-old child with autisticlike behaviors. He was abused by his natural parents before being placed in a foster home. The abuse resulted in broken bones and cigarette burns. Steve now spends time in class drawing pictures of fire and weapons and destroys classroom materials by throwing them or stomping on them.
3. Fred is a 12-year-old adolescent with a moderate mental disability who lives with a large extended family in a remote geographical setting. He often makes

obscene gestures in the classroom setting and was stopped by the teacher when he was discovered simulating a sexual act in the back of the classroom with a female student who also had a moderate mental disability.

4. Brenda is a 13-year-old adolescent with a moderate mental disability who lives in poverty conditions with her extended family. Her brother recently was released from prison, where he served a sentence for attempting to kill a law officer. Brenda has come to school and confided in the paraprofessional that she is excited because her brother has promised to help her make a baby.

5. Betsey and Ron are 16 and 18 years old, respectively. They both have a moderate mental disability. They like to tell classmates and school staff that they are in love and want to get married. When they have the opportunity, they hold hands with each other.

References

Abramson, P. R., Parker, T., & Weisberg, S. R. (1988). Sexual expression of mentally retarded people: Educational and legal implications. *American Journal on Mental Retardation, 93,* 328–334.

Adler, E. (1998, Oct. 18). Jim, Jodi's wedding is a sign of change. *Lexington Herald-Leader,* pp. J1–2.

Beck, M. (1999). *Expecting Adam.* New York: Random House.

Bell, M., & Stoneman, Z. (2000). Reactions to prenatal testing: Reflection of religiosity and attitudes toward abortion and people with disabilities. *American Journal on Mental Retardation, 105,* 1–13.

Blanchett, W. J. (2002). Voices from a TASH forum on meeting the needs of gay, lesbian, and bisexual adolescents and adults with severe disabilities. *Research & Practice for Persons with Severe Disabilities, 27,* 82–86.

Blanchett, W. J., & Wolfe, P. S. (2002). A review of sexuality education curricula: Meeting the sexuality education needs of individuals with moderate and severe intellectual disabilities. *Research & Practice for Persons with Severe Disabilities, 27,* 43–57.

Bowe, F. G. (1995). Ethics in early childhood special education. *Infants and Young Children, 7* (3), 28–37.

Brantlinger, E. (1992). Professionals' attitudes toward the sterilization of people with disabilities. *Journal of the Association for Persons with severe Handicaps, 17,* 4–18.

Breeze, P. (1997). A woman's choice (p. 2). *Roe v. Wade.* Lexington, KY: Lexington Planned Parenthood Center.

Brown, S. E., & Valluzzi, J. L. (1995). Do not resuscitate orders in early intervention settings: Who should make the decision? *Infants and Young Children, 7,* 13–27.

Caspar, L. A., & Glidden, L. M. (2001). Sexuality education for adults with developmental disabilities. *Education and Training in Mental Retardation and Developmental Disabilities, 36,* 172–177.

Collins, B. C. (1992). Reflections on "Teaching a generalized response to the lures of strangers to adults with severe handicaps." *Exceptionality, 3,* 117–120.

Collins, B. C., Hall, M., Rankin, S. W., & Branson, T. A. (1999). Just say "No!" and walk away: Teaching students with mental disabilities to resist peer pressure. *Teaching Exceptional Children, 31,* 48–52.

Collins, B. C., Nelson, C. M., & Ryall, C. (1992). Challenges to generalization in adults with severe disabilities. In R. B. Rutherford, Jr. & S. R. Mathut (Eds.), *Severe Behavior Disorders of Children and Youth*, vol. 15, pp. 116–124. Reston, VA: Council of Children with Behavioral Disorders.

Collins, B. C., Schuster, J. W., & Nelson, C. M. (1992). The in vivo use of a constant time delay procedure and multiple exemplars to teach a generalized response to the lures of strangers to adults with mental handicaps. *Exceptionality, 3,* 67–80.

Committee on School Health and Committee on Bioethics. (2000). Do not resuscitate orders in schools. *Pediatrics, 105,* 878–879.

Coulter, D. L. (1988). Beyond Baby Doe: Does infant transplantation justify euthanasia? *Journal of the Association for Persons with Severe Handicaps, 13,* 71–75.

Davis, L. A. (2000). Serious issues facing today's victim and offender with mental retardation. *TASH Newsletter, 26* (8), 14–16.

Developmental disabilities and puberty (2005). Planned Parenthood of Connecticut, Inc. Retrieved July 5, 2005, from www.ppct.org/education/resources/ddpuberty.htm.

Do-Not-Resuscitate orders for medically fragile students (2000). *School Nurse.* Retrieved September 6, 2004, from www.schoolnurse.com/med_info/drno.html

Dubin, M. (2003). Violence against women with disabilities. *TASH Connections, 29* (8/9), 34–35.

Dukes, C. (2004). Making social relationships an integral part of sex education. *TASH Connections, 30* (7/8), 14–17.

Eight things that need to happen to safeguard against non-voluntary euthanasia in the U.S. (2005). Not Dead Yet Web site. Retrieved July 5, 2005, from www.notdeadyet.org/docs/drmwants0305.html.

Elkins, T. E., & Andersen, H. F. (1992). Sterilization of persons with mental retardation. *Journal of the Association for Persons with Severe Handicaps, 17,* 19–26.

Epps, S., Stern, R. J., & Horner, R. H. (1990). Comparison of simulation training on self and using a doll for teaching generalized menstrual care to women with severe mental retardation. *Research in Developmental Disabilities, 11,* 37–66.

Ferguson, P. M., & Ferguson, D. L. (1992). Reader response: Sex, sexuality, and disability. *Journal of the Association for Persons with Severe Handicaps, 17,* 27–28.

Focht-New, V. (1996). Beyond abuse: Treatment approaches for people with disabilities. *Mental Health Nursing, 17,* 427–438. Retrieved July 5, 2005, from http://greg.quuxuum.org/journal/focht_new.html.

Fredericks, B. (1992). Reader response: A parent's view of sterilization. *Journal of the Association for Persons with Severe Handicaps, 17,* 29–30.

Gartin, B. C., Murdick, N. L., Thompson, J. R., & Dyches, T. T. (2002). Issues and challenges facing educators who advocate for students with disabilities. *Education and Training in Mental Retardation and Developmental Disabilities, 37,* 3–13.

Garwood, M., & McCabe, M. P. (2000). Impact of sex education programs on sexual knowledge and feelings of men with a mild intellectual disability. *Education and Training in Mental Retardation and Developmental Disabilities, 35,* 269–283.

Goeke, J. (2003). Parents speak out: Facial surgery for children with Down syndrome. *Education and Training in Developmental Disabilities, 38,* 323–333.

Harley, D. A., Hall, M., & Savage, T. A. (2000). Working with gay and lesbian consumers with disabilities: Helping practitioners understand another frontier of diversity. *Journal of Applied Rehabilitation Counseling, 31,* 4–11.

Hingsburger, D. (1995). *Hand made love: A guide for teaching about male masturbation through understanding and video.* Eastman, Quebec: Diverse City Press.

Hingsburger, D. (2004). Sexuality conflict. *TASH Connections, 30* (7/8), 26–27.

Hingsburger, D., & Haar, S. (2000). *Finger tips: Teaching women with disabilities about masturbation through understanding and video.* Eastman, Quebec: Diverse City Press.

Hingsburger, D., & Tough, S. (2002). Healthy sexuality: Attitudes, systems, and policies. *Research & Practice for Persons with Severe Disabilities, 27,* 8–17.

Hingsburger, D., VanNoort, D. S., & Tough, S. (2000). But I thought . . . Sexuality and teens with developmental disabilities. *TASH connections, 26* (5), 8–11.

Hodapp, R. M., & Fidler, D. J. (1999). Special education and genetics: Connections for the 21st century. *Journal of Special Education, 33,* 130–137.

Irwin, M. M. (1997). *Sexuality and people with disabilities.* Bloomington, IN: Center for Disability Information & Referral, Institute for the Study of Developmental Disabilities. Retrieved September, 6, 2004, from www.iidc.indiana.edu/cedir/sexuality.html

Kelly, K. A. (2003). The victimization of individuals with Fetal Alcohol Syndrome/Fetal Alcohol Effects. *TASH Connections, 29* (8/9), 29–30.

Kennedy, C. H., & Niederbuhl, J. (2001). Establishing criteria for sexual consent capacity. *American Journal on Mental Retardation, 106,* 503–510.

Keyes, D., Edwards, W., & Perske, R. (1997). People with mental retardation are dying, legally. *Mental Retardation, 35,* 59–63.

Keyes, D., Edwards, W., & Perske, R. (2002). People with mental retardation are dying, legally: At least 44 have been executed. *Mental Retardation, 40,* 243–244.

Knight Ridder News Service (2003, February 4). Down syndrome dolls help children identify. *Lexington Herald-Leader,* p. E8.

Kocher, G. (2004, May 2). It's the victim who got a 'life sentence.' *Lexington Herald-Leader,* pp. A1, A4–5.

Lannen, S. (2000, March 7). Mother, daughter found dead in home: Property manager discovers apparent murder-suicide. *Lexington Herald-Leader,* p. B4.

Lee, Y. K., & Tang, C. S. (1998). Evaluation of a sexual abuse prevention program for female Chinese adolescents with mild mental retardation. *American Journal on Mental Retardation, 103,* 105–116.

Lesseliers, J., & Van Hove, G. (2002). Barriers to the development of intimate relationships and the expression of sexuality among people with developmental disabilities: Their perceptions. *Research & Practice for Persons with Severe Disabilities, 27,* 69–81.

Linhorst, D. M., Bennett, L., & McCutchen, T. (2002). Development and implementation of a program for offenders with developmental disabilities. *Mental Retardation, 40,* 41–50.

Lusthaus, E. (1985). "Euthanasia" of persons with severe handicaps: Refuting the rationalizations. *Journal of the Association for Persons with Severe Handicaps, 10,* 87–94.

Mahowald, M. B., Verp, M. S., & Anderson, R. R. (1998). Genetic counseling: Clinical and ethical challenges. *Annual Review of Genetics, 32,* 547–559.

Matthews, P. (2004, May 5). Father of abused child denied parole: Mother of invalid girl, 10, speaks at hearing. Lexington, KY: *Lexington Herald-Leader,* pp. A1, A7.

May, D. C. (1988). Plastic surgery for children with Down syndrome: Normalization or extremism? *Mental Retardation, 26,* 17–19.

McAfee, J. K., & Wolfe, P. (2000). Individuals with significant disabilities and consent to sexual activity. *TASH Newsletter, 26* (5), 33–35.

McCabe, M. P. (1994). Sexual knowledge, experience and needs scale for people with intellectual disability (Sex Ken-ID) (4th Edition). Melbourne: Psychology Research Centre, Deakin University.

More deaths and abuse in Illinois institutions (2005). Equip for equality calls for the closure of the Choate Developmental Center. The Arc of Illinois Web site. Retrieved July 5, 2005, from www.thearcofil.org/document.asp?did=114.

Mostert, M. P. (2002). Useless eaters: Disability as genocidal marker in Nazi Germany. *The Journal of Special Education, 36,* 155–168.

Nathanson, R. (2004). Interviewing children with disabilities. *Children's Law Manual, 31.*

National Association of Counsel for Children (2005). Training and Technical assistance: Children's law manuals. Retrieved July 5, 2005, from http://naccchildlaw.org/training/manuals.html.

'Normal' circumstances. (2003, February 9). Your Sunday. *Lexington Herald-Leader,* p. A2.

Oliver, M. N., Anthony, A., Leimkuhl, T. T., & Skillman, G. D. (2002). Attitudes toward acceptable socio-sexual behaviors for persons with mental retardation: Implications for normalization and community integration. *Education and Training in Mental Retardation and Developmental Disabilities, 37,* 193–201.

Pease, T. (2003). Helping people who have been hurt: Adaptations to cognitive therapies for people with developmental disabilities and post traumatic stress disorder. *TASH Connections, 29* (8/9), 16–19.

Perske, R. (1991). Unequal Justice? What can happen when people with retardation or other developmental disabilities encounter the criminal justice system. Nashville, TN: Abingdon Press.

Plaute, W., Westling, D. L., & Cizek, B. (2002). Sexuality education for adults with cognitive disabilities in Austria: Surveys of attitudes and the development of a model program. *Research & Practice for Person with Severe Disabilities, 27,* 58–68.

Poirot, C. (1998, November 3). A trend toward life: More parents choosing to keep, raise children born with Down syndrome. *Lexington Herald-Leader,* p. 3.

Powell, T. H., Aiken, J. M., & Smylie, M. A. (1982). Treatment or involuntary euthanasia for severely handicapped newborn: Issues of philosophy and public policy. *Journal of the Association for Persons with Severe Handicaps, 6,* 3–10.

Prenatal Genetic Screening (1992–1994). American Medical Association, CEJA Report D-I-92.

Roberts, C. D., Stough, L. M., & Parrish, L. H. (2002). The role of genetic counseling in the elective termination of pregnancies involving fetuses with disabilities. *The Journal of Special Education, 36,* 48–55.

Ronai, C. R. (1997). On loving and hating my mentally retarded mother. *Mental Retardation, 35,* 417–432.

Sandon, L. (2004, November 13). Abortion debate is about more than ending pregnancies. *Lexington Herald-Leader,* pp. H1, H4.

Schaffer, J., & Sobsey, D. (1990). A dialogue on medical responsibility. In L. H. Meyer, C. A. Peck, & L. Brown (Eds.), *Critical Issues in the Lives of People with Severe Disabilities* (pp. 601–606). Baltimore: Brookes.

Smith, J. D. (1989). On the right of children with mental retardation to life sustaining medical care and treatment: A position statement. *Education and Training in Mental Retardation, 24,* 3–6.

Smith, J. D. (1994). Reflections on mental retardation and eugenics, old and new: Mensa and the Human Genome Project. *Mental Retardation, 32,* 234–238.

Sorenson, D. D. (2003). Invisible victims – 2003. *TASH Connections, 29* (8/9), 31–33.

Stothers, W. G. (2005). Why Schiavo case worries the disabled. *The Toronto Star.* Retrieved July 5, 2005, from www.thestar.com/NASApp/cs/ContentServer?

pagename=thestar/Layout/Article_Type1&c=Article&cid=1111704609865&call_pagei
d=968256290204&col=968350116795.

Strickler, H. L. (2001). Interaction between family violence and mental retardation. *Mental Retardation, 39,* 461–471.

The faces of Down syndrome are reflected in new line of dolls (1998, spring). For disabled children. *Counterpoint,* p. 11.

Turnbull, H. R., Guess, D., & Turnbull, A. P. (1988). Vox populi and Baby Doe. *Mental Retardation, 26,* 127–132.

Valenti-Hein, D. (2002). Use of visual tools to report sexual abuse for adults with mental retardation. *Mental Retardation, 40,* 297–303.

Vig, S., & Kaminer, R. (2002). Maltreatment and developmental disabilities in children. *Journal of Developmental and Physical Disabilities, 14,* 371–386.

Walker-Hirsch, L., & Champagne, M. P. (1991). The circles concept: Social competence in special education. *Educational Leadership, 49,* 65–67.

Ward, K. M., & Bosek, R. L. (2002). Behavioral risk management: Supporting individuals with developmental disabilities who exhibit inappropriate sexual behaviors. *Research & Practice for Persons with Severe Disabilities, 27,* 27–42.

Ward, K. M., Trigler, J. S., & Pfeiffer, K. T. (2001). Community services, issues, and service gaps for individuals with developmental disabilities who exhibit inappropriate sexual behaviors. *Mental Retardation, 39,* 11–19.

Whitehouse, M. A., & McCabe, M. P. (1997). Sex education programs for people with intellectual disability: how effective are they? *Education and Training in Mental Retardation and Developmental Disabilities, 32,* 229–240.

Willard, E. (2004). Respecting, supporting and honoring the sexuality of all people. *TASH Connections, 30* (7/8), 18–19.

Wolfe, P. S., & Blanchett, W. J. (2000). Moving beyond denial, suppression and fear to embracing the sexuality of people with disabilities. *TASH Newsletter, 26* (5), 5–7.

CHAPTER FOURTEEN

FACILITATING THE FUTURE:
Self-Determination

On completion of this chapter, the reader will meet the following objectives:

- Define the term *self-determination* as it applies to the lives of persons with moderate and severe disabilities.

- Describe ways in which self-determination can be incorporated in the education of students with moderate and severe disabilities.

- Describe ways in which preferences can be determined with persons who have diminished cognitive skills and limited communication skills.

- Describe how persons with moderate and severe disabilities can be taught to indicate choices.

Chapter 13 examined three basic human rights that affect quality of life and raise a number of ethical issues in the field of special education, especially in regard to persons with moderate and severe disabilities. These included the right the sexual fulfillment, the right to personal safety, and the right to life. This chapter will explore another human right that also affects the quality of life for persons with moderate and severe disabilities—the right to self-determination.

Chapter 1 set the foundation for this text by describing a shift in paradigms in special education from facility based to services based to supports based to empowerment (Polloway, Smith, Patton, & Smith, 1996). Empowerment is based on the premise that all persons have the right to make choices in their lives instead of having those choices made for them. This includes the right to make poor choices as well as good choices. In a classic position paper, Bannerman, Sheldon, Sherman, and Harchik (1990) focused on "the rights of people with developmental disabilities to eat too many doughnuts and take a nap" (p. 79) when they explored the basic right to personal liberties. At the time they published their article, the authors noted that service providers tended to choose goals and instructional procedures, determine schedules, and regulate access to personal liberties for persons with developmental disabilities while failing to provide opportunities for them to communicate preferences or to make choices. Thus, they asserted the need for a balance between habilitation and personal liberty based on the premise that the right to make choices has been guaranteed by legislation and prepares persons for less restrictive environments. They then suggested such a balance can be achieved by (a) teaching independent living skills that are preferred, (b) giving persons with disabilities input as to what skills they will be taught and how, (c) teaching choice, and (d) providing opportunities to make choices across settings and activities.

In reflecting on the risk involved in giving choice to persons with disabilities, Sobsey (2001) made the points that restrictions on personal freedoms should be minimal because they are disempowering and that restrictions should be used only when personal harm is likely and a less intrusive strategy is not available. For example, running in front of traffic may be a personal choice that puts a person in harm's way. Simple redirection or saying "stop" may not be as effective as physically preventing a person from stepping in front of a car. Physical intervention, however, is a temporary measure while safe pedestrian skills are being taught and mastered so a person may cross streets alone. Although instruction diminishes risk, it cannot prevent the possibility that an accident still could occur.

In 1997 TASH reprinted a classic article by Kennedy and Shoultz that supported the position of Bannerman et al. (1990). In this article the authors stated that all people should have the right to make choices even if they make mistakes and that choices should be "real," not just selected from options given by others. For example, a caregiver stocking the refrigerator and taking two items from the refrigerator and asking which a person with a disability would like for dinner would be a "choice given by another," but a person with a disability receiving support necessary to select items at a grocery store then go to the refrigerator and make a choice from those items would be a "real choice." Activity 14.1 highlights how personal choices can affect the life of a person with a disability.

ACTIVITY 14.1   Personal Liberties in the Life of a Woman with Disabilities

In writing about her life, Obermayer (2001) described the ways in which choice has allowed her to experience personal liberties in her life. As you read through her list, think about your own life—where you live, who your friends are, where you work, etc. Are there personal rights and choices that you take for granted that may not be honored if you had a disability? Here is Obermayer's list:

1. *Freedom*—She lives in an environment where she can choose to come and go at will instead of an institution where all choices are controlled.
2. *Authority*—She has the final say on decisions in her life, such as selecting the apartment where she lives, instead of living where others dictate.
3. *Support*—She has formed a circle of friends to provide natural support for her instead of relying on persons who are paid to provide support.
4. *Responsibility*—She chooses to contribute to her community and to earn her own living instead of living on the charity of others.
5. *Self-advocacy*—She is adamant in exercising self-determination in her life instead of allowing others to make choices for her.

In the field of special education, *self-determination* (a term that has been used throughout this text) refers to the rights of people with disabilities to exercise control in their lives (Wehmeyer & Schwartz, 1998). Deci and Ryan, two psychologists renowned for their research on self-determination, have stated that those who are self-determined "experience a sense of freedom to do what is interesting, personally important, and vitalizing" ("Self-determination theory," 2005). Since the 1990s the field has begun to embrace practices that support the right to a self-determined life, as evidenced by a growing research base in the professional literature and the development of specialized curricula that focus on self-determination. This focus has been supported by federal funding for projects through the Department of Education, such as the Self-Determination Synthesis Project (Test, Browder, Karvonen, Wood, & Algozzine, 2002), and through the enactment of federal legislation (Wehmeyer, Field, Doren, Jones, & Mason, 2004). First, the 1997 Amendments to the Individuals with Disabilities Education Act (IDEA) included language requiring that the IEPs of all students receiving special education services should state their ability to progress in the general education curriculum with adaptations and modifications and all students should be part of the accountability system. Then, No Child Left Behind legislated that all students should meet the same high standards in the accountability process, further ensuring that students with disabilities have access to core content in the general education curriculum. These two pieces of legislation set the stage for self-determination to be infused in the curriculum by ensuring access to inclusive environments in which "real choices" can be made.

Subsequent standards by which all students are to be measured have included self-determination (Wehmeyer et al., 2004). At the national level, the Council for Exceptional Children has developed standards for special education teachers that relate self-determination to instructional planning and strategies, learning environments, and collaborative teaching. At the state and local levels, standards for all students have included goals and objectives related to self-determination, such as problem solving, decision making, and goal setting.

In spite of current legislation and a focus on standards related to self-determination, not all families and teachers have adopted self-determination as an integral facet of the quality of life for persons with moderate and severe disabilities. Based on a survey of 234 parents and teachers of adolescent students with disabilities, Grigal, Neubert, Moon, and Graham (2003) found that self-determination skills were more likely to be taught to students with high-incidence disabilities who were in career tracks than to students with low-incidence disabilities who were in life-skills programs. Cultural differences also may influence whether or not self-determination is valued and embraced. For example, the Navajo culture does not have a term for disabilities but values all people as unique individuals and encourages children to become self-aware and self-sufficient at an early age (Frankland, Turnbull, Wehmeyer, & Blackmountain, 2004). The following sections will focus on additional variables that facilitate self-determination in students with moderate and severe disabilities during the educational process and the transition process, including methods to identify preferences and to facilitate choice making.

SELF-DETERMINATION AND THE EDUCATIONAL PROCESS

A number of factors contribute to an educational setting that incorporates self-determination for its students. For example, Karvonen, Test, Wood, Browder, and Algozzine (2004) identified and analyzed six sites that included students with mild to severe disabilities that were considered to be models of good practices in self-determination. They found that the sites had the following characteristics: (a) students with a perception that they were successful self-advocates; (b) curricula emphasizing self-advocacy and choice and the coaching of these skills in activities, such as IEP meetings; and (c) teachers and parents who served as mentors for self-determination. Based on these models, the authors concluded that strong leadership is needed for putting self-determination into practice and that students with the most severe disabilities benefit from person-centered planning and methods that incorporate opportunities for making choices.

Self-Determination and IEPs

IDEA mandated that all students with disabilities be involved in the IEP process, thus giving them a choice in their educational goals and objectives (Bremer, Kachgal, & Schoeller, 2003). This fostered participation in the IEP process and thought regarding the goals and objectives that result from the process. In analyzing the online survey responses of 523 special and general educators, administrators, related services personnel, student teachers, and staff from institutions of higher education, Mason, Field, and Sawilowsky (2004) found that, although self-determination is considered important, there is a high degree of dissatisfaction with its instruction and implementation. Most of the respondents addressed self-determination in only an informal way, and most did not fully include students in the IEP process even though they considered this to be beneficial in making students better self-advocates. While those involved with secondary school students tended to be more satisfied with the manner in which self-determination was included in the curriculum, half of the respondents voiced the need for better training in self-determination and the ways in which self-determination was addressed in their programs.

A self-determined model begins with the development of the IEP and the involvement of students in the process, taking into consideration the preferences and choices of students for the goals, objectives, and activities that are developed during the IEP meeting. Wood, Karvonen, Test, Browder, and Algozzine (2004) provided examples of how self-determination skills can be incorporated as IEP goals and objectives for students with disabilities, including the following four examples for students with moderate or severe disabilities:

1. To address choice for a student with a severe mental disability, a goal could be to indicate choice for leisure activities and objectives could be to make one consistent request for a preference and to protest if the request is not honored.

2. To address goal setting and attainment for a student with a moderate mental disability, a goal could be to develop an action plan for getting a job and objectives could be to develop an interest portfolio, select and visit work experience sites, analyze work skills needed for the sites, develop goals for attaining those skills, develop an action plan to meet the goals, and monitor progress as action is taken.

3. To address self-regulation for a student with a moderate mental disability, a goal could be to independently maintain reading and writing skills and objectives could be to construct a data sheet, evaluate performance using the sheet, create a schedule for working on skills, and determine mastery or the need for assistance.

4. To address self-advocacy and self-awareness for a student with a moderate mental disability, a goal could be to have active participation in a transition IEP meeting and objectives could be to introduce team members, express preferences for goals, address personal strengths and weaknesses, and identify supports during mock IEP meetings (pp. 13–15).

Self-Determination and Instruction

Self-determination is still a relatively new concept for many teachers and may not have been included in their preparation programs. When 1,219 teachers of adolescent students with disabilities (including a large portion who worked with students with moderate and severe disabilities) were asked for information regarding self-determination, 60% responded that they were familiar with the term, and most cited sources of information as articles in professional journals followed by conferences or workshops (Wehmeyer, Agran, & Hughes, 2000). The same sample of teachers considered the following components of self-determination to be very important: (a) decision making (73.6%), (b) problem solving (73.5%), (c) choice making (73.2%), (d) self-management (65.8%), (e) self-awareness (64.4%), (f) self-advocacy (59.3%), and (g) goal setting (56.0%). The strategies most frequently taught to students with severe disabilities, however, were self-reinforcement and self-evaluation.

Teachers have incorporated self-determination in instruction in a number of ways that include (a) embedding it as an integral part of the curriculum across domains and (b) including self-determination as a targeted skill in direct instruction. In an example of embedding self-determination across the curriculum, Mithaug and Mithaug (2003) found that student-directed instruction for two primary school students with autism that consisted of the teacher prompting the students to set goals, make work assignments, and record their results resulted in more self-management skills being evidenced across nontraining activities than did teacher-directed instruction. During instruction, the students used self-recording cards on which they circled pictures of the areas in which they would work (e.g., math, reading, science, social studies, writing) and the number of worksheets they planned to complete as well as the number they actually completed. Example 14.1 shows a similar sheet that can be used by students with moderate and severe disabilities for planning, monitoring, and evaluating. Even if the student does not have written communication skills, the sheet can be completed by circling a response or using an ink dabber to select a response.

EXAMPLE 14.1 A PLANNING, MONITORING, AND EVALUATION SHEET FOR STUDENTS WITH MODERATE AND SEVERE DISABILITIES

Science Class

I will work on a report on:

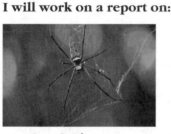
Spiders

Frogs

Chickens

I will use these materials:

Pencil and Paper

computer

library books

globe

I will work on the following behavior:

Raising my hand

Being on time for class

Bringing materials to class

This how I performed in science class:

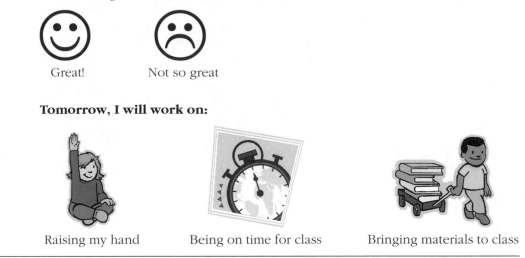

Great!   Not so great

Tomorrow, I will work on:

Raising my hand   Being on time for class   Bringing materials to class

As students with moderate and severe disabilities enter adolescence, self-determination gains importance as students work to attain the highest degree of independence possible before they transition to adulthood. Beneficial skills include choice making, decision making, goal setting, goal attainment, problem solving, self-evaluation, self-management, self-advocacy, and self-awareness (Test et al., 2002). Several researchers have investigated the effectiveness of teaching self-determination to adolescents with disabilities, including those with moderate and severe disabilities. For example, Wehmeyer, Palmer, Agran, Mithaug, and Martin (2000) field-tested a Self-Determined Model of Instruction that included three phases: (a) setting goals, (b) taking action, and (c) adjusting the plan or goal. When implemented with 40 adolescents with disabilities, including those with various degrees of mental retardation, 55% of the students met the individual goals they had set. Palmer, Wehmeyer, Gipson, and Agran (2004) had similar results when they implemented the Self-Determined Model of Instruction with 22 adolescents with mild to moderate mental disabilities. In addition to improving their knowledge of self-determination skills, the students achieved their goals tied to general education core content standards.

Test et al. (2002) provided a sample format of a lesson plan for teaching self-determination skills to students with disabilities. The lesson plan began with defining the various rights of all citizens: (a) rights to which persons are entitled as members of society, such as the right to get married; (b) rights to which persons are entitled when living in the community, such as the right to secure a job; (c) rights to which persons are entitled as consumers of services, such as the right to secure appropriate services; and (d) rights to which persons are entitled as buyers of products, such as the right to be told the truth about products. The lesson then presented conditions for obtaining rights. For example, marriage requires a license, a blood test, a fee, and the completion of various forms. Finally, the lesson ended with a model of role-playing a scenario where these rights are violated (e.g., persons being denied the right to vote due to a mental disability) and a behavioral rehearsal of dealing with the rights violation.

Direct instruction can provide the opportunity for students with moderate and severe disabilities to practice self-determination by making choices. As previously described in Chapter 8, Cooper and Browder (1998) provided multiple opportunities to make choices by pointing, touching, or moving toward an object in teaching restaurant skills to three adults with severe disabilities. These included choices regarding which door to use to enter the restaurant, which foods to order, which sweeteners or condiments to use, and where to sit to consume the meal.

Self-Determination and Transition

As adults, persons with disabilities are entitled to make the same choices as persons without disabilities, including where they will live, with whom they will live, the friendships they will make, how they will participate in the community, the type of assistance or support they will secure, the type of sexual relations in which they will engage, where they will work, and the type of medical treatment they will receive (Taylor, 2001, p. 8). The ability to make choices increases factors associated with quality of life, such as emotional well-being, interpersonal relationships, material well-being, personal development, physical well-being, and social inclusion (Wehmeyer & Schwartz, 1988, p. 4). According to Wehmeyer and Schwartz, other self-determined acts include the following:

1. The ability to act autonomously (i.e., perform acts according to one's own preferences, interests, or abilities independent of external influences),
2. The ability to self-regulate (i.e., make decisions regarding skills to be used in situations, then evaluate and make revisions),
3. The ability to initiate and respond to events in an empowered manner (i.e., act on the belief that one has the capacity to perform a behavior to influence outcomes), and
4. The ability to act in a self-realizing manner (i.e., use knowledge of strengths and weaknesses in a beneficial way) (p. 4).

Taking each of these factors into consideration, Wehmeyer and Schwartz (1998) interviewed 50 adults with mental retardation who lived in group homes and found that self-determination contributed to a positive quality of life. In addition, Wehmeyer and Palmer (2003) found a better quality of life for adults who had more self-determination in their lives when they collected follow-up data on 94 students, including those with mental disabilities, one to three years after they transitioned from secondary school. The adults with a higher degree of self-determination were more likely to be financially independent (e.g., have bank accounts and pay bills), hold jobs with benefits (e.g., vacation and sick leave, health benefits), and live independently. A specific example of a young man whose life was impacted by the use of a self-determined model of transition can be found in Example 14.2.

EXAMPLE 14.2 AN EXAMPLE OF A SELF-DETERMINED LIFE

The story of John Jones is an example of a self-determined transition (Held, Thoma, & Thomas, 2004). John Jones was a young man with autism who was enrolled in a transition program for students between the ages of 18 and 21 years. He worked at a bookstore, took adult classes at the library, lived in an apartment with a roommate, and received support from a local provider. John needed support in developing friendships, liked music, made his own decisions, and was showing improvement in his communication skills.

Prior to adopting a self-determined way of life, John had been in a high school program where he was unsuccessful in inclusion classes due to his behavior and participated in work experiences at a store, a restaurant, and a radio station. He was not good at communicating his likes and dislikes, and his teacher wrote his IEP without his input. Through a desire to improve the quality of John's life, the teacher began to research ways to implement a self-determined model. She built on his interest in music to help him find employment and enroll in music lessons. She facilitated John's communication by having him dictate into a microphone. When the time arrived for his transition meeting, John directed the meeting with a computer-based PowerPoint presentation that he developed with peers. The peers labeled this "The John Jones Show."

Comments following John's presentation included "I had no idea that John was so skilled at the computer!" and "I think it's great that John wants to be a rock star!" (Held et al., 2004, p. 183). These comments illustrate how the practice of self-determination made a positive change in John's perception by others.

As illustrated in Example 14.2, the quality of adult life through self-determination can be enhanced through the development and implementation of the ITP in secondary school. Transition meetings for students with moderate and severe disabilities, however, may fail to use a self-determined focus, as demonstrated in an investigation conducted by Thoma, Rogan, and Baker (2001). In the investigation the authors observed transition meetings, interviewed participants, and analyzed documents for students with moderate to severe disabilities between the ages of 18 and 21 years over a 15-month period. First, they found that there was a high degree of variance across transition meetings, with more participation by parents and teachers than by students. Most students were not informed of their transition meetings, and only one meeting used person-centered planning. Second, the transition meetings were most often scheduled during school hours at the convenience of professionals and focused on the deficits, rather than the strengths, of the students. Third, communication during meetings was often strained, rushed, hostile, and filled with technical jargon, with more time spent talking to parents than to students. Finally, students met the goals on the transition plan, but the goals failed to focus on student preferences for employment. Based on these results, Thoma et al. recommended that (a) students be given a greater role in the overall planning and that their preferences be included, (b) strategies be used to facilitate communication by the students and personal advocates be invited, and (c) outcomes focus on the preferences, interests, and dreams of students.

A chief focus of transition meetings is determining where students will work in adulthood, and a self-determined model takes student preferences into consideration during initial job placements during the secondary school years. McGlashing-Johnson, Agran, Sitlington, Cavin, and Wehmeyer (2003) used the Self-Determined Model for Instruction in the job placements of four secondary school students with moderate and severe disabilities between the ages of 16 and 20 years. During a baseline condition, the researchers taught the students to make goals and developed monitoring sheets with task analyses of their jobs. During training, they guided the students through implementing their plans related to their goals and through using their monitoring sheets to evaluate their performances on their jobs (e.g., packaging bread for patients at a hospital, pricing items at a gardening center, sweeping floors at a bus terminal). As a result, the students showed increases in their targeted behaviors across jobs.

Chapter 11 described strategies for incorporating person-centered planning in transitioning that included developing a personal profile (e.g., circle of support, community presence map), determining a future lifestyle, identifying action steps and the parties responsible, identifying needed service system changes, and following up on recommendations (Miner & Bates, 1997). According to Schwartz, Jacobson, and Holburn (2000, p. 238), there are eight hallmarks of a person-centered approach:

1. Activities, services, and support based on a person's dreams, interests, preferences, strengths, and capacities

2. Inclusion of those who are close to a person in lifestyle planning

3. Meaningful choices based on experiences

4. Use of natural and community supports

5. Fostering of skills to achieve personal relationships, inclusion, dignity, and respect

6. Maximization of opportunities and experiences

7. Planning that is collaborative, recurring, and involves ongoing commitment

8. Satisfaction of the person with supports and services

CHOICES AND PREFERENCES

Implementing a self-determined model with persons with moderate and severe disabilities can be challenging. This is because, due to limitations in cognitive ability and communication skills, it can be difficult for persons with moderate and severe disabilities to communicate choices and preferences, especially for those with the most severe disabilities. Researchers, however, have identified methods through which preferences and choices can be assessed for both children and adults. In most cases this involves interviewing those who have experience with the person, such as caregivers who know which foods the person accepts or rejects or job coaches who know which tasks the person completes or refuses to complete. Preferences also can be identified by systematically presenting potential stimuli then cuing into behaviors that indicate a preference. In some cases it may be necessary to teach the skill of making choices. The following investigations demonstrate these methods across age levels.

Gast et al. (2000) determined the preferences of four students with profound and multiple disabilities, ages 6 to 9 years, by presenting preferred stimuli (e.g., bouncing, being tickled, watching videotape, listening to audiotape) and neutral stimuli (e.g., singing, bubbles, country music, vibrator) and measuring student responses, which included laughter, smiles, and eye gaze. Specifically, the researchers began sessions by first identifying preferred or neutral stimuli based on whether or not these elicited a targeted response. They then presented four stimuli (two preferred and two neutral) and measured the duration of the response to each to determine which was preferred.

Like Gast et al. (2000), Stafford, Alberto, Fredrick, Heflin, and Heller (2002) also presented paired sets of stimuli when they taught five students with severe disabilities, ages 6 to 10 years, to make choices across five phases. To begin, the researchers first identified preferred items (e.g., cookies and bubbles), neutral items (e.g., chips and music), and nonpreferred items (e.g., Froot Loops and a doll). The researchers then began by providing an easy choice between a preferred and a nonpreferred item, moved to a choice between a preferred and a neutral item, then introduced a more difficult choice between two preferred items. Using a constant time delay procedure, a researcher prompted the student through indicating a choice if the student did not first initiate an independent choice. Although the procedure was effective in teaching choice making across students, the researchers found that preferences for the stimuli varied from week to week; thus, they recommended that there is a need to reassess preferences on a regular basis.

Investigations on indicating preferences and choices with adults have focused on more age-appropriate stimuli. In assessing prework task preference across three men with autism, severe or profound disabilities, and nonverbal communication skills, Lattimore, Parsons, and Reid (2002) presented paired materials needed for office cleaning tasks (e.g., dusting, mopping, vacuuming, cleaning sinks). They waited for each of the men to indicate task preferences by touching or pointing to the task materials then observed them to determine the duration of their engagement with the selected tasks. Once preferences for jobs were established, the researchers paired preferred tasks with less preferred tasks on the job and found that the men most frequently chose the same tasks that they had selected during the prework assessment. Thus, the researchers concluded that definite work preferences can be identified prior to the actual work setting.

Next, Lim, Browder, and Bambara (2001) investigated the establishment of preferences in grocery shopping for two adults with severe disabilities who resided in a community-based home. During baseline condition, the men failed to indicate preferences when presented with four types of fruit juices in containers. After the men were given small samples of each drink, however, they indicated definite preferences that generalized to choosing from fruit juices on the shelf of a community grocery store. Based on this outcome, providing samples of choices in advance may facilitate later choices.

Finally, Yu et al. (2002) used observation to determine the preferences of 19 adults with developmental disabilities from a residential community center based on indexes of happiness (e.g., smile, vocalization, clapping). Using an interval system, the researchers recorded whether or not the adults appeared happy as they engaged in work activities (e.g., sorting, shredding, matching) and leisure activities (e.g., listening to music, watching television, attending a concert, taking a lunch or coffee break). They found that the adults displayed higher percentages of happiness during leisure activities than they did during work activities. While happiness appeared to be related to leisure activities in the study by Yu et al., Schwartzman, Martin, Yu, and Whiteley (2004) did not find that happiness was an indicator of preference in the selection of edibles. Schwartzman et al. measured similar indexes of happiness when presenting edibles to four adults with severe or profound disabilities from a residential training facility. With an array of edibles selected on the recommendations of others, the researchers conducted preference assessments by presenting two of the edibles at a time and waiting 10 seconds for the adults to make a choice between the two. Even when presented with edibles known to be preferred, the adults only occasionally displayed indicators of happiness, causing the researchers to conclude that happiness may not be related to choice.

Based on these studies, it appears that preferences can be identified through observation and systematic presentation of choices and that the duration of a response or engagement may be more reliable than looking for a change in affect. Once preferences are established through observational measures, it is possible to teach physical responses for making choices through systematic prompting procedures, such as constant time delay.

Best Practices
Self-Determination

1. Facilitate self-determination by including opportunities for choice making in the curriculum for students with moderate and severe disabilities at an early age.
2. Realize that some students may need to be taught how to make choices.
3. Be aware of ways that persons with moderate and severe disabilities, especially those with significant cognitive disabilities, indicate preferences, including facial expression, vocalizations, body language, acceptance or rejection of stimuli, and duration of engagement.
4. Use IEP and ITP meetings as opportunities for students to exercise self-determination.
5. Use a Self-Determined Model of Instruction across the curriculum.

Conclusion

This chapter concludes this text by focusing on the latest trend in special education for persons with moderate and severe disabilities—empowerment through self-determination. Through making their choices and preferences known, persons with moderate and severe disabilities can lead a life that is richer in quality. The process of self-determination can be facilitated by embedding it throughout the curriculum, and students can be provided with opportunities to make choices from an early age. These can be present in the selection of activities and classes in the daily schedule, in the selection of partners in cooperative groups, in the selection of foods at snack and mealtime, and in the selection of ways to spend leisure time. As students grow older, self-determination becomes greater in importance if personal liberties are to be present in adulthood. The process of transition provides the opportunity to make vocational and residential choices and to form circles of natural supports that will be needed for maximum independence. Even those persons who have pervasive need for supports in their lives can still retain human dignity by making choices within a self-determined model.

In addition to creating opportunities for choice in instruction and transition, self-determination skills can be taught through direct instruction. For example, students can be shown how to become self-advocates in making their choices known and how to attain a higher degree of independence through the processes of self-management, including self-monitoring, self-evaluation, and self-reinforcemnt. It is important for caregivers, teachers, and others who work with persons with moderate and severe disabilities to be sensitive to the need to a self-determined life and to be aware that this is a basic human right.

Questions for Review

1. What is meant by the term *self-determination?* How does it apply to the lives of persons with moderate and severe disabilities?
2. What are some ways in which a person with cognitive and communication deficits might communicate preferences?

3. What is a self-determined model of instruction? How can the phases be implemented in the instructional setting?

4. How can choice making be taught? How can choice making be embedded in the daily schedule?

5. How can the IEP and ITP processes provide the opportunity to practice self-determination?

6. Discuss the right of persons with moderate and severe disabilities to make bad choices.

Performance-Based Assessment

Chuck is a young man with a moderate disability who is nearing 30 years of age. He has severe communication deficits and becomes frustrated and angry when he attempts to communicate and others do not understand him. Chuck is on medication for seizures. He received special education services for students with moderate and severe disabilities throughout his school career that provided him with basic functional academic skills and a sufficient repertoire of basic life skills. During high school, Chuck earned money by taking in the trash cans for his neighbors and used this money to buy equipment for his bicycle.

After completing high school, Chuck remained at home for several years. He continued to receive speech therapy and also participated in weekly counseling for anger management. Chuck held several jobs that resulted in his being fired for behavior. For example, he became angry at a customer while bagging groceries and pushed the grocery cart into her car. Without a job, Chuck began following the garbage truck through town each day on his bicycle. The sanitation workers began to talk to Chuck and bought him an orange safety vest for him to wear when he accompanied them.

When Chuck's parents decided to downsize and move into a new home, Chuck moved into an apartment run by an agency that offered 24-hour supervision. Because he did not have a job, he enrolled in art classes and enjoyed this activity. In time, however, the agency determined that Chuck's behavior issues required more supervision than they were able to offer, so Chuck was forced to return home. At present, Chuck spends his days standing on the street in front of his parents' new home, waiting for the garbage truck to arrive.

Imagine that you are a case worker for an adult agency. How might you facilitate Chuck's right to a self-determined life?

References

Bannerman, D. J., Sheldon, J. B., Sherman, J. A., & Harchik, A. E. (1990). Balancing the right to habilitation with the right to personal liberties: The rights of people with developmental disabilities to eat too many doughnuts and take a nap. *Journal of Applied Behavior Analysis, 23,* 79–89.

Bremer, C. D., Kachgal, M., & Schoeller, K. (2003). Self-determination: Supporting successful transition. *Research to Practice Brief: Improving Secondary Education and Transition Services Through Research, 2.* Retrieved July 6, 2005, from www.ncset.org/publications/viewdesc.asp?id=962.

Cooper, K. J., & Browder, D. M. (1998). Enhancing choice and participation for adults with severe disabilities in community-based instruction. *Journal of the Association for Persons with Severe Handicaps, 23,* 252–260.

Frankland, H. C., Turnbull, A. P., Wehmeyer, M. L., & Blackmountain, L. (2004). An exploration of the self-determination construct and disability as it relates to the Dine (Navajo) culture. *Education and Training in Developmental Disabilities, 39,* 191–205.

Gast, D. L., Jacobs, H. A., Logan, K. R., Murray, A. S., Holloway, A., & Long, L. (2000). Pre-session assessment of preferences for students with profound multiple disabilities. *Education and Training in Mental Retardation and Developmental Disabilities, 35,* 393–405.

Grigal, M., Neubert, D. A., Moon, M. S., & Graham, S. (2003). Self-determination for students with disabilities: Views of parents and teachers. *Exceptional Children, 70,* 97–112.

Held, M. F., Thoma, C. A., & Thomas, K. (2004). "The John Jones Show": How one teacher facilitated self-determined transition planning for a young man with autism. *Focus on Autism and Other Developmental Disabilities, 19,* 177–188.

Karvonen, M., Test, D. W., Wood, W. M., Browder, D., & Algozzine, B. (2004). Putting self-determination into practice. *Exceptional Children, 71,* 23–41.

Kennedy, M., & Shoultz, B. (1997). Thoughts about self-advocacy. *TASH Newsletter, 26*(2), 7–8.

Lattimore, L. P., Parsons, M. B., & Reid, D. H. (2002). A prework assessment of task preferences among adults with autism beginning a supported job. *Journal of Applied Behavior Analysis, 35,* 85–88.

Lim, L., Browder, D. M., & Bambara, L. (2001). Effects of sampling opportunities on preference development for adults with severe disabilities. *Education and Training in Mental Retardation and Developmental Disabilities, 36,* 188–195.

Mason, C., Field, S., & Sawilowsky, S. (2004). Implementation of self-determination activities and student participation in IEPs. *Exceptional Children, 70,* 441–451.

McGlashing-Johnson, J., Agran, M., Sitlington, P., Cavin, M., & Wehmeyer, M. (2003). Enhancing job performance of youth with moderate to severe cognitive disabilities using the self-determined learning model of instruction. *Research and Practice for Persons with Severe Disabilities, 28,* 194–204.

Miner, C. A., & Bates, P. E. (1997). Person-centered transition planning. *Teaching Exceptional Children, 30*(1), 66–69.

Mithaug, D. K., & Mithaug, D. E. (2003). Effects of teacher-directed versus student-directed instruction on self-management of young children with disabilities. *Journal of Applied Behavior Analysis, 36,* 133–136.

Obermayer, L. (2001). Self-determination. *TASH Connections, 27*(2), 14, 27.

Palmer, S. B., Wehmeyer, M. L., Gipson, K., & Agran, M. (2004). Promoting access to the general curriculum by teaching self-determination skills. *Exceptional Children, 70,* 427–439.

Polloway, E. A., Smith, J. D., Patton, J. R., & Smith, T. E. C. (1996). Historic changes in mental retardation and developmental disabilities. *Education and Training in Mental Retardation and Developmental Disabilities, 31,* 3–12.

Schwartz, A. A., Jacobson, J. W., & Holburn, S. C. (2000). Defining person centeredness: Results of two consensus methods. *Education and Training in Mental Retardation and Developmental Disabilities, 35,* 235–249.

Schwartzman, L., Martin, G. L., Yu, C. T., & Whiteley, J. (2004). Choice, Degree of Preference, and Happiness Indices with Persons with Intellectual Disabilities:

A Surprising Finding. *Education and Training in Developmental Disabilities, 39*(3), 265–269.

Self-Determination theory: An approach to human motivation & personality Web site (2005). Retrieved July 6, 2005, from www.psych.rochester.edu/SDT/.

Sobsey, D. (2001). Reflections on risk. *TASH Connections, 27*(2), 11–12.

Stafford, A. M., Alberto, P. A., Fredrick, L. D., Heflin, L. J., & Heller, K. W. (2002). Preference variability and the instruction of choice making with students with severe intellectual disabilities. *Education and Training in Mental Retardation and Developmental Disabilities, 37,* 70–88.

Taylor, S. J. (2001). On choice. *TASH Connections, 27*(2), 8–10.

Test, D. W., Browder, D. M., Karvonen, M., Wood, W., & Algozzine, B. (2002). Writing lesson plans for promoting self-determination. *Teaching Exceptional Children, 35*(1), 8–14.

Thoma, C. A., Rogan, P., & Baker, S. R. (2001). Student involvement in transition planning: Unheard voices. *Education and Training in Mental Retardation and Developmental Disabilities, 36,* 16–29.

Wehmeyer, M. L., Agran, M., & Hughes, C. (2000). A national survey of teacher's promotion of self-determination and student-directed learning. *The Journal of Special Education, 34,* 58–68.

Wehmeyer, M. L., Field, S., Doren, B., Jones, B., & Mason, C. (2004). Self-determination and student involvement in standards-based reform. *Exceptional Children, 70,* 413–425.

Wehmeyer, M. L., & Palmer, S. B. (2003). Adult outcomes for students with cognitive disabilities three years after high school: The impact of self-determination, *Education and Training in Mental Retardation and Developmental Disabilities, 38,* 131–144.

Wehmeyer, M. L., Palmer, S. B., Agran, M., Mithaug, D. K., & Martin, J. E. (2000). Promoting causal agency: The self-determined learning model of instruction. *Exceptional Children, 66,* 439–453.

Wehmeyer, M., & Schwartz, M. (1998). The relationship between self-determination and quality of life for adults with mental retardation. *Education and Training in Mental Retardation and Developmental Disabilities, 33,* 3–12.

Wood, W. M., Karvonen, M., Test, D. W., Browder, D. M., & Algozzine, B. (2004). Promoting student self-determination skills in IEP planning. *Teaching Exceptional Children, 36*(3), 8–16.

Yu, D. C. T., Spevack, S., Hiebert, R., Martin, T. L., Goodman, R., Martin, T. G., Harapiak, S., & Martin, G. L. (2002). Happiness indices among persons with profound and severe disabilities during leisure and work activities: A comparison. *Education and Training in Mental Retardation and Developmental Disabilities, 37,* 421–426.

GLOSSARY

A-B-C analysis: A direct observational technique to determine the antecedents that precede and the consequences that follow targeted behaviors.

Absolute profound range: A range of profound mental retardation in which persons are viewed as lacking all adaptive behavior skills and as being in a medically fragile state.

Acquisition: Initial learning of response or behavior.

Active euthanasia: The termination of a life through an act of commission.

Aggressive behavior: Category of challenging behavior that is directed toward persons or objects within the environment, injury to others in the environment, and is intended to cause harm; may be physical or verbal.

Antecedent: The stimulus that elicits a behavior or response.

Antecedent-prompting procedures: Instructional strategies (e.g., stimulus shaping and stimulus fading) that use stimulus prompts to increase the likelihood that the student will make the correct response.

Antecedent prompts: Events that are added to the stimulus to increase the likelihood that the students will make the correct response; stimulus prompts.

Applied behavior analysis: A body of research based on behavioral principles that has been effectively applied in the field of special education.

Arena assessment: The practice of evaluating a student's instructional needs in which professionals on a team release their roles to observe a single individual working with the student.

Attentional cues: Events that focus a student's attention so learning can take place.

Augmentative communication system: A means of communicating that replaces or supplements verbal communication; may consist of using manual signs or gestures, low-technology devices, or high-technology devices.

Backward chaining: Instructional format in which instruction occurs on the final step of a chained task until the step is mastered then proceeds in a backward fashion, teaching prior steps.

Behavior: The response that occurs following the presentation of a stimulus and an antecedent.

Bottom-up approach: A developmental approach to determining a curriculum.

Bright line test: Legal distinction as to whether or not schools are responsible for delivering and funding medical services as related services based on whether or not they must be delivered by a physician.

Case consultation: Related service delivery personnel provide one-time consultation for single students, provides recommendation for the student's programming, then withdraws.

Chained behaviors: A series of discrete responses or steps linked together in a sequence that results in a single skill.

Chronic illnesses: Conditions, injury traumas, or illnesses that last for an extended amount of time (e.g., months or a lifetime).

Colleague consultation: Model of related service delivery in which therapists provide information for groups of teachers who then deliver services to students based on what they have learned.

Community-based instruction (CBI): In vivo instruction; the practice of teaching in the natural environment to increase the likelihood that generalization occurs.

Community-referenced instruction: Simulation; the practice of teaching with stimuli (e.g., materials, cues) that would be found in the real world to increase the likelihood of generalization.

Complex health care needs: A heterogeneous category composed of chronic illnesses, technology-dependent conditions, or medically fragile conditions.

Comprehensive integration: Collaboration between service delivery personnel and teachers to deliver services to students with disabilities in natural environments with peers without disabilities.

Concurrent instruction: The practice of teaching skills in both classroom simulation and the community at the same time.

Consecutive instruction: The practice of teaching skills in classroom simulation prior to teaching them in the community.

Consequence: The event that follows a behavior or response that affects whether or not the behavior will recur (e.g., a reinforcer or a punisher).

Constant time delay (CTD): Response-prompting strategy that uses a single controlling prompt that is faded over a dimension of time by increasing the delay interval for a student to independently respond from zero seconds to a set interval of time (e.g., three seconds) across sessions.

Consultation: In regard to health care services, those that can be delivered by the educational team with a nurse acting as consultant to school.

Consultation therapy model: Related service delivery personnel train others to implement procedures from their discipline then withdraw.

Contingency contracts: Documents that specify the consequences of appropriate and inappropriate behavior as agreed upon by all who are involved in the behavior intervention plan.

Controlling prompt: The least intrusive prompt that ensures that a correct response will occur.

Criterion of least dangerous assumption: The concept that, in the absence of conclusive data, educators should make decisions based on assumptions that, if incorrect, will have the least dangerous effect on the student.

Criterion of ultimate functioning: The goal for students with moderate to severe disabilities to be able to function to their full potential as adults in least restrictive environments with their peers without disabilities.

Curriculum catalog: A large document containing a variety of task-analyzed activities that occur in the local environments of students across domains.

Developmental approach: A bottom-up approach to instruction in which students are taught skills in a predetermined sequence that is typical of the development of children without disabilities.

Developmental disability: A severe, chronic disability manifested before age 22 that is attributable to a mental and/or physical impairment and results in substantial functional limitations in three or more adaptive areas.

Differential reinforcement: A behavioral intervention strategy in which inappropriate behaviors are decreased by reinforcing appropriate behaviors; variations of the procedure include reinforcing alternate behavior (DRA), other behavior (DRO), incompatible behavior (DRI), and low rates of a behavior (DRL).

Direct care: Personal health care service delivered by a physician, nurse, or other licensed health care professional.

Direct therapy model: Related services delivered by service delivery personnel within their discipline.

Disability: A reduction of function or absence of a body part or organ.

Discrete behaviors: Responses that consist of a single step.

Disruptive behavior: Category of challenging behavior that prohibits learning within the enviornment.

Distributed trial instruction: Instructional format in which trials are interspersed at naturally occurring times throughout the day.

Ecological inventory: An assessment tool that enables the teacher to determine an individualized functional curriculum across community, domestic, recreation/leisure, and educational/vocational domains.

Education: Meaningful progress in a positive direction.

Educational synthesizer: The role of the teacher who gathers information from a variety of disciplines (e.g., occupational therapy, physical therapy, speech/language pathology) to design and implement a coordinated educational program for a student.

Effectiveness: If a procedure has the desired outcome.

Efficiency: If a procedure compares better to others in terms of learning (e.g., time to criterion, number of sessions to criterion, number of errors to criterion).

Eugenics: A theory based on the idea that persons with mental retardation give birth to persons with mental retardation.

Euthanasia: "Mercy killing," the deliberate termination of a life.

Extensive support: A level of support in the 1992 AAMR definition of mental retardation that is provided on a regular basis for long periods of time.

Extinction: A mildly punishing procedure in which inappropriate behavior is decreased by withholding the reinforcer that is maintaining the behavior.

Extinction burst: The possibility that a challenging behavior that is being extinguished may occur at a greater intensity in an effort to access a previously available reinforcer.

Family stress: The physiological or psychological response of family members to a stressor that may be delayed or immediate, such as the response to the stressor of a child with disabilities.

Family stressor: Crisis-provoking event for which a family has little or no preparation, such as the birth of a child with a disability.

Fluency: How well a response or behavior is performed.

Form: The way in which a skill is performed; what it looks like as it is performed.

Forward chaining: Instructional format in which instruction occurs on the first step of a chained task until the step is mastered then proceeds in a forward fashion, teaching remaining steps.

Full integration: Placement in a general education setting for the entire school day that is not in the student's neighborhood school.

Function: The outcome of a skill when it is performed; what it accomplishes.

Functional approach: A top-down approach to instruction in which students are taught functional skills that are immediately useful and are typical of their same-age peers without disabilities.

Functional behavioral assessment: The process of determining the antecedents, functions, and consequences of a person's challenging behavior with the goal of identifying an appropriate behavioral intervention; composed of a combination of interviews, observations, and systematic functional analyses.

Functional communication training: Teaching a person to communicate in an appropriate manner, often with the result of a decrease in inappropriate behavior.

Functional curriculum: A curriculum with a focus on age-appropriate life skills.

Functional exclusion: Physical integration of persons with disabilities without social or instructional integration.

Functional integration: The delivery of services in the natural environment where they are needed.

Functional mental disabilities: A classification for students with moderate to severe disabilities based on the need for a functional curriculum.

Functional skills: Meaningful life skills; skills that are immediately useful in the environment.

General attentional cues: Events (e.g., telling student to look, calling a student's name) that focus a student's attention for learning without requiring a specific action on the part of the student.

General case instruction: Teaching with multiple exemplars that sample the range of stimuli in a class to facilitate generalization.

General education placement: Placement of students with disabilities in classes with students without disabilities with less than 21% of the time spent in a segregated class setting.

Generalization: The application of a response or a behavior in the natural environments.

Graduated guidance: Response-prompting strategy that typically uses a prompt of physical guidance and shadowing of the student's movements, providing assistance as needed.

Handicap: A limitation imposed by a lack of accommodations within the environment.

Impairment: A lessening or weakening in ability or state of health.

In vivo instruction: Community-based instruction (CBI); the practice of teaching in the natural environment to ensure that generalization occurs.

Incidental teaching Naturalistic or milieu response-prompting procedure typically used to expand a child's repertoire of language skills during natural activities based on child interest by prompting a child to elaborate on a response.

Inclusion: Full integration of students with disabilities in general education classes in their neighborhood schools.

Indirect care: Health care service delivered by educational team under supervision of nurse.

Individualized curriculum sequencing model (ICS): A way of delivery instruction by embedding it in ongoing routines and activities.

Instructional integration: Instruction that occurs when students with and without disabilities are taught together.

Instructive feedback: The placement of nontargeted information in the antecedent, prompt, or consequence of an instructional trial.

Interdisciplinary team model: Model of service delivery in which representatives from various disciplines provide collaborative input to a child's educational program but deliver services independent of other team members.

Intermittent support: A level of support in the 1992 AAMR definition of mental retardation that is provided on an as-needed basis and is episodic in nature.

Least dangerous assumption: The belief that, in the absence of conclusive data, one should make the decision that will result in the least harm if the decision turns out to be wrong.

Limited support: A level of support in the 1992 AAMR definition of mental retardation that is delivered consistently over time.

Logic of heterogeneity: The assumption that students are better served in groups composed of those with and without disabilities because they can learn from each other and because integrated settings facilitate generalization by mirroring the real world.

Logic of homogeneity: The assumption that students are better served when educated in segregated settings with other students with disabilities.

Longitudinal programming: The process of selecting target skills for instruction that will lead to independent functioning in the next environment.

Longitudinal transitions: Changes over time that are planned and involve preparation for future environments or stages prior to transitioning so transitions are smooth instead of abrupt.

Mainstreaming: Physical placement of persons with disabilities in settings with persons without disabilities; physical integration.

Maintenance: The performance of a response or behavior over time.

Mand-model: Naturalistic or milieu response-prompting procedure typically used to teach fluency of language skills during natural activities base on child interest by providing a mand when the child does not initiate language and providing a model when a child does not respond to a mand.

Massed trial instruction: Instructional format where trials occur in quick succession, one immediately after the other.

Meaningful skills: Functional skills; skills that produce an effect on the environment.

Medical services: Those services that must be provided by a licensed physician for diagnostic or evaluation purposes.

Medically fragile: Term referring to students who require constant medical supervision to prevent life-threatening situations.

Mental retardation: A term that refers to substantial limitations in functioning manifested prior to age 18, including significantly subaverage intellectual functioning with related limitations in two or more adaptive skill areas.

Mild mental retardation: A classification of mental retardation falling within an IQ range of 55 to 75 or 2 to 3 standard deviations below the mean, according to the 1983 AAMR definition.

Milieu teaching strategies: Naturalistic teaching procedures; response-prompting strategies typically embedded in natural activities to facilitate communication skills.

Missed participation: The lack of an opportunity for students with disabilities to participate in general education activities because adaptations were not made to allow them to participate independently.

Modeling: Naturalistic or milieu response-prompting procedure typically used to teach acquisition of language skills during natural activities by modeling language based on child interest.

Moderate mental retardation: A classification of mental retardation falling within an IQ range of 35 to 55 or 3 to 4 standard deviations below the mean, according to the 1983 AAMR definition.

Moderate and severe disabilities: A classification for persons who, prior to adulthood, are identified as having cognitive disabilities consistent with an IQ below 50–55 or a severe developmental disability that limits their functional ability to this range, having two more disabilities that contribute to their ability to function, and needing varying levels of lifelong support in two or more areas of adaptive behavior.

Monitoring therapy model: Service delivery personnel develop strategies from their discipline and train others to implement them under continued supervision.

Most-to-least prompting: Response-prompting strategy that typically uses prompts from a hierarchy from most to least intrusive and is faded by offering less assistance over time.

Multidisciplinary team model: Model of service delivery in which representatives from various disciplines provide input to a child's educational program and deliver services with little, if any, collaboration between team members.

Multiple exemplars: Teaching with two or more examples of a class of stimuli that may or may not sample the range of stimuli as a strategy to facilitate generalization.

Multiple impairments: A combination of orthopedic and other health impairments.

Myopic participation: The practice of limiting the involvement of students with disabilities in the general education curriculum to minimal opportunities.

Naturalistic teaching strategies: Milieu teaching strategies; response-prompting strategies typically embedded in natural activities to facilitate communication skills.

Naturalistic time delay: Naturalistic or milieu response-prompting procedure typically used to teach a child to apply language skills during natural activities based on child interest by inserting a time delay interval within an activity and, if necessary, prompting a child to initiate.

Negative reinforcer: An aversive consequence that increases that likelihood that a behavior will occur in order to avoid the consequence.

Neighborhood school: The school that a student would attend if he/she did not have a disability; local school or home school.

Noncompliant behavior: Category of challenging behavior that is in opposition to directions or instructions.

Nonseclusionary timeout: Punishment procedure in which challenging behavior is decreased by removing the opportunity for accessing reinforcement within the environment where the behavior is occurring.

Nontargeted information: Information that students learn through observation or as instructive feedback in addition to target skills.

Observational learning: The acquisition of nontargeted information by watching or listening to others.

Orthopedic impairments: Physical impairments related to the skeletal structure.

Other health impairment: A term referring to limited strength, vitality, or alertness due to chronic or acute health problems that adversely affect a child's educational peformance.

Partial integration: Placement in a general education setting for part of the school day that is not in the student's neighborhood school.

Partial participation: The act of taking part in activity even if the entire activity cannot be completed with independence.

Passive euthanasia: The termination of a life through omission of an act to sustain the life.

Passive participation: The practice of physically placing students with disabilities in natural environments where they observe typical peers but do not interact with them.

Peer integration: The placing of peers with and without disabilities in the same physical setting.

Pervasive support: A level of support in the 1992 AAMR definition of mental retardation that is consistently provided with high intensity over time.

Physical impairments: Orthopedic impairments.

Physical integration: Physical placement of persons with disabilities in settings with persons without disabilities; mainstreaming.

Piecemeal participation: The practice of involving students with disabilities in general education activities on an irregular basis.

Positive practice overcorrection: A behavioral intervention to decrease challenging behavior by forcing the person exhibiting the behavior to practice appropriate behavior for a long duration of time.

Practice integration: Collaboration between service delivery personnel and teacher to deliver services.

Premack Principle: A behavioral contingency in which a high-frequency behavior following a low-frequency behavior serves as reinforcer to increase the probability that the low-frequency behavior will be performed.

Primary reinforcer: An unconditioned or unlearned reinforcer whose value is innate to the individual.

Principle of natural proportions: The premise that the percentage of students with disabilities placed in educational settings should reflect the percentage found in the real world.

Principle of parsimony: When two procedures are equally effective, use the one that is simpler and takes less effort to implement.

Principle of partial participation: The philosophy that all persons with disabilities can participate, with or without adaptations, in activities with their peers and should not be excluded.

Profound mental retardation: A classification of mental retardation falling below an IQ of 20 or more than 5 standard deviations below the mean, according to the 1983 AAMR definition.

Progressive time delay (PTD): Response-prompting strategy that uses a single controlling prompt that is faded over a dimension of time by increasing the delay interval for a student to independently respond in small increments of time across sessions.

Prompt: An event (e.g., verbal direction, gesture, physical guidance) that is added to a trial presentation prior to the response to increase the likelihood of a correct response.

Punisher: A consequence following a behavior or response that decreases the likelihood that it will recur.

Reframing: The capability of the family of a child with disabilities to redefine stressful events in order to make them manageable.

Reinforcer: A consequence following a behavior or response that increases the likelihood that it will recur.

Relative profound range: A range of profound mental retardation in which persons are viewed as being more competent and as having some degree of ambulation, language, communication, and self-help skills.

Resource room placement: Placement of students with disabilities in general education with 21% to 60% time spent in a segregated class.

Response: The behavior that occurs following the presentation of an antecedent or stimulus.

Response cost: A mildly punishing procedure in which inappropriate behavior is decreased by removing a reinforcer.

Response generalization: The occurrence of a class of behaviors in response to a single stimulus.

Response-prompting procedures: Instructional strategies (e.g., most-to-least prompting, simultaneous prompting, system of least prompts, time delay) that insert prompts between the stimulus and the response to increase the likelihood that the student will make the correct response.

Response prompts: Events that are inserted between the stimulus and the response to increase the likelihood that the students will make the correct response.

Restitutional overcorrection: A behavior intervention to decrease challenging behavior by forcing the person exhibiting the behavior to restore the effect of their behavior on the environment above and beyond the original state of the environment.

Role release: Practice in service delivery in which a professional from a specific discipline shares expertise with another team member who will provide the service.

School health services: Those services that can be provided in the educational setting by a nurse or other qualified person.

Seclusionary timeout: Punishment procedure in which challenging behavior is decreased by removing the person exhibiting the behavior from the environment where reinforcement is available.

Secondary reinforcer: A conditioned or learned reinforcer that acquires value from being paired with a primary reinforcer.

Self-determination: Combination of skills, knowledge, and attitudes that allow persons with disabilities to participate in planning their lives.

Self-injurious behavior: Category of challenging behavior that is harmful or life threatening to the person who performs it in that it results in physical injury or tissue damage.

Separate class placement: Placement of students with disabilities in a segregated setting for 60% or more of the school day.

Separate school placement: Placement of students with disabilities in a segregated school setting for 50% or more of the school day.

Severe developmental disabilities: A proposed umbrella term to label those with autism, severe mental retardation, and multiple disabilities.

Severe mental retardation: A classification of mental retardation falling within an IQ range of 20 to 35 or 4 to 5 standard deviations below the mean, according to the 1983 AAMR definition.

Shaping: The delivery of reinforcement for successive approximations of a behavior over time until the target behavior is performed.

Simulation: Community-referenced instruction using stimuli (e.g., materials, cues) that would be found in the real world.

Simultaneous prompting (SP): Response-prompting strategy consisting of probe trials that are followed by training trials that use a single controlling prompt that is delivered following a zero-second delay interval; training trials are discontinued when criterion performance occurs during probe trials.

Slippery slope: The gradual extension of a cutoff point for terminating rights, such as the right to sexual fulfillment or the right to life.

Social integration: Interactions that occur between persons with and without disabilities when they are placed in the same physical setting.

Social stressor: Circumstances that require a change in an individual's ongoing life pattern, such as those associated with a child with disabilities and the child's family.

Social withdrawal: Category of challenging behavior that restricts a person due to their inability to interact with others within their environment.

Spaced trial instruction: Instructional format in which there is a brief interval between trials.

Specific attentional cues: Events that focus a student's attention for learning by requiring the student to perform an action (e.g., making a verbal response, pointing to task materials) that demonstrates the student is focused.

Spontaneous recovery: The possibility that a challenging behavior that has been extinguished will recur over time when it is inadvertently reinforced.

Stereotypic behavior: Category of challenging behavior that is disruptive to the learning environment due to its frequency.

Stimulation programming: The use of therapy (e.g., physical, occupational) to improve the quality of life for persons with profound disabilities.

Stimulus: The antecedent that elicits a response or a behavior.

Stimulus control: The consistent occurrence of a response or behavior following a stimulus or antecedent.

Stimulus fading: Antecedent-prompting strategy in which an irrelevant feature of the stimulus is highlighted to increase the likelihood that a correct response will occur.

Stimulus generalization: The occurrence of a single behavior in response to a class of stimuli.

Stimulus prompts: Events that are added to the stimulus to increase the likelihood that the students will make the correct response; antecedent prompts.

Stimulus shaping: Antecedent-prompting strategy in which a relevant feature of the stimulus is highlighted to increase the likelihood that a correct response will occur.

Superimposition: Antecedent-prompting strategy that combines stimulus shaping and stimulus fading to increase the likelihood that a correct response will occur.

Supported employment: Work option that takes places in an integrated, community setting with wages paid at the prevailing rate and where the level, frequency, and type of support is provided as needed.

Supported living: Living option within a community setting where the level, frequency, and type of support is provided as needed.

System consultation: Related service delivery personnel provide one-time consultation for school or agency, make recommendations, then withdraw.

System of least prompts (SLP): Response-prompting strategy that typically uses prompts from a hierarchy from least to most intrusive and is faded by offering only the level of assistance a student needs on each trial.

Task analysis: The breaking down of a chained behavior into its component steps.

Teaching programming: Instruction that focuses on teaching skills to persons with disabilities.

Technology dependent: Term referring to the need for a medical device to compensate for the loss of a vital body function and substantial, ongoing nursing care to avert death or further disability.

Time delay: Response-prompting strategy that uses a single controlling prompt that is faded over a dimension of time.

Token economies: The use of secondary reinforcers to delay access to primary reinforcers within the context of a behavior intervention plan.

Top-down approach: A functional skill approach to determining a curriculum.

Total task presentation: Instructional format in which instruction occurs simultaneously on all of the steps of a chained task until mastery occurs.

Transdisciplinary team model: Model of service delivery in which representatives from various disciplines provide collaborative input to a child's educational program and collaborate with other team members to deliver services using role release.

Transition: The process of moving from one state of being to another in a progressive fashion over the life span.

Trial: A single episode of instruction on a skill.

Zero degree of inference: The practice of inferring nothing when working with students with moderate and severe disabilities.

Zero reject: The principle that, even though a child will never become self-sufficient, the child still can benefit from services that maintain the status quo and provide a stable quality of life.

NAME INDEX

Subject Index